101 837 934 7

POLITICAL INSTITUTIONS IN
THE UNITED KINGDOM

ONE WEEK LOAN

D1342468

POLITICAL INSTITUTIONS
IN THE UNITED KINGDOM

David Judge

OXFORD
UNIVERSITY PRESS

OXFORD

UNIVERSITY PRESS

Great Clarendon Street, Oxford OX2 6DP

Oxford University Press is a department of the University of Oxford.
It furthers the University's objective of excellence in research, scholarship,
and education by publishing worldwide in

Oxford New York

Auckland Cape Town Dar es Salaam Hong Kong Karachi
Kuala Lumpur Madrid Melbourne Mexico City Nairobi
New Delhi Shanghai Taipei Toronto

With offices in

Argentina Austria Brazil Chile Czech Republic France Greece
Guatemala Hungary Italy Japan Poland Portugal Singapore
South Korea Switzerland Thailand Turkey Ukraine Vietnam

Oxford is a registered trademark of Oxford University Press
in the UK and in certain other countries

Published in the United States
by Oxford University Press Inc., New York

© David Judge, 2005

The moral rights of the author have been asserted
Database right Oxford University Press (maker)

First published 2005

British Library Cataloguing in Publication Data

Data available

Library of Congress Cataloging in Publication Data

Data available

ISBN 0-19-924426-X   978-0-19-924426-3

10 9 8 7 6 5 4 3 2 1

Typeset by Laserwords Private Limited, Chennai, India

Printed in Great Britain
on acid-free paper by
Ashford Colour Press Ltd, Gosport, Hampshire

CONTENTS

LIST OF BOXES   ix

LIST OF TABLES   ix

PREFACE   xi

ACKNOWLEDGEMENTS   xiii

1   Making Sense of Institutions   1
    Overview   1
    Introduction   1
    What is an institution?   2
    What is an institution: 'old' and 'new' institutionalism   4
    New institutionalism   5
    Conclusion   21

2   Institutions of Representation: The UK Parliament   23
    Overview   23
    Introduction   23
    The Westminster model   24
    The House of Commons   32
    The House of Lords   64
    The monarchy   76
    Conclusion   79

3   Institutions of Representation: Parties and Groups   82
    Overview   82
    Introduction   82
    Models/types of party systems   83
    The Conservative party   85
    The Labour party   89
    The party and electoral systems   94
    Other parties   95

Subnational party systems 97

Groups 103

Networks and governance 106

Conclusion 114

4 **The Executive and Core Executive** **117**

Overview 117

Introduction 117

Departments and ministerial accountability 120

Departments 123

Non-departmental public bodies 138

Modernising government/wiring it up 142

Joining it up: Coordination old and new 143

The combined centre 151

The Treasury 158

Conclusion 160

5 **Territorial Institutions** **163**

Overview 163

Introduction 163

Pre-1999: Simple but not undifferentiated institutions 165

The institutions of devolution post-1999 177

New institutions 183

Conclusion 217

6 **Judicial and Regulatory Institutions** **221**

Overview 221

Introduction 222

Judicial and political institutions 223

Judicial review 226

Human Rights Act 1998 229

Asymmetry and judicial institutions 234

Supreme Court 236

Regulation 239

Ombudsmen   252

Inspection   256

Inquiries   257

Conclusion   258

7 **Conclusion**   **262**

Overview   262

Introduction   262

Extent of institutional change   263

Precipitants of institutional change   266

Coherence: Where's the blueprint?   273

Change and continuity   275

REFERENCES   281

INDEX   307

LIST OF BOXES

2.1 The Pre-eminence of the House of Commons   26
2.2 Legislative process in the House of Commons   46
4.1 Ministerial Code   120
4.2 Ministerial Departments 2004   125
4.3 Non-Ministerial Departments   134
4.4 A Week is a Long Time in Politics   145
4.5 Ministerial Committees   150
4.6 Delivery and Reform Team   155
5.1 *Your Region, Your Choice* (Cm 5511 2002)   212

LIST OF TABLES

2.1 MPs are expected to represent a number of different interests in Parliament. How important are the following interests in determining your role as a representative? (N 179)   33
2.2 Seats won at the 1997 and 2001 General Elections   38
2.3 Success Rates of Public Bills   48
2.4 Replies to Questions appearing in Hansard and indexed in POLIS   52
2.5 Departmental Select Committees   61
2.6 Peers By Type (December 2004)   68
5.1 Scottish Parliament Election Results 1999 and 2003   184
5.2 Welsh National Assembly Election Results 1999 and 2003   194
7.1 Institutional Change Post-1997   264

PREFACE

There are many books dealing with political institutions in the United Kingdom. At an introductory level most of the 'block busters' written for first year undergraduates provide pre-digested descriptions of how UK institutions operate. At a more advanced level, political scientists dispute amongst themselves how political institutions operate and interact with each other and with other institutions in civil society. This disputation has resulted in the UK in a series of conceptualizations of institutional interactions revolving variously around notions of 'governance', 'differentiated polity', 'hollow state', 'regulatory state', 'power dependency models of the core executive', or even 'union state' and 'multi-level governance'. Each model privileges, respectively, the position of some institutions above others—whether of groups or associations, or executive, or regulatory, or territorial institutions—in complex interconnections in networks or resource dependency relationships. While each model or perspective analyses institutions and institutional effects, none are explicitly 'institutional' in themselves. However, what unites these various models is their conscious rejection of the traditional 'institutional' approach encapsulated within the 'Westminster model'.

So where does this book fit with existing studies? The short answer is 'somewhere in between'. It is neither 'introductory' in the sense noted above, nor is it 'advanced' in the sense of dismissing the precepts of the Westminster model. This book starts from a recognition of the revival of interest in, and importance afforded to, institutions in political science. It poses the basic question of 'what is an institution?' and provides an answer through an exposition of 'new institutional' theories. While the analysis is informed by institutional theories, this book also provides a basic description of how institutions in the UK work in practice. Indeed, some readers who prefer 'theory-lite' analysis may wish to skip chapter 1 and proceed directly to the more empirically based chapters. What they will find, however, is that they cannot escape the core themes identified in chapter 1.

One theme of this book is the interconnectedness of political institutions in the UK—and how they operate as part of a wider institutional complex. Another related theme is the exploration of how and why this particular institutional configuration developed; and how and why it changed over time. In part, this is an historical institutionalist account, but one that also draws upon the insights of other strands of institutional theory in explaining how institutional rules and norms are constructed and conceived.

A third, unremitting theme is that institutions operate in accordance with routines and rules reflecting 'normatively appropriate behaviour'. Such behaviour is guided both by norms and values that provide internal 'interpretation of meaning' for members of particular institutions, and by wider societal understandings and expectations. This links to a further theme, that the Westminster model, as an organizing perspective, still retains its significance in prescribing a set of norms, values and meanings that legitimate the actions and prescribe the interactions of UK political institutions. The Westminster model continues to delimit the activities of major political actors—politicians, civil servants and judges—and how they relate to each other, and how institutional norms—of the executive, legislative and judicial branches—are conceived in the UK. In reaching this conclusion the paradoxical nature of the translation of the prescriptions of a 19th century Westminster model into 21st century institutional practice is highlighted. Indeed, one of the most pressing challenges for 21st century UK governments is to reconnect the daily interactions of political institutions to the 'appropriate behaviour' prescribed in the 'Westminster model'.

DJ

ACKNOWLEDGEMENTS

This book stems from an invitation by Peter Mair to contribute to the *Comparative Politics Series*. So I suppose it is his fault! Equally blame should be apportioned to the various editors at Oxford University Press, Angela Griffin, Sue Dempsey and Ruth Anderson, who resolutely failed to give up on this book despite every missed deadline by the author.

The catalogue of culpability extends to Matt Flinders, Oonagh Gay, Brian Hogwood, James Mitchell, Dave Richards, Michael Rush and Mark Shephard who provided, respectively, comments on one or more chapters, none of which were sufficiently damning to stop the project in its tracks. Nor can Fiona Macintyre escape censure, as she decided that taking time out to have a baby was more important than helping to format the final manuscript.

The true fault, however, rests with Lorraine, my wife, for not persisting with her advice that I 'should get a life' and stop writing books. Only my children, Ben and Hannah, are above reproach as both of them resolutely refuse to read anything written by their father or to take any of his ideas (about politics, life or the universe) seriously.

While I might wish to heap opprobrium on the aforementioned people, I have to concede that their efforts have only improved this book. Any faults of interpretation, fact or argument remain mine alone. Though, if any praise is to be received, I might wish to accept that alone as well!!

The following Crown copyright material is reproduced with the permission of the Controller of HMSO and the Queen's Printer for Scotland:

Box 2.1 Cm 5291 (2001) *The House of Lords: Completing the Reform*

Box 4.1 *Ministerial Code*

Box 4.3 *List of Ministerial Responsibilities*

Box 4.4 *Ministerial Code: Ministerial Committees*

Box 5.1 Cm 5511 (2002) *Your Region, Your Choice*

Parliamentary copyright material from the following sources is reproduced with the permission of the Controller of Her Majesty's Stationery Office on Behalf of Parliament:

Table 2.3 *House of Commons Sessional Information Digests*

Table 2.4 *House of Commons Sessional Information Digests*

Table 2.6 *House of Lords: Analysis of Composition*

Data in Table 2.1, derived from *The Challenge for Parliament: Making Government Accountable* (2001), is reproduced with the permission of Dod's Parliamentary Communications.

1

Making Sense of Institutions

Overview

This chapter seeks to answer the question: what is an institution? It is essential for a book on political institutions to provide a basic introduction as to how institutions have been conceived by social scientists. The initial objective, therefore, is to provide an overview of the academic discussion about the nature of political institutions, and to examine the contested nature of various conceptualizations of institutions. A second objective is to explain how major variants of 'institutional' and 'new institutional' theory deal with the questions of how institutions form, how they develop, and how they change? At the core of institutional studies is a concern with 'rules of the game'. How these rules are interpreted is examined in relation to the major variants of new institutionalism: rational choice, historical, normative and empirical perspectives. The basic, but vital, point is that institutions do not exist in isolation and that they have to be studied in their relations with other institutions and the social, economic and political contexts in which they operate. The interconnectedness of institutions, the importance of historical trajectories, and the contingencies of social, economic and political change provide analytical pointers to explaining institutional form.

Introduction

The most fundamental question underpinning any book with the title *Political Institutions in the UK* is: what is an institution? If the question is simple the answers (in the plural) are complex. Indeed, it is worth spending some time thinking about what an institution *is* before attempting to understand the specific nature of political institutions in the United Kingdom. In providing an overview of the academic discussion of political institutions, this chapter highlights the contested nature of the definitions and analyses of institutions. It is important to recognize these differences from the outset because ideas about how institutions form, how they develop, and how they change vary from one academic perspective to another.

It will become clear that some perspectives or models are more appropriate for this book than others. Nonetheless, if, in the process of defining an institution, some notions are preferred to others and the relative importance of some ideas are privileged over others, then the reasons why this is the case also have to be made clear. In doing so, various organising frames can be identified that will help to guide the description and analysis of UK political institutions. In essence, this chapter maintains that, while institutions 'exist', how we interpret their existence is dependent upon how we conceive of institutions in the first place. This is not to make a particularly profound philosophical point, but simply to acknowledge that institutions do not exist in isolation, either from each other, or from the social, economic and political contexts in which they operate, or from wider values and norms.

It is also worth spending some time thinking about 'institutions' in order to appreciate that, on the one side, the academic discussion of 'institutionalism' is often focused upon institutions in general (rather than the operation of specific institutions), and, on the other, that although there are many descriptions of UK institutions, most of them do not adopt an explicit 'institutionalist' perspective. The paradox, therefore, is that rarely do theories about institutions and the detailed analysis of specific political institutions coincide. But before examining complexities and paradoxes let us start by attempting to determine the meaning of 'institution'.

What is an institution?

One starting point is what has been termed a 'brass plate' definition of institutions (Fox and Miller 1995:92). This refers to the brass plate on the entrance to a building denoting the institution in question. Nowadays the name plate is as likely to be an illuminated laminate emblazoned with a designer logo as brass, but, whatever the material of the name plate, the building upon which it is affixed signifies the existence of 'an institution'.

Thus in London, for example, Westminster Palace houses the institution of Parliament (Commons and Lords); Whitehall is the physical location of the central departments of state; and nestling at its heart is Downing Street and the home of the Prime Minister. Just around the corner at the other end of the Mall is Buckingham Palace (one of the physical locations of the monarchy). Similarly, the major institutions of the legal system—the Central Criminal Court at the Old Bailey and the Royal Courts of Justice in the Strand; of local government—the strikingly modern City Hall of the Greater London Authority, of the political parties respectively—Old Queen Street, the home of the Labour Party, Victoria Street for the Conservative party, Cowley Street for the Liberal Democrats—all have physical identities. In Edinburgh, Scottish political institutions have their own array of impressive buildings: the Scottish parliament building located at Holyrood, St Andrews House and Victoria Quay are the homes of the Scottish Executive, and Holyrood Palace is one of the official residences of the monarch in Scotland. In Cardiff, Cardiff Bay is the location of the National Assembly for Wales and the National Assembly Government.

One advantage of a brass plate or 'architectural'/'spatial' approach to institutions is that at least there is some physical manifestation that they exist. Certainly, before the advent of telephony and electronic communications the very proximity, or otherwise, of buildings also provided some indication of the interactions and interconnections between institutions and their members.

Another advantage of an 'architectural' or 'brass plate' perspective is that it points both to stability and change. The historic buildings of Westminster and Whitehall both point to the importance of history, and to the longevity of many of the UK's political institutions (with Westminster Hall dating back 900 years for instance), but also the significance of change (typified both by the relocation of some departments of state to new or different buildings and the frequent changes of name plate on some buildings, with, for example, the Department for Education and Skills changing its remit and title several times in recent years). Buildings can also be the symbols of institutional innovation or renewal, as, for example, the Holyrood building in Edinburgh; or the new Greater London Authority building which symbolizes the phoenix-like rise of a London regional authority after the Greater London Council was terminated in 1986 and its landmark building, County Hall, was redeveloped to become a leisure complex.

But this is about as far as an architectural perspective on institutions takes us, because nobody would claim that the buildings themselves are institutions. All that is claimed is that they are the physical location of institutions. What matters is what happens inside the buildings. Moreover, some institutions are not encompassed by a single building, or even physically located in buildings. Some notions of institutions transcend spatial location, for example, the 'bureaucracy', the 'executive', or the 'judiciary'.

As soon as attention moves beyond architectural artefacts to what happens inside the buildings, then people (actors) and their interconnections through formal rules and informal norms and values come into analytical view. How these people are organized, how they interact with each other internally within an organization and with others externally, and how their expectations of these interactions are structured becomes the focus of attention.

What is an institution: 'old' and 'new' institutionalism

The discussion of 'institutions' is now inextricably linked with 'institutionalism' as an academic perspective—or more accurately academic perspectives. A distinction is normally drawn between 'old' institutionalism and 'new' institutionalism.

'Old' institutionalism has been caricatured as atheoretical, formalistic, hyperfactual, outmoded, normative and descriptive (for summaries see variously Peters 1996, 1999; Rhodes 1995a, 1997, Lowndes 2002); so much so that there is a real danger that modern students (or at least those who are unwilling to read the small print of these overviews) are likely to construct a 'straw man version' of old institutionalism. So-called 'critics of traditional institutionalism' are credited with the view that its 'focus was upon formal rules and organizations rather than informal conventions; and upon official structures of *government* rather than broader institutional constraints on *governance* (outside as well as within the state)' (Lowndes 2002:92).

Yet, having identified the critics' position, most commentators then proceed to note that the old institutionalists were far more analytically astute and sophisticated than their 'critics' countenanced. Thus, Peters (1996: 205) cautions that a blanket dismissal of the value of old institutionalism would undervalue the work of some of the major scholars of political science of the early 20th century. Similarly, Rhodes (1997:69) cites the work of Herman Finer in the 1930s as an example of an institutionalist who 'contextualizes institutions, explores the relationship between formal requirements and informal behaviour, and seeks to explain cross-national institutional differences and their consequences for democracy'. Even further back Lawrence Lowell (1920), with the professed purpose of 'describing' English political institutions, was well aware that formal structures and constitutional documents alone revealed little about political institutions. Instead, he had an acute awareness of institutional adaptation and of political institutions resembling 'living organisms' (1920:14), of institutional interconnectedness, and of the importance of ideas and values—of 'the customary aspects of the constitution'. Further back still, Redlich (1908), and Dicey ([1885] 1959) both examined the embeddedness of British institutions in their cultural, historical and socio-economic environments. This was not a concern simply with the formal structural aspects of institutions but was also a concern with theory (or proto-theory) if not actually theorising. It was also a concern with informal norms as much as formal rules, and with actors as much as with organizations. What underpinned many early institutionalist analyses, therefore, was an 'organising perspective' (Gamble 1990:405).

New institutionalism

The rediscovery of institutions in the 1980s was dependent in part upon exaggeration: exaggeration of the extent to which the analysis of institutions was neglected in the preceding decades, and exaggeration of the failings of old institutional analysis in the first place. In fact, institutional analyses continued to be a prominent aspect of many sub-disciplines of political science (for example, legislative studies) especially beyond the United States, throughout the behavioural and rational choice revolutions, and many institutional studies were explicitly concerned with theorising and with the deployment of methodologies normally ascribed to 'new' institutionalists.

In other words, while new institutionalism claimed to have 'rediscovered' institutions, institutions and their analysis had never actually disappeared. Rather, they had simply 'receded in importance from the position they held in earlier theories', and had been 'supplanted by a conception of political life that is non-institutional' (March and Olsen 1989:1–3). When a new generation of political scientists looked up from the analytical maps provided by behaviouralists and first generation rational choice political scientists, they discovered that the political topography was not as simple as these maps suggested. In the jargon of social scientists these approaches to the discipline were 'under socialized' (Lowndes 2002:91). Political life was far more than the aggregation of individual preferences, and it became apparent to new institutionalists that individual preferences in isolation did not account exclusively for political outcomes, but that these preferences were rooted in, and reflected in mediated form, the structures and organizational biases of institutions.

In recognising the complexity of political topography new institutionalists then sought to devise new conceptual maps to locate institutions. Various different categorizations were identified by different institutional 'cartographers'. Lowndes (2002:95) has identified a basic dichotomy between 'normative' and 'rational choice' perspectives; Hall and Taylor (1996) identified three new institutionalisms; Reich (2000) argued that there were four forms; whereas Peters provided both a five-fold (1996) and a six-fold (1999) typology of versions of new institutionalism. What all of these variants of new institutionalism share, however, is a common concern to locate institutions at the centre of political analysis. What differentiates them is why they believe that institutions play this central role.

Rules of the game

According to Bo Rothstein (1996:145), '[t]here seems to be a general agreement that, at their core, political institutions are the "rules of the game"'. But as Rothstein immediately points out, this raises the question of what should then be included in the rules? Not surprisingly the answers have varied significantly among new institutionalists.

At one extreme is the expansive notion provided by 'sociological institutionalism'. Although this variant will not feature significantly in this book it is useful as a perspective from which to identify the further horizons of institutional study. Indeed, what needs to be noted generally is that the sociological variant is far broader than the new institutionalisms adopted by political scientists. Institutions for 'sociological institutionalists' are delimited by norms, cognitions, culture, symbols, habits or even 'myths' and ceremonies (see Rothstein 1996:145; Hall and Taylor 1996:946; Peters 1999:105–6; Lowndes 2002:103). The term 'delimited' is used consciously here, rather than the word 'defined', simply because this view is non-definitional in so far as nothing is left out of consideration (Peters 1999:106). This does not mean that such an approach is without merit for political scientists. Rather the opposite, as it prompts awareness that institutions are not simply to be understood in terms of formal rules, organizations and procedures, but also that the broader cultural context within which institutions operate needs to be taken into account. This is not, however, to go as far as some sociological institutionalists and to argue that culture and institutions shade imperceptibly into each other, nor to conceive of culture as 'institutions' (Hall and Taylor 1996:947–8).

Sociological institutionalism is also of relevance for its emphasis upon how institutions influence behaviour by 'providing the cognitive scripts, categories and models that are indispensable for action' (Hall and Taylor 1996:948). They 'influence behaviour not simply by specifying what one should do but also by specifying what one can imagine oneself doing in a given context' (Hall and Taylor 1996:948). In this sense, institutions assign meaning to social life. Individual action is thus socially constituted by and through institutions. In reverse, institutions are themselves 'socially constructed' (Hall and Taylor 1996:950).

At one level, what this suggests is very simple—that individuals and institutions are inextricably linked and that, as systems of meaning, institutions shape the behaviour of individuals within them. Yet, at another far more complex level, exactly what distinguishes institutions—from norms, values, culture and other organizational forms—remains indeterminate. The inherent danger of sociological institutionalism is that if the conception of institutions 'means everything then it means nothing' (Rothstein 1996:103). If the 'orthodoxies' of political science in the 1970s and 1980s were deemed to be 'under socialized' then the sociological institutionalist response can be criticized for being 'over socialized' (Rothstein 1996:148).

Rational choice institutionalism

If the sociological variant is too broad, for present purposes at least, then rational choice institutionalism is too narrow. Starting from the proposition that individual preferences are endogenous and hence not determined by institutions, rational choice theorists seek to explain how individuals make decisions if they know that the outcome will also be influenced by other individuals (Aspinwall and Schneider 2000:10–11). Despite the starting precept of methodological individualism, and the view of individuals as utility maximizers who rank their priorities in accordance with exogenous preference scales, the ultimate assumption is that individuals interact and are interdependent. In which case some structuring of individual interactions is required to achieve common decisions.

From rational choice perspectives institutions provide the rules, procedures and informal practices within which individuals interact. Individuals seek to maximize utility but their options are simultaneously constrained by the rules and enhanced by the incentives provided by the 'political space' of institutions (Peters 1999:44–5). Individuals accept these institutional constraints out of recognition that their individual goals can be maximized within the rules and procedures collectively affecting other political individuals. In other words, the recognition that institutional rules also constrain their competitors provides the rationality required for actors to accept the limitations on individual choice incurred by institutional membership. At the core of rational choice institutionalism, therefore, is a view of institutions as a set of rules that structure individual behaviour and decision making. At its most basic the definition relies 'on rules in separating the institutional from the non-institutional' (Peters 1999:54).

Of course, political analysis is never quite so simple as this last sentence suggests. While most rational choice institutionalists would start from this basic premise, most would also seek to qualify it in some way. In essence there are four types of qualification, associated in turn with four major schools of rational choice models: institutions as rules, principal-agent, game-theoretic and rule-based models (for overviews see Hall and Taylor 1996:942–6; Peters 1999:43–62). The details need not detain us here, other than to note that that what these approaches have in common are: i) a conception of institutions as rules; ii) the identification of political activity as a series of collective action dilemmas with institutions providing the context within which these dilemmas can be resolved; iii) agreement that institutions structure strategic interactions of individuals and reduce uncertainty; and iv) a deductive approach to the origins of institutions that produces 'a stylized specification of the functions that institutions perform' (Hall and

Taylor 1996:945). What they also have in common is a loose connection to the 'real world'.

Historical institutionalism

In contrast to rational choice, approaches historical institutionalists claim that they 'address real-world questions' (Pierson and Skocpol 2002:697). At its broadest as Thelen and Steinmo (1992:2–3) point out:

> historical institutionalism represents an attempt to illuminate how political struggles 'are mediated by the institutional setting in which [they] take place.' In general, historical institutionalists work with a definition of institutions that includes both formal organizations and informal rules and procedures that structure conduct . . . What is implicit but crucial in [most] conceptions of historical institutionalism is that institutions constrain and refract politics but they are never the sole 'cause' of outcomes.

Clearly, by this definition, historical institutionalism is an institutionalist perspective, but how distinctive is it from sociological or rational choice variants? One answer is: not very. This is the answer ascribed to Hall and Taylor by Hay and Wincott (1998). The latter pairing of authors accuse the former pairing of locating both rational choice and sociological institutionalisms within the 'canon' of historical institutionalism, and, in so doing, 'imply that historical institutionalism is not a distinctive approach to institutional analysis in its own right' (Hay and Wincott 1998:953). While willing to concede that historical institutionalism is something of an 'amalgam' of 'calculus' and 'cultural' approaches, Hall and Taylor argue that these approaches are not simply coterminous with 'rational choice' and 'sociological' perspectives. Ultimately, however, they recognize that historical institutionalism is not 'a fully-realized alternative to either of these approaches' (1998:958). In part, this is because 'a growing number in both schools share the core contentions of the other' (1998:959), and because 'in short, some intellectual borrowing has been going on all round' (1998:960). The extent of this borrowing is acknowledged in Peters' (1999:63) conclusion that: 'it is difficult to separate this version of institutionalism from the others'.

Historical and rational choice versions start with the question: how do institutions affect political strategies and political outcomes? (Thelen and Steinmo 1992:7). In answer, some rational choice models recognize that institutions are 'culturally constructed', and, in return, many sociological institutionalists see activity within institutions as 'strategic and bounded by the mutual expectations of others' (Hall and Taylor 1998:959). On both counts historical institutionalists would find these assumptions unproblematic. Indeed, a key premise of historical institutionalists is that institutions provide the strategic context in which political actors formulate their strategies and pursue their interests.

In trying to distance themselves from these other institutionalisms those of the 'historical' persuasion point to at least three fundamental differences. First, historical institutionalists generally find the strict rationality assumptions of rational choice to be overly reductionist. Thus, they are willing to see individuals more as 'rule-following satisficers' than as rational maximizers. In other words, they are willing to countenance individuals following societally defined rules even when to do so might not be in the individual's own best interest (Thelen and Steinmo 1992:8). A second difference, and the 'most central' for Thelen and Steinmo at least (1992:8), concerns preference formation. For historical institutionalists preference formation is problematic rather than a given. Preferences are seen to be socially and politically constructed. In this manner, both strategies and goals (and not just the former as in rational choice) are shaped by political institutions.

A third and generic difference is the 'broader' perspective offered by historical institutionalism. This broadening/expansion takes several different forms. One is a broader understanding of 'how the structure of ideas embodied in the institutions of a polity may affect individual action' (Hall and Taylor 1998:961). Indeed, ideas are central to this perspective (Peters 1999:71). This enables historical institutionalists to identify that 'exposure to new ideas can alter the basic, as well as strategic, preferences of actors' and also to have a more expansionist notion of the types of ideas that 'might matter to actors, ranging from causal relations that govern the world and the likely behaviour of other actors (on which rational choice analysis often concentrates), to moral visions about what is good or just that speak to the self-identities of many political actors' (Hall and Taylor 1998:961). This, it is maintained, gives them a 'good basis for an increasingly sophisticated understanding of the relationship between structures and agents' (Hall and Taylor 1998:961).

A second distinguishing feature claimed for historical institutionalism 'is the prominent role that power and asymmetrical relations of power play in such analyses' (Hall and Taylor 1996:940). In contrast to the focus of rational choice perspectives upon freely-contracting individuals, historical insti-tutionalists acknowledge the capacity of institutions to reflect inequalities of power and access afforded to different individuals and collective organizations.

These concerns with ideas and power point to a much broader concern with the relationship between institutions and macro-level processes and social forces. In the words of Pierson and Skocpol (2002:702) historical in-stitutionalism has 'macroscopic inclinations'. As such it is interested in 'in-teraction effects' and 'overarching contexts' (Pierson and Skocpol 2002:711) and so sets historical institutionalism apart from individual-level behaviour or micro-processes evident in, for example, rational choice institutionalism.

If, as historical institutionalists claim, they are interested in 'explaining variations in important or surprising patterns, events or arrangements—rather than on accounting for human behaviour without regard to context or modeling very general processes' (Pierson and Skocpol 2002:696–7), tackle 'big, real-world questions' (2002:713), and seek to highlight relatively broad social contexts—'they look at forests as well as trees' (2002:711, original emphasis), then what is the specific 'institutional' dimension of their re-search agenda?

The very fact that the concern is macroscopic—and is with broad sets of organizations and institutions and how they relate to each other; overarch-ing contexts; and looks for patterns over time (2002:709)—clearly identifies the approach as 'historical' but still leaves unspecified what the 'institution-al' dimension is. At one level it is possible to argue that historical institution-alists are primarily concerned with the effects of institutions rather than with the institutions themselves. Many of the leading historical institutionalist studies have been focused upon explaining the policy outcomes of different institutional complexes and configurations, and explaining policy continu-ities and variations both within and across countries. While historical insti-tutionalism has increased the understanding of the impact of institutional arrangements for political and social outcomes, it still has problems in 'treating institutions as themselves important objects of explan-ation' (Pierson 2000:475).

In the first instance, the basic question of 'what is an institution?' often leads to under-conceptualized answers. Certainly, as Peters notes (1999:65), the answers provided by historical institutionalists are 'more vague than in most approaches'. Indeed, Lieberman (2001:1013) seeks to argue that a historical institutionalist 'definition is necessarily vague because analysts working within this framework conceptualize and define institutions in more precise ways according to their own questions and theories'. But this seems to suggest that there is no coherent historical institutionalist theory only 'theories' in the plural.

Yet a starting point for a common definition stems from the assumption that the institutional structure shapes collective behaviour and generates different policy outcomes, in which case at least 'structure' and 'organization' can be discerned as key parts of the definition of an institution. This structuralist dimension is emphasized by Hall and Taylor (1996:937) in their recognition that historical institutionalists see 'the organization of the polity or political economy as the principal factor structuring collective behaviour and generating distinctive outcomes'. This leads to a definition of institutions as 'the formal or informal procedures, routines, norms and conventions embedded in the organizational structure of the polity or political economy' (1996:938). Institutions are thus 'associated' with 'organizations and the rules or conventions promulgated by formal organization' (1996: 938). This developed Hall's earlier definition of 'formal rules, compliance procedures, and standard operating practices that structure the relationship between individuals in various units of the polity and economy' (1986:19). Most particularly it expanded the notion of rules to include informal rules, though it did lose the concept of 'standard operating procedure' (which is of some significance for the discussion of empirical institutionalism, see below). Nonetheless, most historical institutionalists would be willing now to 'work with a definition of institutions that includes both formal organizations and informal rules and procedures that structure conduct' (Thelen and Steinmo 1992:2). Though exactly where to draw the line between organizational rules and broader norms and conventions remains open to dispute (see Thelen and Steinmo 1992:2; Peters 1999:67–8). The ultimate problem is that historical institutionalists tend to accept 'commonsense concepts of formal institutions' (Peters 1999:67) yet wish to embed notions of 'ideas' and 'power' in these already nebulous definitions.

Paradoxically, although historical institutionalists may not exhibit a firm grasp on what an institution 'is' they are more precise on how and why institutions come into being, persist and change over time. Though, even here, they are more explicit about explaining persistence than institutional formation and change. Peters (1999:67) claims that 'to some extent the emphasis on embodying ideas in the structures that support institutions may be taken as a definition of the formation of institutions. It can be argued that when an idea becomes accepted and is embodied into structural form the institution has been created'. Yet, the tautological dimension of this statement is apparent, as an institution exists when an idea is accepted, yet acceptance is signified by the presence of an institution. Another problem entails identifying the exact period when an institution takes on its organizational or structural form. The centrality of this issue for historical institutionalists is highlighted by Lieberman:

> The most important starting point for estimating the impact of institutions on outcomes is through the comparison of periods prior to and subsequent to the creation of the relevant political institutions central to the HI [historical institutionalist] argument. Simply put, if HI scholars want to claim that a particular set of institutions matters for a particular set of outcomes, it is necessary to show that such outcomes were not already in place prior to the establishment of such institutions. Thus the identification of moments of institutional origination is a preliminary point of departure for the analysis.
> (Lieberman 2001:1020)

Yet the potential for error in identifying such 'moments of institutional origination' are high (Peters 1999:67; Lieberman 2001:1020). It should be remembered here that much of the attention of historical institutionalists has been focused upon policies (for example, health provision, taxation policy, trade policy, unemployment insurance schemes) and a desire to explain development of these policies both cross-time and cross-nationally.

In explaining policy development the notion of 'path dependency' has become locked into many historical institutional analyses. As a general observation 'formal political institutions are usually change resistant' (Pierson 2000:490). In part, this is because political institutions are often consciously designed to constrain future change and so make reversal unattractive or difficult for future actors (see Pierson 2000:491). 'Path dependence' thus stipulates that initial institutional choices and structures become self-reinforcing over time. This 'self reinforcing dynamic' means that 'once actors have ventured far down a particular path . . . they are likely to find it very difficult to reverse course' (Pierson and Skocpol 2002:700). All of which seems to emphasize institutional continuity and persistence, and requires some reconceptualization of institutional development if change is to be accounted for.

Historical institutionalists have addressed the 'problem' of change in various ways. One is to argue that 'path dependency' can explain political change as well as inertia. Thus, for example, Pierson and Skocpol (2002: 701–2) argue that the timing and sequencing of events may have a fundamental impact on institutional development; as some specific political arrangements may 'prove to be particularly vulnerable to some event or process emerging at a later stage in political development'. Though exactly why still remains undisclosed in this statement. Pierson (1996) had earlier sought to explain institutional change in an evolutionary model. At the heart of this model is incremental adjustment in response to dysfunctional elements or unanticipated consequences arising out of the initial institutional design (see Peters 1999:70, Lowndes 2002:105). Institutions have the capacity 'to learn' and to modify behaviour as a result. All that historical institutionalists would maintain, however, is that the efficacy of such learning mechanisms is subject to 'considerable limitations' in the political world (Pierson 2000:490).

Other historical institutionalists have sought an answer in the idea of 'critical junctures'. This postulates that institutional development may be characterized by periods of continuity punctuated by 'moments when substantial institutional change takes place thereby creating a "branching point" from which historical development moves onto a new path' (Hall and Taylor 1996:942). This notion is paralleled in turn by the very similar idea of 'punctuated equilibria'. As outlined by Krausner (1984:242) this notion accepts that an institution will exist for long periods in an equilibrium state—operating in accordance with its initial institutional arrangements (or those formulated in response to a preceding 'punctuation')—but that 'rapid bursts of institutional change' may punctuate the existing equilibrium. Of course this then raises the questions of what precipitates such 'punctuation'? And how profound does the punctuation have to be unhinge the existing equilibrium? Indeed, judging the magnitude of difference and the trajectory of change can be problematic as, almost by definition in historical institutionalism, 'outcomes are heavily influenced by the past, they tend to change more at the margins than with complete disjunctures' (Lieberman 2000:1021).

In contrast, Peters and Pierre (1998) identify a 'disruptive model' of institutional change in historical institutionalism. Change involves a sharp break with the past and 'results largely from the necessity of adapting to changed external factors, whether those factors are empirical . . . or more ideational'. In this view, institutional change is conceived as a response to external change in the environment of an institution. In fact, Peters (1999:70) argues that, generally, explanations of change in historical institutionalism have to be sought outside of the approach itself as there is no internal dynamic for change (other than the dysfunctions of initial design noted by Pierson).

Normative institutionalism: March and Olsen

March and Olsen have been credited both with the revitalization of the study of political institutions as well as with coining the phrase 'new institutionalism' (Peters 1999:25; Lowndes 2002:94). They are also identified as leading exponents of 'normative institutionalism' and the belief that institutions 'are collections of standard operating procedures and structures that define and defend values, norms, interests, identities and beliefs' (March and Olsen 1989:17). The adjective 'normative' is used to 'reflect the central role assigned to norms and values within organizations in explaining behaviour' (Peters 1999:25). In choosing to label March and Olsen as 'normative institutionalists' the emphasis is placed upon norms rather than upon 'organizational forms' (March and Olsen 1989:22) or 'collections of . . . structures' (March and Olsen 1989:22). In March and Olsen's own words, however, it is these organizational forms and structures which 'define and defend' (1989:17) norms and values—not the other way round.

Indeed, it is worth spending some time to differentiate 'rules', 'organizations' and 'norms' at this stage. If Peters and Lowndes are prone to emphasize the 'normative' dimensions of March and Olsen's perspective over and above the 'organizational' or 'structural' dimensions, others such as Lane and Ersson want to make a clear distinction between institutions as rules and institutions as organizations. In fact they argue that it is 'crucial . . . to make the separation between these two definitions [as rules or organizations]' (Lane and Ersson 2000:26), and are openly critical of March and Olsen's linkage of rules and organization. Lane and Ersson's basic claim is that if an institution is constituted by rules then it cannot also be 'behaviour' or an actor in its own right. If institutions are both, then 'maybe institutions are everything and by entailment nothing' (Lane and Ersson 2000:30).

The starting proposition of March and Olsen, however, is that 'institutions can be treated as political actors' (1989:17). Institutions are capable of 'making choices on the basis of some collective interest or intention' (1989:18) if they exhibit institutional coherence and autonomy. Such coherence and autonomy stems from the fact that 'much of the behaviour we observe in political institutions reflects the routine ways in which people do what they are supposed to do' (1989:21). These 'routines' constitute 'standard operating procedures' whereby 'actions are fitted to situations by their appropriateness within a conception of identity' (1989:38). This 'logic of appropriateness' is identified as 'a fundamental logic of political action' (1989:38). In turn, 'action' is conceived 'as institutionalized through structures of rules and routines' (1989:38).

Rules are identified both as 'routines, procedures, conventions, roles, strategies, organizational forms, and technologies around which political activity is constructed', and as 'beliefs, paradigms, codes, cultures, and knowledge that surround, support, elaborate, and contradict those roles and routines' (1989:22). They are important in enabling actors to identify 'normatively appropriate behaviour' (1989:22); so that 'what is appropriate for a particular person in a particular situation is defined by political and social institutions and transmitted through socialization' (1989:23). While determining what is 'appropriate' at any particular time is not unproblematic, the rules and routines reflect historical experience, allow for variability as well as standardization, and sustain sufficient trust to build 'confidence that appropriate behaviour can be expected most of the time' (1989:38). 'Institutions define individual, group, and societal identities, what it means to belong to a specific collective' (1989:17). The cumulative result is 'political structures' which create and sustain 'islands of imperfect and temporary organization in potentially inchoate worlds' (1989:16).

If a stipulative definition of an institution is easy to discern in March and Olsen's perspective—of rules, norms, standard operating procedures, and organizational forms and structures—determining how institutions arise in the first place is a little more difficult to discover. As Lowndes (2002:105) notes, normative institutionalists 'do not have an easy answer as to why institutions in general (or particular political institutions) come into being'. In fact, the answer to the question 'why' is largely treated as self evident—to bring 'order and stability in an interactive world that might otherwise appear quite chaotic' (March and Olsen 1989:53). Indeed, the question 'why' is largely subsumed within the question 'how do institutions form?'.

The concept of the 'elaboration of meaning' is used by March and Olsen to explain how institutions form. In essence, institutions 'strengthen pre-existing structures of related values and cognitions' (1989:41). The structure of meaning of institutions derives from pre-socialized individuals with previous understandings (see Peters 1999:32). These shared meanings lead to a 'tendency to partition a population of individuals into groups or institutions that share interpretations and preferences within groups but not across groups' (March and Olsen 1989:45). Institutions are vitally important, therefore, for the 'organization of belief' (1989:45). 'By shaping meaning, political institutions create an interpretive order within which political order can be understood and provided continuity' (1989:52).

When it comes to accounting for change March and Olsen provide what they call an 'institutional perspective on institutional change' (1989:53). The starting premise is that 'not all rules are necessarily good ones, least of all indefinitely' (1989:54), therefore, institutions are led to act as 'routine adaptive systems' (1989:58) responding to environmental signals and learning from the process of change itself. 'Institutions develop and refine goals while making decisions and adapting to environmental pressures' (1989:66). In the long-run the development of political institutions is seen 'less as a product of intentions, plans and consistent decision than incremental adaptation to changing problems with available solutions within gradually evolving structures of meaning' (1989:94). In this sense, Peters and Pierre identify the normative institutionalist perspective on institutional change as an 'organic conception' and one characterized by 'continual incremental reassessment of performance' (1998). But it should be remembered that March and Olsen do not believe that the outcomes of change are certain and predestined, as they are subject to: embedded historical experience (1989:167), the exercise of power based upon possession of political, economic and social resources (1989:59), the intermeshing or 'nesting' of institutions in complex systems of governance (1989:170), or even 'comprehensive shocks' (1989:58).

Empirical institutionalism

In many ways 'empirical institutionalism' continues many of the more positive aspects of the analytical tradition of 'old' institutionalism. Empirical institutionalists start from the assumption that 'institutions matter' and that 'the formal structuring of interaction does determine, or at least influence behaviour' (Peters 1999:95). Like 'old' institutionalism there is a tendency for other political scientists to dismiss it as atheoretical and descriptive, and for it to be deterministic in the belief that formal structures impact upon individual behaviour and collective choices.

Empirical institutionalists usually take the existence of institutions as pre-given — they are simply a fact of political life (Peters 1999:89). Often what is of more interest than the formation of institutions, therefore, is how institutions can be classified and how their interactions can be monitored; and how constellations of institutions can be categorized. The desire to develop typologies is evident in the empirical institutionalists' distinctions between, variously, 'parliamentary' or 'presidential' systems (Lijphart 1992); 'majoritarian' or 'consensual' parliamentary systems (Lijphart 1984, 1999); 'policy making' or 'policy influencing' legislatures (Packenham 1970, Mezey 1979, Norton 1990) 'arena' or 'transformative' parliaments (Polsby 1975); or of implementation structures (Pressman and Wildavsky 1974).

In part, the desire to categorize institutions and to fit them into typologies stems from a concern to establish the relative 'effectiveness' of differing institutional configurations. 'Effectiveness' has been conceived variously as the performance of the political system (Pasquino 1997), or of the types of policies enacted (Weaver and Rockman 1993), or of the policy performance of democratic governments (Lijphart 1999). In each case the basic question posed is: Do institutions matter? Indeed, this question provided the title of Weaver and Rockman's book published in 1993. Their main concern was to investigate 'institutional influences' on governmental policymaking capabilities. The basic hypothesis was that 'political institutions shape the processes through which decisions are made and implemented and that these in turn influence government capabilities' (Weaver and Rockman 1993:7). Their initial focus was to compare presidential and parliamentary systems, but they were sensitive to the variations within these systems (what they termed 'regime and government types' (1993:8)). Moreover, they were aware also that 'the effects of political institutions can be mediated both by the broader social milieu in which those institutions function and by their historical development' (1993:10). In line with normative institutionalists they acknowledged that 'institutions reflect not just legal forms but also normative understandings and expectations' (1993:10). In line with historical institutionalists they were also willing to acknowledge the importance of 'the histories of programs, successful responses in the past, [and] dominant beliefs among leaders' (1993:11) to the functioning of institutions.

For Weaver and Rockman a full answer to the question of 'do institutions matter?' requires, therefore, an understanding of institutional constraints, decision making processes and 'other influences' such as political, socio-economic and demographic conditions (1993:30). For our purposes it is worth noting that Weaver and Rockman point implicitly to the importance of *interinstitutional* connections in highlighting the different institutional rules that characterize executive-legislative relationships in presidential and parliamentary systems (including party cohesion, executive recruitment, patterns of accountability, and processes of decision making). Their analysis is also of importance in identifying the significance of *institutional context* and of how 'social conditions and organizations' (1993:35) can impact upon institutional effects. Equally important is the conclusion that, while institutional effects are 'real and significant', they are also often 'indirect and contingent' (1993:39). This *contingency* of institutions—upon wider political, economic and social conditions and forces—is of significance in helping to explain institutional variation across time and across political systems. If the question 'do institutions matter? is simple; then what the Weaver and Rockman volume, and the works of other 'empirical institutionalists', such as Lijphart, illustrate is that the answers are far from simple.

Lijphart, at various stages in his career, has studied the consequences of different institutional configurations. He has been concerned to expose the relative merits of parliamentary and presidential systems (1992) and the 'most important institutional difference among them: the relationship between the executive and the legislature' (1992:1), and to analyse the broader institutional patterns associated with 'majoritarian' and 'consensual' democracies (1984, 1999). Lijphart maintains that clear patterns and regularities appear when political institutions 'are examined from the perspective of how majoritarian or how consensual their rules and practices are' (1999:1). A basic division is discernable between the principles of the

'majoritarian model' with its concentration of political power, and its exclusive, competitive and adversarial institutional structures and practices,
and those of the 'consensus model' which is characterized by 'inclusiveness, bargaining and compromise' (1999:2). From these principles can be
deduced 'ten differences with regard to the most important democratic institutions and rules' (1999:2). In turn, these ten differences can be grouped
according to two dimensions: an 'executive-parties' dimension and a
'federal-unitary' dimension.

The first dimension distinguishes between: first, the extent of the concentration of executive power either in single-majority cabinets or in broad
multiparty power sharing coalitions; second, executive-legislative relations
in which the executive is dominant or those where there is a balance of
power between the two institutions; third, two-party versus multiparty systems; fourth, disproportional versus proportional electoral systems; and
fifth, pluralist versus corporatist systems of interest representation (1999:3).

On the second 'federal-unitary' dimension Lijphart identifies five differences between: first, unitary and centralized, and federal and decentralized governments; second, unicameral versus bicameral legislative systems;
third, flexible as opposed to rigid constitutions; fourth, the absence or presence of judicial review; and, fifth, central banks which are dependent on the
executive versus independent central banks. (1999:3–4).

In noting these differences the first half of each pairing is associated with
majoritarian democracies and the second with consensus models. While
Lijphart seeks to demonstrate that consensus democracies do 'outperform
majoritarian democracies with regard to the quality of democracy and the
kindness and gentleness of their public policy orientations' (1999:301), the
significance of his work for our purposes is that it reveals the interconnectedness of institutions in major constellations (two in Lijphart's case).
Moreover, it acknowledges the significant interactions between political
structure and political culture (1999:307) but also recognizes the complexity and multi-directionality of these interactions. Perhaps, of equal import, is the fact that Lijphart can only identify one majoritarian democracy,
(not surprisingly given its alternative title of the 'Westminster model') that
closely approximates the ten interrelated elements of the model identified
above, and this is the British institutional system (New Zealand and Barba-
dos are two others but both deviate markedly from key aspects of the majoritarian model).

Conclusion

If we treat new institutionalism as an 'organising perspective' (Gamble 1990:405), as a 'framework for analysis, a map of how things relate, a set of research questions', rather than testable theory as such, then at least we can define the boundaries of our study of institutions using some of the 'boundary posts' provided by new institutionalism. At this point it is simplest to stipulate where the boundaries of analysis will be drawn. Political institutions will be conceived as:

- Formal organizations and structures.

- These formal structures operate in accordance with standard operating procedures reflecting the acceptance of routines and rules that prescribe 'normatively appropriate behaviour'.

- 'Appropriate behaviour' reflects the norms and values of the (most powerful) actors within the organization and provides internal 'interpretation of meaning' for members of the organization.

- Internal organizational norms and values in turn reflect wider societal understandings and expectations. Institutional *context* is thus of significance.

- There is a *contingency* to institutional structures—their form is mediated by wider social, economic and political conditions and forces, both contemporarily and historically.

- Formal organizations operate within institutional constellations, wherein *interinstitutional* interactions help to delimit and define the activities of any particular institution within the configuration.

It is apparent that these stipulations are drawn from a range of new institutional models (and for that matter old institutionalist perspectives). What they point to is a notion of political institutions that includes both structures and rules, and recognizes the importance of both structure (organization) and agency (individuals). The notion of institutions is inclusive in accepting both formal rules and routines and informal norms and values. It recognizes the importance of history and the 'constraints' associated with path dependency, but is not deterministic in allowing for changing social, economic and political forces and associated recalibrations of power relations and 'ideas' to impact upon organizational form. Moreover, it recognizes that, while political institutions are located in their historical and social context, the notion of constellation also points to the fact that they are interconnected.

....

KEY TERMS

- critical junctures
- empirical institutionalism
- historical institutionalism
- institutional change
- institutional context
- institutional formation
- institutionalism
- interinstitutional interactions
- logic of appropriateness
- majoritarian model

- new institutionalism
- normative institutionalism
- parliamentary systems
- path dependency
- presidential systems
- punctuated equilibria
- rational choice institutionalism
- rules of the game
- sociological institutionalism
- standard operating procedures

....

GUIDE TO FURTHER READING

LANE, J-E and ERSSON, S. (2000) *The New Institutional Politics: Performance and Outcomes*, (London, Sage).

An advanced, comparative study of theories about, and the policy effects of, institutions.

MARCH, J. G. and OLSEN, J. P. (1989) *Rediscovering Institutions: The Organizational Basis of Politics*, (New York, Free Press).

March and Olsen were at the forefront of the 'rediscovery' of institutions, and this book provides one of the clearest expositions of the importance of the 'logic of appropriateness'.

PETERS, B. G. (1999) *Institutional Theory in Political Science: the 'New Institutionalism'*, (London, Pinter).

The best and most comprehensive introduction to new institutionalism.

STEINMO, S., THELEN, K. and LONGSTRETH, F. (eds.) (1992), *Structuring Politics: Historical Institutionalism in Comparative Analysis*, (Cambridge, Cambridge University Press).

A collection of essays that became central to the broader dissemination of historical institutionalism in political science.

WEAVER, R. K. and ROCKMAN, B. A (1993) *Do Institutions Matter?*, (Washington, D. C., Brookings Institution).

A classic institutionalist study examining the different impact of presidential and parliamentary systems upon policies enacted.

2

Institutions of Representation: The UK Parliament

Overview

This chapter examines the 'Westminster model'. This is a model in which the House of Commons occupies a pivotal institutional position in the UK state and has engendered a specific pattern of interinstitutional interactions and specific notions of 'appropriate behaviour'. If it is accepted that the Westminster model is of value as an organising perspective—in the sense of identifying a 'set of norms, values and meanings'—then it is important to understand how and why this particular perspective came to dominate political discourse in the UK. In this sense, understanding the modern institutional form of parliament requires some understanding of what has gone before. The simple, but essential, analytical point made in this chapter is that parliament has to be conceived within a constellation of institutions; and is inextricably linked with the executive on the one side and parties as representative institutions on the other. In turn, these institutions operate within a system of ideas and perspectives on legitimate government. These assumptions and understandings have institutional implications in terms of how parliament interacts with other institutions, how it operates as an organization, and how its members conceive of their roles (as revealed in their norms and values, and notions of 'appropriate behaviour').

Introduction

It might seem perverse to start the examination of political institutions in the UK with an analysis of the Westminster parliament. Most standard texts relegate the study of parliament way down their list of chapter priorities (see Budge et al 2004:chapter 18; Jones et al 2004:chapter 17), or do not even accord parliament a separate chapter at all (Dearlove and Saunders 2000). Others, while dutifully recording the role performed by the UK parliament, accord it the status of the 'living dead of the constitution' (Kingdom 2003: 347). Still others seek to reveal 'the myths about Parliament which can produce exaggerated and unreal ideas about what it can and cannot do' (Riddell 2000:6); and willingly conclude that some 'cornerstones' of British constitutional debate, such as the notion of parliamentary sovereignty, are frankly 'nonsense' (Riddell 2000:1). If these were not sufficient reasons to start our analysis somewhere else then the model upon which the claims to significance of the institution is founded, the 'Westminster model', has been roundly dismissed as 'oversimplified', as holding 'crude assumptions about the nature of power' and of creating 'false dualities' (Smith 1999a:36; see also Rhodes 1997:5–7; Richards and Smith 2002:47–8). So why start with parliament and the 'Westminster model'?

The Westminster model

The first reason is simply the 'centrality of the institutional approach to the Westminster model' (Rhodes 1997:6). As Smith (1999a:10) notes, the model is 'institutional in its concern with the workings and power of particular institutions'. The second reason is that despite all of the criticisms of this model it has not 'been replaced by a coherent alternative' (Gamble 1990: 419). Despite its perceived failure to provide an accurate description of how UK institutions work and interact, 'the most important feature of this model is that it reflects how most politicians and officials perceive the system' (Richards and Smith 2002:48). It continues, therefore, 'to inform and condition the way in which [these] actors operate' (Richards and Smith 2002:48). Given the fact that the Westminster model 'embodies political traditions which continue to shape political behaviour' (Rhodes 1997:199) even its critics acknowledge that it is, therefore, 'the inevitable starting point' (Rhodes 1997:198) for an analysis of UK political institutions.

As a 'legitimizing mythology' (Richards and Smith 2002:48) the Westminster model continues to be of elemental significance in the 21st century. And rooted at the centre of that 'mythology' the House of Commons provides 'the absolutely indispensable legitimation for the government of the country' (Miliband 1982:20; see Judge 1993:2). In this sense the Commons is 'by far the most important institution in the British political system' and 'has been at the core of the theory and practice of British government for over three hundred years' (Miliband 1982:20).

In the Westminster model the House of Commons is literally at the centre of the state's institutional constellation. Parliament is identified as the ultimate source of sovereignty (supreme authority) with all other 'branches of the state ... subordinate to it' (Gamble 1990:407). Its pivotal institutional position has engendered a specific pattern of institutional interactions and specific notions of 'appropriate behaviour' related to those interactions. These interactions are characterized by Richards and Smith (2002:48) as:

> all decisions are made within Parliament and there is no higher authority. Legitimacy and democracy are maintained because ministers are answerable to Parliament and the House of Commons is elected by the people. Decisions are taken by Cabinet and implemented by a neutral Civil Service.

Rhodes (1997:198–9) derives a slightly different institutional profile for the Westminster model: 'cabinet government, parliamentary sovereignty, majority party control of the legislature, institutionalized opposition, ministerial responsibility, and a neutral civil service'. But the interconnectedness of institutions, the focus upon institutions as organizations and structures operating in accordance with wider societal understandings and meanings, and with their own internal standards of 'normatively appropriate behaviour', are implicit features of both Rhodes' and Richards and Smith's versions of the Westminster model. Moreover, both identify the model as an 'organising perspective' which 'identifies what is important and worthy of study' (Rhodes 1997:6). While accepting that it directs our attention to a particular institutional configuration, the difficulty with the discussions of Rhodes and Smith and Richards is that they then take the prescriptions of the model to be empirical facts. Yet, as Rhodes (1997:6) acknowledges at one point, the usefulness of the model does not 'lie only in its factual accuracy'. Indeed, it is possible to go further and claim that its usefulness is not rooted 'even in its factual accuracy'. It is a set of norms, values and meanings prescribing legitimate government. Its democratic credentials rest in an acceptance of representative government (not even necessarily representative democracy) and prescriptions about how state power *should* be apportioned and operate. Moreover it is a 'legitimizing mythology' deployed explicitly by the UK government itself (see Box 2.1):

BOX 2.1   **The Pre-eminence of the House of Commons**

The United Kingdom is a Parliamentary democracy. Sovereignty rests with the Crown in Parliament. Law making rests with the tripartite sovereignty of Crown in both Houses of Parliament. . . .

In practice, the powers of the three parts are uneven. The Crown, or Executive, has over the centuries become increasingly accountable to Parliament for its exercise of its powers. Within Parliament, power has transferred from the Lords to the Commons. The basis on which the Commons asserted its right was always its position as the representative body of the people, even in the days when the people who elected it comprised a small minority of even the adult male population. . . .

The House of Commons has thus long since been established as the pre-eminent constitutional authority within the UK. The Government is formed by the Party which can command the support of the House of Commons. A Government which loses the support of the people's elected representatives in the Commons cannot remain in office. General Elections return individual MPs who are expected to look to the interests of their constituents irrespective of Party affiliation. There are also contests between political parties vying for supremacy in the House of Commons. The Party which secures a majority has the right to form a Government and, subject to sustaining its Parliamentary majority, to carry through the programme set out in its election Manifesto. Ministers are continuously accountable to the House of Commons through debates and votes; a process formalised and fortified by the role of the non-Government Parties in forming an Opposition, with the largest non-Government Party occupying the position of Official Opposition. . . .

This constitutional framework, founded on the pre-eminence of the House of Commons, has provided Britain with effective democratic Government and accountability for more than a century, and few would wish to change it. . . .

Source: Cm 5291 2001:paras 13–17

The importance of history and ideas

If we are to accept that the Westminster model is of value as an organising perspective—in the sense of identifying a 'set of norms, values and meanings'—then it is important to understand how and why this particular set came to dominate political discourse in the UK. Indeed, it is worth stressing here that the value of this perspective is not as a description of reality, for it has not corresponded to UK practice for well over a century; and, even then, the practice was exceptional in the general historical pattern of executive dominance and was confined to a very short period in the 19th century—in essence between 1846 and 1868. Thus, those who criticize it because 'it no longer provides either an accurate or comprehensive account of how Britain is governed' (Rhodes 1997:3) fail to recognize that even in the late 19th century it 'was in fact an idealized view' (Birch 1964:74), and that for most of the 20th century 'adherents to the Liberal theory of the state [encapsulated in the Westminster model] have been regretfully aware that political practice has departed from [these] principles' (Birch 1964:80). The importance of the Westminster model, therefore, is not its descriptive accuracy but rather that 'it captures the institutional continuities of the [UK political] system'; and that 'whoever seeks to understand British government must understand this strand of the British political tradition' (Rhodes 1997:3).

The parliamentary state

A basic tenet of historical institutionalism, as noted in chapter 1, is that an understanding of modern institutional forms requires some understanding of what has gone before. Historical institutionalists emphasize the relationship between institutions and macro-level processes and social forces, and the importance of ideas and power. The notion of 'path dependency' has become locked into many historical institutional analyses and the belief that initial institutional choices and structures become self-reinforcing over time. While institutional continuity and persistence is to be expected from this perspective, then change, when it occurs, has to be accounted for. One way has been to build institutional change into an evolutionary model, with institutions having the capacity 'to learn' and to modify behaviour. Another has been to identify 'critical junctures' and to argue that periods of continuity may be punctuated by substantial institutional change. This notion is paralleled in turn by the very similar ideas of 'punctuated equilibria', and 'disruptive models' of institutional change which identify sharp breaks with the past as institutional responses to external change in their environment.

Aspects of historical institutionalism are of value in analysing and understanding the development of the UK parliament. Not surprisingly, the origins of parliaments have attracted the attention of historical institutionalists, with the emergence of representative institutions being linked to a 'bargaining model' whereby 'the ruler trades a parliament for revenue' (Herb 1999:4; see also Bates 1991; Tilly 1992). Certainly such a 'bargain' helps to explain the origins of the English parliament. Intermittent meetings of Parliament in the 13th century served the expedient purpose of enabling the king simultaneously to extend not only the scope of taxation, but also consent to such taxation. Yet securing consent, whereby the solicitation of the views of the 'political nation', as constituted by the king's most powerful subjects, on important policy matters certainly pre-dated parliament as an institution. Indeed, the principle of consent to taxation was itself a feudal principle which had been written into the Magna Carta in 1215, and was, therefore, a recognized preserve of parliaments when summoned by the monarch. Meeting as a collective body, parliament demonstrated that the advice and counsel offered to the king was not individual in character but derived from collective discussion and deliberation. The notion of parliament as a corporate body, as the focus of discussion of common business, and of the aggregation of 'informed' opinion was thus apparent at the end of the 13th century.

What is equally noteworthy is that these principles of consent and representation were invoked in support of, and not as a challenge to, strong executive government. The distinguishing feature of the English (later British) state since the 13th century, and the origins of parliament itself, is the emphasis placed upon government rather than parliament. Representative government in Britain has historically been conceived, and functioned, as a means of legitimating executive power. What the parliamentary tradition in Britain has been concerned with is the transmission of opinion between 'political nation' and governors, the controlling of government to the extent that governmental actions require the consent of the representatives of that 'nation', and the legitimation of changes of governors. Almost from the outset these have been the essential characteristics of the English (later British) state and the reason why it warrants the title: 'The Parliamentary State' (Judge 1993). The importance of the parliaments summoned towards the end of the 13th century is that they set precedents for future parliaments, or, in historical institutionalist terminology, they helped to map the 'path' of future institutional development.

Thus, one reason for the distinctive pattern of English state development after the 17th century, when recognizable features of the modern state become pronounced, stems from a remarkable continuity with medieval political forms. Importantly, in England the medieval political system already rested on the premise that monarchical (executive) power was conditional.

It was not until the 16th century (and the Tudor period), however, that the practice of government conformed more systematically to this premise. The restructuring of the state under the Tudors confirmed the supremacy of the executive working through a representative parliament. At this time the unity of crown-in-parliament was largely taken for granted given the policy consensus between crown and the dominant economic class. Out of this unity the Crown was able to increase its power—conditional upon the consent of parliament. At the same time as the monarch's power was elevated within the state so too was there an incremental restructuring of power differentials within parliament itself. The relationship between the king's ministers in his council and parliament was reoriented to ensure that ministers sat in the House of Commons rather than in the Lords, and that they were expected to seek election to the House. In securing a place for the council in the Commons, executive responsibility to the legislature was thus institutionalized in tandem with a responsibility of the legislature to support and control the executive. In these circumstances, a limitation was placed upon 'irresponsible' opposition arising out of the very unity at the centre of government.

In accordance with the historical institutionalist view of 'disruptive' change, the inversion of the power relationship between the crown and parliament during the Civil War in the 17th century reflected a wider transformation of economic, social and political forces in the state. The institutional unity of 'crown-in-parliament' was fractured primarily because the 'objectives of the king's policies no longer suited the interests and the political notions of the classes represented in the House of Commons' (Butt 1969:43). Hence, the political fragmentation of the state reflected a wider fragmentation of economic interests—between the continuing feudal claims and requirements of the monarch and his supporters, and the emergent demands of sections of the landed classes allied to a gentry commercialising and capitalising agricultural production. Divisions in Westminster reflected divisions in the country with MPs, as a cross-section of an economically dominant class, themselves divided. Attendant upon these wider economic and social transformations came institutional change.

These changes found confirmation, eventually, in the Constitutional Set-tlement of 1689. The true significance of 1689 is that the historic political principles of consent, representation, and the sovereignty of the crown-in-parliament were attuned to the emergence of a new liberal economy and developing principles of a liberal society. In this sense the Revolution of 1688 was both political and economic. After 1689 it was indisputable that legal supremacy rested in parliament rather than in any other state insti-tution—whether monarch or courts. The boundaries of legitimate power were thus marked out. What subsequent centuries witnessed was the chan-ging coalitions of economic forces capable of operating within those bound-aries to advance their own interests. Parliament was an institution linked also to wider civil society. As that society changed, so the framework of the constitutional settlement of 1689 proved capable of redirecting state policy to reflect those changes. The subsequent history of state development in Bri-tain was to retain parliament at the centre of the state but, inevitably, par-liament was not to be sustained as *the* centre of state decision making. What parliament proved capable of doing was accommodating revolutionary eco-nomic development within an evolutionary political framework.

Indeed, the very centrality of parliament in this framework focused the political demands and political aspirations of the emerging industrial classes upon Westminster. Both the reality of political power and the lo-gic of liberal theory led, therefore, to the incremental admission into the franchise of the new industrial classes after 1832. In turn, the admission of the urban and industrial classes into parliament had repercussions for the party system therein. As Norton (1998:18) notes, 'the external environ-ment was to shape parliamentary developments in the 19th century'. Party became the major force in parliamentary politics and brought attendant institutional change. The essence of 'party government', with parties iden-tified with both government and opposition and each party seeking to form a government through securing an electoral majority, was apparent by the mid-1830s. However, mobilization of opposition was to prove more prob-lematic and it was not until the closing years of the century that party op-position became a structural feature of British parliamentary government. The restructuring of the Conservative and Liberal parties after 1867, to form mass-membership organizations and to ensure adherence to party policy on the part of their elected representatives, in combination with the earlier development of party government, ensured consistency of support for executive measures. The important point is that from 1867 onwards, if not before, governments could depend upon consistent support within the House of Commons for the passage of legislation. Moreover, the gradual 'democratization' of the House of Commons associated with franchise reform enhanced its claims to supremacy over the unelected House of Lords.

As party government developed, so parliament began 'to legislate with considerable vigour, to overhaul the whole law of the country' (Maitland 1908:384). Increasingly, general acts of parliament were introduced to structure and regulate economic and social relations in a rapidly industrialising nation. Legislative 'activism' brought with it three major consequences. First, more regulatory responsibilities accrued to the executive as a result of the legislation passed by parliament. Second, a host of organized, sectional and functional representative organizations began to emerge. The characteristics of modern British government—the ascendancy of the executive and the system of interest representation—were thus foreshadowed in the very 'golden age' of parliament in the mid-19th century. Third, there was an incremental extension of the executive's control over the proceedings of the House. Time, as well as party support, was also required to ensure the expeditious processing of legislation. Accelerated industrialization and its attendant social consequences in subsequent decades simply accelerated the transition to an executive-centric state. By the end of the 19th century, and certainly by the end of the first decade of the twentieth, the modern British state was inimitably structured in its present institutional form: parliament was sovereign in constitutional theory but the executive was 'sovereign' in practice (see Griffith 1982). In terms of the central relationship between parliament and government the imbalance has never subsequently been redressed. This is because in Walkland's (1979:2) opinion:

> This structure has changed little in its basic assumptions concerning the role of parliament for much of the [20th] century, and has proved equally attractive to modern governments which have felt little impulse to change a set of understandings and conventions which serve their purposes so well.

Understandings and conventions

From this brief historical review certain ideas and assumptions about the institution of parliament have been identified. Before listing these, however, the essential analytical point to be made is that parliament has to be conceived within a constellation of institutions, wherein it is inextricably linked with the executive on the one side, and parties as representative institutions on the other. The elemental interconnectedness of institutions is captured in the formal designation of parliament as the 'crown-in-parliament'. While the pre-eminence of the House of Commons had been confirmed in practice by the 19th century, and by statute in the Parliament Act of 1911, the House of Lords still retains residual legislative powers and the monarch is still represented nominally in the Commons by 'ministers of the crown'.

In turn, these institutions operate within a system of ideas and perspectives on legitimate government, and encompass a series of understandings upon the location of legal authority (sovereignty), the representativeness of parliament and the responsibility of the political executive to that representative institution (encapsulated in the term 'representative and responsible' government), and the sustaining of the executive through parties (in the notion of 'party government').

These assumptions and understandings have institutional implications in terms of how parliament interacts with other institutions, how it operates as an organization, and how its members conceive of their roles (as revealed in their norms and values, and notions of appropriate behaviour). These assumptions and understandings will be used to structure the following examination of the modern UK Parliament.

The House of Commons

The House of Commons can be conceived in terms of a series of interconnected institutional roles—as a representative, deliberative, legislative, and legitimating institution—which refract the norms, values, and ideas about 'appropriate behaviour' identified in the preceding sections.

Representative institution

Linkage and territory

Throughout its history the House of Commons has been identified as a representative institution. Indeed, the core principles of parliamentary government in the UK—of consent, legitimation and authorization of executive actions—were built upon territorial representation (see Reeve and Ware

TABLE 2.1	MPs are expected to represent a number of different interests in Parliament. How important are the following interests in determining your role as a representative? (N 179)

How important	Very	Quite	Very/Quite
Geographical constituency	67.6	25.1	92.7
Individual constituents	47.5	33.5	91.0
Nation as a whole	58.1	31.3	89.4
Political party	26.8	44.7	71.5

Source: Hansard Society 2001:138–9

1992:46; Judge 1999:149–50). From the outset, as Manin advises (1997:3), 'we need to remind ourselves that certain institutional choices made by the founders of representative government have virtually never been questioned'. One of the 'choices' made in the UK was the territorial basis upon which MPs were to be elected. In the modern House, individual Members of Parliament continue to represent a territorial constituency, and cumulatively the House of Commons represents 659 constituencies (646 after 2005) throughout the UK. The significance of the territorial basis of representation is underlined daily in debates in the Commons' chamber when MPs still address each other in the third person and by constituency. Despite accusations that this arcane mode of address is an anachronism, the Modernisation Committee of the House forcefully upheld the tradition: 'Members do not sit in the House as individual citizens, they are there as representatives of their constituents; and it is in that capacity that they should be addressed' (HC 600 1998:paras 37–9).

The principle of territorial representation—of the representation of collective interests of a geographical area and the interests and opinions of individuals within a geographical area—thus affects directly the institutional norms of the Commons. The strength of these norms is illustrated in Table 2.1, where it can be seen that constituency and constituents are still identified by MPs as the primary foci of representation in the 21st century.

The size and number of constituencies are determined by a Boundary Commission in each of the four countries of England, Scotland, Wales and Northern Ireland. Reviews of constituency boundaries since the 1940s have been undertaken at periodic intervals of between eight and twelve years. The fifth general review conducted by the Boundary Commission for England started in February 2000 and a final report is scheduled to be produced by the end of 2005 or early 2006. In undertaking its reviews the Boundary Commission is generally sensitive to the principle of maintaining 'community of interests' and 'local ties' within constituencies (Boundary Commission for England 2000:13). It also seeks to keep the size of the electorate as 'close as practicable' to a quota, set at 69,932 electors in 2000 (Boundary Commission for England 2000:11). Upon completion of the fifth review, the functions of the four Parliamentary Boundary Commissions will be transferred to a new Electoral Commission charged with, amongst other tasks, the responsibility to modernize the electoral machinery of the UK and to promote greater public awareness of the democratic process.

If the importance of locality in electoral apportionment is evident in the Boundary Commissions' work, then so too is the importance of constituency representation evident in the role orientations of MPs themselves (see Table 2.1). Stemming from this emphasis upon locality/constituency are concomitant institutional implications. One consequence is the channelling of citizen-representative interactions through the 'gatekeeper' of constituency, another is a 'social understanding' of the representative role which pre-dates the modern dominance of party representation, and a third impacts on the organizational structures and rules of the Commons itself in terms of working patterns and working time (see below).

Exclusion: 'principle of distinction'

> Another inegalitarian characteristic of representative government ... was deliberately introduced after extensive discussion, namely that the representatives be socially superior to those who elected them. . . . Representative government was instituted in the full awareness that elected representatives would and should be distinguished citizens, socially different from those who elected them. We shall call this the 'principle of distinction'. (Manin 1997:94)

In England (and later Britain) territorial representation was taken to be self-evident from the medieval period onwards, with geographical communities believed to be inextricably linked with economic interest—be it land or commerce—and with the beneficiaries of those interests believed to be the 'natural' representatives of those interests. Before the franchise reforms of the 19th century, electorates were small in number and economically and socially dominant in each constituency. Representatives in turn were even smaller in number and even more elitist (see Manin 1997:96). Membership of parliament was thus socially exclusive, 'distinctive' and clearly bounded. In this sense one of the basic requirements of 'institutionalization' (Polsby 1968:145)—of becoming an institution—was met. Uncontested elections and low turnover of MPs helped to secure the 'institutional boundaries' of the Commons before the gradual democratization of the franchise after 1832. Perhaps, ironically, 'uncompetitive elections' and low turnover arising from the nature of party competition and 'safe seats' in elections since 1945 have helped to replicate the boundedness of pre-democratic parliaments. The parliamentary elite now represents the 'meritocracy'—the beneficiaries of the post-war expansion of welfare provision and educational opportunities. Equally, this elite reflects the opportunities available to pursue a full-time and long-term 'political career'. As Michael Rush (2001:137–8) observes:

> MPs now fulfil their roles in a manner akin to that of many occupations: being a Member of Parliament is their only or overwhelmingly principal occupation and in terms of salary they are treated as full-time; in the provision of services and facilities they are treated as professionals.

The salary of an MP after April 2004 was £57,485. All MPs receive the same salary but ministers and other paid parliamentary office holders receive an additional salary for their office. The salary of an MP is in itself a partial reflection of the distinctiveness of MPs from the average income earner of under £20,000 in the same year (and for that matter from the top earners!). In addition, each MP can claim between £66,458 and £77,534 a year to employ up to the equivalent of three full-time members of staff, a further £19,325 for 'Incidental Expenses Provision' (in essence 'office costs'), as well as up to £20,902 for 'additional costs' incurred when staying away from their main home while performing parliamentary duties. MPs also receive a standard package of office equipment worth about £3,000 (PCs, printers, scanners, copiers, laptop, associated software, answer machines etc), as well as free stationery, UK phone calls and postal services (for details see Cm 4997 2001; House of Commons Department of Finance and Administration 2004).

In the House of Commons elected in 2001 the typical (almost identikit) MP was middle class, university educated and overwhelmingly male (even the females resembled the males in terms of occupational and educational background). What is also notable is the increased numbers of new MPs who had held political positions before becoming MPs. The intakes of newly elected MPs at the 1997 and 2001 elections reflected the growth of the 'career politician', that is 'the individual who lives for politics, who seeks entry to the House of Commons as early as possible and who seeks to stay in the House for as long as possible' (Norton 2004:396). What also helps to define and differentiate the 'career politician' is their 'ambition for ministerial office' (Rush 2001:135, Norton 2004:396; Rush 2005:124−5). The significance of these aspirations for the performance of parliamentary roles will be examined shortly, but, for now, let us simply note that the 'exclusiveness' of MPs continues in the 21st century and that the institutional boundedness of the Commons is preserved and, in fact, reinforced by the very processes of representation that are supposed to open and link the institution to wider civil society. Dominant ideas about the bases of representation—'party' and 'constituency'—undermine alternative conceptions—microcosmic representation—and help to sustain the exclusionary dynamic of parliamentary government. Manin (1997:232 original emphasis) captures this point succinctly in his conclusion that:

> Representative government remains what it has been since its foundation, namely a governance of elites distinguished from the bulk of citizens by social standing, way of life and education. What we are witnessing today is nothing more than *the rise of a new elite and the decline of another.*

The importance of the prevailing ideas about representation in the UK, therefore, is that they provide a justification of, and defence against, what to many diverse groups in society (most particularly women and ethnic minorities) seem to be palpably undemocratic practices (see Judge 1999).

Party representation

If elections simply involved selecting individuals who came together in Parliament after the election in order to form a government, nobody would know in advance what their policy would be and electors would lose their opportunity to influence government policy. It is no coincidence, therefore, that the slow extension of democracy in Britain over the last century and a half has been bound up with the consolidation and growth of political parties and the intensification of national competition between them for office. (Budge et al 2004:439)

There is little dispute that the practice of modern representation in the UK revolves around party politics, and that by extension modern parliamentary politics is party politics, and that, in turn, modern parliamentary government is also party government. Thus, as Klingemann et al note (1994:5), 'Political parties are the main actors in the system that connects the citizenry and the governmental process. . . . political parties aggregate demands into coherent policy packages—a process that gives voters a choice in elections. Political parties form governments and act as opposition in legislatures'.

Party representation conceives of a process of responsibility: of party leaders to party members and of party governments to party voters. The congruence (or disjunction) of party promises and party performance; the articulation of promises in an electoral programme; the translation of promises into policies within the framework of the manifesto; and the correspondence of voters' preferences and policy outputs, all direct attention to the central concepts of 'manifesto' and 'mandate' in modern British representative government.

The idea of the electoral mandate is deceptively simple and follows a logical sequence: first, each party presents to the electorate a policy programme in the form of a manifesto; second, voters make an informed choice between the competing parties on the basis of this programme; third, the successful party seeks to translate this programme into practice once in government; and, fourth, the governing party is then judged by the electorate on its success in implementing its promises at the next election. What this perspective offers, in effect, is an idealized view of responsible government: one where the actions of parliamentary elites are legitimized by the electoral choice of voters mediated through the programmes of parties.

Ultimately, however, the core element of 'party' interpretations of representation is the justification of party discipline within Parliament. What unites all parties in the UK is the defence of the idea of party discipline based upon the notion of the electoral mandate. Despite routine infringements in practice this conceptual base remains largely unquestioned amongst the parliamentary elite (see Topf 1994:150). What party theory justifies, in essence, is a 'system in which the elected representative may be forced by his party managers to vote for a policy which is contrary to the apparent interests of his constituents, contrary to the prevailing opinion in his constituency, and contrary to his own personal judgement about what is best for the country' (Birch 1971:97). The fact that 71 per cent of MPs in 2001 (see Table 2.1) believed 'party' to be important in defining their representative role reveals the continuing strength of the *idea* of party representation in the face of sustained empirical undermining of its theoretical foundations (see chapter 3).

Party composition of House of Commons

Since 1997 the House of Commons has been dominated by the Labour party.

TABLE 2.2 Seats won at the 1997 and 2001 General Elections		
	1997	**2001**
Labour	418	412
Conservative	165	166
Liberal Democrat	46	52
Ulster Unionist	10	6
Democratic Unionist	2	5
Scottish National	6	5
Plaid Cymru	4	4
Sinn Fein	2	4
Social Democratic & Labour	3	3
Independent	1	1
UK Unionist	1	0
Speaker (Stood as 'Speaker seeking re-election')	1	1
Total	659	659
Government majority	179	167

Usual Channels

The dominance of party is reflected in the organization of the House itself. Yet, as Rogers and Walters (2004:86) observe: 'Given the enormous importance of political parties in Westminster politics, it is perhaps surprising that they are not more explicitly recognised in the rules of the . . . House'. However, without party organization and the associated norms and conventions that have developed around it the House would fail to operate. As Wright (2000:108) notes: 'All the essential features of the House of Commons are structured by the realities of parties'. The organizational impact of parties is obvious even in the very seating arrangements in the Commons chamber, with the division between the parties reflected in the location of the governing party on one side (on the benches to the right of the Speaker) and the opposition parties on the benches facing the government. Correspondingly, committees of the House (see below) reflect the 'composition of the House' and thus reflect the party balance in the wider House.

While the House is structured in accordance with the fundamental division between government and opposition, and its formal procedures reflect this basic adversarial relationship, the daily routine of the Commons is determined by informal consensual understandings reached between the respective party managers. These managers are known as the 'whips'—after the 'whippers-in' who controlled fox-hounds at hunt meetings (before the banning of fox hunting under the Hunting Act 2004). The control analogy points to two dimensions of the whips' role, one is control over the arrangement of the collective business in the Commons, the other is control over the individual activities of party representatives. While the notion of control attracts most attention and criticism, the notion of management best encapsulates the role of the whips. Whips of all parties cooperate through the 'usual channels' to manage the business of the House. While backbench MPs are prone to criticize the 'usual channels' for being 'too cosy' and too secretive, nonetheless, such co-operation is necessary for the business of the Houses to be completed. Thus, for example, the schedule of daily business, the timetabling of bills, membership of committees, and the distribution of select committee chairs are normally determined through the 'usual channels' (see Rush and Ettinghausen 2002:7–8).

The other main management function of the whips is the internal management of the respective parties. The management of votes is particularly important, both in ensuring that party members vote in the required numbers and in the right way. Each party needs to keep its own members informed of the scheduling of business and the significance of that business. As Philip Norton noted: 'the greater the volume of business transacted, and the greater the complexity, the greater the need for guidance' (1981:30).

Traditionally this information has been conveyed through a system of un-derlining of items of business (from one to three lines) on the daily or-der paper. The partisan significance of any particular item is indicated by an increasing scale of underlining, with a 'three-line whip' indicating the highest priority accorded to attendance and voting by the party leadership. This method was supplemented in the 1997 parliament by the issuing of telephone pagers to Labour MPs. Despite widespread press cynicism about the use of such technology, it simply constitutes, at one level, an updating of traditional means of managing backbench participation and voting in the House.

The first objective of the party whip is to secure the requisite numbers of MPs to vote; on the government side to ensure the necessary majority in support of a motion or legislative proposal, and on the opposition side to re-cord the degree of dissent from the government's proposals. Given the size of Labour majorities in the 1997 and 2001 parliaments (see Table 2.2), secur-ing attendance of the Parliamentary Labour Party (PLP) might have been expected to have been simply a routine and mechanical process, nonethe-less, some judicious management of backbenchers was still required. The Labour whips had to counteract the powerful backbench logic that 'if I miss that vote that is OK, my vote will be neither here nor there' (Labour MP quoted in Cowley 2002:164).

A second part of the management role of the whips is the communic-ation of the programme of the party leadership to backbenchers, and, in return, the conveying of the opinions of backbenchers back to the leadership. Related to this communication function is the management of consensus within the party and the maintenance of voting unity. While seeking to be 'consultative and inclusive' (Cowley 2002:150) the whips are also willing to deploy 'persuasion and coercion' when called upon to do so. Whips have a range of incentives and disincentives at their disposal to forestall persistent dissension, and to inculcate loyalty. Ultimately, however, MPs primarily support their party leaderships not out of fear, or out of inducement, but simply because they share a common overarching perspective on politics, and because they wish to appear united (Cowley 2002:178). When this consensus fractures, however, as it did over the issue of Iraq in the spring of 2003, then the per-suasion, negotiation and intimidation of the whips is insufficient to prevent backbench rebellions. In votes on Iraq, in February and March 2003, 122 and 139 Labour MPs respectively voted against their own government's policy. While these were the largest dissenting votes recorded against a modern government, they were simply the most dramatic examples of a tendency of Labour MPs since 1997 to rebel infrequently but to do so in sizeable numbers. As Philip Cowley's research (2002) demonstrates, some 50 per cent of Labour backbenchers voted against the government at some stage in the 1997–2001 parliament and to some effect on a range of policies. This pattern continued after 2001 with 191 separate backbench rebellions involving 211 Labour MPs in the three sessions between June 2001 and November 2004, Cowley and Stuart 2004:2–3).

Nonetheless, it is worth stressing the general claim that 'political parties are built on an overwhelming consensus of opinion and sense of identity' (Weir and Beetham 1999:373). It is also worth emphasising that this relatively tight consensus has organizational and institutional ramifications (for example, impacting upon the division of labour within parties and the Commons more broadly, and upon norms about parliamentary career trajectories (see below)).

Deliberative institution

The interconnectedness between ideas and institutional practice is revealed further in the emphasis placed upon deliberation in the House of Commons. What might appear to many in the 21st century to be an illogically time-consuming activity—interminable debate—is still entirely reasonable in terms of the institutional norms and values inherited from preceding centuries. The emphasis upon deliberation is closely linked to ideas about what MPs, individually, and the House, collectively, should be doing. Indeed, the contemporary strength of these ideas is worth noting at this point. As Table 2.1 reveals, MPs in the 21st century still subscribe overwhelmingly (89 per cent) to the view that elected representatives should represent the interests of the nation as a whole. Equally significantly 81 per cent of MPs believed that their decisions to act and vote in parliament were strongly influenced by their own opinions (this was nearly as strong as the influence exerted by party leadership at 87 per cent). These two factors—'nation' and 'own judgement'—coalesce in trustee notions of representation (see Judge 1999:47–69).

The best known formulation of trustee theory was provided by Edmund Burke, in his famous *Address to the Electors of Bristol* in 1774, who argued that

'Parliament is a *deliberative* assembly of one nation, with one interest, that of the whole—where not local prejudices ought to guide, but the general good, resulting from the general reason of the whole' ([1774] 1801 vol 3:20). This *Address* linked the style of representation (the 'how'—trusteeship) with the focus of representation (the 'what'—the nation) and, in so doing, provided a theory of legitimate government. Parliamentary outputs, primarily in the form of legislation, were deemed to be legitimate precisely because they had been subject to the process of deliberation by representatives of all sections of the 'political nation' (however defined at the time). Similarly, the principle of trusteeship was also evident a century later in the writings of John Stuart Mill. His view of what a parliament should do was conditioned by what the British parliament already did: 'in reality the only thing which [it] decides is which of two, or at most three, parties . . . shall furnish the executive government' ([1861] 1910:234); and that 'the only task to which a representative assembly can possibly be competent is not that of doing the work, but of causing it to be done; of determining to whom or to what sort of people it shall be confided, and giving or withholding the national sanction to it when performed' ([1861] 1910:237). The truly effective function of a representative assembly, therefore, was deliberation:

> Representative assemblies are often taunted by their enemies with being places of mere talk and *bavardage*. There has seldom been more misplaced derision. I know not how a representative assembly can more usefully employ itself than in talk, when the subject of talk is the great public interests of the country, and every sentence of it represents the opinion either of some important body of persons in the nation, or of an individual in whom some such body have reposed their confidence. A place where every interest and shade of opinion can have its cause even passionately pleaded, in the face of the government and of all other interests and opinions. ([1861] 1910:240)

Whilst the starting premises, and, indeed, the location of ultimate political responsibility, differentiated their conceptions of representation, nonetheless, Burke and Mill were agreed that representatives should *not* be bound by instructions from the represented. Equally, they agreed that the best interests of the nation could be established and promoted through parliamentary deliberation.

The continued relevance of trustee notions of representation has been chronicled elsewhere (see Judge 1999:58–68) but one recent example was found in the Report of the Select Committee on Modernisation and its statement that: 'All Members of Parliament bring to deliberations their independent judgement and their assessment of constituency interest' (HC 224 2002: para 11).

Type of debate

Much of the time of the Commons is occupied by debate of some description—whether of the general legislative programme (in debates on the Queen's Speech), the principles of specific legislative proposals (in debates at second reading), of the concerns of the opposition parties (in opposition day debates), emergency debates, or constituency matters (in adjournment debates). Indeed, since November 1999 opportunities for debate have expanded with the introduction of a parallel chamber known as 'Westminster Hall' (which meets in the Grand Committee Room just off of Westminster Hall). The format of debates in Westminster Hall ranges from adjournment debates on subjects raised by individual MPs, general debates on a topic chosen by the Speaker, 'cross-cutting debates' and the discussion of policies straddling more than one government department, through other general debates determined by ballot, to debates on select committee reports chosen by the Liaison Committee (see below). The additional time for debate, made available through this forum, is some 27 per cent, or an estimated extra 333 hours of debate on average per session (Rogers and Walters 2004:270).

While deliberation in Westminster Hall has been applauded as a 'success' in enabling backbenchers 'to initiate debate on topics of their choice and to explore that topic in a more rational atmosphere than is possible in the more partisan environment of the Chamber' (HC 1168 2002:para 97–8), the actual impact of the 'parallel chamber' has been relatively limited. Few MPs attend such debates—with an average of between 10 and 12 MPs present at general debates—and proceedings in 'Westminster Hall' have attracted relatively little media coverage (HC 906 2000:para 20).

Although considerable time is devoted by MPs to deliberation there is a widespread perception that much of this time is wasted. Attendance at debates in the main chamber is generally low, 'on most days MPs addressing the House do so to rows of empty green benches' (Norton 2004:408). Moreover, 'Members appear in the Chamber to speak rather than listen. It is a forum for making a case but for most of the time has only marginal effect on major decisions' (Cm 4997 2001:32). Perhaps, not surprisingly, the public has a jaundiced view of parliamentary deliberation (gleaned largely from media coverage). As the Hansard Society (HC 1168 2002:8) noted, the public perception is largely of confrontational clashes between party MPs engaged in 'squabbling' and 'arguing', and the Society concluded more generally that: 'It may be that debates are no longer suitable for today's politics. In an era of soundbite politics and 24 hour news, the idea of debating a single issue for six hours is alien to most MPs and their electorate' (Hansard Society 2001:51). However, there are some notable occasions when parliamentary debates do register more positively with the public, as with the debate on 'Iraq and Weapons of Mass Destruction' held when MPs were recalled from their summer vacation on 24 September 2002. A year earlier, the House had been recalled three times immediately after the events of 11 September 2001 (14 September, 4 and 8 October 2001) to debate international terrorism and the attacks in the USA on the World Trade Centre and the Pentagon and the responses to these terrorist attacks. Certainly, the debates on waging war in Iraq in March 2003 attracted widespread and intensive media and public attention. This debate also provided a vivid example of how debate may 'serve to challenge, in a public way, the policies and actions of the Government and to put forward alternative suggestions which, in turn, are subject to challenge' (HC 333 2003:para 4).

Legislative institution

Every Act of Parliament starts with the words:

> Be it enacted by the Queen's most Excellent Majesty, by and with the advice and consent of the Lords Spiritual and Temporal, and Commons, in this present Parliament assembled, and by the authority of the same, as follows . . .

The significance of this preamble is that it makes explicit that laws are made *collectively* by parliament. However, as noted above, traditionally parliament—although nominally a legislature (literally a 'maker of law')—served not to 'make' statutes but rather to consent to, and authorize the executive's legislative proposals. Parliament's legislative role was thus conceived in terms of amending, improving and authorising laws by allowing for scrutiny and for the expression of public opinion to be brought to bear in the process. Hence, the primary 'legislative' function of parliament came to be the legitimation of government legislation. The 'democratic' credentials of the legislative process rest, therefore, upon the mechanisms by which public influence, control and scrutiny are exercized. Within the Commons the protracted five-stage process—of first and second readings, committee and report stages, and third reading of bills—is a procedural reflection of the importance accorded to legitimization (see Box 2.2).

Certainly much of the time of both the Lords and the Commons is spent in processing legislation. In session 2002–3 some 490 hours, or approximately 38 per cent of the time of the House, were expended on the consideration of bills (House of Commons 2004). Most of this time, in turn, was devoted to the consideration of government legislation (public bills), with non-government bills (private members bills) accounting for only about 19 per cent of the time spent on legislation as a whole.

According to the Modernisation Committee: 'the core of parliamentary business is making law' (HC 1168 2002:para 25). Yet, within the collective institution of parliament some institutional elements are more important than others. Thus, the Commons is pre-eminent over the Lords, and within the Commons the government is pre-eminent within its own party and over other parties. Moreover, when 'making' law, it is the executive that formulates and initiates legislation, controls the processing of legislation, and determines the ultimate outputs of that process:

> Once Bills are formally introduced they are largely set in concrete. There has been a distinct culture prevalent throughout Whitehall that the standing and reputation of Ministers have been dependent on their Bills getting through largely unchanged. As a result there has been an inevitable disposition to resist alteration, not only on the main issues of substance, but also on matters of detail. (HC 190 1997:para 7)

As the Modernisation Committee proceeded to note, a major factor sustaining the current mode of processing legislation (and also of constraining procedural change) was the 'culture of the House' (HC 190 1997:para 17). Notably absent from this culture are 'those values enhancing detailed scrutiny and criticism of executive actions by Parliament as a collectivity . . . the idea of "Parliament" as a political force, or as a whole, is therefore simply a myth. Parliament in this sense simply does not exist' (Weir and Beetham 1999:376). Yet it is only if these ideas are treated seriously (and they have to be treated seriously in terms of legitimation) that the time spent by the Commons in processing legislation makes much, or any, sense.

BOX 2.2   **Legislative process in the House of Commons**

Draft Bill Scrutiny: According to the Modernisation Committee pre-legislative scrutiny 'provides a vehicle for the careful, planned consideration of bills before they reach the floor of the House' (HC 1222 2003:para 15; see also HL 173 2004:paras15–28). In which case, the Modernisation Committee attached the 'highest importance' to such scrutiny and willingly endorsed it as a 'core task' of Select Committees (HC 1168 2002:paras 28–9). Indeed, the active engagement of select committees at a pre-legislative stage had been an aspiration of parliamentary reformers since the inception of departmental committees some two decades earlier. Only gradually did this aspiration become reality—with government departments increasing the numbers of draft bills from 18, between 1992–1997, to 42, between 1997 and 2004. (The Queen's Speech in November 2004 announced a further eight draft bills). In addition to scrutiny by Select Committees, draft legislation may also be considered by joint committees of both Houses, including the Joint Committee on Human Rights. Despite this increased activity, however, the extent to which legislation is shaped 'decisively' by parliamentarians remains indeterminate (see HC 558 2003:paras 31–6).

First Reading: marks the formal introduction of a bill. The title of the bill is read out, a notional day for a 'Second Reading' is named, and the bill is ordered to be printed. The first reading stage is merely a formality with no debate and no decision recorded.

Second Reading: the principles of the bill are debated (normally either half a day or a full day is scheduled for debate, though constitutional bills may be scheduled for two or more days). Some non-controversial bills are dealt with in a second reading committee. Second reading debates tend to be wide ranging. The opposition may table a 'reasoned amendment' at this stage. This allows the reasons why the opposition objects to the bill to be stated (but is not technically an amendment to the bill itself). Only three times in the past century has a government lost a vote on second reading (1924, 1977 and 1986). As Norton (2004:405) observes 'a government sometime loses the argument but not usually the vote'.

Committee Stage: Once approved in principle at second reading the bill is sent to committee for detailed scrutiny. There are three choices of committee. First, and most frequently, bills are considered in standing committees. Although the word 'standing' seems to indicate some permanence to these committees they are constituted afresh for each different bill. At any one time there may be five or more separate committees examining separate legislative proposals. The membership of each committee is appointed for the duration of the consideration of each bill, and

_ continues

Box 2.2 continued

usually ranges from 16 to 30 members (with 18 being the average membership). Most importantly membership reflects proportionately the party composition of the Commons as a whole. In turn the procedures adopted in committee reflect the adversarial divide of the chamber. While the purpose of committee stage is to enable legislation to be subjected to detailed clause-by-clause scrutiny, and where appropriate to amendment, the organizational rules and the norms of MPs serving on these committees militate against effective scrutiny. Thus, as Griffith (1974:38) observed in his seminal study, much of what takes place during committee is an extension of the adversarial conflict in the chamber and 'there is little or no intention or expectation of changing the bill. The purpose of many Opposition amendments is not to make the bill more generally acceptable but to make the Government less acceptable'. Some 30 years ago Griffith observed that 70 per cent of amendments moved in committee came from opposition members, yet only eight per cent of these were accepted (compared to a success rate of 99.9 per cent for ministerial amendments). The figures have not changed much over time (see Rush 2005:183–4).

Very occasionally a bill may be considered by a Special Standing Committee. These committees were designed 'to encourage more informed discussion on Bills which were not highly politically controversial' (HC 190 1997:para 9) and allowed for limited investigation of the issues before detailed consideration of each clause. While the Modernisation Committee favours greater use of such committees they continue to be used rarely. In its first parliament the Labour government committed only one bill—the Immigration and Asylum Bill in session 1998–99—to a special standing committee, and in the 2001 parliament the Adoption and Children Bill was referred to such a committee.

Bills may also be referred to a select committee. Apart from the Armed Forces Bill which is published every five years and which is considered by a specially constituted select committee, there have only been isolated occasions when other bills have been sent to select committees. In sessions 2000–01 and 2001–02, for example, the Adoption and Children Bill was sent to an *ad hoc* select committee (but the committee did not complete its consideration of the bill before the 2001 general election and, thereafter, the measure was sent to a special standing order committee in the new parliament (see above)).

An alternative to sending a bill 'upstairs' (committees have met traditionally in rooms situated along second and third floor corridors) is to consider the bill in the Commons' chamber in a Committee of the Whole House. Such committees are used primarily for bills of constitutional significance, such as the House of Lords Bill 1998–99 and the Scotland Bill 1997–98, or for part of the annual Finance Bill, or for other measures requiring rapid processing, such as the Anti-Terrorism, Crime and Security Bill 2001 or the Northern Ireland Assembly Elections Bill 2003.

Report Stage: All bills, except those unamended by a Committee of the Whole House and which proceed directly to third reading, return to the floor of the House

continues

Box 2.2 continued

for 'consideration'. At this stage, further amendments may be made by members who were not directly involved in the committee stage. Primarily, however, the Report Stage presents another opportunity for the government to make last-minute amendments, or to reverse changes made at committee stage.

Third Reading: marks the final stage of the Commons' process before it is sent to the House of Lords for its consideration of the bill. In essence it provides the opportunity to take an overview of the bill after amendment. Third Reading Debates are normally very short and no further amendment of the bill may be made at this stage.

The results of this extensive process of legislative scrutiny are, however, normally and overwhelmingly predictable. Governments get their way and do so increasingly on schedule (see Table 2.3)

TABLE 2.3	Success Rates of Public Bills			
	Government bills introduced	% Successful	Private member's bills introduced	% Successful
1992–3	52	100.0	157	10.5
1993–4	25	100.0	106	13.8
1994–5	38	94.9*	104	14.5
1995–6	43	100.0	80	17.5
1996–7	37	100.0	69	21.7
1997–8	53	98.1	134	6.0
1998–9	31	87.1**	93	7.5
1999–00	40	97.5	97	5.2
2000–01	26	80.7***	61	0.0
2001–02	39	100.0	109	6.4
2002–03	36	97.2****	93	14.0

*One bill withdrawn and one hybrid bill 'carried over'
**One bill carried over under new procedure
***Short session due to General Election
****Two bills carried over
Source: House of Commons Sessional Returns

Since session 1997–98 most major public (government) bills have been subject to 'programme motions' that provide a timetable for each bill in an attempt to encourage more balanced consideration of its contents. The initial experiment was designed to seek cross-party agreement, through the usual channels, about the amount of time to be spent after second reading in the various stages of the bill (for details see HC 190 1997, HC 589 2000, Blackburn and Kennon 2003:314–16, HC 325 2004). Enthusiasm for programme motions failed to gain momentum and, indeed, appeared to be faltering as their number declined from 11 in 1997–98 (in addition there were three guillotines, where time is allocated by the government without prior opposition approval), four in 1998–99 (11 guillotines), and four in 1999–2000 (eight guillotines). In these circumstances, the Modernisation Committee reviewed the programming of legislation and proposed, in the face of opposition from the Conservative members of the Committee, the introduction of a new sessional order to allow for the programming of most government bills. In session 2000–01, 20 out of 21 Bills were programmed without consensus. In the new parliament revised sessional orders were adopted and, by mid-2004, 67 out of a total of 84 bills had been programmed (HC 325 2004:para 6).

The significance of programming was neatly summarized by Sir Alan Haslehurst (Chairman of the Ways and Means Committee):

> If the basic idea behind the concept of programming has been to achieve balanced consideration of legislation, progress to date can frankly and brutally be described as nil. . . . What has happened as a result of recent changes is that the Government gets its legislation with less delay and Members go home earlier. (HC 1168 2002:Appendix 42, para 22)

Haslehurst's plea was that legislative scrutiny could be improved only if government and opposition 'abandon their entrenched positions'. In 2004 the Procedure Committee expressed a similar opinion:

> We believe that, if programming were used as originally envisaged by the Modernisation Committee, namely only when there is cross-party agreement, it would have the potential to be a more effective way of considering, and improving, legislation, and we regret that it has come to be seen as the same as the guillotine, though more widely applied. (HC 325 2004:para 18)

The Procedure Committee recommended a change in the sessional orders to allow programming motions to be used routinely only if there was cross-party support, otherwise the government would have to justify such a motion in debate (HC 325 2004: para 18). In its response, the government pointed to the 'strong political pressures' militating against likely consensus: 'While the Opposition may be willing to adopt a pragmatic approach in informal negotiations through the usual channels, it would be very difficult for it to sign up publicly to a programme for scrutiny of a Bill to which it is opposed in principle' (HC 1169 2004:para 3). In these circumstances, the government proposed a motion to incorporate programming within the Standing Orders of the House and, in doing so, pointed out that some 70 per cent of programme motions had been achieved consensually in the preceding session (HC Debates 26 October 2004 vol 425: col 1309). Nonetheless, many MPs feared that significant portions of major Bills would continue to 'leave this House . . . unexamined and not discussed, which means that the Government [would not have] been held to account' (Sir Patrick Cormack, HC Debates 26 October 2004 vol 425: col 1310).

Delegated legislation

> It would be inaccurate to suggest that the bulk of the laws under which the British people now live have been subject to searching Commons scrutiny . . . This is due [in large part to] the government's increasing tendency to promote Bills which delegate secondary law-making power to ministers through the mechanism of 'regulations' or 'statutory instruments'. (Loveland 2003:132)

Delegated legislation (also referred to as secondary or subordinate legislation) takes several different forms, the most important of which are Statutory Instruments, and Deregulation and Regulatory Reform Orders. Such legislation allows for the provisions of an Act of Parliament to be changed, or brought into effect, without having to pass a new law. On average each year some 1,500 statutory instruments are laid before Parliament (see HC 48 2000:para 25), but this is only about half of the annual output (estimated to be around 3,000 by Beetham et al (2002:141)). Much delegated legislation, therefore, is not considered by Parliament and, in fact, some instruments are not even printed (see Blackburn and Kennon 2003:346).

Of those Statutory Instruments that do reach Parliament only about 15 per cent require approval before they become law (through an 'affirmative procedure'). The vast majority of such instruments are subject to a 'negative procedure' whereby they come into force on a specified date unless a motion for annulment is passed. Even when such a motion is tabled it is at the discretion of the government as to when and where the instrument is debated and voted upon (in a standing Committee on Delegated Legislation, or on the Floor of the House). In either location 'the government is able to prevent criticism of its delegated legislation despite the fact that statutes provide formally for such criticism' (Blackburn and Kennon 2003:488).

Not surprisingly, the system for scrutiny of delegated legislation is widely condemned as 'woefully inadequate' (HC 300 2000:para 24) or 'palpably unsatisfactory' (HC 152 1996:para 1, HC 48 2000:para 53). Of no less surprise is that the Procedure Committee has proposed reform of the scrutiny system of delegated legislation three times in recent years (in 1996 [HC 152 1996]; 2000 [HC 48 2000] and 2003 [HC 501 2003]). Equally unsurprising is that the governments of the time, Conservative in 1996 and Labour in 2000 and 2003 have been hesitant in their responses. The 1996 proposals were not implemented, and the Labour government, in 2002, stalled consideration of the issue (HC 1168 2002:para 53), and, in 2003, remained unwilling to introduce a sifting committee in the Commons as suggested by the Procedure Committee (HC 684 2003:Annex A).

Remedial orders

A new variant of delegated legislation known as 'remedial orders' was introduced in the Human Rights Act 1998. Such orders provide ministers with a procedure to amend primary legislation when a court has ruled that an Act of Parliament is incompatible with the European Convention of Human Rights (see chapter 6). Two types of remedial order are noted in the 1998 Act. A non-urgent procedure requires a draft order to be introduced but can only be 'made' after approval by affirmative resolution of each House. After a period of 60 days in which representations can be made, the draft order is scrutinized by the Joint Committee on Human Rights, and then requires approval by resolution of each House. In urgent cases, under a 'fast track' procedure, an order may be made with immediate statutory effect, but the order ceases to have effect unless approved by affirmative resolution of each House within 120 days (for details see HL 58/HC 473 2001). The first, and only, remedial order to be made in the first four years of the operation of the Human Rights Act, was introduced in 2001 and amended the Mental Health Act 1983.

Legitimation

The time spent on debate and the processing of legislation is frequently derided as a 'waste of time'. Certainly, in terms of observable influence upon public policy, the Commons in its collective guise as deliberator and legislator is a remarkably ineffective institution. But despite this, the emphasis upon deliberation and the careful processing of legislation remains of axiomatic importance in sustaining the legitimacy of public policies. As argued elsewhere, and at length, there is no other institution in the UK with the formal capacity to confer such legitimation (see Judge 1990:18–44; Judge 1993: Judge 1999; Judge 2004). It is in this sense that, 'as the body accepted by both mass and elites for legitimating measures of public policy, Parliament is a powerful body' (Norton 1993a:145).

Scrutiny/control institution

Parliamentary questions

In the 1997–2001 parliament ministers were required to answer on average 40,000 questions in each session (see Table 2.4), and cumulatively had to be present in the chamber to answer questions for over 500 hours in that period. With each oral question costing on average £345 and each written question £148 to answer (as at April 2004, see HC Debates 19 January 2005: col 986W), and with the total costs of administering the questions system estimated at over £8 million per session (see HC 622 2002:para 20, Cm 5628

TABLE 2.4	Replies to Questions appearing in Hansard and indexed in POLIS						
Type							Total
	1997–98	1998–99	1999–00	2000–01	2001–02	2002–03	1997–2003
	n	n	n	n	n	n	n
Oral	8,132	4,774	5,343	2,591	6,392	6,272	33,504
Written	51,451	31,649	36,067	16,687	67,651	51,614	255,119

Source: House of Commons Sessional Information Digests 1997–2003
N.B. *oral replies include supplementary answers/POLIS doesn't record all written answers (multiple questions on same topic may have been recorded as one answer)*

2002:para 4), then, if 'some members view [Question Time], especially Prime Minister's Question Time, as a farce' (Norton 2004:409), it is an expensive farce.

But, as with so many of the proceedings in the House of Commons, questions are an institutional reflection of the formal interinstitutional relationships between legislature and executive as well as of informal intrainstitutional partisan relationships.

As a procedure, questions developed initially 'as an irregular form of debate' (House of Commons Information Office 2004:2). They were a relatively informal means of asking ministers to account for their actions. Indeed, questioning remains a relatively informal procedure as it is only partly regulated by Standing Orders, and Question Time itself is not recorded in the Votes and Proceedings or the Journal (HC 622 2002:para 7). The rules governing questions were subject, between 1945 and 2003, to no less than 13 select committee enquiries and consequent constant procedural tinkering. Nonetheless, despite substantial procedural change, the practice and purpose of questioning 'is not in essence different' from the immediate post-war period (House of Commons Information Office 2004:3). The purpose remains the same: 'to press for action or seek information' (Principal Clerk HC 622 2002:para 28). Or, in a more elaborate formulation, to bring particular issues to the attention of ministers, to obtain information about ministerial activities not previously on the public record, to require ministers to defend their positions in a public and critical forum, to press for governmental action, and to subject government as a whole to 'critical interrogation' (Norton 1993b:198). In other words, questions serve as a means of securing ministerial accountability. There are five basic types of questions. Oral questions are asked and answered on the floor of the House. Written questions are the most numerous, and receive written responses—the texts of which are published in Hansard. Prime Minister's questions are directly targeted at the PM and range cumulatively and widely over all aspects of government policy. Urgent questions (known before 2002–03 as Private Notice questions) raise matters of immediate public importance. Finally, in January 2003 a new form of question time was held for the first time in Westminster Hall. This involved ministers from a number of government departments answering 'cross-cutting' questions about their 'joined-up' responsibilities (see chapter 4). Four such cross-cutting sessions are to be scheduled each parliamentary year.

One positive assessment of the value of questions was offered by Tony Wright, Chairman of the Public Administration Committee, who emphasized in the House: 'We know that parliamentary questions are a vital instrument in the hands of Members of Parliament. In fact, written questions are probably the most vital instrument of sustained accountability that Members of Parliament have' (HC Debates 21 March 2002:Col 137WH). (When combined with provisions of the 1998 Data Protection Act and the Freedom of Information Act 2000 written questions can be used effectively to secure the release of information previously withheld by departments (see HC 136 2002:para 6)). In addition, the government, when withholding information requested in questions, has agreed that it will cite the relevant exemption in the *Code of Practice on Access to Government Information* 'this is to ensure that Ministers cannot evade accountability by hiding behind vague phrases such as "not normal practice to provide this information" when they refuse to answer' (HC 136 2002:para 3)). Similarly, the government rates questions as a 'highly effective means of holding the Executive to account' (Cm 5628 2002:para 2). Yet the effectiveness of questions in attaining their purpose remains open to dispute. MPs collectively are generally a little less generous in their assessment than the government. For example, only 43 per cent of a sample of 167 MPs in 2002 rated oral questions as 'very' or 'quite' effective'; though 60 per cent believed written questions to be 'very' or 'quite' effective' in fulfilling the purpose of holding the executive to account (HC 622 2002:Annex B). Cynics beyond the House of Commons might want to discount, or at least deflate, these assessments still further (for reasons see below) but ultimately, and residually, there is an institutional significance attached to the procedure of questions that cannot be discounted.

First, there is the symbolic significance of questions in that ministers are routinely subject to appear before MPs to account for the actions of their departments. Ministers know that they will normally be required to answer questions for the best part of an hour once a month. Second, and perhaps more importantly, civil servants and agency officials also know this to be a fact too (see chapter 4). Equally the prime minister knows that for at least two hours a month he or she will have to answer questions in the House. The PM presently answers questions at 12 noon for half an hour on Wednesday afternoons.

The fact that Tony Blair as prime minister arbitrarily adopted the new timing, moving from two 15 minute slots on Tuesdays and Thursdays without prior consultation within the House, both points to the relative informality of the procedure itself as well as to a belief that the PM was attempting to manipulate the procedure to his own partisan advantage. Indeed, the reform of Prime Minister's Questions reveals both the centrality of the principle of ministerial accountability—in the acceptance that the highest minister in the land must attend parliament—but an equal and countervailing acceptance that the PM will seek to minimize partisan embarrassment in so doing. The institutional precept of the open scrutiny of the executive by the legislature is inverted by the partisan precept that the former should be shielded from (and 'closed' to) the effects of partisan cross-examination in the House. While-ever it is accepted as 'inescapable' that questions, particularly oral questions 'will in many cases be employed for essentially party-political purposes' (HC 622 2002:para 30) then there is every prospect that despite procedural changes—to shorten the deadlines for notice, to introduce electronic tabling, to enhance the topicality and relevance of question time, to curb long and rambling questions and more particularly ministerial replies (see HC 622 2002:33–8)—the partisan techniques of shielding ministers from penetrating scrutiny will continue to be deployed. Planted questions, sycophantic questions, syndicated questions, sympathetic supplementary questions, and organized pre-briefing sessions of backbenchers by frontbenchers and whips have all been used as partisan devices to protect government ministers, as party politicians, from embarrassment by opposition MPs, who are also acting as party politicians. In this process the interests and norms and values of party as an organization override the interests and norms and values of parliament as an institution. This is one of the fundamental paradoxes at the heart of the institution of parliament (see Judge 1993:197–216).

Select Committees

[T]here is more to life, in terms of ministerial accountability, than parliamentary questions alone. Questions and answers are integral to the accountability process, but they are not the only way in which Members may request information from the Government. . . . the Select Committee system offer[s] other means. (Christopher Leslie, Parliamentary Secretary, Cabinet Office, HC Debates 21 March 2002:col 173WH)

The then Leader of the House, Robin Cook, went one step further than his junior ministerial colleague and maintained that: 'Departmental Select

Committees are the most developed vehicle through which MPs can carry out detailed scrutiny of Government Policy and Ministerial Conduct' (HC 440 2001:para 5).

Departmental select committees are of relatively recent origin. Created in 1979 they operate alongside two other types of select committees. The first, often referred to as investigative committees, include the Public Administration, Public Accounts, European Scrutiny, Regulatory Reform, and Environmental Audit Committees. These committees monitor particular areas of governmental activity and produce concise, regular reports. The second type of committee deals with 'internal matters' of the Commons—and includes the Administration, Catering, Modernisation, and Standards and Privileges Committees. There is a third type of 'joint committee' of both Houses, the most visible examples of which are the Human Rights Committee, the Joint Committee on House of Lords Reform, and the Statutory Instruments Committee.

The sheer number and proliferation of committees in recent years in the House of Commons reflects the general observation that 'Committees are, by broad consensus, among the most significant internal organizational features of modern parliaments' (Strøm 1998:55). Yet, historically, for the reasons noted above, 'the British Parliament has always been a chamber-oriented institution. Though it has ... variously made use of committees the emphasis has always been on the chamber' (Norton 1998:143). Nonetheless, by the late 1990s, Norton (1998:151) maintained that, as a result of the developing committee system, the Commons 'was more specialised and institutionalised than ever before in its seven century existence'. But this was not saying much in comparison with most other western parliaments (see Bergman et al 2004:172–3).

At the very time, in the early 1980s, that the system of departmental select committees was being introduced some commentators pointed out that the reasons why the House had displayed a traditional resistance to a systematic division of labour, and why the impact of the new system was likely to be constrained in the future, reflected three central elements of the organizational and normative systems of the UK's legislature. These were identified by Judge (1981) as the adversarial nature of partisan competition, the conjunction of executive and House leadership roles, and the weakness of supportive theories of representation in the House. In particular Judge noted that, 'the normative system of the House, as with any other dominant value system, reflects the predilections of the most powerful actors and supports the existing distribution of power: in other words, the norms, aspirations and practices of most backbenchers are defined by reference to the executive' (Judge 1983:190; 1993:215).

Nonetheless, in 1979 the introduction of a new system of 14 departmentally-related select committees was heralded as a new dawn in the relationship between the executive and legislature (St John Stevas HC Debates 1979 vol 969 col 35). The new system followed a report from the Select Committee on Procedure in 1978. This Committee openly avowed that its aim was to strike a new balance in the relationship between the executive and the legislature. Indeed, the Procedure Committee had a grand vision which started from an appreciation that: 'The essence of the problem . . . is that the balance of advantage between Parliament and Government in the day-to-day working of the constitution is now weighted in favour of the Government to a degree which arouses widespread anxiety and is inimical to the proper working of our parliamentary democracy' (HC 588 1978:viii) And which finished with the belief that: 'a new balance must be struck . . . with the aim of enabling the House as a whole to exercise effective control and stewardship over Ministers and the expanding bureaucracy of the modern state for which they are answerable, and to make the decisions of Parliament and Government more responsive to the wishes of the electorate' (HC 588 1978:viii).

Now it should be made clear that neither the Procedure Committee of 1978, nor the then Leader of the House, Norman St. John Stevas, countenanced a redistribution of decision-making power to the House. Instead the ability—the power—of the Commons to scrutinize and so to influence the executive was to be enhanced. It was realized at the time that if 'the impact of a committee on central government is a self-inflicted blow' (Study of Parliament Group 1976:37), then only a restatement of the powers of the new committee system would increase the masochistic tendencies of governments. To this end the Procedure Committee recommended, amongst other things, that select committees should be empowered to order the attendance of ministers to give evidence, to order the production of papers and records by ministers, to require government observations to be produced within two months of the date of publication of a report, and to set aside eight days per session for debates on committee reports. Moreover, a challenge to executive normative ascendancy in the House was posed by proposing the payment of chairmen of select committees. This was believed to be 'both desirable for its own sake, and could also provide some element of a career opportunity in the House not wholly in the gift of the Party Leaders' (HC 588 1978:lxxix). Thus, for all that the Procedure Committee sought to present its proposals as an evolutionary change, the radical threat to executive hegemony was apparent in its report (see Judge 1981:192).

In 1979 this challenge was implicitly recognized by the government in its careful circumscription of the powers of the new committees: their chairmen were not to be paid; the power to compel the attendance of ministers was denied; no time limit was specified for the submission of departmental observations nor were eight days set aside for the discussion of committee reports. It is against these restrictions that the committees have chafed ever since.

The continued significance of these restrictions featured in two major internal reviews of the committee system (HC 19 1990 and HC 300 2000). While both internal reviews concluded respectively that there was 'no doubt' that the post-1979 system was 'a success' (HC 19 1990:para 357; HC 300 2000:para 4), both recognized that the 'success was not unalloyed' (HC 300 2000:para 6). In making suggestions to 'make the system more effective and independent; to make it a better scrutineer of Government' the Liaison Committee revisited several of the proposals made some two decades earlier by the 1978 Procedure Committee.

Like its predecessor in 1978, the Liaison Committee in 2000 recognized that any reform proposals needed to be made in the context of the 'realities' of parliamentary life. Pre-eminent amongst these realities was the fact that 'Ministers are also Members of Parliament, and are sustained in office by Parliament' and that 'party loyalty and organisation . . . structure the way in which Parliament and its institutions work' (HC 300 2000:para 9). Yet, having recognized these realities, the Committee's report acknowledged that executive dominance and party control were precisely the main constraints upon the effective operation of the committees. Thus, it was 'wrong that party managers should exercise effective control of select committee membership' (para 13) and hence a new 'non partisan' nomination system should be adopted (para 15). Equally, the dominant conception of a parliamentary career in terms of 'ministerial office', and the fact 'that able and effective select committee members—and sometimes even Chairmen—are so easily tempted by the lowliest of government and opposition appointments' (para 29), had both to be conceded and yet counteracted. The Committee recognized that: 'We must be realistic about this; many Members understandably aspire to be Ministers' (para 29), but concluded (as indeed had the Procedure Committee nearly a quarter of a century earlier) that one way to redress the imbalance—between the attractiveness of executive and parliamentary positions—was to build an alternative career-path based on committee service which was to be acknowledged at its peak in the payment of committee chairs.

The Government's reply was rapid and rejected virtually every recommendation made by the Liaison Committee. The Committee found the reply: 'both disappointing and surprising':

> We found it disappointing because our proposals were modest ... And we found it surprising that a Government which has made so much of its policy of modernising parliament should apparently take so different a view when its own accountability and freedom of action are at issue. (HC 748 2000: para 3)

Yet such a response should come as no surprise to readers of this book in view of the analysis outlined above.

Perhaps more of a surprise was that, within 11 months of the Liaison Committee's report, many of its recommendations were adopted by the Modernisation Committee and, in turn, accepted by the House itself. The circumstances under which this apparent reversal occurred are not the major concern here, other than to note four interconnected factors. First, of some significance, was the contemporaneous publication of two influential external reports by the Norton Commission (2000) and the Hansard Society (2001)—both of which stressed the centrality of departmental select committees to the effective scrutiny of executive actions. Second, the intermeshing of external and internal reformist arguments and personnel proved to be important (and was acknowledged by, amongst others, the chairman of the Liaison Committee, Robert Sheldon, (HC 224 2002:ev21; see also Kelso 2003:59). A third contributing factor was the miscalculation of party managers in seeking to prevent the reappointment of two outspoken Labour Committee chairpersons (Donald Anderson and Gywneth Dunwoody) at the start of the new parliamentary session in July 2001. And, fourth, and of crucial importance, was the appointment of a 'modernising' Leader of the House, Robin Cook, who was committed to accelerating the reformist dynamic within the Commons (see Cook 2003).

The Modernisation Committee published its Report on Select Committees in February 2002 (HC 224 2002). Although it made 22 recommendations—including a change of title of investigatory committees to 'scrutiny committees', an agreed statement of core tasks, the employment of specialist support staff, a standard committee size of 15, the revamping of reports, and the possibility of all committee reports being debated in Westminster Hall—the main proposals of interest for present purposes were those dealing with the appointment of committee members and the payment of committee chairs.

The Modernisation Committee recommended that appointment should be the responsibility of a 'Committee of Nomination'. This meant that while 'it is natural that the selection of nominations to the places allocated to each party should in the first instance be conducted within that party', ultimately appointments would be confirmed by an impartial Nominations Committee (HC 224 2002:paras 7–23). The Modernisation Committee also recommended that 'the value of a parliamentary career devoted to scrutiny should be recognised by an additional salary to the chairmen of the principal . . . committees [both 'scrutiny' and 'investigatory']' (HC 224 2002: para 41).

In the event, in a vote in the House of 14 May 2002, MPs accepted most of the package of reforms recommended by the Modernisation Committee but ultimately voted against (209 vs 195) the creation of an independent Nominations Committee. During the vote one Labour MP, Gordon Prentice, asked the Speaker if 'on a free vote, is it in order for the Government Whips to point to the No Lobby saying "PLP this way"?' (HC Debates 14 May 2002 vol 385 col 720). After the vote, several MPs more directly attributed the defeat to the influence of both sets of whips (see *The Guardian* 15 May 2002:9; *Daily Telegraph* 15 May 2002:10; Kelso 2003:65–6). And it was left to Tony Wright (Chair of the Public Administration Select Committee) to ask ruefully, 'Where were the massed ranks of parliamentary reformers . . . [the motion] was lost, and it was lost because all the whip fraternity organised to vote it down, and the forces of progress, where were they?' (quoted in Kelso 2003:66). Indeed, failure to curb the control of party managers over the appointment process has implications for the other parts of the package. Kelso, for example, notes that members of the All-Party Group for Parliamentary Reform were worried that the payment of committee chairs in the absence of an impartial Nominations Committee might be 'used by the whips' offices as a sweetener for compliant MPs seeking placement on particular select committees, and potentially render those committees less powerful than before the reforms were proposed'. Precisely these fears were articulated in October 2003 when the decision was taken to pay select committee chairmen an additional salary of £12,500 (see for example HC Debates 30 October 2003: cols 449–50; 455; 459; 475–8).

There were 18 departmental committees in existence in 2004 (see Table 2.5). These shadowed the major departments of state and hence were subject to reorganization in the wake of departmental restructuring (as occurred with the creation of the Office of Deputy Prime Minister in May 2002, and the Department for Constitutional Affairs in June 2003). Standing Order 152 states that the role of departmental select committees is 'to examine the expenditure, administration and policy of the principal government departments'.

TABLE 2.5	Departmental Select Committees	
Name of Committee	Principal government departments concerned	Members
1 Constitutional Affairs	Department of Constitutional Affairs	11
2 Culture, Media and Sport	Department for Culture, Media and Sport	11
3 Defence	Ministry of Defence	11
4 Education and Skills	Department for Education and Skills	11
5 Environment, Food and Rural Affairs	Department for Environment, Food and Rural Affairs	17
6 Foreign Affairs	Foreign and Commonwealth Office	11
7 Health	Department of Health	11
8 Home Affairs	Home Office	11
9 International Development	Department for International Development	11
10 Northern Ireland Affairs	Northern Ireland Office	13

continues

Table 2.5 continued

Name of Committee	Principal government departments concerned	Members
11 Office of the Deputy Prime Minister: Housing, Planning, Local Government and the Regions	Office of the Deputy Prime Minister	11
12 Science and Technology	Office of Science and Technology	11
13 Scottish Affairs	Scotland Office	11
14 Trade and Industry	Department of Trade and Industry	11
15 Transport	Department for Transport	11
16 Treasury	Treasury, Board of Inland Revenue, Board of Customs and Excise	11
17 Welsh Affairs	Welsh Office	11
18 Work and Pensions	Department for Work and Pensions	11

According to the Liaison Committee: 'The work of select committees tends to be seen by government as a threat rather than as an opportunity' (HC 300 2000:para 56). That this threat is still perceived by ministers and officials confirms the continuing strength of an 'executive mentality' (see Judge 1981; 1990; 1993; Flinders 2002:27). Equally, under the leadership of the House by Robin Cook, there was a positive attempt to emphasize the 'opportunities' afforded by select committees. There is no doubt that committees have increased the flow of information about executive activities both in the collection and dissemination of that information, that they have enhanced the information networks linking parliament and organized publics, and that they have subjected government policies to more rigorous scrutiny than before. Equally, there is no doubt that MPs believe that select committees were 'far and away the most effective way in which Parliament held Government to account' (Hansard Society 2001:43). Indeed, 84 per cent of the 179 MPs in the Hansard Society's (2001:131) survey rated select committees as 'effective or very effective' in securing information and explanation from the government. Moreover, there is strong external support for the views that 'the departmental committees introduced in 1979 have been a major success' (Norton Commission 2000:29), 'a successful innovation' (Hansard Society 2001:), and are 'Parliament's most effective device for holding government to account' (Wright 2000:218). This matches the House's own assessments that the committees have 'made notable contributions to parliamentary and public debates' (HC 224 2002:para 3), and that generally they have 'shown the House of Commons at its best: working on the basis of fact, not supposition or prejudice; and with constructive co-operation rather than routine disagreement' (HC 300 2000:para 5).

But each of these favourable assessments is tempered by recognition that the actual 'success of the committee system is limited' (Hansard Society 2001:29), and that in 'terms of parliamentary scrutiny they represent the classic half full, half empty bottle' (Norton Commission 2000:29). The annual reports from the departmental committees provide an insight into the practical limitations encountered by select committees (for an overview see HC 590 2002; HC 588 2003, HC 446 2004). While much reformist attention has been focused on enhancing the operational capabilities of committees (through more staff, more resources, more coordination, more coherence in structure, increased size, better reporting etc), the major impediments of party competition and executive dominance (and associated norms) still remain as significant obstacles to sustained and rigorous scrutiny. These impediments shone through the evidence provided by the Leader of the House, Peter Hain, to the Liaison Committee in October 2004. On the positive side, the government expressed its willingness to revise the advice provided to civil servants on 'providing evidence and responding to select committees' to make clearer the presumption in favour of attendance, provision of information and cooperation, as well as encouraging 'departments to be proactive in providing relevant information and documents to Committees' (HC 1180 2004:Q1). Yet on the specific issue of select committees gaining access to civil service 'advice to ministers', Hain sought to justify the non-disclosure of such advice by invoking the principle of ministerial accountability (see chapter 4):

> Officials have a relationship with Ministers where we are the ones who are publicly accountable and they are the ones who professionally advise in accordance with the traditions and the rules of the Civil Service . . . because if I take a decision that one of your Select Committees thinks is wrong, or any

of my ministerial colleagues, then we [ministers] are the ones who should be answerable; that is the principle of ministerial accountability. (HC 1180 2004: Q5–6)

The House of Lords

The UK Parliament represents a form of 'asymmetric bicameralism' (Patterson and Mughan 2001:41) where the upper chamber, the House of Lords, is subordinate to the lower chamber, the House of Commons. Unlike other asymmetric systems (France, Ireland, Japan, Poland, and Russia) in which the Upper House is not only called a Senate but has restricted legislative powers or simply advisory powers, the House of Lords 'remains an anachronism' (Patterson and Mughan 2001:44) in performing a substantial legislative function.

If the House of Lords replicates the legislative role of the Commons, as indeed it does in its five stage processing of legislation—through first reading, second reading, committee stage, report stage and third reading—then the most fundamental question is why have a second chamber at all? Indeed, critics have never tired of citing Abbe Sieyes words from the 18th century that 'if a second chamber dissents from the first, it is mischievous; if it agrees it is superfluous'. The answer to this fundamental question can be found, however, in three of the themes of this book: in history, in interinstitutional interactions, and in ideas and 'social understandings' about the roles of political institutions.

History

As noted in chapter 1, history is a powerful variable explaining modern institutional form, and especially in revealing the 'path dependent' nature of formal political institutions. Historical institutionalists maintain that initial institutional choices and structures become self-reinforcing over time. Certainly, the existence and modern role of the Lords makes little sense without some understanding of its historical development.

The House of Lords has its origins in the Anglo-Saxon *Witenagemot* and the *Curia Regis* (Court of the King) in the 12th and 13th centuries. Both the Lords Temporal (the magnates, the great earls and barons with their private armies) and the Lords Spiritual (the archbishops,

bishops and abbots who represented the church as the major landowner of the time) were needed by monarchs for consent to, and authorization of, their policies. As noted earlier, the 'Commons' (the representatives of cities and counties) were later summoned to Parliament. Initially, however, they were not allowed to speak in the presence of their more powerful feudal superiors. For this reason the Commons began to meet separately and, ultimately, after 1377 to elect a 'Speaker' to speak on their behalf to the monarch. Thus, by the end of the 14th century, a two chamber parliament had emerged with each House exercising a 'definite power' and each with a recognized 'legitimacy' (Shell 2001:8). From the 14th century members of the House of Lords received individual summonses to attend (with the emerging presumption that such summonses would be subject to the principle of hereditary succession). Those summonsed attended as 'Peers'—as nobles of equal status. They were men of property and power in their own right and served not as 'representatives' in the sense increasingly adopted in the Commons (see above). Indeed, as Norton (2004:431) notes: 'Any sense of representativeness was squeezed out' and 'the lack of any representative capacity led to the House occupying a position of political—and later legal—inferiority to the House of Commons'. While this might be true at an individual level, collectively, however, the Lords represented the interests of property, land and privilege and acted as 'an institution independent of the crown, one representing property over and against the community as a whole' (Shell 2001:9). In fact, the dominance of this notion of the collective representation of landed, aristocratic interests was to last well into the 19th century. However, as the principles of liberal democratic representation were asserted incrementally after 1832, and as the legitimatory defence of the non-democratic, heredity basis of representation in the Lords was undermined, so the wider institutional role of the Lords came increasingly into question.

Throughout its history the composition of the Lords has been inextricably entwined with its institutional role. Before examining this fundamental linkage it is worth noting the impact that its composition has had upon its internal organization and procedures. Given the principle of the equality of its members—of nobility sharing the same essential privileges—the Lords was 'uniquely in the world amongst legislative chambers—a self-regulatory body' (Wheeler-Booth 2001:82). This meant that the Lords has 'never delegated its powers to regulate its own proceedings to any other authority'

(Wheeler-Booth 2001:82). Yet the traditional principles of self-regulation and of equal rights of initiation and participation in business have been eroded with the changed composition since 1999 (see below, see Wheeler Booth 2001:87–8).

Composition

> Largely hereditary and permanently pro-Conservative, the House of Lords before 1999 was self-evidently an anachronism in a democratic age. (Budge et al 2004:452)

If the composition of the Lords affected its internal organization it also, and more significantly, impacted upon wider interinstitutional interactions with the House of Commons, and, therein, the executive and the majority party. Given the huge preponderance of Conservative supporters amongst hereditary peers before 1999, there was an inbuilt Conservative majority in the upper chamber irrespective of the outcome of any particular general election for the Commons. With the rise of party government in the 19th century came the potential for heightened policy and legislative conflict between a lower chamber dominated by one party and an upper chamber dominated by another. Thus, in the late 19th century the convention arose that the Lords would not block government legislation that was 'backed by the opinion of the people' (Lord Lyndhurst 1858 cited in Loveland 2003:157). Exactly what constituted 'the opinion of the people' led to some speculation at the time, with the Third Marquis of Salisbury, the then leader of the Tory Peers, espousing a 'referendal theory' whereby legislation could be opposed unless an explicit commitment was included in the government party's election manifesto (see Shell 1992:10). The paradox of an unelected House sustaining the democratic claims of an electoral mandate was not lost on critics at the time.

When the Lords refused to pass the 1909 Finance Bill (which sought to raise taxes to fund the Liberal government's social policy reform programme), on the grounds that its provisions had not featured explicitly in the 1906 electoral campaign, then the partisan fault-line of the composition of the two Houses opened up the institutional fault-line over the respective powers of the two Houses. These cumulative constitutional tremors led to the passage of the Parliament Act of 1911. The Act removed the capacity of the Lords to block 'money bills' for more than one month, and restricted the powers of delay on other public Bills (other than one to extend the life of parliament beyond five years) to a maximum of two parliamentary sessions. The period of delay was reduced further, to a maximum of one parliamentary session, by the Parliament Act of 1949. The circumstances surrounding the introduction of the 1949 Act mirrored those of the 1911 Act, this time with a majority Labour party in the Commons fearing obstruction from Conservative peers in the Lords. Both Acts revealed the consequences of the interconnectedness of the interinstitutional relations between the two Houses of Parliament, the executive and parliament, and the parties within parliament. Equally the Parliament Acts point to the analytical utility of the notion of 'disruption' or punctuated equilibria' in explaining institutional change.

When it comes to explaining the House of Lords Act 1999, however, the notions of 'crisis' or 'disruption' provide little analytical purchase (see chapter 7 for a discussion of institutional change under New Labour). The 1999 Act sought to fulfil the Labour party's 1997 manifesto commitment to remove the right of hereditary peers to sit and vote in the House of Lords. In the event, as a result of an expedient amendment to forestall Conservative opposition, 92 hereditary peers were retained in an 'interim second chamber' that came into existence in November 1999. They were elected by their hereditary colleagues and were returned, with no little irony, as the only 'elected' members of an undemocratic interim House. The number of hereditary peers was thus reduced by nearly 90 per cent from the 759 who had sat in the old House. In turn, the total membership of the House was virtually halved from 1,295 to 695. The composition of the interim House can be seen in Table 2.6:

As Table 2.6 reveals, around 80 per cent of peers of the 'interim House' were 'life peers'. Life Peers had been introduced by the 1958 Life Peerages Act which allowed the Prime Minister to advise the monarch on the appointment of peers who would sit, speak and vote in the Lords but who could not pass on their titles when they died. In 1963 a Peerage Act allowed hereditary peers to renounce their titles (in order to be eligible to sit in the Commons) and enabled female hereditary peers to sit in the Lords for the first time. (Four women hereditary peers retained membership in the interim House alongside 109 female life peers).

TABLE 2.6	Peers By Type (December 2004)

Archbishops and Bishops	26
Life peers (Law Lords)	29
Life Peers (under Life Peerage Act 1958)	561
Peers (under House of Lords Act 1999)	91
Total	707

Peers By Party

Party	Cons	Lab	Lib Dem	Cross	Other	Total
Life Peers	155	197	64	152	9	577
Hereditary Peers	48	4	4	33	1	90
Total (Party)	203	201	68	185	10	667
Bishops						26
Absent on leave						14
Total (All)						707

Source: www.publications.parliament.uk/pa/ld/ldinfo/ldanal.htm

Composition and powers

The removal of the hereditary peers, whilst envisaged as an 'initial, self con-tained reform' (Labour Party 1997a:32), was also seen as the precursor of other steps to make the Lords 'more democratic and representative'. Exactly how was not specified at the time. Indeed, subsequently, the pledge for fur-ther reform was to haunt the Labour government. Initially the government produced a white paper, which was published in January 1999 alongside the House of Lords Bill, and which proposed 'a far-reaching examination of the long-term future of the House of Lords following the removal of the hered-itary peers' (Cm 4183 1999:ch 2 para 17). To this end, a Royal Commission, chaired by Lord Wakeham, was established in February 1999 to examine the future role, functions and composition of the House of Lords and its report was published in January 2000 (Cm 4534 2000). What is notable, for the present discussion, was the government's insistence that:

> The House of Commons will continue to be the more important chamber, with the final say on whether legislation is passed. On the basis of the outcome of a general election, the Commons will determine the party of government and it will be able ultimately to insist on the form in which legislation will be passed . . . (Cm 4183 1999:ch 4 para 5)

This insistence on the maintenance of the existing dominance of the majority party in the Commons and, in turn, the dominance of the Commons over the Lords found reflection in every subsequent official document. Thus the terms of reference of the Wakeham Commission started with the clear statement: 'Having regard to the need to maintain the position of the House of Commons as the pre-eminent chamber of Parliament and taking particular account of the present nature of the constitutional settlement . . .' (Cm 4534 2000). Members of the Commission noted the impact that this presumption had upon their final report:

> In particular, we wanted to produce recommendations which would illustrate the crucial trilateral relationship between the Government, the House of Commons and the new second chamber. We took into account the fact that the stability of the trilateral relationship could be affected by the powers of the new second chamber and also by the way its members are selected. (Cm 4534 2000:2–3)

Manifestly, the composition of the reformed Lords could not be considered in isolation from this trilateral institutional relationship and an attendant specification of institutional roles. In which case, a second chamber should not pose a threat to the Common's pre-eminence but should 'augment and complement the Commons' work' (Cm 4534 2000:25). Perhaps not surprisingly, therefore, the Commission recommended that there 'should be no significant changes in the second chamber's law-making functions' (Cm 4534 2000:4); and judged that, in respect of primary legislation, 'the current balance [between the two Houses] is about right and should not be radically disturbed' (Cm 4534 2000:4.7). The role of the Lords was thus conceived in traditional terms as a revising and scrutinising chamber which ensures that the government has the opportunity to 'reconsider and adequately justify its position' (Cm 4534 2000:4.12).

Given the desire to maintain the 'balance' between the Houses, in effect the dominance of one over the other, the starting proposition about membership was to rule out a directly elected second chamber. The reason flowed from the Commission's conception of role and the fact that an elected chamber 'would by its very nature, represent a challenge to the pre-eminence of the House of Commons and make it difficult to strike the balance between the powers of the two Houses that our terms of reference require and that we recommended' (Cm 4534 2000:11.6). The result was a recommendation in favour of an upper chamber of around 550 members with a minority of elected regional members. In other words, the Commission did not recommend that the membership should be 'wholly or largely directly elected' (Cm 4534 2000:11.36).

Though derided in the press and by reformist groups, the Wakeham report and its recommendations were supported in the 2001 Labour party manifesto which included a commitment 'to implement them in the most effective way possible' (Labour Party 2001:35). In November 2001 the government published a white paper *Completing the Reform* (Cm 5291 2001). The principles of reform again started from the premise that the Lords should be a 'revising and deliberative assembly not seeking to usurp the role of the House of Commons as the pre-eminent chamber' and whose membership was not a 'duplicate or clone of the Commons' (Cm 5291 2001:para 8). This meant that 'the role, functions and powers of the House of Lords should remain largely unchanged' (para 10) and that the Wakeham Commission's recommendations on membership were broadly endorsed. Specifically the White Paper proposed a House of 600 members, with 20 per cent elected from regional lists, and with possible term limits of five, ten or 15 years with the government inclined towards the shorter options (HC Debates 16 November 2001 c105W). An Independent Appointments Commission would only select independent members and not party members. It would, however, determine the numbers of party members in the light of the preceding general election.

The response to the White Paper, both in Westminster and beyond, was at best guarded and more generally hostile (see HC Research Paper 02/002 2002:17–26; HC 494 2002, HC Debates 10 January 2002, HL Debates 9 and 10 January 2002). Even Lord Wakeham criticized the specifics of the White Paper (see HC 494 2002:para 16). The Commons' Public Administration Select Committee responded to the White Paper with its own report *The Second Chamber: Continuing the Reform* (HC 494 2002). In that report the Committee reproduced the results of a survey of MPs which revealed starkly that 'only 19 out of 409 Labour MPs and not one out of 164 Conservative [respondents]' favoured a majority appointed second chamber. The

Committee concluded that 'Wherever else it lies, the centre of gravity clearly does not lie with the White Paper' (HC 494 2002:para 42).

Given the unfavourable response to its White Paper the government proposed the appointment of a Joint Committee with 12 members from each House. The Joint Committee's terms of reference included the familiar recitation: 'to consider issues relating to House of Lord reform . . . within the context of Parliament as a whole, having regard in particular to the impact which any proposed changes would have on the existing pre-eminence of the House of Commons' (HL 151/HC 1109 2002:para 3). The primary task of the Committee, however, was to report on the options for composition. In its First Report, published in December 2002, it identified seven options, ranging from a fully appointed to a fully elected second chamber, and recommended that both Houses should vote in a series of motions on each option sequentially (HL 17/HC 171 2002:para 61–78).

On 4 February 2003 both Houses voted on the seven options. The Commons also voted on an amendment on the abolition of the Lords. The Lords, perhaps not surprisingly given its almost wholly appointed membership, voted in favour of a wholly appointed upper chamber, and opposed all options for election. In the Commons the amendment to abolish the upper house was defeated, as, indeed, were all of the seven other options. The outcome was that the Commons vote produced the 'contradiction of voting for the status quo by voting against the status quo' (McLean et al 2003:308). At the end of the vote the initial comments made by Mr Cook in opening the debate sounded eerily prescient:

> there is a real possibility that we could drift into House of Lords reform becoming our parliamentary equivalent of 'Waiting for Godot', as it never arrives and some have become rather doubtful whether it even exists, but we sit around talking about it year after year. (HC Debates 4 February 2003: col 152)

When the Joint Committee reconvened in the aftermath of the Commons' indecisive vote it started from the proposition that: 'Even if the engines had not fallen off the [reform] train, their thrust has been diminished' (HL 97/HC 668 2003:para 2). It maintained that, in the absence of common ground on the reform of the long-term composition of the Lords, progress would be made only incrementally and through the investigation of and reporting on 'certain specific issues' (HL 97/HC 668 2003:para 14). It also chose to highlight the 'significant roles that the House does and could in future fulfil' (para 15). In essence these supplemented the roles performed by the Commons: deliberation, scrutiny, enhanced legislative efficiency and effectiveness through introducing, revising and amending legislation. Because these supplemented rather than supplanted the roles of the Commons, the government believed that, in the absence of a consensus on composition, it should concentrate its efforts upon making the Lords work effectively in the performance of its existing roles (HL 155/HC 1027 2003:para 14).

The government, faced with a lack of consensus, had in Lord Falconer's (Lord Chancellor, and the Secretary of State for Constitutional Affairs) words: 'two stark choices: do nothing or seek to move forward where we can' (CP 14/03 2003:foreword). In choosing the latter option the government made two controversial announcements and initiated, subsequently, two 'consultation' processes. The first announcement came in June 2003 and proposed the removal of the Law Lords (the Appellate Committee) and the creation of a new Supreme Court for the United Kingdom (see Chapter 6). In opening the consultation process, the government made clear its intention to 'put the relationship between the executive, the legislature and the judiciary on a modern footing' (CP 11/03 2003:10). What was also clear was that other constitutional changes—devolution to Wales, Scotland and Northern Ireland (see chapter 5), the passage of the Human Rights Act 1998 (see chapter 6) and the growth of judicial review (see chapter 6)—had been the major precipitants of this reform rather than Lords' reform as such.

The second announcement came in September 2003 and proposed the abolition of the remaining hereditary peers and the creation of a statutory Appointments Commission (CP 14/03 2003:para 23). In the absence of agreement on how to implement further reform, the government claimed that it 'should consolidate the reforms which have already been made' (CP 14/03 2003:para 23). In March 2004, in the face of continuing disagreement about even this consolidationist proposal, the Secretary of State for Constitutional Affairs acknowledged that it was 'abundantly clear' that a Lords Reform Bill, to remove the remaining hereditary peers and to create a statutory Appointments Commission, would not be passed by the Upper Chamber. 'In these circumstances', Lord Falconer announced that, 'there is no point in committing further legislative time to this issue at this stage', but also promised that the government would 'return to it in our manifesto for the next election' (Department for Constitutional Affairs 2004).

Indeed, one former adviser to the Leader of the House, Meg Russell (2003:311), maintained that even in the penumbra of the debacle of the February 2003 vote there were sufficient grounds to argue that 'the House of Lords might in important ways be considered already reformed'. But Russell's case was made on the basis that the Lords already had adequate powers, that its composition remained distinct from that of the Commons and that its 'perceived legitimacy' had increased sufficiently for it to exercise its existing powers more effectively. On the issue of perceived legitimacy Russell (2003:316) claimed that the most 'obviously illegitimate group—the hereditaries—had for the most part been removed; and that the resultant change in party balance 'may have acted to further boost the public's perceptions of the legitimacy of the chamber as it is now' (2003:317). But this supposition finds no empirical substantiation in Russell's article, and indeed it runs counter to the fundamental, historical and institutional logic of representative government in the UK that legitimacy derives from the electoral process. This was acknowledged by both proponents and opponents of a reconstituted House of the Lords. Indeed, throughout, the government's case had been based upon its fundamental belief in:

> the Commons as the pre-eminent chamber, . . . we do not wish to undermine that pre-eminence or make any proposal that would achieve an equivalence between the Commons and the Lords. Anything that makes the House of Lords more representative, more democratic, more legitimate, is likely to produce some shift in the relative position of the House of Lords. What we must take care to do is not to achieve a second chamber which over a period of time would seek parity with the Commons and perhaps not even stop at parity. (Robin Cook, HC 494–II 2002:Q194)

In this statement legitimacy is linked to democratic processes of representation and democracy (through competitive elections). An un-elected chamber did not become any more legitimate (in representative democratic terms) simply by being the default option in the debacle of the government's attempted second phase of reform.

'Proper role and functions'

If little consensus was evident about the future composition of the Lords, there was more common ground upon the 'proper role and functions' of the upper chamber. The extent of this agreement could be gauged from the Wakeham Commission Report (see Cm 4534 2000), the Joint Committee's Reports (see HL 17/HC 171 2002:paras 9–10; 19–24; HL 97/HC 668 2003:paras 18–19), and the government's white papers and consultative documents (Cm 4183:chapter 7, paras 7–18; Cm 5291 2001:paras 19–24; CP 14/03 2003:paras 2–3). It was agreed that the primary roles of the Lords were to hold ministers to account, to deliberate on public issues, and to scrutinize and amend legislation. Of these, 'the most important role of the Lords is to be a revising chamber for legislation' and a chamber which would provide a 'distinctive perspective, and not simply duplicate the work of the Commons' (CP 14/03 2003:para 3).

In practice, over half of the time of the Lords (60 per cent in 2002–03) is devoted to processing legislation. Given that the House of Lords 'is one of the busiest Parliamentary chambers in the world' (House of Lords 2003: para 4)—sitting for 174 days in 2002–03 (12 days more than the Commons) and on average for seven hours a day—the importance of legislative work to the internal schedule of the second chamber is beyond doubt. Equally, the number of bills processed by the Lords is impressive in quantitative terms. In session 2002–03, for example, 33 government bills and 13 private members bills received Royal Assent. Ten of these bills were introduced directly in the Lords. On average, one-third of public bills are introduced in the second chamber, and 'recent Governments of all political complexions would not have been able to achieve their legislative programmes without this facility' (HL 97/HC 668 2003:para 18).

A total of 9,659 amendments were tabled to the government bills in session 2002–03, of which 2,925 were accepted. Some 207 amendments were put to a vote, of which 83 were lost by the government. Indeed, bargaining and disputation on the most contested amendments has been a characteristic feature of the 'interim House'. A vivid illustration of this process occurred at the end of the 2001–02 session when, on the very last day of the session in November 2002, 13 public bills received Royal Assent. Four controversial bills were still being debated by the two Houses days before, and in two cases (Animal Health, and Nationality, Immigration and Asylum), just hours before the end of the session. Ultimately, the passage of these bills was secured only after a number of compromises by the government. Indeed, in the case of the Anti-Terrorism, Crime and Security Bill the government suffered 13 defeats and the bill was passed only after the Home Secretary had been forced to make 'a humiliatingly large number of concessions' (Cowley and Stuart 2003:195). In November 2004 five bills received their royal assent on the last day of the parliamentary session after disputation between the two chambers. The Hunting Act 2004, which banned fox hunting in England and Wales, was only passed using the provisions of the 1949 Parliament Act (see above).

Most of the amendments tabled in the Lords are moved by the government itself, though a sizeable proportion are in response to comments made by non-government Members. Moreover, of the non-government amendments made, ministers are more prone to respond positively than they would be in the Lower House. Indeed, this revising function, of submitting government legislation to a 'second look', is one that is central to the case for the retention of a second chamber. As Norton argues (2004:438): 'It is not a function that the House of Commons can carry out, since it is difficult if not impossible for it to act as a revising chamber for its own measures; that has been likened to asking the same doctor for a second opinion'.

The Lords also has a significant role in scrutinising secondary legislation. The House has procedures whereby all bills are examined initially by the Delegated Powers and Regulatory Reform Committee 'to report whether the provisions of any bill inappropriately delegate legislative power, or whether they subject the exercise of legislative power to an inappropriate degree of parliamentary scrutiny' (HL 9 2003:para 4). For each bill the relevant government department provides written evidence to the Committee about the provisions for delegated legislation and why such provisions are necessary. The Committee then advises the House on the appropriateness of such provisions and draws attention to so called 'Henry VIII' powers (under which primary legislation may be amended or repealed by subordinate legislation without further parliamentary scrutiny). Notably there is no corresponding scrutiny process in the Commons. There is no Commons' committee dealing with delegated powers in primary legislation.

There is, however, a corresponding Commons' Committee dealing with regulatory reform proposals. Both Houses consider whether such proposals meet the technical requirements of the Regulatory Reform Act 2001, especially whether the government is entitled to do what the order proposes, that adequate consultation has taken place, and that the order removes a burden without removing 'any necessary protection'. In 2001–02 the Lords' Delegated Powers and Regulatory Reform Committee considered powers in 55 bills, and in 2002–03 in 57 bills; and reported, respectively, on eight and 16 sets of government amendments. The government 'almost invariably accepts' the recommendations of the Committee (HL 9 2003:para 29). Indeed, the Committee has 'earned a formidable reputation as a watchdog over the use of ministerial power' (House of Lords 2004:7)

The capacity of the Lords to 'hold the government to account' is enhanced by the expertise and experience brought by its members to deliberation and scrutiny. In the less partisan setting of the Lords, the range of professional occupations represented in the chamber allows for more detailed examination of the technical details of policy than is often evident in the House of Commons. Similarly, extensive expertise is displayed in the upper chamber's investigative committees, such as the European Union Committee and the Science and Technology Committee, as well as in other ad hoc committees such as those dealing with Stem Cell Research and Animals in Scientific Procedures in session 2001–02. In this respect the Lords (through its different composition) supplements, rather than replicates, the expertise and experience brought to bear in the consideration of public policy; and proponents of an unelected second chamber consider this a positive virtue of the present House of Lords.

The monarchy

The final stage of the legislative process in parliament is the royal assent, whereby a bill is accepted with the words '*La Reyne le veult*'—the Queen wills it. These words still symbolize the fact that the UK remains a constitutional monarchy. The crown symbolizes the fusion of the legislature and the executive. The history of the UK demonstrates the pivotal position of the monarchy in melding the institutional relationship between parliament and the executive into 'parliamentary government'. On the one side, as noted earlier in this chapter, parliament was convened initially to grant supply and offer support to the monarch (as the formal and functional executive of the state). As parliament sought to enhance its control over the monarch, so the monarch—in deciding major matters of policy—became simultaneously more dependent upon a group of 'privy councillors', part of whose responsibilities was also to mobilize support for these policies within parliament. Moreover, by the 17th century, there was a developing expectation that such councillors would sit in the House of Commons rather than in the Lords and would seek election to the lower house. In this manner, a process of the institutionalization of executive responsibility to the legislature was initiated in tandem with a responsibility of the legislature to support and control the executive. The necessity for the executive to evolve methods for retaining parliamentary support was simply heightened by the constitutional settlement of 1689.

If 1689 defined the relationship between parliament and the 'executive' (as embodied in the monarch), the years thereafter witnessed the gradual redefinition of the relationship between the executive and parliament through the constitutional disembodiment of the monarch. Stated at its simplest, a transfer of executive power was made from the individual person of the monarch to the collective entity of 'ministers of the crown'. Ministers, as leaders of political parties, ultimately came to hold office, not at the discretion of the monarch, but at the discretion of voters and to be responsible, in a staggered relationship, to parliament and to the electorate (see chapter 4). In this process, the crown was effectively short-circuited from the flows of institutional power in a 'democratizing' UK state.

The question is frequently raised: 'Given that the powers of the crown have almost wholly passed to the government, what then is the role of the monarch? (Norton 2004:368). The answers neatly divide those who wish to consign the monarchy to the 'living dead of the constitution' (Kingdom 2003:347) and those who identify continuing and important symbolic and representative roles for the monarch. The latter roles include: representing the UK as head of state as a 'symbol of the nation'; setting standards of citizenship and family life; acting as a focal point of national unity; symbolising continuity through the performance of ceremonial duties (for example, opening parliament and awarding honours); and even preserving Christian morality as supreme governor of the Church of England (see Norton 2004:368–76; Johnson 2004:57–76). While supporters of a constitutional monarchy maintained that Queen Elizabeth II had performed these duties assiduously, and so sustained the credibility of the monarchy into the 21st century, more sceptical observers cautioned that 'it is only by accident that the present Queen [has been] able to do this' (Blackburn and Plant 1999:142). As Blackburn and Plant (1999:142) proceeded to note: 'If we want a head of state who can symbolise the whole nation, or at least a majority in it, then this is probably a stronger argument in favour of an elected head of state than an hereditary one'. Taken to its extreme this view underpins the republican position that the monarchy in the UK is an unnecessary institution in a democratic, multi-cultural, secular and multi-national state (see Nairn 1988; Benn 2003:191–3, 233–6).

If the monarchy attracts disputation about the value of what it 'does', the institution also draws criticism for what it 'does not do' (and what it has not been expected to do in an era of elected parliamentary government). The essence of this latter argument is that major executive powers still reside with the crown, yet they are not exercised by the monarch in person. These are known as 'prerogative powers'. There are two main types of prerogative powers: 'constitutional' and 'executive'. The constitutional category includes the monarch's rights to assent to legislation; to prorogue or to dissolve parliament; and to advise, encourage and warn ministers in private; as well as to appoint the prime minister and other ministers. Conventionally the monarch accepts the advice of ministers in exercising these powers. Similarly, the advice of ministers is the crucial determinant in the exercise of prerogative executive powers. Such powers include: making and ratification of treaties; conduct of diplomacy; declaration of war; deployment and use of the armed forces; appointment and removal of ministers; recommendations for dissolutions, peerages, and honours; appointment of senior judges; and the organization of the civil service.

Not surprisingly, given their scope and importance, these powers have attracted critical attention. On the one side, their exercise raises the question that, 'by virtue of the absence of personal choice, [are they not] a waste of time and something of which the monarch should be shorn?' (Norton 2004:376). On the other side, more profound questions are posed about the contemporary relationship between the executive and legislature through the continued interposition of prerogative powers. In essence, the problem distils into the fact that these powers 'are among the most significant that governments possess, yet Ministers regularly use them without any parliamentary approval or scrutiny' (HC 422 2004:para 1). In fact, not only do prerogative powers offer significant scope for ministers to act without parliamentary approval, but parliament does not even have the right to know what these powers are. In this sense, '[t]his is unfinished constitutional business. The prerogative has allowed powers to move from the monarch to Ministers without Parliament having a say in how they are exercised' (HC 422 2004:para 61). This 'unfinished business' and the extent to which 'royal prerogative' powers should be conceived as 'ministerial executive' powers

(HC 422 2004:para 8) will be considered further in chapter 4. For now, how-ever, it is sufficient to note that the monarchy still retains its location as part of the tricorporal institution of parliament, and as the titular apex of 'Her Majesty's Government' in whose name 'Ministers of the Crown' oper-ate, and whose 'Queen's Speech' nominally identifies the government's ses-sional legislative programme.

Conclusion

The continuing centrality of the Westminster Model to the official discourse of ministers has been apparent throughout this chapter. In prescribing a series of interinstitutional interconnections between the related institutions of parties, legislature and executive as the kernel of legitimate government in the UK, the model influences internal organizational structures and spe-cifies 'appropriate behaviour' within those structures, as well as structuring the external interactions among institutions. If institutions help to define individual and group identities—of what it means to belong to a 'specific collective' (March and Olsen 1989:17)—then the identities of Members of Parliament are defined in terms of their party affiliation and their rela-tionship to the executive, ironically by the norms of institutions exogen-ous to the 'specific collective' of the House of Commons itself. This is why it is worth repeating the point made earlier that: 'the normative system of the House, as with any other dominant value system, reflects the predilec-tions of the most powerful actors and supports the existing distribution of power' (Judge 1993:215). This fact is evident in the culture and career as-pirations (and hence, intrinsically, aspirations for the institution itself) dis-played by most MPs. The norms of party loyalty are evident in a series of surveys and academic studies (see, for example, Searing 1994; Rush 2001; Cowley 2002). While these norms are not absolutes, it remains the case that the 'overwhelming desire on the part of the vast majority ... [is] not to do anything that might make their party appear divided' (Cowley 2002:182). When factored into legislative-executive interactions the institu-tional norms of party find reflection in the broader institutional norms of parliament. This conjunction was succinctly expressed by one Labour MP who described his role as: 'to provide the executive with a permissive envir-onment in which they can do their work' (quoted in Cowley 2002:106).

The culture of the Commons as 'institutionalized' in parliamentary procedure is, in theory, an endogenous collective culture. As Blackburn and Kennon (2003:247) note: 'All institutions need clearly recognised processes for the transaction of their business', but what is of paramount importance about parliamentary procedure is that it is 'the House which is master and the House which can do what it likes, not individual Members, not majority or minority groups' (2003:247–8, on the importance of procedure as a constraint on government see also Norton 2001). Yet, in practice, the Commons is bifurcated by reinforcing exogenous norms derived from 'party' and 'executive' roles. As noted earlier in this chapter, the inhibitions of this 'culture' on institutional change has been consistently identified within the House itself (see for example HC 190 1997:para 17; HC 1168 2002:para 48). Thus, Tony Wright, Chair of the Public Administration Committee, pointed directly to this fundamental paradox when questioning the Leader the House about the government's White Paper on completing the reform of the House of Lords:

> Just to get a sense of where you and the Government are coming from on this, on the basis of the proposals in the White Paper, . . . the section in there which talks about the pre-eminence of the House of Commons is entirely about not upsetting these balances in the system. Could I put this to you . . . surely we do need to upset the balances in the system and overwhelmingly we need to upset the balance between Parliament as a whole and the Executive. Is that not what reform should be about? (HC 494–II 2002:Q194)

For Wright this was a rhetorical question. For the government it posed an elemental challenge to the institutional norms and values associated with the 'Westminster model', and was thus a question best left unanswered.

....

KEY TERMS

- asymmetric bicameralism
- crown-in-parliament
- delegated legislation
- deliberation
- electoral mandate

- interim house
- interinstitutional relations
- legislative process
- legitimation
- Lords' reform

- monarchy
- parliamentary state
- party government
- party representation
- party whips
- peers
- principle of distinction
- representative democracy
- representative government

- responsible government
- prerogative powers
- scrutiny
- select committees
- sovereignty (supreme authority)
- standing committees
- territorial representation
- usual channels
- Westminster model

GUIDE TO FURTHER READING

BLACKBURN, R. and KENNON, A. (2003) *Parliament: Functions, Practice and Procedures*, (London, Sweet and Maxwell).

An encyclopaedic and detailed exposition of the workings of the UK parliament

COWLEY, P. (2002) *Revolts and Rebellions: Parliamentary Voting Under Blair*, (London, Politicos).

Combines searching academic analysis of voting in the House of Commons with enjoyably irreverent prose.

JUDGE, D. (1993) *The Parliamentary State*, (London, Sage).

Provides a distinctively different approach to the study of the UK parliament!

ROGERS, R. and WALTERS, R. (2004) *How Parliament Works* (5th edn.), (London, Pearson, Longman).

A comprehensive and enlightening introduction to the internal operations of parliament written by two insiders.

RUSH, M. (2005) *Parliament Today*, (Manchester, Manchester University Press).

Provides a detailed understanding of how parliament operates on a day-to-day basis and of how its working patterns are structured by broader political and institutional forces.

3

Institutions of Representation:
Parties and Groups

Overview

This chapter examines the institutions of representation and of 'linkage' between government and the governed. Its primary focus is upon political parties and organized groups. It locates both parties and groups within a wider institutional frame, and assesses how the 'Westminster model' continues to influence the development of institutions of representation within the UK. The questions of how parties form and how they develop organizationally are examined, alongside consideration of how far the notion of a 'two party system' is still relevant at the UK and subnational levels. While the two major parties still uphold the Westminster model and adhere to its principles, the practice of modern UK government is now commonly conceived to revolve around 'groups' and 'associations' and their interactions with governing institutions. The related notions of 'networks' and 'governance' have become something of an analytical orthodoxy, and have served as an explicit critique of the Westminster model. The orthodoxy of 'networks' is challenged in the light of the continued significance of the institutional prescriptions of established notions of representative government in the UK, and by the institutional development of networks themselves.

Introduction

It is apparent that the party system can best be understood as part of a wider political and institutional settlement. (Webb 2000:3)

Indeed, given the centrality of parliament to the 'institutional settlement' in the UK, it has been argued that 'the party system in Britain can best be understood in terms of its relationship with parliament. . . . Parliament matters therefore because it provided the structural context for the development of political parties' (Judge 1993:68). Similarly, Hill (1976:15) is in no doubt of the importance of the institutional context of the formation of political parties in Britain, for him, 'the beginnings of the party system of modern Britain coincided with the emergence of a Parliament as a permanent institution'.

In turn the importance of institutional context to the formation of political parties found reflection in a variety of theories/models on party formation. In words resonant of historical institutionalist analysis Panebianco (1988:50) maintains that: 'A party's organizational characteristics depend more upon its history, i.e. on how the organization originated and how it consolidated, than upon any other factor. . . . Every organization bears the mark of its formation, of the crucial political-administrative decision made by its founders'. Others have argued that once a party adopts a particular organizational form then that structure may be '"frozen" and therefore become resistant to change' (Gunther and Diamond 2003:173). This does not mean that organizational change does not occur; only that the starting points and the initial constellations of organizational norms and membership values affect the direction and pace of change within different parties. Thus, although parties have had to react to changing socio-economic contexts (in, for example, the rise of 'identity politics', post-materialist values, class dealignment) and developing communication technologies (most particularly the pervasiveness of television and the internet), and, although there is some apparent convergence in organizational style, nonetheless, there remain identifiable differences between the major parties in Britain stemming from their diverse origins.

Models/types of party systems

One classic theorization of the development of parties is provided by Duverger (1959). His basic contention was that two types of parties could be discerned: those that originated inside parliaments and those with extra-parliamentary origins. On the one side, parties created before the development of the mass franchise and which arose from the activities of representatives within parliament displayed elitist, organizational characteristics of a 'cadre party'. Thereafter, their origins continued to affect the parties' behaviour and organization. The Conservative and Liberal parties in the UK conformed to this ideal type. On the other side, parties created after the development of the mass franchise and formed outside of parliament tended to be markedly different in their organizational structure. Indeed, one of Duverger's more lasting contributions to the debate on party development was his identification of 'externally created' parties as being more centralized, more ideologically coherent and less disciplined, and their parliamentary members more actively controlled by the extra-parliamentary organization (see Duverger 1959:xxx; LaPalombara and Weiner 1966:10). Duverger also argued that such parties, especially socialist parties, would be less willing to ascribe major importance to parliament and be less deferential to the institution and its members. However, as with all generalizations, reality is a little more complicated, and certainly the British Labour party has 'always been an unorthodox mass party' (Webb 2000:199).

Parties in the 21st century

Typologies, like Duverger's, that might be of value in explaining the initial development of parties are not necessarily appropriate for categorising the same parties in the 21st century. Indeed Gunther and Diamond categorize both the modern Labour and Conservative parties in the UK as different types of 'electoralist parties'. This categorization is similar to Panebianco's (1988:262–7) model of 'electoral professional' parties. Both types emphasize the role of professional campaigners, the pre-eminence of public representatives and a highly personalized leadership, and de-emphasize the role of activists and party bureaucrats. Still other analysts identify a trend beyond 'electoral professional' parties to the creation of 'modern cadre parties' which are characterized by 'being elite driven, top down organizations, and lacking a genuine mass membership base' (Heffernan 2003:126). While both UK major parties have never approximated very closely to an authentic mass party, they have not yet reverted to a cadre form. What is beyond dispute, however, is that both major parties have witnessed significant organizational change in recent decades. As Richard Heffernan

(2003:139) concludes: 'British political parties are no longer what they used to be'.

The Conservative party

The Conservative party at its origin in the 17th century constituted a classic 'cadre party' (in Duverger's terms) as it developed out of parliamentary alliances and its principle organizational objective was to ensure support for the party's leadership and the securing of executive office. Indeed, after 1688, a primary goal of parties became the manipulation of executive power; and, by this date, a Tory party had developed which was 'held together . . . by a set of political and religious attitudes . . . and also by its ambitions and by a rudimentary party organisation' (O'Gorman 1975:14–15).

Even after the extension of the franchise in 1832 and 1867, the primary organizational goal of the party remained unchanged and the new extra-parliamentary structures, designed to incorporate a new 'mass membership', were still conceived within an over-arching institutional frame centred on parliament. Thus, as McKenzie (1963:146 original emphasis) noted: 'from its earliest beginning the popular organization of the Conservative party *outside* Parliament was conceived as a servant of the party *in* parliament'. In other words, the 'mass organization' was established to mobilize support for parliamentary leaders, and it was a 'top down', hierarchical, and 'organizationally thin' structure.

Before 1997 the leader of the Conservative party was regarded as the 'fount of all policy' (Norton 1994:95) as no other element within the party was vested with the formal power to determine policy. While, before this date, the party made little pretence of subscribing to internal democratic norms and structures (Webb 2000:192–3), in practice, the leader had been forced to rely upon other bodies within the party to assist in policy initiation. Nonetheless, the Conservative party did not have a corporate legal identity and was constituted historically in three separate organizations. First, the National Union of Conservative and Unionist Associations served as the extra-parliamentary arm of the party. It had its origins in the late 19th century and was created in response to the extension of the franchise and the formation of local Associations to coordinate the recruitment of members and the winning of elections. Second, Central Office, served as the professional arm of the party. Central Office was under the direct control of the party leader and provided the organizational link between party members in the country and party leaders in Westminster. The third organization was the parliamentary party with the leader at its head. In this manner the Conservative parliamentary party was formally insulated from the party's professional and voluntary arms, other than through the integration of all three organizational hierarchies in the position of the party leader. Indeed, between 1965 and 1998 the Conservative parliamentary party had sole responsibility for the election of the party leader. Yet, the parliamentary leader alone was vested with responsibility for policy making.

In the absence of a formal constitution no other organization within the party had a responsibility for the determination and implementation of party policy. Even the annual conference was officially only the conference of the National Union, and not of the party as a whole. As such it had often been portrayed as more of a 'rally for the faithful than a deliberative assembly' (Whiteley et al 1994:30) or as an 'exercise in public relations' (Ingle 2000:72). Yet this image of conference's subservience—with control from above and deference from below—did not go unchallenged. Kelly (1989), for example, argued that conference established the mood and receptivity of the party faithful to policy proposals. In this way it had 'considerable influence upon ministerial initiatives' (1989:184) because conference debates provided a sounding board of wider party and public opinion (see also Tether 1996:107). In essence, the leader still led—but on the condition that the advice of the wider party membership was at least listened to. As Michael Trend, then Deputy Chairman of the Conservative party, reminded the 1997 Conference: 'the National Union is not a powerbase in the party as a whole. It is a base, but it has little power' (Conservative Party 1997, Conference Speech 8 October). Trend made this statement in preface to a call for the building of a 'single, strong and unified party' and for a fundamental reorganization of the party's structure.

The Fresh Future and party reorganization

That such a fundamental review was needed was apparent from the result of the 1 May 1997 election (see chapter 2 Table 2:2). Electoral defeat has traditionally provided the spur for parties to reconsider their internal organization. This had occurred most notably in 1945 for the Conservatives, and after successive defeats in 1983, 1987, and 1992 for the Labour party. In both parties the trauma of decisive electoral defeat allowed internal critics to articulate their pleas for greater 'democratization' and to apportion blame to what they perceived to be an irresponsible, unresponsive and divided parliamentary elite. More particularly, the financial difficulties in the Conservative party in the 1990s had been exacerbated by the inability of Central Office to access the funds of local Constituency Associations given the legal autonomy of the latter (see Garner and Kelly 1998:95).

William Hague, as the new party leader, commissioned a fundamental review of the party's internal organization, and proposals for change were presented to Conference in October 1997 in the document *Our Party: Blueprint for Change*. The draftsman of this document, then party Vice-Chairman Archie Norman, believed that it proposed 'a huge extension of democracy' within the party (Conservative Party 1997, Conference Speech 8 October 1997). Following from these proposals, a 'White Paper' on reform of the party, entitled *The Fresh Future*, was published by Central Office in February 1998.

The Fresh Future proposed a constitution which would create a single unified party. For the first time members would join 'the' Conservative party. More particularly the reformed Conservative party was to have 'an open and democratic organization ... owned by its members' (Conservative Party 1998:21). At the centre of the new unified party was a 'Party Board' which was 'the supreme decision-making body on all matters concerning party organisation and management' (Conservative Party 2001:17). In 2004 there were 17 members of the Board with representatives from the voluntary section, the parliamentary party drawn from both Houses, and the professional party.

The declared guiding principle of reform was 'decentralization', whereby there would be 'the fewest possible layers of communication between party members and the party leadership and that there should be a much greater degree of involvement for party members'. To this end the party's regional tier was restructured and replaced by 42 Area Councils designed to serve as coordinating bodies linking the Board to the Associations. Constituency Associations preserved their autonomy to select candidates for elections 'subject to the condition that all selected candidates must be included on the party's approved list of candidates'. Increasingly, however, constituency campaigning became subject to more active central management after 1997 (see Denver et al 2003:546–7).

In pursuing the commitment to make the reformed party 'open and democratic', *The Fresh Future* proposed that, for the first time, every member would have a direct vote in the election of the party leader. The first election under the new rules took place in 2001 when Ian Duncan Smith prevailed over Kenneth Clarke to succeed William Hague as leader. The first stage in the election involved only Conservative MPs. (MPs were also empowered under *The Fresh Future* to trigger the resignation of an existing party leader and to choose the candidates in a leadership contest. This opportunity was taken in October 2003 when 25 Conservative MPs precipitated a vote of confidence in the leader, and which Ian Duncan Smith lost by 75 to 90). At the second stage in 2001, all party members were included in the election process—with the result decided on the basis of one member one vote—and with some 267,797 members voting. In 2003 there was no second stage to the selection process. Michael Howard was returned unopposed by Conservative MPs without the subsequent necessity for a ballot of the wider party membership.

Not only were ordinary members to be involved directly in the choice of the party leader, but the White Paper further proposed a Policy Forum to encourage political discussion throughout the party, and the creation of Regional Policy Congresses to discuss policy proposals. It was envisaged that the Conservative Policy Forum would have 'major input into the annual party conference agenda', yet the party's Committee on Conferences was to determine the final agenda. The annual conference itself was afforded no decision-making capacity and was identified simply as 'the main party gathering of the year'. In this sense, as Webb concludes (2000:197), 'it is unlikely that anything has changed much with the advent of the *Fresh Future* revolution . . . members still lack formal rights of control'.

According to the official version, the post-1998 party structure 'hinges around six basic themes: unity, decentralisation, democracy, involvement, integrity and openness' (Conservative party 2001:16). Certainly after 1998 'democratization' was as much an accepted part of the lexicon of the Conservative party as of the Labour party (see below). Indeed, the transformation of the Labour party's structure in the 1990s was held up as a template by 'modernisers' in the Conservative party (see Norman, Conference Speech

8 October 1997; Kelly 2002:39). Yet, as noted at the time: 'Despite the rhetoric of democracy . . . the thrust of the [modernising] proposals is towards centralisation' (Peele 1998:146). This fits with the observation that: 'the empowerment of the party on the ground remains compatible with, and may actually serve as a strategy for, the privileging of the party in public office' (Katz and Mair 2002:129). Or it can be conceived as part of a process of 'democratisation as emasculation' (Webb 1994:120); and this is a process common to both the Conservative and Labour parties in the 21st century (see below).

The Labour party

The origins of the Labour party are of some significance for the subsequent development of the party. It is conventional to argue that: 'Labour is unique among the major British parties, since it is the only one that originated outside parliament' (Garner and Kelly 1998:125). However, too much should not be made of the extra-parliamentary origins of the Labour party. Ultimately, constitutional orthodoxy and the requirements of operating within a 'parliamentary state' have tended to prevail over party organizational heterodoxy. In other words, decentralization of authority within the party, in theory, has been tempered, in practice, by centripetal pressures sustained by the conjunction of party, parliamentary and, occasionally, state leadership positions in the Parliamentary Labour party.

The Labour party was established to secure the representation of organized labour in parliament. As Ernest Bevin (one time General Secretary of the Transport and General Workers Union) famously claimed, the party had grown 'out of the bowels of the trade unions' (Labour Party 1935:180). The Trade Union Congress's resolution of 1899 in favour of the formation of a Labour Representation Committee (LRC) led directly to the formation of just such a Committee in England and Wales in 1900. The overwhelming majority of the LRC's membership came from the trade unions, with a number of socialists officially attached via the Fabian Society, the Independent Labour Party and the Social Democratic Federation. From the outset the LRC operated primarily as an electoral machine (see Hodgson 1981:14; Fielding 2003:18). Its priorities were to secure support on the basis of policies compatible with existing majority opinion within the electorate;

and to implement ameliorative policies for 'workers' which would generate further electoral support.

With the transformation of the LRC into the Labour party in 1906 the new party inherited the same objective. Hence the party constitution of that year stated simply that its 'object' was: 'To organise and maintain a Parliamentary Labour party [PLP], with its own whips and policy' and to secure election of candidates for this purpose (Labour Annual Conference Report 1906 quoted McKenzie 1963:470). From the outset the advancement of specific trade union interests through parliament gave the Labour party a recognisably labourist and parliamentarist character (see Judge 1993:86–8).

Not surprisingly, given the pre-eminence of trade unions in this alliance, the new party adopted many organizational characteristics of the trade unions themselves. In practice, therefore, the LRC, and later the Labour party, simply adopted many existing procedures of the TUC in evolving its own constitution and standing orders (see Minkin 1992:279–80). These procedures included: the 'block vote'; the determination of policy by an annual conference composed of delegates from affiliated organizations; and a distinct set of attitudes to leadership—where leaders were accorded no higher status than rank and file members; and where each member had the right to submit resolutions to conference through their affiliated organization. In this manner the sovereignty of conference came to be an accepted and integral part of Labour's organizational structure.

When the Labour party adopted its formal constitution in 1918 the new organizational structure combined a framework of local constituency parties and individual members with trade unions and socialist organizations affiliated at both local and national levels. Indeed, it was not until 1918 that constituency parties were established throughout the country to create a mass membership base of individual members. Even then, it remained, 'a somewhat unorthodox mass party' (Webb 2000:199). In turn, conference combined both delegates from local constituency parties and nationally affiliated groups. Conference authority was proclaimed in Clause 5(1) of the new constitution. Yet, despite the formal restatement of conference sovereignty, the 1918 constitution did little to resolve the practical ambiguities of authority within the party.

What was foreshadowed in 1918 was a widening of the representational focus of Labour MPs beyond the specific aims of organized labour, a broadening of the party's electoral appeal, and a reaffirmation of the centrality of the existing institutions of parliamentary democracy to the attainment of the party's objectives. In this process of refocusing and reaffirmation, the delegatory relationship between the labour movement and its representatives in parliament became obscured. As the party's objectives widened beyond the simple representation of labour in the political process, so the scope increased for PLP interpretation of party policy and discretion as to implementation. As a general rule, what transpired was that Labour leaders in government (with the exception of the Attlee administrations of 1945–51 which were uniquely attuned to the interests dominating the wider movement) emphasized their policy independence; and, in opposition, the party conference took the opportunity to remind the PLP leaders of the error of their ways in government (see Minkin 1980; Coates 1975:31–41, 86–9). In this regard, Conferences in the 1970s and early 1980s were particularly proactive and sought the reassertion of intra-party democracy and the restoration of conference authority. And, for a relatively brief period in the early 1980s, the 'customary balance' between the PLP leaderships and conference was inverted (see Webb 2000:202).

Significantly, although the underpinning debate in the party in that period was primarily about ideology, the need for reform was articulated in terms of party organization and the style of Labour representation in the Commons. In the intra-party conflict the 'new left' reformers identified mandatory reselection of MPs as their priority for controlling the PLP. This priority was later accompanied by demands for other internal organizational changes including the extension of the franchise for the election of the party leader beyond the PLP, and for the party's National Executive Committee to have the final say on the contents of the manifesto. The success of the 'new left' can be gauged from the fact that the reforms on reselection and the electoral college for the party leader were accepted at successive conferences between 1979 and 1981.

In fact, as soon as it was apparent that mandatory reselection would occur, a proposal was made that the general membership of constituency parties should make the final selection through the principle of One Member One Vote (OMOV). This proposal reappeared in 1984 when Neil Kinnock, as party leader, proposed a system of 'voluntary OMOV' which was rejected by Conference, but Kinnock returned to the subject in 1987. This time he proposed a 'compromise OMOV' which took account of the sensitivities of the Trade Unions. As a compromise this system satisfied no-one and in 1990 the NEC voted for its discontinuance. After Labour's fourth consecutive general election defeat in 1992, and the replacement of Neil Kinnock by John Smith as leader of the party, the issue of OMOV was revived. The 1993 Conference was persuaded to adopt OMOV for candidate selection, with a minor concession to a continuing special role for the unions. This concession was soon discarded under Tony Blair's leadership. Thereafter only ordinary individual members retained the franchise. In addition, as part of a wider programme of organizational reform, Blair reduced the weight of the union's block vote at conference to 50 per cent (down from the 70 per cent negotiated by John Smith in 1993) and secured the agreement of trade unions, in the same year of 1996, to giving financial support to the party centrally.

Party organization in the 21st century

'Democratization' within the party was advanced further in 1997 in three inter-related ways. The Labour leadership extended the plebiscitary tendencies in the party; residualized further Conference's role; and created a Joint Policy Committee to have 'strategic oversight of policy development in the party and the rolling programme' (for details see Panitch and Leys 1997:233–6; Webb 2000:202–9; Shaw 2002). The new system of 'democratic' policy-making was outlined in *Partnership in Power* which was endorsed at the 1997 Conference.

Partnership in Power stated that: 'Conference would remain the sovereign policy- and decision-making body of the party' (Labour Party 1997b:1). Nonetheless, it was apparent that Conference's role was to be limited in practice to 'agreeing' decisions taken elsewhere and to orchestrating the publicising of 'Labour's achievements and plans'. 'Annual conference should reflect all that is best about the party and its values'. While acknowledging that there would continue to be 'debate and sometimes strong differences of opinion', *Partnership in Power* maintained that such debate 'needs to rest upon a clear understanding, and acceptance, of the respective roles and responsibilities of the party on the one hand and of the government on the other'.

In explaining how the *Partnership in Power* system works the Labour Party identifies the Joint Policy Committee (JPC) and the National Policy Forum (NPF) as the 'key institutions' (www.labour.org.uk/howdoespartnershipinpowerwork). The JPC is chaired by the party leader and oversees the *Partnership in Power* process. Its members are government ministers, and members of the National Executive Committee (NEC), and the NPF. The NPF is composed of 183 members from all 'stakeholder groups in the party' (CLPs, regional representatives, trade unions, socialist societies, the NEC, and MPs, MEPs and representatives from local government). In turn, the NPF is assisted by eight Policy Commissions focused on specific policy areas.

The task of the NPF is to draft consultative policy documents and amend the documents once the consultation process is completed. The consultation process operates in a series of rolling 'waves'. Each 'wave' lasts two years, with the first year devoted to wide-ranging consultation that encourages submissions from party members and non-members alike. The second 'wave' produces 'policy documents' after the consultative documents have been amended by the NPF in the light of submissions received during the consultation period. These policy documents are then circulated internally within the party. The JPC then makes the final revisions and is charged with reaching agreement on the policy documents. The process culminates with the presentation of the JPC's final reports to Conference. Once endorsed by Conference, the policy proposal becomes eligible for inclusion in the next manifesto.

Essentially, reforms throughout the 1990s and into the 21st century have relocated the locus of authority within the party away from the organized party on the ground towards individual members. As Peter Mair (1994:16) observed in his comparative study of party organizations in western democracies, this phenomenon is not restricted to the British Labour party but is part of a more general trend in which 'ordinary' members are empowered while activists become marginalized. This has led to accusations that the PLP leadership has pursued a strategy of 'democratization as emasculation' (Webb 1994:120); and that the cumulative effect has been to produce a 'new democratic centralism' within the party's organization (Shaw 2002:164–5). It is 'democratic' in providing individual members opportunities to influence candidate and leadership selection and to be consulted on policy formulation. It is 'centralist' in enhancing leadership autonomy in policy-making, and in developing a 'highly concentrated system of command and control' within the party (Shaw 2002:165).

The party and electoral systems

The fact that the discussion thus far in this chapter has focused exclusively on the Conservative and Labour parties at the 'national level' is in itself a reflection of the continuing salience of the notion of Britain as a 'two-party system'. In terms of the outcomes of Westminster elections this remains the case; as either one or other of the main parties has formed a single party government since 1945. Yet, in terms of electoral competition and proportion of votes cast, Westminster elections have produced a 'two-party-plus' system. Whereas in 1951 the Labour and Conservative parties accumulated nearly 97 per cent of the vote between them, by 2001 the corresponding figure was just under 75 per cent. Correspondingly, the percentage of the vote at general elections secured by the main 'third' party, the Liberal Democrats, has increased from 2.5 per cent in 1951 (competing as the Liberal party) to just under 19 per cent in 2001. Moreover beyond Westminster, in elections to devolved parliaments and assemblies in Scotland, Wales, and Northern Ireland (see chapter 5) multi-party systems now operate, both in terms of electoral competition and representation in these bodies. While this is not the place to investigate the reasons for this transformation it is worth reminding ourselves of Webb's statement, produced at the start of this chapter, that the party system has to be set within its broader political and institutional context.

Since the 1970s there has been a significant decrease in levels of class and partisan identification (Heffernan 2003:122) to the extent that less than half of the UK electorate now have any form of stable identification with either of the major parties. Whatever the causes (and these are many and complex (see Webb 2000:38–79)), there is no doubt that the parties' tasks of aggregating the demands of various 'stakeholders' into coherent programmes, sustaining intra-party cohesion, and developing an effective political marketing strategy has become both more exacting and necessary in these circumstances. In various ways these changes in the electoral bases of the two major parties have impacted upon cohesion within the parliamentary parties (see chapter 2), upon the relative positions of party leader and other senior party figures, given the elevation of the party leader and the increased 'presidentialization' of electoral contests (see chapter 4), as well as upon the organizational structures of the parties themselves (see above).

Yet if electoral volatility, partisan realignment and dealignment, and declining participation levels (down to 59 per cent turnout in the 2001 general election), have fundamentally dislocated the two-party system as an electoral construct at the UK level, the simple plurality (first-past-the-post) electoral system has secured the continuance of a two-party system within Westminster itself. In making the case that the argument about electoral reform for the House of Commons 'is central to the future of the British political system' Pippa Norris (2001a:881) was moved to note that:

> the Westminster system had arguably not changed fundamentally on the executive-party dimension. Britain retains single-party majority cabinet government in Whitehall not coalitions, a dominant cabinet rather than executive-legislative balance, two-party predominance of government and opposition at Westminster despite the rise of popular support for other parties ... and above all a majoritarian electoral system for Westminster, buttressing and supporting all of the above.

For supporters of the present first-past-the-post system these characteristics of a two-party system are to be appreciated rather than denigrated (see Norton 1997:84–8). Certainly the Labour governments after 1997 appeared to become increasingly appreciative of the virtues of the existing system of elections for Westminster as successive commitments were discarded: to holding a referendum on voting reform in the lifetime of the 1997 parliament; to consider seriously the recommendations of the Jenkins' Commission for an Alternative Vote-plus system, and to 're-examine' voting reform in 2003 (for details see Forman 2002:309–12).

Other parties

Liberal Democrats

The Liberal Democratic party was formed in 1988 by the merger of the Liberal party and the Social Democratic party (SDP). These two parties had formed an alliance in 1981 after the formation of the SDP by a number of former Labour party members who had left the party in the wake of the ideological and organizational restructuring in the late 1970s (see above). In terms of ideology the new Liberal Democratic party could be located within the stream of 'left-of-centre social liberalism which has been prominent in Britain for more than a century' (Webb 2000:106). According to the 2001 Manifesto: 'Three simple words. Freedom, honesty, justice. These sum up what the Liberal Democrats stand for' (Liberal Democrats 2001:1). But the problem for the Liberal Democrats, almost from its inception, was that the Labour party chose, through its 'Third Way' rhetoric, to compete on very similar ideological terrain (see chapter 7). What used to be distinctive about the Liberal Democrats in the early years was the advocacy of environmentalism and constitutional reform. Constitutional reform was advanced on both principled and pragmatic grounds; the former emphasized core values of individual liberty, democratic civic engagement and an 'enabling state', the latter recognized the benefits proportional systems of voting, and devolved assemblies, offered to secure enhanced representation and executive positions for Liberal Democrats. But significant sections of the Liberal Democrats' reformist proposals were appropriated by the Labour party, with the commonalties of interest finding reflection in institutional form in a joint consultative committee pre-1997 and the special cabinet committee immediately post-1997 (see chapter 4).

The constitution of the federal party of the Liberal Democrats (2003:2.1) makes clear that the party is a federation with discrete Scottish, Welsh, English, and Federal components. The reserved functions of the Federal party are the determination of policy (within the remit of federal institutions) and of the party's overall strategy, overall preparations for Westminster and EP elections; and the overall 'presentation, image and media relations of the party' (2003:2.3). Membership of the party is gained through a local party or a specified associated organization. Generally the Liberal Democrats have been adjudged to be a 'membership-orientated phenomenon' (Webb 2003:21). This is reflected in the election procedures for leader and president, the selection of parliamentary candidates, and the election of conference representatives (all by OMOV). The Federal Conference, which meets twice a year, is, according to the Federal Constitution, the 'sovereign representative body of the Party, and shall have the power to determine the policy of the Party' (2003:6.7). But the responsibility for 'developing policy and overseeing the policy-making process' resides with the Federal Policy Committee (FPC). The FPC also has responsibility for preparing the party's UK manifesto.

Given these responsibilities the FPC exerts considerable influence in the party's policy-making process, not least because it appoints policy working groups to take submissions and produces consultation papers for dissemination within the party before agreeing a final draft to be sent to the Federal Conference. As the leader of the party chairs and directs the work of the FPC he (as to-date all leaders have been male) in turn retains considerable autonomy, to the extent that Ingle (2000:194) maintains that the leader's policy formulation role 'has been enormous'. Similarly in the sphere of constituency campaigning 'the Liberal Democrats have not been immune to the centralizing trend seen in other parties' (Denver et al 2003:547). But here the limited resources of the party's central organization means that responsibility for constituency campaigns, beyond key target seats, still remains primarily devolved to local constituency parties.

Overall, therefore, the Liberal Democrat party, like the two other major parties in Britain, confirm pronounced features of the 'electoral-professional' model of party organization. While ideas of 'democratization' are privileged within the party, and while the party 'may speak with many voices', it 'remains the case that fewer voices than ever seemingly determine its policy direction' (Heffernan 2003:131).

Subnational party systems

If the term 'two-party system' has lost much of its descriptive accuracy at the UK national level, other than in the sense of the two largest parties dominating the distribution of seats within Westminster, it is meaningless in the party systems in the devolved electoral systems of Scotland, Wales and Northern Ireland. In Scotland in 2003 15 parties contested the election and six found representation in the Scottish Parliament. In Wales five parties contested the 2003 election and four were returned to the Assembly. In November 2003 19 parties contested the Northern Ireland Assembly elections and eight were returned to Stormont. Indeed, the party system in Northern Ireland has long been distinct from the 'normal' dynamics and characteristics of party interactions in the rest of the UK (see Webb 2000:20). In the 2001 general election, for instance, 11 parties contested the election and four were returned under the single transferable vote system to Westminster (see chapter 5).

Party organization in Scotland

Long before devolution, the Labour and Conservative parties had acknow-ledged the distinctiveness of Scottish politics and political institutions (see chapter 5) through the decentralization of their organizations in Scotland (see Kellas 1989:114).

Scottish Labour Party: A Scottish Labour party was initially formed in 1888, which then merged with the Independent Labour Party in 1894. Five years later in 1899 an initiative by the Scottish TUC created the Scottish Workers' Parliamentary Committee (SWPC) to coordinate labour repres-entation (this predated by a matter of months the initiative of the TUC Con-gress to establish the Labour Representation Committee in England and Wales). In 1906 the SWPC changed its name to the Scottish Labour party and in 1909 merged with the wider British Labour party. Thereafter, a Scot-tish Advisory Committee was created in 1915, later changing its name to the Scottish Council of the Labour party. Upon the adoption of the 1918 La-bour party constitution, the Scottish Council was deemed to be a 'regional' party and was granted some degree of organizational differentiation in an essentially centralized party. A Scottish Annual Conference provided the opportunity to debate Scottish issues (and, indeed, until 1968 there was a prohibition upon the discussion of non-Scottish topics at conference). The existence of a separate Scottish conference provided a forum in the 1980s and 1990s for the propagation of ideas about a distinct a Scottish Labour identity (through calls for greater autonomy for the party), devolution and the nature of representation in a future Scottish Parliament (see Hassan 2002:31). Nonetheless, the Scottish party remained constrained within the broader centralized British party structure.

The adoption of *Partnership in Power* by the British party in 1998 brought about parallel organizational change in the Scottish party. While the Na-tional Policy Forum has the responsibility for developing policy for the UK manifesto, a Scottish Policy Forum (SPF) formulates policy for the Scottish manifesto. In a two-year 'wave' cycle the SPF, assisted by local policy for-ums, produces detailed policy reports that are then debated and voted upon at the Scottish Conference. With the advent of a Scottish parliament the Scottish party conference is restricted to the consideration of devolved mat-ters, matters of shared responsibility, and issues dealt with by the European Parliament and local government.

According to the party, the policy documents produced for the 2003 Conference were 'the culmination of over 250 local policy forums, a process involving 11,000 party members and over 300 submissions' (see www.scottishlabour.org.uk/policydocuments). In practice, however, the centralizing tendencies (noted above) in the British party are apparent in the Scottish party. As Hassan (2002:32) observes:

> The Policy Forum is widely seen by party members as a top-down process, involving greater centralization and the party leadership managing relations with the party. With the advent of the Scottish parliament, these processes have become ministerially focused and influenced, with ministers, advisers and parliamentary researchers becoming the key shapers of documents and debates at the Forum.

Scottish Conservative and Unionist Party: The National Union of Scottish Associations was formed in 1882. Upon merger with the Liberal-Unionists in 1912 it became the Scottish Unionist Association and in 1965 it was renamed the Scottish Conservative and Unionist Association. In Scotland the term 'Unionist' traditionally invoked Westminster sovereignty; opposition to Home Rule both in Scotland and, more particularly, in Ireland; and presbyterian social philosophy (see Mitchell 1990:8–14; Midwinter et al 1991:21–2; Hutchinson 2001:14–20).

In 1997, after the worst electoral performance since 1865, and the failure to return a single Conservative MP in Scotland, the party embarked upon organizational reform. As with the Labour party the reforms in Scotland paralleled the organizational changes in the British party. Thus a single organization was fashioned out of the existing three-legged structure of the voluntary, professional and parliamentary organizations. The leader of the Scottish party was to be elected by a college of party members (30 per cent) and Members of the Scottish Parliament (70 per cent). Policy for the Scottish Conservatives was to be formulated along similar lines to policy formulation in the British party—through a Scottish Policy Forum, the Scottish Executive (elected by party members) and the Scottish Conference (see Ingle 2000:69; Seawright 2002:73–4).

Scottish National Party: The organization of the SNP traditionally displayed its 'non-parliamentary' origins in the fact that: 'Annual conference is supreme with activists having considerable power' (Mitchell 2003a:35). Delegates from Branches and Constituency Associations are represented on the various national bodies that help to determine the policy and direction of the party: the National Assembly, the National Council and the Annual Conference. The National Assembly is the forum for the development of policy prior to approval by the National Council or the Annual National Conference. The Council is the governing body between conferences and as such is empowered to make policy. The National Executive Committee is responsible for overseeing the organization and administration of the party, and for devising the SNP's national political strategy. The pre-parliamentary origins of the party, and the fact that the party's constitution had remained largely unreformed since its electoral rise in the 1960s, left the national leadership exposed to factional disputes and activist discontent. John Swinney, after protracted dissent and a formal challenge to his leadership in September 2003 resigned in June 2004, but before doing so secured reform of the party's constitution at a special conference in April 2004. The main elements of reform included the introduction of one-member-one-vote for candidate selection and for choice of the leader. Indeed, the formal position of leader was established to replace the former position of 'national convenor'. The nomination process for the leadership was tightened to prevent frivolous challenges, and the national executive was reduced in size from 32 to 21 members and was to be chaired by a new Business Convenor. In September 2004, Alex Salmond was elected leader (for the second time) under this new process.

Scottish Liberal Democrats: As noted above, the Liberal Democratic party is a federation composed of Liberal Democrats in England, Scottish Liberal Democrats and Welsh Liberals Democrats. The Scottish party has it own constitution which affirms that it is 'an independent constituent part of a federation'. As in the federal party, Conference is deemed to be the 'governing body' of the Scottish party with the power 'alone' to make policy, and is required to meet at least twice a year. The Leader of the party has to be a member of the Scottish Parliament; while the Deputy Leader is expected to be a Member of the House of Commons representing a Scottish Constituency. In practice, membership of the governing coalition in the Scottish Executive has enhanced the position of the party leader who also serves as Deputy First Minister. The Liberal Democratic position in the coalition proved pivotal in defining the distinctive Scottish policies on university tuition fees and free personal care (see Simeon 2002:229–30). Indeed, as Lynch (2002:93) points out, 'the constitutional independence of the Scottish party has enabled a considerable level of Scottish policy autonomy to be practiced and, indeed, the [federal] party has made a virtue out of allowing the Scottish party to do its own thing'.

Scottish Green Party: The Scottish Green Party traces its origins back to 1979 and the creation of the Scottish Ecology Party in 1979. It changed its name to the Scottish Green Party in 1986 and in 1990 became a separate party from the Green Party in England and Wales. In 1999 Robin Harper was elected as the first Green Party Member of the Scottish Parliament (and indeed the first Green elected member in the UK). In 2003 seven Green MSPs were elected to the Scottish Parliament and became a formal parliamentary party for the first time.

Scottish Socialist Party: The Scottish Socialist Party (SSP) was formed in 1998 out of the Scottish Socialist Alliance (SSA). The SSA had itself been formed two years earlier out of an alliance of various socialist organizations operating in Scotland. The primary objectives of the SSP are to secure the socialist transformation of society within an independent Scottish republic. At the 1999 Scottish Parliament election the SSP's charismatic leader, Tommy Sheridan was returned from the regional list for Glasgow, and after the 2003 election he was joined by five other SSP representatives.

Given the party's extra-parliamentary origins, its diverse factional membership, and its radical ideology, it is unsurprising that the SSP's Constitution emphasizes the role of individual members organized at branch and regional levels, and headed by a sovereign conference. Conference is assisted by the National Council which has responsibility for implementing party policy between conferences and monitoring the work of the Executive Committee. The Executive Committee provides political and strategic leadership and is responsible for the day-to-day running of the party.

The factional nature of the party is reflected in the right of members to organize intra-party 'platforms' or tendencies'. Indeed, making a virtue out of the deep differences over ideological strategy in the party, the Constitution notes that the SSP 'as a pluralist party, recognizes that a range of political points of view is a healthy source of debate and new ideas' (Scottish Socialist Party 2003:para 14.1). Moreover as 'a new, developing party ready to learn from our members' experience of campaigns and struggle, as well as from those outwith the party', the Constitution envisages that the party's 'structures will continue to develop over time in the light of circumstances, experience and full consultation with the membership' (Scottish Socialist Party 2003:Preamble). With the resignation of Sheridan as party leader in November 2004 the factional intra-party differences intensified and speculation about the continued electoral viability of the party mounted.

Party organization in Wales

Wales Labour Party: The Wales Labour party historically has been characterized by a weak party organization, but one that has been dominated by grassroot activists (Laffin et al 2003:4). In parallel with the implementation of *Partnership in Power* nationally, the Welsh party established a Welsh Policy Forum, its own Policy Commissions and a Welsh Joint Policy Committee (WJPC). As Laffin et al (2003:11) note the WJPC has, outside of the manifesto writing cycle, become the effective policy making body of the party. Significantly the WJPC has a substantial ministerial presence from the Assembly Government (see chapter 5), and ministers have a direct and decisive input through the WJPC into the policy-making process. The end result has been the process of emasculation of party activists as the decentralising logic of OMOV in internal party election and selection procedures has circumvented the power base of activists, while the democratization of policy making processes has served to enhance the capacity of leaders to shape party policy. The increased propensity of Welsh Labour leaders to emphasize their policy divergences from the national party has raised the issue of a formal federalization of the Labour party's structure. However, although the central party has 'accepted some degree of informal regionalisation and devolution within the party, . . . no formal steps have been taken in terms of internal devolution' (Laffin et al 2003:22).

Plaid Cymru: Plaid Cymru was founded in 1925 and its prime contemporary objective is: 'To promote the constitutional advancement of Wales with a view to attaining Full National Status for Wales within the European Union' (www.plaidcymru.org). The Constitution of Plaid Cymru states that the party will 'pursue its aims by means of political activity, democratically organized by members of the party freely associating together' (Constitution 3.1, www.plaidcymru.org/1.1.html). As with the SNP, Conference is deemed to be the 'highest authority of the party and is responsible for determining Plaid Cymru's policy'. The National Council debates and determines strategy and tactics, and approves the party's election manifestos. A smaller National Executive Committee is responsible for strategic management and for the implementation of Conference policies. In turn, a National Policy Forum researches and develops policy options for debate by the National Executive Committee, the National Council and Conference.

Welsh Liberal Democrats: The Welsh Liberal Democrats are part of the federation of UK Liberal Democrats. As with the Scottish party, the Welsh party has it own constitution (which was amended at the Spring Conference in March 2004). As in the federal party, Conference is deemed to be the 'supreme decision-making body of the party' charged with the formulation of policy, and is required to meet at least twice a year. Unlike the Scottish party however, the Leader can be an MP, MEP or Member of the Welsh National Assembly. Unlike the Scottish Liberal Democrats the Welsh party has not been a consistent member of a coalition executive. Although a formal coalition partner in the first Assembly, the Liberal Democrats were excluded from office after the second Assembly elections in May 2003. Lacking policy focus after 2003, 'the future salience and impact of the Liberal Democrats [in Wales] remains contingent upon the return of coalition politics' (Osmond 2004:58).

Groups

The major political parties at the UK level still subscribe to the essence of the Westminster model (outlined in chapter 2). They contest elections in the expectation that a plurality of votes will secure government office for one of them. Once the plurality of votes is recalibrated into a majority of seats through the first-past-the-post electoral system then the benefits of centralized executive control accrue to the largest party (see chapter 4). Not surprisingly, therefore, both the Labour and Conservative parties in power have articulated the virtues of the Westminster model and subscribed to the institutional norms associated with that model. Yet, while the two major parties still uphold the model and adhere to its principles, the 'reality' of modern UK government for many influential academic observers is not centred upon parties as representative organizations, or upon manifestos as the literal embodiment of the linkage between party electors, party members and party representatives in government, or other associated precepts of party government. Instead, the 'reality' is of 'groups' and 'associations', of 'governance' rather than 'government', of consensual policy-making in networks rather than adversarial partisan posturing in parliament, and of a 'differentiated', 'fragmented' and 'decentred' polity rather than the centralized, unitary political system prescribed in the Westminster model.

In examining the competing models based upon networks and governance what follows is an elliptical analysis of groups as institutions/organizations. The focus of the following discussion is not primarily upon the organizational characteristics, or upon the different functional categorizations of groups, but rather upon the interactions between groups/associations and formal institutions of government. In preface to that discussion, however, it is worth making a few terminological clarifications.

The first is the distinction traditionally drawn between political parties and groups. In practice this distinction is relatively clear cut, as the first-past-the-post electoral system, in conjunction with the nature of internal party organization, provide few incentives for groups to operate on the same electoral terrain as parties. In essence, the distinction can be drawn between parties which contest elections with the objective of securing representatives to pursue a programme across a broad spectrum of public policies, and groups which have a narrower policy focus and seek to influence policy-making in specific sectors without routinely contesting elections. Although this distinction is blurred at the margins, with single-issue groups occasionally contesting elections (see Grant 2000:13), and with some groups affiliated with parties (the classic example is the formal position of trade unions within the Labour party), nonetheless, a discrete 'institutional identity' is retained by groups beyond the electoral process and the party system (see Baggott 1995:6).

A second distinction routinely made in academic analyses is between different types of groups. Normally variations around dichotomotous categorizations are noted. One of the longer standing distinctions is between 'sectional' and 'cause' groups (Stewart 1958). The former represent the interests of a particular social or economic group and have 'closed' or restricted membership (for example, the British Medical Association or the National Farmers Union each with a membership of over 100,000); whereas the latter promote a common cause and normally have a broad membership base (for example, the Royal Society for the Protection of Birds with a membership of over 1,000,000). Variations around this basic distinction have been provided with the adjectives 'interest' offered instead of sectional, and 'promotional' or 'attitude' instead of cause group (see Baggott 1995:13–14). A further elaboration upon this basic distinction has been made between 'primary' and 'secondary' groups (see Coxall et al 2003:137–8). The former are defined in terms of their pursuit of primary 'political objectives' and of political lobbying. The latter are concerned primarily with the provision of some common service to members, though they might engage intermittently in 'political activities' (for example, motoring organizations such as the Automobile Association, or professional associations such as the Association of University Teachers or the Royal College of Nurses).

A more telling distinction, however, has been made between 'insider' and 'outsider' groups. Wyn Grant (1978) in formulating this classification made a distinction on the basis of 'alternative group strategies and on the receptivity of governments to those strategies'. Insider groups are seen by governments to be 'legitimate' and are integrated into consultative relationships; outsider groups may be seen as 'protest groups', often with objectives 'outside the mainstream of political opinion', and so find it difficult to gain, or do not even seek, recognition by the government. What is of particular significance in Grant's classification is that group strategies are defined in terms of the institutional 'rules of the game' of the central executive: 'Access and consultation flow from the adoption of a pattern of behaviour which is acceptable to government' (Grant 2000:20). Richardson (1993:4) also underlines the fact that group strategies are devised 'in the context of existing [state] institutional structures and processes'. In this manner the institutional configuration associated with the Westminster model provides incentives for groups to adopt particular political strategies in seeking to influence domestic UK public policies. The value of the insider/outsider distinction is that it 'focuses attention on the choices that have to be made by groups and government, and on the exchange relationship that develops between them' (Grant 2000:27). In turn the notion of 'exchange relationships' opens up possibilities for a wider conceptualization of interactions between state institutions and groups in the form of 'networks' and 'governance'.

Networks and governance

Rhodes (see 1988, 1990, 1996, 1997), in conjunction with Marsh (Rhodes and Marsh 1992) and Bevir (Bevir and Rhodes 2003), has produced the most definitive account of British governance focused on networks. Rhodes starts from a critique of the 'Westminster model'. (Though latterly he has preferred to think of the model 'explicitly as a narrative'. A narrative for Rhodes has the advantages of revealing the 'diversity of beliefs and traditions upon which institutions rest' (Bevir and Rhodes 2003:25)). The Westminster model has a shared set of assumptions about power and about the interaction of ideas and institutions. More particularly it is, as noted in chapter 2, the 'pervasive image shared by British politicians and civil servants' (Bevir and Rhodes 2003:26). Despite this, Rhodes has argued consistently that the Westminster model is an inaccurate portrayal of contemporary UK governance. His starting point is that there has been a 'shift from government by a unitary state to governance by and through networks' (Bevir and Rhodes 2003:6):

> Governance refers to informal authority of networks as constitutive of, supplementing or supplanting the formal authority of government. The concept of governance thus overlaps with those of the core executive, the hollow state and the differentiated polity, all of which point to a more diverse view of state authority as being located at the boundary of state and civil society. (Bevir and Rhodes 2003:6)

The concept of governance is closely linked to the concept of networks (Pierre and Peters 2000:19; Bevir and Rhodes 2003:49). The idea of policy networks initially derived from notions of interest intermediation, of how organized groups are incorporated into government policy-making processes. This idea 'recognizes that in most policy areas a limited number of interests are involved in the policy-making process, and suggests that many fields are characterized by continuity ... in terms of the groups involved in policy making' (Rhodes and Marsh 1992:4). Policy networks reflect the fact that relationships between groups and government are institutionalized but that these interactions are segmented (Richards and Smith 2002:175). In this view networks are treated as institutional structures in themselves. These structures:

limit participation in policy-making, define the role of actors, decide which issues to include and exclude from the policy agenda, shape the behaviour of actors through the rules of the game, privilege certain interests not only by according them access but also by favouring their preferred policy outcomes, and substitute private government for public accountability. (Bevir and Rhodes 2003:50; see also Rhodes 1997:9–10)

This statement raises two major issues about the nature of networks: the extent of limitation and exclusion of 'outsider' groups (and in reverse the degree of incorporation and inclusion of some 'insider' interests) and the insulation of networks from public accountability.

It has become conventional in the literature on networks to locate different types of networks along a continuum according to: the extent to which they have exclusive or inclusive membership (from highly restricted membership to a large number of members), the degree of integration (measured by the frequency, stability, continuity and consensual nature of interactions), and the distribution of resources and power within networks (see Rhodes and Marsh 1992:13–14; Rhodes 1997:43–5; Richards and Smith 2002:175–8; Bevir and Rhodes 2003:50–2). At one end of this continuum are policy communities and at the other are issue networks.

Policy communities

Policy communities are characterized as closed networks within which membership is restricted to a limited number of groups and government actors who share a largely consensual perspective on policy in a particular policy area. Only those insider groups with requisite resources gain access to this segmented world of policy making. Within a community there is mutual dependency between groups and government. There is resource exchange insofar as groups provide information, expertise, support, and facilitate policy implementation (often directly through service delivery); and governments provide, most importantly, 'authoritative allocations' and the legitimation of policy outputs (see Rhodes and Marsh 1992:13; Richards and Smith 2002:177). Some variants of network analysis ascribe to policy communities a 'stability of relationships' (Rhodes and Marsh 1992:13) and a 'consistency in values, membership and policy outcomes which persist over time' (Bevir and Rhodes 2003:50). Indeed, for some, communities are defined precisely because they are 'a special type of *stable* network' (Jordan 1990a:327 original emphasis).

While the notion of policy communities had achieved, by the 1980s, the status of both 'an empirical model' and 'a new conventional wisdom . . . about how policies are made' (Jordan 1990b:471) it also came under increased scrutiny both as a 'model' and an accurate representation of 'how policies are made'. As a model it came under sustained and withering critique (along with broader conceptions of policy networks) from Keith Dowding (1995; 2001). Dowding maintained that typologies of networks (with policy communities as one polar position) did not constitute a model as such. In UK network analyses generally there was no attempt to distinguish between dependent and independent variables; or to 'causally relate' network characteristics to each other and to different types of policy (Dowding 1995:141). In other words the categories 'policy community' and 'issue network' did not explain differences between policy formation in different policy sectors. If networks were to explain policy outcomes then there should be some independent variable stemming from the collective characteristics of the network at work.

Similarly the initial conceptualization of 'policy community' asserted the stability of memberships and relationships as one of the defining characteristics of a community. As a description of some relationships at a particular period in UK post-war history this characterization had some resonance. However, in itself, it was incapable of explaining change and instability, let alone providing the analytical foundations for *theorising* dynamic and changing interactions and policy outcomes. As one of the initial proponents of the notion of 'policy community' came belatedly to acknowledge, the assumption of stable policies, stable relationships and stable memberships and the subsequent inability to account for change was the 'Achilles heel' of the concept (Richardson 2000:1007). Indeed, Richardson (2000:1010) conceded that: 'It is difficult to accommodate [the significant policy changes since 1979] within any policy community or network "model"'. Similarly, Marsh et al (2001:235; 2003:317–8) found in their study of policy-making in four UK departments between 1974–1997 that only one policy community persisted throughout this period. Their conclusion was that 'it appears that there are relatively few tight policy networks, or policy communities in the terminology of Marsh and Rhodes' (Marsh et al 2003:317).

While maintaining that policy networks did still play an important role in the British political system in the 21st century Marsh et al were 'wary of over-emphasising that importance' (2001:236; 2003:319). Whereas Rhodes persisted in residualising the importance of formal government actors in his claims that networks were self organising, regulated by rules devised and agreed by their participants, with a significant degree of autonomy from the state—so much so that they 'are not accountable to the state' (Bevir and Rhodes 2003:53), other network analysts gradually came to acknowledge that 'we need to take the role of government, or rather departments, in policy networks more seriously than the network literature generally, or the differentiated polity model specifically suggests' (Marsh et al 2003:319).

Marsh et al recognize that there are asymmetries of power and resource mobilization in networks. These asymmetries find reflection in the exchange relationships in networks, with government, or more specifically departments, tending to be the more important actors (2003:319). Thus, while there is no dispute that government is locked into myriad networks, and is often dependent upon non-governmental actors for the delivery of services and the implementation of government programmes, nonetheless, government possesses 'a unique set of resources' (2003:320). Unlike Rhodes who maintains that, at best, governments can only 'indirectly and imperfectly steer networks' (Rhodes 1997:53; Bevir and Rhodes 2003:53) Marsh et al argue that for much of the time the central executive in the UK is still strong enough, and possesses sufficient resources, to ensure that it wins policy battles 'most of the time' (2001:248; 2003:320).

Key amongst governmental resources is the authority to introduce and pass legislation (Marsh et al 2001:236; 2003:319). Uniquely among network participants, government actors can claim legitimacy derived ultimately from the ballot box.

Insulation from public accountability

If the policy network is the best encapsulation we have of the policy-making process in Britain, there are normative grounds for concern. (Grant 2000:51)

Certainly in the early British analyses, networks were identified unambiguously as a challenge to the Westminster model and traditional notions of representative government. Policy communities, at one end of the network continuum, were defined in terms of their distance from established modes of parliamentary representation.

Richardson and Jordan, who were at the forefront of network analysis in the UK, started from the premise that the simplistic theory encapsulated in the 'Westminster model' contrasted sharply with the complexity of the practice of a segmented policy process 'with communities organised around individual government departments and their client groups, and with policy making generally impenetrable by "unrecognised groups" or by the general public' (Richardson and Jordan 1979:174). One consequence of the 'notion that policies are the product of sectoral bargaining in which ministries have clientelistic orientations to the major groups' was a reduction in the importance of legislatures, parties and the formal institutions of government (Jordan 1990b:473). Indeed, throughout their joint work Jordan and Richardson contrasted the 'clear-cut and traditional principles of parliamentary and party government' (Richardson and Jordan 1979:74), 'traditional notions of democracy, accountability and parliamentary sovereignty' (Jordan and Richardson 1987:288), and 'traditional notions of parliamentary and electoral democracy' (Jordan and Richardson 1987:289) with the reality and practice of group politics in Britain. In so setting the practice of groups against the theory of parliamentary democracy Richardson and Jordan characterized the British system of government as 'post-parliamentary' (see also Richardson 1993:90; 2000:1006). Similarly, Rod Rhodes was relentless in pointing out that networks were 'invariably' insulated from parliament and the public (1988:78; 1990:204; Rhodes and Marsh 1992:13; 1997:38).

Yet, the extent to which a 'different world of power—essentially a post-parliamentary polity' (Richardson 2000:1006) had emerged in the wake of networks came under increasing scrutiny. Judge (1990a; 1993; 1999) was one of the earliest and most persistent 'revisionists' to this thesis. His basic argument was that 'irrespective of the actual impact of Parliament upon policy-making, there is one fundamental reason why it remains crucial to the whole process. This is simply because no other system of representation has the theoretical legitimacy of parliamentary representation' (1990:39). Without denying the descriptive utility of network analysis or a trend towards complex 'governance' Judge argued that the claims on behalf of new forms of representation through networks—that they are replacing, supplanting, and operating independently of parliamentary representation—needed careful examination.

Indeed, even proponents of network models have been willing to afford some greater recognition to the legitimating frame of representative democracy within which policy networks and structures of governance have to operate. Thus, Richardson (1993:90) acknowledged that 'a useful qualification to the post-parliamentary thesis . . . is [that it is] important to note the symbolic and legitimating functions of parliament'. Daugbjerg and Marsh (1998:62) proceeded to note that: 'Since representative democracy is the major form of governance in Western societies, it does not make sense simply to argue that parliaments are excluded from influence because we cannot observe the direct effects upon the policy outcome'. They conclude that: 'Overlooking the role of parliaments in analyses of policy making is, therefore, a great mistake' (Daugbjerg and Marsh 1998:63). Similarly, Marsh and Smith (2000:8) acknowledge that 'political authority' is perhaps the most important external constraint upon networks. Thus 'if a minister, particularly the Prime Minister, is prepared to bear the costs of breaking up a policy community, he or she has the resources and the authority . . .' (Marsh and Smith 2000:8).

In addition to this growing academic recognition, the practice of UK government continued to reveal the impact that the specific conceptualization of representation incorporated into the Westminster model had upon the practical operation of networks in the UK. As noted in chapter 2 (and as will be seen in chapter 4) contemporary UK governments continue to subscribe to the Westminster model. Indeed, the evidence provided by Marsh et al (2001:244) reveals that this conceptualization of democracy is both an empirical fact accepted by members of the core executive and also a normative aspiration in that they believe that 'this is how it should be'. Moreover, this conceptualization 'legitimises their authority and power. As such it affects how the political system works' (Marsh et 2001:247). Ultimately, Marsh et al conclude that, in accepting this view, politicians and bureaucrats in the UK continue to 'operate . . . with a view which actually fits more happily with the Westminster model than with the Differentiated Polity Model' (Marsh et al 2003:310).

Issue networks and beyond

According to leading networks analysts there has been a general trend in the UK away from policy-making characterized by tightly knit policy communities and stable networks to more loosely organized and less stable 'issue networks'. A step change is normally identified with the Thatcher era when many established policy communities lost control of policy framing and agenda setting (see Richardson 2000:1010; Marsh et al 2001:198–200; Richards and Smith 2002:178–80). Significantly, the Thatcher governments asserted the primacy of the norms and values implicit within the Westminster model over those associated with policy communities (see Judge 1990b:66; Richardson 2000:1009–11). Whereas Labour governments after 1997 have been more disposed to seek the views of groups and to broaden consultation processes and to re-establish networks in some areas such as social policy (Richards and Smith 2002:181–3; Marsh et al 2003:319), this did not necessarily mean a comprehensive return to old-style policy communities. In some sectors (in, for example, GM crops and organic agriculture) policy networks were either 'indeterminate/intermediate' (see Toke and Marsh 2003:238) or took the form of 'issue networks' involving many participants with fluctuating interaction and limited consensus (see Greer 2002:470).

Issue networks are normally conceived as 'open' processes of consultation. According to Rhodes they have the following characteristics:

> many participants, fluctuating interaction and access for the various members; the absence of consensus and the presence of conflict; interactions based on consultation rather than negotiation or bargaining; an unequal power relationship in which many participants may have few resources, little access and no alternative. (Bevir and Rhodes 2003:50; see also Rhodes 1997:45; Marsh 1998:14)

Exactly what constitutes an 'issue network' is open to dispute, as by definition its boundaries are permeable, its membership is fluctuating and variable, and its locus of interinstitutional interactions is diffuse. Indeed, unlike closed policy communities anchored in and around government departments, issue networks transcend formal political institutions and institutionalized patterns of network behaviour and extend into informal institutions and non-institutionalized action (through social movements and direct/protest action).

If the pivotal point on Marsh and Rhodes continuum between policy communities and issue networks has tipped towards the latter in recent years it has brought in its wake a more variegated policy style in the

UK. In part, as noted above, governments have destabilized long-standing policy communities as they increasingly asserted their own policy priorities. Equally, the very dominance of the policy community system led excluded groups to seek admission to the system. Where 'entry' was achieved, the 'new entrants often brought different values, policy frames, demands and modes of behaviour to the negotiating table' (Richardson 2000:1021). In turn, the permissive loosening of policy community norms encouraged some former insider groups to contemplate an increased deployment of outsider strategies of media campaigns, direct action and demonstrations. These strategies were realized in alternative institutional venues (parliament, news media, courts, and increasingly, supranational venues in the EU), and often within a context of a reframing of ideas and policy frames. In practice, the divide between insider and outsider strategies had never been rigid, as the former have traditionally deployed multi-dimensional and multi-arena strategies (see Judge 1990a:34–8; Grant 2000:32–5).

The blurring of insider and outsider strategies was highlighted in the rise of single-issue politics in the UK. Certain specific examples characterize the complexities of government-group interactions in the 21st century: the 'fuel protests' of 2000; and the campaign against genetically modified crops (for details see Grant 2001; Robinson 2002; Doherty et al 2001, 2002; Greer 2002; Toke and Marsh 2003). Both entailed: the dislocation of established networks relationships through changed government priorities (reflected not least in the reorganization of central departments and the repackaging of policy arenas and the reconstitution of department-group relations in, for example, the Department of Environment, Food and Rural Affairs (see chapter 4)); the perceived marginalization of insider groups such as the National Farmers Union and the Road Haulage Association, and the questioning of existing insider strategies by some members in the light of such perceptions; a process of 'learning' from the activities of social movements and the adoption of the tactics of protest and direct action; the adoption of loose and decentralized organizational structures by the new protest movements; and the consistent preference of governments to repatriate, as soon as possible, such contentious issues into an arena of private negotiations with established organizations. In these circumstances Richardson (2000:1008) concludes that: 'whilst there are undoubtedly policy communities and networks which exhibit both stability and exclusiveness and do control policy agendas, there appears to be countertendencies which lead to lack of control, policy instability, and unpredictable outcomes'.

Conclusion

This chapter has underlined the simple point that there is no escape from the Westminster model and its prescribed institutional configuration in the UK in the 21st century.

On the one side, the major political parties—as the beneficiaries in office of the majoritarian Westminster electoral system—still subscribe to the underpinning logic of that system and support its institutional effects (encapsulated within the 'Westminster model'). It is still the case that parties provide the major personnel of government and that 'national governmental policy in Britain is still predominantly party ... policy' (Webb 2000:262). Political parties remain the primary institutional mechanism for the aggregation of political interests. Certainly, by the general election of 2001—given continuing social dealignment, New Labour's colonization of the ideological centre ground (see Norris 2001b:577–9; Bara and Budge 2001:592–6), and the centripetal logic of two-party competition—the interests of 'middle England' found aggregation across all major UK parties. Moreover, the historical development of the parties' own internal organizations has been characterized by the privileging of parliamentary leadership positions (in practice if not necessarily in theory) and resultant, inbuilt dynamic tensions between members, activists and leaders.

On the other side, advocates of a 'network' approach recognize that the 'Westminster model survives in spite of many cracks' but then offer an alternative 'governance as networks' narrative to redress the inadequacies of the traditional model (Bevir and Rhodes 2003:31). The explicit claim is that 'networks' and 'governance' capture recent changes in UK government in a way that the Westminster model cannot (Bevir and Rhodes 2003:54). Indeed, 'governance' is defined as 'governing with and through networks' (Bevir and Rhodes 2003:56). In themselves, networks are seen as institutional structures with their own rules of the game, boundaries (in terms of the patterned inclusion and exclusion of organized interests), and 'appropriate behaviour' for participants. They have proliferated with the 'marketization' and fragmentation of systems for delivering public services in recent decades, with the result that governments have become more dependent on multifarious networks.

Simply because governments have become more dependent on networks does not necessarily mean, however, that networks have superseded or supplanted 'government' and its institutions. The contention of this chapter is that the institutions of government as characterized in the 'Westminster model'—parliament, departments, the core executive, and the civil service—provide the essential legitimating and operating institutional frame within which networks can function. This much is now acknowledged by several leading proponents of network analysis (see Richardson 2000:1010; Marsh et al 2001:310; Richards and Smith 2002:271–2; Marsh et al 2003:319–20). In this practical sense models of 'networks as governance' cannot escape the Westminster model that they were designed to replace. The relationship between the institutions of government and the institutions of governance (primarily networks) remains asymmetrical. Within government the core executive and the departments of state retain a crucial and privileged position. These government institutions have asserted their pre-eminence both within networks, and through their capacity to destabilize and reconstitute government-group interactions. In addition governments have sought to deal with the consequences of fragmentation and new modes of service delivery through various institutional initiatives—the most recent of which has been 'joined-up' government. It is to these issues of the core executive and the differentiated polity that we now turn in chapter 4.

....

KEY TERMS

- annual conference
- block vote
- cadre party
- cause groups
- democratization as emasculation
- electoral professional parties
- electoral volatility
- electoralist parties

- governance
- insider groups
- intra-party democratization
- issue networks
- linkage
- mass membership
- mass party
- multi-party systems

- new democratic centralism
- One Member One Vote
- organized groups
- outsider groups
- partisan dealignment
- partisan realignment
- party system

- policy communities
- policy networks
- political parties
- sectional groups
- single-issue politics
- subnational party systems

GUIDE TO FURTHER READING

BEVIR, M. and RHODES, R. A. W. (2003) *Interpreting British Governance*, (London, Routledge).

A novel, cutting edge analysis of modern UK governance, occasionally 'too sharp' for its own good.

GRANT, W. (2000) *Pressure Groups and British Politics*, (London, Macmillan).

A short, incisive introduction to conceptualizations about, and the contributions of, groups in UK politics

JORDAN, A. G. and RICHARDSON, J. J. (1987) *Government and Pressure Groups in Britain*, (Oxford, Clarendon Press).

Highly influential, if now somewhat dated, analysis of the contribution of groups to the UK's political process.

MARSH, D. and RHODES, R. A. W. (eds.) (1992), *Policy Networks in British Government*, (Oxford, Oxford University Press).

A seminal collection of early essays on networks that continues to structure discussion of interest representation and intermediation in the UK.

WEBB, P. (2000) *The Modern British Party System*, (London, Sage).

A comprehensive overview of the party systems within the UK.

4

The Executive and Core Executive

Overview

This chapter examines the main institutions of the core executive—departments, agencies, and the institutions of coordination centred around the cabinet, the prime minister and the Treasury. It highlights how the norms, beliefs and political culture derived from the parliamentary system affect institutional structures and norms in Whitehall. The cabinet system and central departments institutionalize notions of collective and individual ministerial responsibility to parliament. From these conventions stem associated ideas about the respective responsibilities of elected politicians (ministers) and non-elected officials/bureaucrats (civil servants); and, paradoxically, institutional norms and values which deprive the core principle of accountability of much of its practical meaning.

The continuing centrality of the political accountability of ministers to parliament in the institutional form of departments and the core executive is examined in the context of organizational challenges posed by managerialism, de-layering and agencification. What the chapter emphasizes is that executive institutions in the UK are best understood from an *interinstitutional* perspective, and one that acknowledges the interconnected and complex institutional interactions centred upon Whitehall.

Introduction

For much of the 20th century the terms 'central government', or 'cabinet government', or simply 'Whitehall' served to describe executive politics in the UK. Indeed, 'Whitehall', as the geographical location of the major departments of state, was commonly used as the collective name for central administration in the UK (see Greenwood et al 2002:24). Moreover, the concentration of executive institutions within such a small geographical area was itself symptomatic of the intense centralization of power within the UK state. Yet, by the last decade of the 20th century, the term the 'core executive' came to prominence in the study of UK politics in recognition that the traditional descriptive terms failed to capture the complex web of institutions and interinstitutional interactions focused upon and radiating from Whitehall.

Martin Smith (1999a:1), as one of the main proponents of the term 'core executive', maintains that it 'is at the heart of British government. It contains the key institutions and actors concerned with developing policy, coordinating government activity and providing the necessary resources for delivering public goods'. Yet, exactly which institutions are covered by the term is open to dispute. Rod Rhodes (1995b:12), one of the original analysts of the 'core executive', included the prime minister, the cabinet, cabinet committees, coordinating departments (such as the Cabinet Office, Treasury and Foreign Office), the law officers and the security and intelligence services (see also Hood and James 1997:178). He drew a distinction between those institutions, networks and actors concerned with coordination (the core executive) and those 'centres of political authority which take policy decisions' (primarily departments and associated agencies) (Rhodes 1995b:12). Similarly, Burch and Holliday (2004:3) confine the term core executive to a small number of agencies at the 'very centre of the executive branch of government that fulfil essential policy setting and general business coordination and oversight functions above the level of departments'. Smith, on the other hand, includes departments, and by implication agencies, in his definition of the core executive (1999a:5−6).

Whether the boundaries of the core executive are drawn narrowly or more widely, they map out an institutional configuration that is both complex and contingent. The structure is complex in the sense of incorporating discrete institutions, roles and norms (which are differentiated in other non-parliamentary systems between executive roles performed by party politicians, and executive/bureaucratic roles performed by civil servants and other 'public officials'). It is also contingent in the sense of reflecting perpetually changing relationships both within and between individual institutions and their incumbents at any particular time (prime minister and cabinet, cabinet and individual departments, ministers and civil servants, departments and agencies).

What in the past was treated as a relatively simple undertaking of describing 'the centre' has now become a 'consciously analytical' (Smith 1999b:115) and wide-ranging exercise that acknowledges the importance of history, interinstitutional interactions, and the importance of norms and values. Distinctions that are readily apparent in some other political systems—between political executive and bureaucracy, between policy and administration, between legislative and executive branches, and even of standard institutional terms such as 'government department' and 'civil service' are 'now almost incapable of precise definition' in the UK (Greenwood et al 2002:19).

Despite this imprecision, this chapter aims to examine the main institutions of the core executive—departments, agencies, and the organizations of coordination centred around the cabinet and the prime minister (primarily the Cabinet Office, and the Prime Minister's Office). In so doing it will highlight how the norms, beliefs and political culture derived from the parliamentary system affect institutional structures and norms in Whitehall. This builds upon the view that:

> the organisation and structure of the central state has to be analysed within the prevailing ideas of legitimate—of representative and responsible, of *parliamentary*—government. The argument ... is simple: the central state cannot be examined in Britain without reference to the structural and organising precepts of parliamentary government itself. This is not to argue that central state institutions act consistently in accordance with these precepts, merely that there is a widespread belief, within and beyond the executive that they should. (Judge 1993:132–3)

At the heart of these precepts is the principle of the political accountability of the executive to parliament. Wrapped around, and feeding from, this simple central principle, however, are a series of ivy-like corollaries which give the appearance of growth and life on the surface but have effectively deprived the feeder principle of much of its practical substance. The fundamental precepts are collective and individual notions of ministerial responsibility and their respective institutionalization in the cabinet system and central departments. From these precepts stem associated ideas about the respective responsibilities of elected politicians (ministers) and non-elected officials/bureaucrats (civil servants); and institutional norms and values which deprive the core principle of accountability of much of its practical meaning.

Departments and ministerial accountability

Central departments in the UK are predicated upon the political account-ability of ministers to parliament. The doctrine that the political head of a department is answerable for the actions of that department to parliament is 'a vital part of the Liberal theory of the constitution' (Birch 1964:140). The continuing centrality of this doctrine is evident in the Ministerial Code is-sued by the prime minister (see Box 4.1). In fact, there is unquestioned agreement between the executive and both Houses of Parliament that this should be the case. This fundamental institutional consensus is reflected in the exact correspondence of the wording of the *Ministerial Code* and the

---

BOX 4.1 **Ministerial Code**

■ Ministers have a duty to Parliament to account, and be held to account, for the policies, decisions and actions of their departments and 'next steps' agencies;

■ It is of paramount importance that Ministers give accurate and truthful information to Parliament, correcting any inadvertent error at the earliest opportunity. Ministers who knowingly mislead Parliament will be expected to offer their resignation to the Prime Minister;

■ Ministers should be as open as possible with Parliament and the public, refusing to provide information only when disclosure would not be in the public interest which should be decided in accordance with the relevant statutes and the Government's Code of Practice on Access to Government Information;

■ Ministers should similarly require civil servants who give evidence before Parliamentary Committees on their behalf and under their direction to be as helpful as possible in providing accurate, truthful and full information in accordance with the duties and responsibilities of civil servants as set out in the Civil Service Code.

Source: www.cabinet-office.gov.uk/central/2001/mcode/p01

resolution adopted by the House of Commons in 1997 (HC Debates 19 March 1997:col 1046; HL Debates 20 March 1997:col 1055).

Clearly the emphasis of the *Code* is upon the duty of ministers, and departmental officials speaking on behalf of ministers, to provide full and accurate information and so to account in an 'informatory' or 'explanatory' sense (see Woodhouse 1994:29–30). Beyond that, however, the convention of ministerial responsibility has incorporated, historically, the notion that ministers are required to redress departmental shortcomings; either in a simple act of contrition and apology to the House, or through the instigation of corrective action. This dimension is normally called 'amendatory accountability' and entails taking 'remedial action for revealed errors or defects of policy or administration, whether by compensating individuals, reversing or modifying policies or decisions, disciplining civil servants, or altering departmental procedures' (Turpin 1989:57). In this sense ministers acknowledge departmental blame but not personal criticism. This distinction between organizational and personal culpability was brought into stark relief in the wake of the Inquiry into the Arms for Iraq affair in 1996. In his report into the affair (HC 115 1996) Lord Scott accepted the government's argument that, given the scope and complexity of modern government, and that 'reliance on the advice of officials has become so inevitable', it now meant that it was 'unreal' to attach blame to a Minister simply because something had gone wrong in his or her department (HC 115 1996; K8.16). Ministers could not, therefore, 'reasonably be held to blame for things done or omitted within his department of which he knew nothing at the time and could not have been expected to have foreseen or prevented' (HC 115 1996: K8.16).

If this was the case, then a distinction could, and should, be drawn between 'amendatory accountability' and 'sacrificial responsibility' where a minister is expected to resign in recognition of departmental error or maladministration. Such 'vicarious responsibility' has always been a contested element of the convention (See Marshall 1984:65, Judge 1993:137–40; Woodhouse 2003a:304–10), nonetheless, many analysts of the core executive build just such an absolute requirement into the convention before proceeding to dismiss the entire convention as a 'myth'. The fact that only four ministers had resigned between 1900 and 2004 in recognition of departmental error to which they were 'linked' by commission or omission (Wydham in 1905, Dugdale in 1954, Carrington in 1982 and Brittan in 1986); and that two others (Byres and Morris) resigned in 2002 in recognition of some-what nebulous and cumulative failures to perform their respective minis-terial roles, is used as empirical evidence of the mythical qualities of the convention. Yet, even if it is conceded that 'ministerial accountability may be a myth', nonetheless, it is still possible to argue 'it is a very powerful myth that affects the way ministers and civil servants operate' (Bogdanor HC 238 2000:Q186). Thus, despite its empirical shortcomings, the convention con-tinues to provide 'the rationale for the institutional structure of govern-ment' (Woodhouse 1994:298).

The belief that a minister alone is in some sense accountable for the per-formance of an administrative department is the principle around which the British central state has been organized, and around which the rela-tionship between elected representatives and non-elected bureaucrats has been defined. The constitutional centrality of departments is apparent in Daintith and Page's (1999:6) pronouncement that the UK's executive 'is made up of departments, and it is normally the heads of these departments . . . not the government as a whole, that powers, and resources, are alloc-ated by law'. Thus, although the minister will be acting as a minister of the Crown, his or her powers and duties under an Act are his or hers alone in law. In turn, this legal precedence of the minister has organizational con-sequences for a department itself.

Historically, the principle of accountability helps to explain the rise of the organizational form of ministerial departments. Before the start of the 19th century Britain shared with other European states the common prac-tice of administering executive tasks through boards of public officials (Par-ris 1969:82–4; Chester 1981:42–9). While boards continued to be of signific-ance in Scotland until well into the 20th century (see Mitchell 2003b: 139–41; see chapter 5), there was a general supersession of boards by min-isterial departments in England and Wales, to the extent that the latter be-came 'the norm of British government in the period between the first reform Bill and the Crimean War' (Parris 1969:82). In this period 'MPs began to feel dissatisfied with a form of administration [boards] which omitted to provide for what they regarded as acceptable ministerial representation in the Commons' (Hanham 1969:341). Again to quote Parris (1969:85): 'Responsibility was the crux of the problem'.

The fundamental difficulty with boards was how to make them responsible to parliament. The easiest solution was either to make individual ministers responsible for each board, or to turn a board into a ministry. Hence, administrative boards 'not only went out of fashion but also out of existence' (Fry 1979:159), leaving governmental departments headed by a minister as the predominant organizational form of the central state. Although the organizational monopoly of ministerial departments within the central state was relatively short-lived, central executive institutions continued to be defined in accordance with 'some measure of direct parliamentary and ministerial overview' (Dunleavy 1989:260; see Fry 1979:159). In this sense the precepts of parliamentary government and of ministerial responsibility continue to have a profound effect upon the very organizational topography of the British central executive.

In turn these precepts have impinged directly upon the internal organization of ministerial departments themselves. The constitutional convention of individual ministerial responsibility has provided 'a strong determinant of the structural development of administrative organization and therefore the style of government' (Radcliffe 1991:29). At a micro-level, of internal departmental structure, the model clearly identifies an 'authority hierarchy' headed by a minister. Such a hierarchy 'facilitated both accountability and equity, allowing detailed control of subordinates, and enforcement of rules, through a hierarchic structure' (Greenwood, et al 2002:28–30).

Departments

In 2004 the Labour government identified the department of state as 'the lead element in a linked set of public, private and voluntary sector bodies responsible for delivering services' (Cabinet Office 2004:para 6.5). Indeed, Marsh et al (2001) maintain that the constitutional and political importance of British government departments is 'unquestionable'. For them, departments are 'the source of most policy and they hold overall responsibility for delivering policies. As such, the activities of the core executive occur within the departmental framework' (Marsh et al 2001:1). This location of the core executive within a broader departmental context is important for present purposes because it allows the themes of the impact of ministerial responsibility upon both organizational structure and upon norms, values and 'administrative culture' to be developed further.

In the following analysis several related and directional themes have to be borne in mind. The first is that a simple, uniform 'departmental framework' does not exist but instead there is a multiplex of interlocked frameworks; second, although the 'culture' of Whitehall will be examined, subcultures and overlapping cultures can also be identified in most departments; and third, while concentrating upon the organizational precepts of responsibility and accountability, it has to be recognized that there has been a consistent tension in the major departments between the values of accountability (often associated with a 'public sector ethos') and those of 'service delivery' (commonly associated with a 'managerial ethos' in recent decades). This tension was pre-figured in the 19th century in the operation of public boards, it was observable in the development of public corporations and nationalized industries in the 20th century, and is evident in the 21st century concerns with new public management and agencification. The fourth theme is that, although focusing upon departments as institutions, the discussion will also spill over into a broader analysis of the 'civil service' as an institution.

A department is what a department is!

Although there is wide agreement that departments are at the centre of government, or provide the framework of the 'core executive' (Marsh et al 2001:1), or that 'departmental primacy' (Page and Daintith 2000:64) is the organising principle of the executive in the UK, there is little agreement as to what a department is or how it is defined. As McLean et al (2000:139) note 'the search for a definition of a government department in the British system of government is an elusive and difficult one'. The search becomes even more elusive as the boundaries become blurred by a tendency to switch between the terms 'department' and 'central government' or to use them as synonyms (see Jordan 1994:12–15, McLean et al 2000:140). One common route around this definitional problem has been to adopt a non-definitional perspective. Thus, of the many different organizational forms found at the centre of government, 'only two generalisations can be made: (1) most have links, however tenuous, with ministers; (2) the most politically salient are usually ministerial departments' (Greenwood et al 2002:24–5).

Encompassed within these generalizations is the essence of UK departments and more broadly UK central government. The 'essence' is that ministers remain responsible, no matter how tangentially, for the activities of those organizations. Indeed, perhaps the easiest way to differentiate central government organizations is by the degree of formal linkage between the staff of an organization and a minister. This leads to a four-fold categorization of ministerial departments, non-ministerial departments, agencies, and non-departmental public bodies—as delimited by lessening direct control by ministers (in theory at least).

Ministerial departments

Until relatively recently, discussion of departments tended to focus upon ministerial departments and often implicitly assumed that there was a standard monolithic form of 'department'. Yet, as Hogwood (1995:512) has made clear, such traditional conceptions of a department were, even before the inception of Next Steps Agencies in 1988 (see below), 'the exception rather than the rule'. To start with, a distinction needs to be made between ministerial departments and non-ministerial departments. After the creation of the Department of Constitutional Affairs in June 2003 (which incorporated the territorial departments for Northern Ireland, Scotland and Wales with the legal affairs departments of the Lord Chancellor, the Privy Council Office, and the Law Officers) there were five broad categories of ministerial departments according to basic function (see Box 4.2).

BOX 4.2   **Ministerial Departments 2004**

Economic
   HM Treasury
   Trade and Industry

Defence and External Affairs
   Defence
   Foreign and Commonwealth Office
   International Development

Domestic Affairs
   Culture, Media and Sport
   Education and Skills
   Environment, Food and Rural Affairs
   Health

continues

Box 4.2 continued

Home Office
Transport
Work and Pensions

Organization of Government

Office of the Deputy Prime Minister
Cabinet Office
Prime Minister's Office
Office of the Leader of the House of Commons

Territorial and Legal

Department for Constitutional Affairs
Includes

UK Territorial Departments

Northern Ireland Office
Scotland Office
Wales Office

Legal Affairs

Lord Chancellor's Department
Privy Council Office
Law Officer's Department

What unites these ministerial departments is the simple legal fact that they have a minister at their head. In law it is the ministerial head who is responsible for the actions of the department (see Page and Daintith 2000:64). By convention, holders of ministerial office have been members of either House of Parliament. 'Such membership', as Bradley and Ewing (2003:270) point out, 'is essential to the maintenance of ministerial responsibility'. In most departments the ministerial head is entitled the Secretary of State. In all departments there is a ministerial team of junior ministers (variously ranked and entitled as ministers of state, parliamentary under secretaries, and parliamentary secretaries). Normally there is a formal division of labour amongst the ministerial team, with each post carrying specific duties and mapped out in departmental organigrams. Ultimately, however, the Secretary of State, or designated ministerial head, remains constitutionally responsible for all the work of the department. In turn, this legal precedence of the ministerial head has organizational consequences for a department itself. Historically, government departments were characterized by pyramidal hierarchies. In these steep hierarchies responsibility for administration and finance tended to be concentrated immediately below ministerial level in the authority of the most senior administrator, the permanent secretary.

The continuing significance of hierarchical structures in Whitehall in the 21st century was emphasized by the Performance and Innovation Unit (see below) in its report *Wiring it Up* (PIU 2000a:para 3.1). The traditional vertical management structures of departments were seen to be 'highly effective in delivering many key policies and priorities' and had the specific advantages of providing 'a single, clear line of accountability' and securing control over resources. 'Most areas of government business' were still structured in accordance with ' "vertical" management lines with Ministers at the top and service providers and their clients at the bottom' (PIU 2000a:para 3.1).

This verticality reflects two basic organizational principles. The first is that 'the Minister in charge of a Department is alone answerable to Parliament for the exercise of the powers on which the administration of that Department depends' (Cabinet Office 2001). As a corollary, the convention of individual ministerial responsibility, which defines external relations between department and parliament, clearly assumes an internal hierarchy of decision in which ministers are charged with 'deciding' policy and civil servants with 'advising' and 'administering' policy. Significantly, this prescription still finds reflection in 'official' descriptions of internal departmental relationships, with, for example, the *Ministerial Code* maintaining that: 'the Permanent Secretary has 'general responsibilities for the organisation and discipline of the Department [and] the duty to advise on matters of policy' (Cabinet Office 2001).

Civil service culture

One of the institutional consequences of the convention of ministerial responsibility and the 'external' linkage of departments to parliament has been its impact upon the internal norms and culture of departments. As made clear throughout this book, institutions are the site of interactions guided by norms, rules and beliefs as to 'appropriate behaviour'. This does not mean that there is a universal 'civil service culture' that is equally appropriate to all civil services, but, simply that each bureaucracy reflects the historical development and institutional context of its particular administrative setting. Thus the culture of modern UK civil servants has been affected by the development of a state system that is parliamentary (Judge 1993), elitist and secretive (Marsh et al 2001:28), and which has derived from 'the creation of departments in the 19th century which ensured that decisions were locked into a Whitehall system where ministers adopted the prerogative of the Crown' (Marsh et al 2001:28–9). Traditionally, therefore, 'the recognition that the minister *ought* to exert executive control, and that the higher civil service should be "upward looking", plays a major part in determining the role perceptions of bureaucrats themselves' (Judge 1993:145).

In many ways the relationship between a minister and senior civil servants in a department is one of 'fusion', of 'an ever-present indissoluble symbiosis between minister and civil servants so that they were almost one person' (Foster 2001:726). (The Senior Civil Service Level was created in 1996 and includes the 4,150 or so most senior managers, specialists and policy advisers). In this relationship ministers have been able to exert internal control over departmental affairs, because senior civil servants have conceived of their role as ministerial surrogates or as 'quasi-politicians'. Ministerial control has been exercized indirectly in the department through the self-control exercized by senior civil servants. In this way constant awareness of the external link between the administrative world of Whitehall and the political world of Westminster has impacted upon the internal linkage between the realms of 'administration' and 'policy'. In these linkages, knowledge of the Whitehall machine, appreciation of the policy and political implications of departmental programmes, and a 'public service ethos'—where the integrity of civil servants has been rooted in their partisan neutrality, anonymity and permanence—have characterized the institutional culture of senior civil servants for most of the past century and a half (see Marsh et al 2001:27–31). This culture consciously recognized the importance of 'accountability' of ministers to parliament and of the cascaded relationships within departments stemming from this external accountability (see above). Indeed, this emphasis upon the skills required to operate in an 'accountability' culture centred upon parliament helps to differentiate the UK from other notions of accountable bureaucracies (see Campbell and Wilson 1995:251–2, 260–4; Foster 2001:727).

If, for most of the 20th century, a 'universal' culture transcended Whitehall, it also provided the paradox of simultaneously reinforcing departmentalism and sustaining the values of 'departmentalitis'. The fundamental organizational principle of Whitehall, as Bogdanor notes, is that 'the Civil Service is organised in departments. It advises ministers on departmental matters' (HC 238 2000:Q170). The vertical structures of accountability within departments provided institutional incentives for civil servants to concentrate on 'their' departmental policies, and to work within established departmental perspectives on policy (see Flinders 2002:68), and to confine ministerial initiatives within the boundaries of departmental 'silos' or 'chimneys' (or whatever other analogy of constraint was in vogue at the time).

If the traditional institutional emphasis was upon 'accountability' and steeply hierarchical structures within departments, successive governments since the 1960s have sought to prioritize 'service delivery' and 'managerialism' through structural and cultural reforms within Whitehall. The emphasis upon accountability was deemed to sustain an 'innate conservatism' in Whitehall 'partly because politicians tend not to relish unpleasant surprises and partly because the accountability frameworks are unsympathetic to risks that go wrong' (Bichard 2000:43). To question this conservatism, a series of reviews, headed by outsiders—Fulton in the 1960s, Rayner and Ibbs in the 1980s—provided answers strongly influenced by private sector managerial and efficiency models (see below; for details see Foster 2001:727–41; Hennessy 2001:190–208, 598–627, Richards and Smith 2002:104–19). In turn the reviews led to three major organizational changes within Whitehall: managerialism, de-layering and agencification.

Managerialism

Managerialism places the emphasis upon the control and efficient utilization of departmental resources, both financial and personnel, and the inculcation of a set of skills distinct from policy-making or mere administration (Oliver 2003:222). The overriding objective of successive phases of the 'managerial revolution' in Whitehall has been to promote efficiency through the adoption of private sector management techniques and the employment of private sector personnel. The fact that private sector management had 'more restricted aims' than the public service (Greenwood et al 2002:6), that policy planning and implementation in the public sector tended to be more complicated than in the private sector (Foster 2001:743), and that, generally, the track record of UK managers was less than impressive, made the idea that the civil service would become more efficient if it adopted such practices positively 'bizarre' in the opinion of some commentators (see Bogdanor 2001:293). Nonetheless, successive governments since the 1970s imported private sector management techniques and practices into Whitehall. The extent to which new public management philosophies had permeated the debate about the role of the civil service was neatly summarized by the House of Commons' Select Committee on Public Administration:

> Meeting ... complex and demanding requirements [of modern government] may now demand new skills, and new people, with the central Civil Service moving from being line administrators to being experts in fields such as change management, extended strategic contracting, the development of multi-channel procurement and delivery systems, and so on. (HC 94 2001:para 19)

In his 1999 report to the prime minister on *Civil Service Reform* the then Cabinet Secretary, Sir Richard Wilson, identified the continued need of the civil service to develop stronger managerial competence. He believed that this could be provided through: stronger leadership; better business planning; sharper performance management; improved diversity of personnel; a 'service more open to people and ideas, which brings on talent'; and a better deal for staff (see Cabinet Office 1999). Responsibility for implementing the Wilson Report eventually fell to the Delivery and Reform Team of the Cabinet Office (see below) created by the incoming Cabinet Secretary Sir Andrew Turnbull in 2002. Indeed, the 'vision' of Turnbull was to continue with reform so that, by 2005, the civil service would be 'respected as much for its capability to deliver as for its policy skills' and would 'think creatively and operate strategically' (www.civilservice.gov.uk/reform/about_delivery/vision.asp).

To this end, the Delivery and Reform Team proposed a new 'leadership package' for the Senior Civil Service. The package included an upgrading of the Top Management Programme and introduced a 'High Potential Development Scheme' to expedite the rise of talented managers to the highest 'leadership positions' (see Cabinet Office 2003d:4; Cabinet Office 2004:para 5.17). Whereas much of the reformist emphasis since the 1980s had been upon enhancing management skills and financial capabilities within the civil service, the objectives in the 2000s were to promote leadership and to focus on service delivery (Cabinet Office 2004:para 5.29). The overall changes envisaged for the civil service were encapsulated in tabular form in the document *Civil Service Reform: Delivery and Values* (Cabinet Office 2004:28). Under two columns, headed 'yesterday's success story' and 'tomorrow's equivalent', the role of a Permanent Secretary was listed respectively as 'the Minister's senior policy adviser' and as 'the Minister's senior delivery agent and policy adviser'. Clearly, 'tomorrow's vision' reflected the Labour government's belief in the need to promote more effective leadership and greater risk-taking within the ministerial-civil service partnership at the apex of central departments.

One mechanism for strengthening political leadership and innovation at the top of departments was the employment of special advisers. The use of special advisers is not new, and dates back to the 19th century. The present system was formalized, however, in 1974 when the then prime minister, Harold Wilson, allowed ministers to appoint advisers on a regular basis. In February 2004 there were 83 paid special advisers in post. 55 worked in departments and 28 were employed in Downing Street (HC Debates 22 July 2004 vol 424: col 446W–70W). Special advisers are not employed as civil servants though they have 'civil service like status' (HC 293 2001:para 19). They serve the valuable function of providing 'political' advice and assessments to ministers, and alternative perspectives to those provided by permanent civil servants. Although an established mechanism for widening the advice presented to ministers, the increased numbers of special advisers, the opaqueness of the procedures governing their appointments, and the potentially disruptive effect should they interpose themselves as 'gatekeepers' between ministers and civil servants, raised concerns about 'putting a proper framework of accountability around their activities' (HC 293 2001: para 81; see also Cm 5775 2003:43–53). These concerns found reflection in the proposals for a Civil Service Act (see below) and in the government's intention, should such an Act be passed, to 'clarify what special advisers can do' and equally 'what special advisers cannot do' (Cm 6373 2004: paras 38, 40).

Another mechanism for improving innovation was the widening of the recruitment base of senior civil servants to secure a more diverse and socially representative bureaucracy (see Cm 4310 1999:56; HC 94 2001:paras 28–30; Cabinet Office 2004:17). In addition, recent governments have been attracted to an 'outside' recruitment strategy which encouraged applications from senior private sector executives, and which promoted two-way secondments (of civil servants accepting temporary appointments in the private sector and vice versa). Ultimately, however, the potential managerial and efficiency benefits had to be weighed against the potential 'damaging consequences' to the public sector ethos and to ensuring that 'the core values of the service should not be put at risk' (HC 94 2001:para 31). Indeed, Baroness Prasher, the First Commissioner, in her foreword to the Civil Service Commissioners' Annual Report for 2002–03 recognized that: 'At a time of rapid change there is a need, more than ever, to ensure core values are not eroded. ... These values are neither incompatible with nor peripheral to the process of change' (Office of the Civil Service Commissioners 2003).

Delayering

Quantitatively the civil service has been reduced in size from 735,000 in 1979 to 523,580 in April 2004. Between 1995 and 1997 alone, the senior civil service was reduced by 20 per cent with the removal of an entire tier (Grade 3) from the Whitehall bureaucracy. In this period, as the then Cabinet Secretary observed: 'we did a lot of delayering ... and you find a lot of Departments now have a lot more direct working to Ministers and a lot less people ticking their names as things go forward ... we accept that the sort of traditional hierarchy very often does not fit the needs of what we are trying to do' (HC 238 2000:Q393). This 'delayering' impacted upon senior officials through an increased emphasis upon the performance of more managerial roles and upon lower ranked officials undertaking more detailed policy work (see Richards and Smith 2004:122). While the removal of what some considered to be 'excessive tiers in the old hierarchies' (Foster 2001:733) might be regarded as an organisational advantage, the disadvantage of delayering was that it encouraged 'junior or senior officials ... to send their advice direct to ministers unchallenged by other civil servants, [as a result] mistakes of fact and analysis were more likely to be made' (Foster 2001:733). The real loss, therefore, was an impairment of the 'once ingrained official habit of challenging exactly what every other official (and minister) meant' (Foster 2001:733).

This sense of loss of 'ingrained habits', and of a general threat to the 'civil service ethos', pervades the thoughts of the cautionary critics of the managerial revolution in Whitehall. Their argument is that there is an apparent irony in the fact that managerialism has simply served to illuminate the *requirement* for traditional civil service values. The traditional civil service norms are not out-dated residues from a bygone era of limited and account-able government, but instead are essential values in an executive system rooted in an 'accountability' culture centred upon parliament.

Perceived threats to this accountability culture underpinned, in large part, proposals for the introduction of a Civil Service Act. Indeed, the House of Commons' Public Administration Select Committee, in introducing a draft Civil Service Bill in December 2003 (which, in itself, was a procedural innovation), made clear that in 'an era of rapid, fundamental and often controversial change in Whitehall and beyond' the 'core values' of a professional and politically neutral civil service should be safeguarded in legislation (HC 128 2003:paras 3–5)). The purpose of the Bill was to provide 'a clear framework which would enable Parliament to ensure that public service principles are upheld and that civil servants and others are carrying out their jobs with propriety' (HC 128 2003: para 6).

The government responded to the Public Administration Committee's initiative by publishing a consultation document on a draft Civil Service Bill in November 2004 (Cm 6373 2004). The cautious nature of the consultation process was evident in the statement: 'The Government believes that the current arrangements remain workable and afford welcome flexibility in the way in which the Civil Service can be organised and managed . . . before adopting a statutory approach, the Government would want to be sure that these advantages would be preserved' (Cm 6373 2004:para 14). Notably, the government maintained that the non-statutory approach had stood the test of time and that there had been 'a largely uncontested political consensus on the benefits of an impartial and politically neutral civil service'. More importantly for the analysis of this book, defence of this position was articulated in terms of the Westminster model:

> Parliament's general authority as the ultimate sovereign body and source of the Government's right to govern has ensured that over this entire period successive governments have taken seriously Parliament's concerns about the organisation, management and culture of the Civil Service. (Cm 6373 2004:para 13; see also para 21.1)

Non-ministerial departments

In 2004 21 non-ministerial departments were listed in the *List of Ministerial Responsibilities* (see Box 4.3). As their title suggests they are not headed by ministers. They tend to be established to deliver a specific service and to have specific statutory duties. They are headed by boards, commissioners, or individual office holders; and their staff are civil servants.

BOX 4.3	Non-Ministerial Departments

Charity Commission
Commissioners for the Reduction of the National Debt
Crown Estate
Crown Prosecution Service
Export Credits Guarantee Department
Food Standards Agency
Forestry Commission
HM Customs and Excise*
Inland Revenue*
Office for Standards in Education
Office of Communications
Office of Fair Trading
Office of Gas and Electricity Markets/Gas and Electricity Markets Authority
Office of HM Paymaster General
Office of the International Rail Regulator
Office of the Rail Regulator
Office of Water Services
Postal Services Commission
Public Works Loan Board
Serious Fraud Squad
UK Trade and Investment

*Under the Revenue and Customs Bill introduced in The Queens Speech, November 2004 HM Customs and Excise and the Inland Revenue were to be merged into a single department.

Source: www.knowledgenetwork.gov.uk/eLMR/Minister.nsf/

While the heads of non-ministerial departments report to ministers, ministers do not normally have responsibility for detailed operational matters. The general rationale is to distance day-to-day administration from direct ministerial intervention. This is particularly the case if they perform some regulatory function. Thus, for example, the Food Standards Agency is described officially as 'operating at arm's length from Ministers' (Cabinet Office 2003a:99). Similarly, 'customer confidentiality' and 'keeping ministers' sticky fingers off the tax returns of the citizenry' (Hennessy 2001:478) has been a traditional rationale for non-ministerial revenue departments. This rationale underpinned the recommendation made in March 2004 by the O'Donnell Review. The Review examined the departments dealing with tax policy and administration, and concluded that a single Revenue and Customs Department should be created. Notably, however, the O'Donnell Report also recommended a new framework document 'setting out who is accountable to whom, for what' and which would provide an 'opportunity for Ministers to set out long-term principles to govern the work of the department' (Cm 6163 2004:12). In turn, in November 2004, the proposed new accountability arrangements were generally welcomed by the Treasury Committee (see HC 556 2004:paras 54–57). In between times, on 1 September 2004, David Varney had been appointed Executive Chairman of the new department, and in October 2004 it was announced that the Paymaster General would have strategic oversight of HM Revenue and Customs. The primary legislation to merge HM Customs and Excise and the Inland Revenue was announced in the Queen's speech in November 2004.

Executive Agencies

In November 2004 there were 132 Executive Agencies throughout the UK. In addition, four of the non-ministerial departments (the Inland Revenue, Customs and Excise, Public Record Office and HM Land Registry) operated fully on 'Next Steps lines'. Some 381,260 civil servants, 73 per cent of the total UK civil service, worked in these bodies (see Cabinet Office www.civilservice.gov.uk/management_information/ statistical_information/statistics/index.asp). Of the 132 agencies, 90 reported to ministers in Whitehall departments, the remainder reported to the Scottish Executive, Northern Ireland Executive and the National Assembly for Wales (see chapter 5).

Executive Agencies are based upon a nominal separation of policy and 'operational matters' within departments. This 'separation' was envisaged in, and advanced by, a series of initiatives largely associated with the post-1979 Conservative governments' managerialist and efficiency crusades (for details see Richards 1997:23–39; Richards and Smith 2002:104–8). The antecedents of the idea of agencies, however, can be traced back to the Fulton Report of 1968 and its 'managerialist-inspired' recommendations for the creation of agencies within departments as well as the devolution of some departmental functions to non-departmental agencies. Nonetheless, it was the drive for greater efficiency in service delivery and in the management of public resources, encapsulated in the 'new public management' ethos of the Thatcher era that was the immediate precipitant of the 'Next Steps' agencies. The 'preliminary steps' had been taken in the 1980s in the Rayner Scrutinies, Management Information Systems for Ministers (MINIS) and Financial Management Initiatives (FMI). The 'next step' was to build upon these initiatives and to further 'shift the focus of attention away from process to results' (Efficiency Unit 1998:para 13). What the preceding initiatives had demonstrated was 'how far attitudes and institutions have to change if the real benefits of management reforms, in the form of improvement in the way government delivers its services are to come through' (Efficiency Unit 1988:para 13). Whereas the traditional departmental structure placed the emphasis upon 'process', greater emphasis was now to be placed upon efficient service delivery. What was believed to have inhibited efficient management in the past was the emphasis within departments upon 'policy' development and advice, and upon understanding the 'state machinery' and the 'process of government' rather than upon the management of personnel and resources and efficient service delivery. The convention of ministerial responsibility was deemed responsible in part for the overload experienced at the top of departments (Efficiency Unit 1988:para 7).

If this was the diagnosis, then the cure was to be found in the creation of agencies 'to carry out the executive functions of government within a policy and resources framework set by a department' (1988:para 18). Responsibility for performance was to be placed 'squarely on the manager of an agency' (Efficiency Unit 1988:para 23). In practice, this would entail managers being 'directly responsible for operational matters' (Efficiency Unit 1988:para 23). Such direct responsibility obviously posed a significant challenge to existing notions of ministerial responsibility, and, in a three-page appendix to the Efficiency Unit's report, the changes necessary to the practice of accountability were considered. Yet, the then Prime Minister Mrs Thatcher, sought from the outset to dispel fears about a diminution of ministerial responsibility by maintaining that: 'Each agency will be accountable to a Minister, who will in turn be accountable to Parliament for the agency's performance'. When pressed on this point the prime minister replied: 'There will be no change in the arrangements for accountability. Ministers will continue to account to Parliament for all the work of their Departments, including the work of the agencies . . . I repeat: there will be no change in the arrangements for accountability' (HC Debates 1988 vol 127 col 1151).

The officially proclaimed model of a separation of policy and execution, with agency chief executives having operational autonomy yet working within the overarching direction of and responsibility to ministers, was at best ambiguous and at worse consciously naïve. Predictably, perhaps, the practice turned out to be far more complex and differentiated.

Deploying an historical institutional analysis Francesca Gains (1999, 2004a) has mapped the diversity of the implementation of the agency concept across departments. The essence of her argument is that there 'was path dependency in the adaptation of the agency concept in the UK as change was mediated through the existing constitutional and organizational arrangements and the policy preferences of actors involved' (2004a:57). She notes that the new institutional arrangements were grafted on to existing formal institutional and informal practices (2004a:58). The result was 'vastly different interpretations of the extent of managerial freedom and the meaning of accountability' across departments (2004a:57–58). Equally Gains (1999:210–12) points to the importance of variable understandings of Whitehall's norms and culture in explaining some of the institutional tensions encountered between agencies and their sponsoring departments. In the cases of the Prison Service and the Child Support Agency, at the height of their notoriety in the mid-1990s, Gains notes that their respective Chief Executives (Derek Lewis and Ros Hepplewhite) were both Whitehall 'outsiders', who were unfamiliar with the established 'rules of the game' and who 'appeared to ignore, or be unaware of how to use, more traditional civil service skills, such as caution, co-ordination, and consultation' (Gains 1999:210). In particular, Hepplewhite was adjudged not to 'have properly realized the parliamentary perspective' of her activities (Gains 2004b:559).

While significant differences are apparent in the degree, and manner in which, departments accommodated Next Steps Agencies, the core principle of a 'repositioning of central government executive operations "at arms' length" from departments' remained intact (Greenwood et at 2002:35). What was notable in practice, however, was that the 'arm' proved to be shorter in some departments than in others.

In practice there has been substantial variation in patterns of ministerial involvement with agencies. At one extreme the Prison Service (for England and Wales) and the Child Benefits Agency provide extreme and untypical examples of the involvement of ministers (see Talbot, 1995; Barberis 1998; Gains 1999; Harlow 1999). At the other extreme there has been little ministerial involvement in, for example, many agencies in the Ministry of Defence (see Hogwood et al 2000:213). In between these extremes, ministers are intermittently involved in agencies when politically salient issues are identified in parliament or by the media. Of course, little or no ministerial or parliamentary interest in the activities of agencies does then raise the question of what accountability means in such cases? One answer was provided by Hogwood et al (2000:218–19) who discovered that an absence of ministerial and parliamentary interest did not imply an absence of accountability. Even those agencies that have attracted few parliamentary questions from MPs, or meetings with ministers, have nevertheless been subject to reporting and scrutiny, particularly by the core department, but also through system-wide reviews. In addition, agencies have frequently identified constituencies of responsibility and accountability beyond the department. Many agencies provide their services on a contractual basis. Many have 'customers' within both the core and other departments, and outside government altogether and see themselves as 'accountable' to their customers. In these circumstances while 'Next Steps agencies might be seen as attenuating the responsibility of ministers they may be considered more accountable . . . to consumers' (Flinders 2001:230).

Non-departmental public bodies

In 2004 839 non-departmental public bodies (NDPBs) were sponsored by UK government departments. A further 114 NDPBs were sponsored by the Scottish Executive and 34 by the Welsh Assembly Government (see chapter 5). In addition, under the general heading of 'Public Bodies', there were also nine public corporations (such as the BBC), two nationalized industries (such as British Shipbuilders), and 24 NHS bodies sponsored by UK departments. Collectively, such public bodies have become known as 'quangos'—an acronym for 'quasi-autonomous non-governmental organizations'—though this is basically a misnomer, as, in the case of

NDPBs, departments are responsible for their funding and ensuring their good governance. In turn, ministers are 'ultimately responsible for the activities of the bodies sponsored by their departments' (Cabinet Office 2003b:iv), and appointments to NDPB boards are also normally made by ministers. In this sense NDPBs are part of 'government' even if they carry out their functions at arm's length from central government.

As the Cabinet Office (2003c:Executive Summary 7.ii) notes, 'NDPBs do not exist in isolation from the rest of Government: they contribute to the de-livery of wider departmental and governmental objectives'. Indeed, NDPBs are part of 'big government' as over 19,500 appointed members served on public bodies, including the major types of NDPBs, in 2004 (the Public Ad-ministration Committee estimated that nearly 35,000 appointees sat on NDPBs see HC 165 2003:Table 1), and executive NDPBs spent some 10 per cent of all money voted by parliament (Treasury 2001:para 4.19). Moreover, the official, limited definition of NDPBs restricts the total number listed as public bodies, in part, because of 'the political imperative to keep the quango count low' (Greenwood et al 2002:154).

The Cabinet Office identifies four types of NDPBs. First, Executive NDPBs carry out administrative, regulatory and commercial functions (such as the Arts Council, the Broadcasting Standards Commission, the Higher Education Funding Council for England, and the Environment Agency) and employ their own staff and have their own budgets. Second, Advisory NDPBs provide independent and expert advice to ministers (such as the Advisory Committee on Pesticides, and the Low Pay Commis-sion). Third, Tribunal NDPBs have jurisdiction in specific fields of law (for example Employment Tribunals, or the Appeals Service—which organizes independent hearings for appeals relating to social security matters, or tax credit decisions). The fourth NDPB variant relates specifically to the Prison Boards of Visitors which act as 'watchdogs' for the administration of the prison system.

As with non-ministerial departments there are good reasons why some government sponsored activities should be shielded from direct ministerial intervention through the organizational structure of NDPBs. As Oliver (2003:317) notes: 'the funding of universities and research for instance, or the regulation of health and safety, or of utilities, ... may require an ab-sence of political interference in order to promote public confidence that the function will be discharged objectively and not for partisan or party political advantage or in breach of the laid down criteria for the function'. The problem arises, however, that if these bodies are shielded from direct ministerial and political 'interference' they may also be shielded simultaneously from direct public scrutiny and accountability through the parliamentary system.

Despite frequent calls for a 'cull' or a 'bonfire' of quangos, and despite frequent opportunities to review the appropriateness of NDPB tasks, through quinquennial reviews (see HC 209 1999:paras 29–32), 'it is unlikely that functions performed by NDPBs can easily be absorbed back into government departments. NDPBs perform functions which have been deliberately set apart from Ministerial control' (HC 209 1999:para 28). Put very simply, NDPBs have an intrinsic attraction for governments as they allow for: flexibility and greater efficiency and responsiveness in service delivery; partnership between government and non-government organizations; the inclusion of experts and specialists who bring wider knowledge to decision-making than could be recruited through party political channels; and, alternatively, involve ordinary citizens as lay members of tribunals and as prison visitors (see Cabinet Office 1997:8–9, HC 209 1999:para 22; Weir and Beetham 1999:196–7). Not surprisingly, therefore, such 'public bodies' are a common feature not only in the UK but also in the administrative systems of many other countries such as Denmark, the Netherlands, Germany as well as New Zealand. But if NDPBs solve several linked, management dilemmas for governments—efficiency, innovation, flexibility and implementation capacity—they also generate fundamental accountability paradoxes.

The most striking paradox is that although NDPBs are essentially created to work at arm's length from ministers, ministers and departments often have a vested interest in ensuring that, for large executive NDPBs which involve significant expenditure decisions, there are close working relationships (see HC 209 1999:para 31–35). As Weir and Beetham (1999:203) note: 'The regimes under which many national executive quangos operate is now almost indistinguishable in practice from that of executive agencies'. In which case, perhaps, it is not surprising to find that common issues of accountability link executive agencies and NDPBs (see Hogwood et al 2000:219–221), Certainly, status as an NDPB does not provide protection from parliamentary scrutiny. NDPBs are formally accountable to parliament via ministers in their sponsor department. They have to account for their financial probity and effectiveness to the Public Accounts Committee, and in 2002 the government accepted that all NDPBs should be subject to audit by the Comptroller and Audit General (Cm 5456 2002:para 2.14).

More broadly, beyond financial control, the Labour government recognized the widespread concern about the accountability of NDPBs in its pledge to make 'quangos more accountable, open and capable of being understood' (Cabinet Office 1998:para 3). In particular, it noted that 'as there are no democratic elections to the boards of NDPBs, it is all the more important that the accountability of these bodies to Parliament is strengthened' (para 5). Since the Nolan Report (Cm 2850 1995), appointments to NDPBs have been made in accordance with the 'Nolan principles' (see chapter 6) with a Commissioner for Public Appointments monitoring such appointments. Moreover, since July 2001, and the revision of the Commissioner's Code of Practice, there have been rolling departmental reviews over three-year periods to ensure that departmental appointment procedures comply with the code and standards of good practice. The problem remains, however, that the definitional ambiguities surrounding NDPBs means that there is no consistency as to how the Nolan principles are applied to 'public bodies'. Recognition of this problem led the Public Administration Committee to recommend the 'mapping' of all public bodies attached to central government and the drafting of 'precise, comprehensive and transparent criteria' to define NDPBs (HC 165 2003:para 3.8).

As part of its concern with accountability arrangements in the 21st century the government commissioned a review of audit and accountability in central government with regard to the 'importance of parliamentary scrutiny and accountability in the round' (Treasury 2001:Box A1). The resulting report, *Holding to Account*, while accepting a classic formulation of ministerial responsibility (Treasury 2001:para 3.6), also recognized that 'different forms of accountability are best suited to different purposes' (Treasury 2001:para 3.8). Indeed, in practice, NDPBs are accountable in a variety of ways to a variety of principals and 'stakeholders'—through publication of annual reports and annual accounts, investigation by the Parliamentary Commissioner for Administration (the Ombudsman), departmental reviews, as well as through the traditional processes of parliamentary scrutiny (see Hogwood et al 2000:220–1). To enhance the latter parliamentary dimension, the Labour government persistently promoted the virtues of departmental select committees in monitoring the activities of NDPBs (see Cabinet Office 1997; Cabinet Office 1998:para 5). However, the practicality of this proposed means of effecting enhanced scrutiny was questioned within the House of Commons itself (see HC 209 1999:paras 40–5). Equally the extent to which there was public access to, and openness of, NDPB processes caused continuing concern both inside and outside parliament (see HC 367 2001:paras 34–5; Beetham et al 2002:133).

Modernising government/wiring it up

If the 1990s witnessed the ascendancy of concepts of 'new public management' and the primacy of 'service delivery', and a concomitant 'delayering' of departmental hierarchies and agencification, the 2000s brought a recognition that policy advice and accountability (the traditional organizational principles of Whitehall) were equally important and had been de-emphasized unduly in the preceding decades. This interconnectedness was acknowledged by the Public Administration Select Committee (HC 94 2001:para 5):

> Our key theme is the importance of achieving and maintaining combined progress on two key issues: improving the performance of public services at the same time as maintaining or increasing their public accountability. Both goals are crucial . . . yet they are too often treated separately. Instead we believe they are indissolubly connected. Public services need to deliver performance of a high quality; but they also need to be properly accountable for their performance.

In his evidence to the Public Administration Committee Michael Bichard, formerly Chief Executive of the Benefits Agency and Permanent Secretary of the then Department for Education and Employment, underlined the imbalance: 'Over the last ten to 15 years, there has been a huge emphasis upon delivery, implementation and management. . . . now was the time to think a little bit more about [the quality of policy advice]' (HC 94 2001:Q1003). While Bichard's comments were aimed at reconstituting the relationship between policy advice and delivery within departments, Sir Peter Kemp made the counter case that the dual roles of permanent secretaries — policy adviser and programme manager — could be separated out at the top of departments (HC 238 2000:Q214). In either direction, the focus of attention was clearly intra-departmental. Of greater concern for the

Labour government, however, were inter-departmental interconnections and, in particular, the 'need to challenge departmentalism and the fragmenting consequences of the extensive "agencification" of central government carried out under the "Next Steps" change programme' (HC 94 2001:para 6).

The first Labour government after 1997 subsequently invested considerable effort in trying to 'get different parts of government to work together' (Cm 4310 1999:16) and in promoting 'joined-up government'. Within Whitehall it was believed that ministers and civil servants needed to develop a culture that 'values cross-cutting policies and services'; civil servants needed to develop skills and capacity to address cross-cutting problems; and that 'the centre' (No 10, the Cabinet Office and the Treasury) needed to provide a strategic framework to foster cross-cutting working (PIU 2000a:5). There was of course the obvious difficulty that historically the Whitehall culture emphasized departmentalism and loyalty to departmental ministers (see above). There was equally an exaggeration of the novelty of 'joined-up' thinking. As Ling (2002:639) observes: 'Just as sex was probably going on before it was invented in the 1960s, so too was joined-up government being practiced before it was so named'. Indeed, Flinders (2002:57) notes that every government in the 20th century had called for more cross-departmental coordination. Attempts to counteract the effects of rigid departmentalism thus have a long history. In the 1970s, for example, there were sustained attempts to improve coordination across related policy areas through, variously, the creation of two 'super departments' (Department of the Environment and the Department of Trade and Industry) after the *Reorganisation of Central Government* White Paper, and the introduction of strategic coordination through Programme Analysis and Review (PAR), the Public Expenditure Survey Committee (PESC), and the Central Policy Review Staff (CPRS) (see Cmnd 4506 1970; Radcliffe 1991; Smith 1999a:183–4; Greenwood et al 2002:40–1; Hennessy 2001:220–242).

Joining it up: Coordination old and new

The proponents of 'holistic governance' (see Perri 6 et al 2002) or of 'joined-up government' were explicit in their recognition that the 'culture in which Ministers and civil servants traditionally defend the narrow interests of their department or agencies has to be changed' (HC 94 2001:para 6) and that the vertical organization of departments had inhibited the coordination of service delivery. As the Prime Minister stated in his introduction to the *Wiring it Up* report: 'Many of the biggest challenges facing Government do not fit easily into traditional Whitehall structures' (PIU 2000a:Foreward). An early attempt had been made with the creation, in 1997, of a giant department of the Environment, Transport and the Regions (DETR) and the merging of the two separate departments of Education and Employment into the new Department for Education and Employment (later Education and Skills). These institutional changes reflected the continuing appeal of coordination through integrating existing departments into larger units (and a later redefinition of policy interconnections: environment, food and rural affairs, work and pensions, education and skills). But where the reports *Modernising Government* and *Wiring it Up* went beyond traditional strategies of departmental merger to achieve coordination was in the emphasis placed upon the extension of nondepartmental coordinating mechanisms at the centre, and centrifugal coordination of the activities of public bodies and agencies within and beyond Whitehall.

Traditional coordination: The political executive and cabinet government

Although departments are the pre-eminent institutional form at the centre of the UK government, most recent academic attention has been focused upon the core executive and the institutions of coordination superimposed above departmental level. Indeed, as noted at the beginning of this chapter, some definitions reserve the term 'core executive' exclusively for the institutions and mechanisms of coordination within central government (see Rhodes 1995b:12). Similarly, Burch and Holliday (1996:1) in preferring the term 'cabinet system' to describe the coordinating mechanisms of Whitehall identify the cabinet, cabinet committees, Cabinet Office, Prime Minister's Office, parts of the Treasury, and major government law offices as the key coordinating institutions. In either case—core executive or cabinet system—there is a clear belief that the idea of cabinet government, with the cabinet as a solitary and pre-eminent coordinating institution, is both descriptively inaccurate and analytically unrefined. Instead, both terms explicitly acknowledge that coordination in Whitehall is *interinstitutional*, and as such involves interconnected and complex institutional interactions.

Dispensing with the debate about cabinet vs prime ministerial government

One advantage of an interinstitutional perspective in analysing the core executive is that it identifies a series of institutions that are locked into complex and variable interactions. In which case it makes little sense to characterize coordination at the centre of UK government exclusively in terms of the activities of any single institution. In turn, this means that the debate about whether or not UK central government is best characterized as 'prime ministerial', or 'presidential' (see Foley 2000, Foley 2004), or as 'cabinet government' is, if not 'irrelevant' as Smith (2003:62) suggests, then at least is restricted in its analytical utility. In practice it is not the case that the institutional relationship is zero-sum—either there is prime ministerial government or there is cabinet government—but rather it is possible to have both. The relationship between the two institutions is contingent and may fluctuate even within the tenure of office of any individual prime minister let alone between the tenures of successive prime ministers. Indeed, the events of May 2003 seemed to indicate that the relationship could change even within the space of a week (see Box 4.4).

BOX 4.4   **A Week is a Long Time in Politics**

On 12 May 2003 Claire Short resigned as Secretary of State for International Development in the aftermath of the invasion of Iraq by the United States and the United Kingdom. Short's public disagreement with UK government policy over intervention in Iraq, and, in particular, the organization of the subsequent reconstruction programme, made her 'position impossible' and hence she maintained that she had 'no alternative than to resign from the government' (HC Debates 12 May 2003:col 37). What was of special significance for the present discussion, was her belief that the 'errors that we are making over Iraq' stemmed primarily from 'the style and organisation of our Government'. Her diagnosis was that:

the problem is the centralisation of power into the hands of the Prime Minister and an increasingly small number of advisers who make decisions in private

continues

Box 4.4 continued

without proper discussion. It is increasingly clear, I am afraid, that the Cabinet has become, in Bagehot's phrase, a dignified part of the constitution—joining the Privy Council. There is no real collective responsibility because there is no collective; just diktats in favour of increasingly badly thought through policy initiatives that come from on high. (HC Debates 12 May 2003:col 38)

However, an official spokesman responded to Short's accusations by pointing out that there had been recurring discussion on the specific issue of reconstruction policy in Iraq at ministerial meetings and in cabinet itself (specifically at a meeting that Ms Short had failed to attend (see *The Guardian* 14 May 2003:8)).

On the general issue of cabinet decision-making, by May 15, only three days after Short's resignation, there was widespread press coverage of the fact that the full cabinet was to make the final decision on whether a referendum would be announced on entry into the euro (see *The Guardian* 15 May 2003:13). As one cabinet member, John Reid, stated: 'The aggregate of their [ministers'] decisions will be the collective decision of the cabinet. It will be a cabinet decision' (see *The Guardian* 15 May 2003:13). Indeed, *The Guardian* leader-writer was willing to concede that the process of decision making over the euro pointed to the conclusion that 'cabinet government still means something real' (16 May 2003:25).

Nonetheless, the issue of the relative power of the prime minister and the cabinet continues to attract the attention of leading commentators (see, for example, Foley 2000). For Hennessy (2000:11) the debate still matters as 'it is a kind of running commentary. It is about a governing state of mind, about process as much as policy, about the nature of political power and its arbitration as the epicentre of British government'. For others, such as Richard Rose (2001:3), the debate is of importance in conceding that: 'in the world of Westminster politics, leaders such as Margaret Thatcher and Tony Blair have made obsolete the Victorian dictum that the Prime Minister is first among equals. Today he or she is first without equal'. But this stops short of identifying a process of presidentialization in the UK, for in Rose's (2001:234) words, 'Downing Street will remain the home of a prime minister rather than a president'. The 'bottom line' is that the different institutional and 'constitutional architecture' of the UK serves to distinguish the office of prime minister from that of a president. Ultimately, therefore, the debate is not simply about 'prime minister versus cabinet' but is also about institutional configurations and interactions at the centre of UK government.

This simple fact is best summarized in Smith's observation that:

> In understanding the changing role of the Prime Minister it is important not
> to oversimplify the argument. To see the core executive as dominated by an
> over-powerful Prime Minister is to misunderstand the complex networks of
> relationships that are essential to the running of the modern state. ... The
> core executive approach suggests that the Prime Minister is one actor, albeit
> a significant actor, within the institutions and relationships that make up the
> core executive. (Smith 2003:61–2)

Whereas 'personality' tends to be privileged in the 'classic' debate about the
differentials of power between cabinet and prime minister, modern analyses
of the core executive emphasize institutions, institutional norms, interinstitutional processes and resource transactions. The 'classic' debate that has
raged intermittently since the 1960s has often been ahistorical. Certainly, the
concern over the pre-eminence of Margaret Thatcher or Tony Blair is nothing new. Over a century ago Sydney Low (1904:158) noted, for example, that:
'The precise amount of authority exercised by a prime minister must depend
upon circumstances and his own character. If he is a Pitt, a Peel, a Palmer-
ston, a Disraeli, or a Gladstone, he may come near to being a dictator'.

Not surprisingly, therefore, the starting premise of core executive analysts is that the 'nature and form of the core executive is not dependent on
the personality of any one actor' (Smith 2003:62). Ministers have resources
whether as prime minister, as constituted collectively in the cabinet, or
as political heads of departments. Certainly any prime minister has an
impressive array of resources stemming from his or her institutional
position as head of government and leader of the party. These include patronage (especially the appointment of ministers to specific posts), the definition and interpretation of procedural guidelines (most importantly in the
Ministerial Code and the *Civil Service Code* (see Hennessy 2000:65–6)), the
determination of the structure of government, control of the conduct of
cabinet and parliamentary business (including the convening of cabinet, the
number and composition of cabinet committees and the final determination of the government's legislative programme). But, equally, departments
and their ministerial heads have their own institutional resources; not the
least of which are specialization, administrative capability, policy expertise
and departmental networks. Put very simply, despite sporadic prime
ministerial interventions, 'departments control the policy process' (Marsh

et al 2001:109). Each department operates within a relatively autonomous policy space (which in itself may constitute a problem—as acknowledged in various attempts to encourage 'joined-up government' (see below)). The sheer scope and complexity of modern state activity means that no single person or institution can exert influence, let alone exercize control, across the full range of government policies. In which case, if the prime minister has to engage in 'time sharing' with departments in the formulation and implementation of policy he or she is also 'necessarily engaged in power-sharing' (Rose 2001:154).

In a devolved system of decision-making through departments, the organizational conundrum has always been how to ensure that the centrifugal forces of departmentalism did not override the requirement for policy coherence and coordination of government programmes. Traditionally, in an era of limited government, the cabinet served as a collective mechanism of coordination and for the resolution of inter-departmental disputes. The convention of collective responsibility provided the normative underpinnings of executive institutional coordination (ensuring justifiable and defendable collective executive policies) in the face of parliamentary responsibility. Thus the thesis of the 'decline of the cabinet' has resonance beyond the confines of the prime ministerial debate, as such a decline is deemed to exacerbate the problem of coordination at the centre of government.

Coordination

> Coordination is fundamental to public administration; without it, policy-making and administration would be conducted without reference to different governmental components or overall goals. In British central government, however, it is especially important. (Greenwood et al 2002:48)

In the 19th century the cabinet developed into the primary institution of coordination in UK central government. It served as a means both of resolving interdepartmental disputes and imposing collective agreement upon ministerial departments. The cabinet was identified as the apex of the executive providing a forum for senior departmental ministers to discuss, decide and coordinate policy. The convention of collective responsibility simply underscored the need for effective coordination. As the Haldane Committee's (Cmnd 9230 1918) famous specification of the cabinet's functions made clear, the cabinet was charged with 'the continuous co-ordination and delimitation of the activities of the several departments of state' (along with the 'final determination of policy' and 'supreme control of the national executive').

Throughout the 20th century, however, the relative emphasis moved from the cabinet to the cabinet *system* in the processes of coordination. While politicians and commentators alike bemoan the 'decline of the cabinet'—as quantified in the declining number of formal meetings, the reduction in their duration, and the amount of business brought before it for decision (see Greenwood et al 2002:54)—nonetheless, other 'compensatory' institutional processes have operated to offset any residualization of coordination at the centre. The cabinet may still be the ultimate point of decision and coordination for policies which prove too intransigent or politically contentious for the other coordinating institutions to resolve, but in most instances coordination will be attempted through the wider core executive or the broader cabinet *system*. In other words 'coordination has shifted elsewhere' (Smith et al 1995:56) beyond the cabinet itself.

Coordination beyond the cabinet is conducted through an extensive range of established institutions as well as new institutions and processes. The 'old' include bilateral negotiations between departments, interdepartmental committees, cabinet committees, the Cabinet Office, the Treasury and the Prime Minister's Office. The 'new' include a variety of 'taskforces' and 'units' incorporated within the 'old' institutional structures of the Cabinet Office and Prime Minister's Office.

Bilateral discussions between departments, at both official and ministerial levels, account for much routine coordination within Whitehall. The institutional norm is to settle 'at as low a level as possible' in departmental hierarchies and, wherever appropriate, through informal processes (see James 1999:49–56). In some policy areas informal networks of civil servants offer flexible means of coordination within and across departmental boundaries (Marsh et al 2001:124–9; Greenwood et al 2002:50). Where these informal processes prove incapable of resolving issues, more formal institutionalized processes are deployed. These include interdepartmental committees, official committees, and cabinet committees.

Interdepartmental committees draw together civil servants from those departments concerned with mutually relevant cross-cutting policies. There are a vast and fluctuating number of these committees in reflection of the sheer volume of issues requiring coordination between two or more departments. Most interdepartmental committees deal with routine matters, but a few have attained notoriety—as in the case of the committee of officials from the Department of Trade and Industry, Ministry of Defence and the Foreign Office which operated in the mid-1980s to review arms export licences to Iraq. In the interests of 'efficiency', civil servants attempted to reach decisions in this interdepartmental committee without referring the matter to ministers. As the Scott report concluded, the officials treated 'the need for expedition in order to further the interest of defence sales ... as of greater importance than Ministerial approval of IDC [interdepartmental committee] licensing decisions' (HC 115 1996:D1.140).

Official Committees are, as their name suggests, also composed of civil servants, but rather than operating at an interdepartmental level they are part of the wider cabinet system. They mirror ministerial cabinet committees (see below) both in structure and duration. Ad hoc committees usually operate on a temporary basis and deal with a specific issue, while standing committees, as their name suggests, tend to be more permanent. Usually Official Committees collect and collate information, present options for ministers, investigate issues and, on occasion, may have decision-making capacities.

Cabinet Committees are essentially ministerial committees whose composition and structure is determined by the prime minister. The official statement of their purpose is outlined in the Ministerial Code (see Box 4.5).

BOX 4.5   Ministerial Committees

The Cabinet is supported by Ministerial Committees (both standing and ad hoc) which have a two-fold purpose. First, they relieve the pressure on the Cabinet itself by settling as much business as possible at a lower level or, failing that, by clarifying the issues and defining the points of disagreement. Second, they support the principle of collective responsibility by ensuring that, even though an important question may never reach the Cabinet itself, the decision will be fully considered and the final judgement will be sufficiently authoritative to ensure that the Government as a whole can be properly expected to accept responsibility for it. When there is a difference between Departments, it should not be referred to the Cabinet until

— continues

Box 4.5 continued

other means of resolving it have been exhausted, including personal correspondence or discussions between the Ministers concerned.

   If the Ministerial Committee system is to function effectively, appeals to the Cabinet must be infrequent.

Source: www.cabinet-office.gov.uk/central/2001/mcode/p02.htm

In November 2004 there were 32 Ministerial Committees and Groups and
a further 25 ministerial sub-committees listed on the Cabinet Office web site
(www.cabinetoffice.gov.uk/cabsec/index/index.htm). The core ministerial
standing committees in the second Labour government were those dealing
with Public Services and Public Expenditure (PSX), Defence and Overseas
Policy (DOP), Economic Affairs (EAPC), Legislative Programme (LP), and
Domestic Affairs (DA). There were some 14 miscellaneous (MISC) committees dealing with particular tasks (for example, on Animal Rights Activists [MISC13] or on the Ageing Society [MISC29]). In addition, a Joint
Ministerial Consultative Committee was still listed in 2004. Originally created in 1997 to consider constitutional issues with the presence of senior
Liberal Democratic Party members, the Consultative Committee was suspended in September 2001 but 'remains available to resume its work if
further constitutional items become ready for discussion' (www.cabinet-
office.gov.uk/cabsec/2003/cabcom/jcc.htm).

The combined centre: The Cabinet Office, the Prime Minister's Office and the Treasury

The 'combined centre' is a term used by the Cabinet Office to delineate the
organizations covered by the Delivery and Reform Team and other central
units identified in Box 4.6. However, the term is of wider utility in revealing
the interinstitutional connections at the core of the core executive and will
be used here to reveal the intertwined roles of the Cabinet Office, the Prime
Minister's Office, the Deputy Prime Minister's Office and the Treasury, as
well as in the more specific usage to describe the work of the Delivery and
Reform Team.

The Cabinet Office

The Cabinet Office has responsibility for the coordination of cabinet business. A basic task of the Cabinet Office is to act as a secretariat to the prime minister and ministers who chair cabinet committees. In this capacity the Cabinet Secretariat arranges meetings, sets agendas, drafts papers, briefs chairs, circulates documents, takes minutes and records and transmits decisions to departments. The Secretariat is composed of six individual secretariats. In turn these reflect the changing priorities of government. In response to fuel protests and severe floods in 2000, and the outbreak of foot and mouth disease in 2001, a Civil Contingencies Secretariat (CCS) was created in July 2001. The work of the CCS increasingly focused upon coordinating the review and enhancement of civil contingencies arrangements after the terrorist attacks on 11 September 2001 (Cm 5429 2002:15). Similarly the work of the Defence and Overseas Secretariat and the Assessments Staff and Intelligence Support Secretariat has been of increased significance in the 'post 9/11' era. (In April 2003, the Machinery of Government Secretariat, which had recently changed its name from the Central Secretariat, had its work transferred to other parts of the Cabinet Office). The Economic and Domestic Secretariat covers all other domestic issues, while the Ceremonial Secretariat is responsible for the preparation of the PM's Honours list and Honour's policy work, and the European Secretariat coordinates EU business.

A second major task of the Cabinet Office is 'to provide a strategic lead at the centre of government and to support the Government collectively in delivering its priorities' (Cm 5429 2002:13). Whereas, traditionally, the Cabinet Office served to ensure 'the operation of collective responsibility' (Smith 1999a:165) and to resolve disputes between departments by brokering agreements, increasingly since 1997 the emphasis has been upon the pursuit of 'effective coordination of issues which cut across departments, the wider public sector and beyond' (Cm 5429 2002:14). Thus, the Cabinet Secretariat identifies as one of its key roles 'taking the lead in co-ordinating work affecting the interests of several departments, in order to ensure progress on a policy initiative' and the 'undertaking of short-term projects into crosscutting issues' (www.cabinet-office.gov.uk).

However, the first objective identified by the Cabinet Office itself was to 'support the Prime Minister in leading the Government' (Cm 6226 2004:21).

Indeed, in the *Cabinet Office Departmental Report 2004*, under the heading of 'The work of the Cabinet Office', the duties and organization of the Prime Minister's Office featured prominently. While maintaining a separate institutional identity it is clear, nonetheless, that 'the Prime Minister's Office, No 10', works with the Cabinet Office to provide central direction for developing, implementing and presenting governmental policy' (Cm 6226 2004:23). The fact that the prime minister has been at the forefront of these organizational initiatives has led Kavanagh (2004:469) to conclude that: 'To all intents and purposes Blair has formed a Prime Minister's Department. Some units and most of the staff are based in the Cabinet Office, simply because they cannot be accommodated in Downing Street. Blair does not call it a Prime Minister's Department because that would raise so many constitutional objections'. This view had been expressed earlier by one Whitehall 'insider' who declared that the debate about a Prime Minister's Department was 'academic . . . because we already have one. It's a properly functioning department with a departmental head . . . with a sense of being *the* central machinery of government' (quoted in Hennessy 2001:485).

Indeed, the prime minister did little to dispel this belief when he appeared before the House of Commons' Liaison Committee in July 2002. (In itself, this was an historic appearance, as it marked the first time that a prime minister had appeared before a select committee of the House of Commons to answer questions on the role of the Head of Government). Mr Blair made 'no apology for having a strong centre. I think you need a strong centre . . . the reality is for any modern Prime Minister you want to know what is happening in your own Government, to be trying to drive forward the agenda of change on which you were elected' (HC 1095 2002:Q5 and Q4; see also HC 310 2004:Q93). Certainly Mr Blair was an enthusiast for strengthening the core of the core executive in driving institutional innovation and organizational change in the Prime Minister's Office, the Cabinet Office and the Treasury (see below).

The Prime Minister's Office

The Prime Minister's Office is headed by a Chief of Staff and, in 2004, was organized around a number of different units. At the centre of the Office, the Policy Directorate served to 'develop new ideas'; prepare policy advice on domestic and economic policy; convey the PM's decisions and views, and ensure the necessary follow-up. The Policy Directorate combined the functions previously carried out by the Private Office and the Policy Unit and linked them to No 10's core management and support functions. Advice on EU business and foreign affairs was provided by the European and Foreign Policy Advisers' Office. The Parliamentary Section handled the parliamentary aspects of the PM's role; while the Appointments and Honours Sections, as their titles suggest, advised on a range of honours and appointments, most particularly Crown appointments.

The communications function was performed by three units. The Strategic Communications Unit devised and coordinated the communication strategy, the Press Office provided the (not always smooth) interface between the PM and the press and broadcast media, and the Corporate Communications Division processed the PM's correspondence and maintained the No 10 website. In turn, the Events and Visits Office arranged the large number of official visits, receptions and events focused on No 10.

Office of the Deputy Prime Minister

In May 2002 the Office of the Deputy Prime Minister (ODPM) was hived off from the Cabinet Office to create a new department in its own right. Two other units that had formerly been located in the Cabinet Office—the Women and Equality Unit and the Equality Coordination Unit—were transferred at the same time to the Department of Trade and Industry. The ODPM was given a key coordinating role in ensuring 'joined-up government' through overseeing the work of a range of specialist issue-oriented units. In 2004 the ODPM was organized around five groups: Sustainable Communities (including the Thames Gateway Delivery Unit); Tackling Disadvantage (including Homelessness and Housing Support, Neighbourhood Renewal, and the Social Exclusion Unit), Local Government and Fire; and Regional Development (including the Regional Coordination Unit). In addition to these specialist units in the ODPM the Blair governments also instigated a range of ad hoc policy reviews, commonly known as taskforces (see Richards and Smith 2002:244–6).

Delivery and Reform Team

On becoming Cabinet Secretary and Head of the Home Civil Service in 2002 Sir Andrew Turnbull established a Delivery and Reform Team (DRT) to coordinate the activities of a diverse set of Units and Groups that had developed in the Cabinet Office under Labour Governments since 1997. This was necessary, in the opinion of veteran Whitehall observer Peter Hennessy, because the system that had developed after 1997 had produced 'the most disjointed Government I have ever observed' (Hennessy HC 238 2000:Q191).

BOX 4.6   **Delivery and Reform Team**

The Delivery and Reform Team is based in the Cabinet Office and reports to the Head of the Home Civil Service. Its stated task is 'to lead and support delivery and reform across the Civil Service and the wider public sector'.

Strategy Unit (SU)

Carries out strategic reviews and works with departments to improve policy.

Prime Minister's Delivery Unit (PMDU)

Seeks to ensure that the Government achieves its delivery priorities across key areas of public services. It is charged with ensuring delivery of the Prime Minister's 'top public service priority outcomes'.

Reform Strategy Group (RSG)

Responsible for defining the overall reform strategy for the Civil Service, co-ordinating and communicating the work of the Delivery and Reform group and working with departments on Performance Partnerships and baseline reviews.

Corporate Development Group (CDG)

Responsible for improving the management and development of public servants. It includes the Centre for Management and Policy Studies (CMPS).

e-Transformation work of the Office of the e-Envoy (OeE)

Responsible for focusing government on the customer through electronic delivery.

Office of Government Commerce (OGC), an office of HM Treasury

Responsible for the improvement of the Civil Service's capability to commission and deliver major projects.

Office of Public Services Reform (OPSR)

Promotes the four principles of reform and customer focus, and developing models for improving public service delivery, for example, in the health service, schools, local policing and local government.

continues

Box 4.6 continued

Efficiency Review Team

A joint Cabinet Office and Treasury team created in 2003 to conduct efficiency reviews across public services to identify potential for recycling administrative resources into 'frontline' services.

Other central units working with the Delivery and Reform Team are

Regulatory Impact Unit—Cabinet Office
Economic and Domestic Secretariat—Cabinet Office
No 10 Policy Directorate
HM Treasury

The Strategy Unit (SU)

The Strategy Unit was established in 2002 and merged the Performance and Innovation Unit (PIU), the Prime Minister's Forward Strategy Unit (FSU) and parts of the Centre for Management and Policy Studies (CMPS). The PIU had been created in 1998 out of a desire 'to rebuild [government's] capacity to do long-term thinking and strategic policy work', as well as to provide a way to 'tackle issues that cut across departmental boundaries' (Strategy Unit Briefing 2004:2). Direct parallels were drawn between the PIU and the earlier strategic cross-cutting institution of the Central Policy Review Staff in the 1970s (see Flinders 2002:60; SU Briefing 2004:2). As part of the drive for more joined-up government the PIU produced the *Wiring it Up* Report on Whitehall's management of cross-cutting policies and services, along with other reports on more specific projects, including electronic commerce, active aging, the 'joined-up' delivery of central government policies in regions and localities, e-governance, and the pursuit and seizure of criminal assets (see PIU 2000a:77–8). In 2001 the PIU was supplemented with another unit—the prime minister's Forward Strategy Unit (FSU). The prime purpose of the FSU was to provide strategic reviews of the long-term options in specific policy areas, for example in transport policy and the future of health care. The third constituent element of the Strategy Unit was parts of the Centre for Management and Policy Studies (CMPS). The CMPS is based in the Cabinet Office and was established in 1998 through the incorporation of the Civil Service College. Within the CMPS a Policy Studies Directorate (PSD) was established to coordinate networks of policy makers and provide advice and consultancy across government. PSD became part of the Cabinet Office Strategy Unit in 2002. Its stated objective was the continuous improvement in government policy-making and the encouragement of new and better ways of working on the part of departmental policy makers (www.cabinet-office.gov.uk/innovation/psd/index.shtml). One way in which the PSD sought to achieve this objective was through provision of a 'policy hub'—a web-based portal that provides access to developments in policy making and delivery (www.policyhub.gov.uk).

The Strategy Unit has a staff at any one time of between 70 and 80 people drawn from the private and public sectors. Its approach is consciously cross-departmental and strategic. It brings together teams from different departments and has developed a comprehensive web-based 'toolkit for strategists' which provides materials on project design, project management, analysis, and communication issues (Strategy Unit 2004:6). In 2003 the Strategy Unit undertook a major 'Strategic Audit' of UK government performance and future policy challenges.

Prime Minister's Delivery Unit (PMDU)

The Prime Minister's Delivery Unit was established in 2001 with a team of around 40 people whose prime purpose was to monitor, assess and support progress on the implementation of policies in the priority areas of education, health, crime and transport. In 2002 its remit was expanded to include the other main domestic delivery departments. The PMDU also shares responsibility with the Treasury for securing the target Public Sector Agreements (see below).

Reform Strategy Group (RSG)

As part of Andrew Turnbull's reorganization of the Cabinet Office in 2002 a new unit, the Reform Strategy Group, was created. The RSG has among its responsibilities the definition of an overall reform strategy, coordination of the work of the other Delivery and Reform Units, the communication of 'the reform message' throughout the civil service, the development of Performance Partnerships with departments, and the improvement of coordination within the 'wider centre' (defined as the Delivery and Reform Team, No10 Directorate and the Treasury) (www.civil-service.gov.uk/reform/delivery_reform/reform_strategy.asp).

The Treasury

> Discussion of the Treasury's role is necessarily related to the respective roles of the other central offices of the Government—the Cabinet Office and the Prime Minister's Office. (HC 73 2001:para 41)

Long before the term became *de riguer* in Whitehall, the Treasury had been concerned with 'joined-up government'. Historically, the Treasury had served as the central coordinating department, in part by default, in the absence of other consistent mechanisms of coordination. In its role as a surrogate Ministry of Finance, the Treasury was involved both with revenue raising and the supervision of expenditure by other departments and public agencies, and as such it assumed responsibility for 'the efficiency of the government machine as a whole and for its effective operation and coordination' (Greenleaf 1987:250). In this sense, it was 'the department of departments' and constituted a 'ubiquitous bureaucratic focus' (Greenleaf 1987:250).

This continued centrality was acknowledged by the Treasury Select Committee in 2001 when it described the Treasury as 'one of the central offices of State, lying at the heart of Government. It is the Government's financier, responsible for raising revenues . . . , disbursing funds to the spending departments, and keeping the Governments' accounts' (HC 73 2001:para 5). In late 2004 the Treasury also assumed responsibility for tax policy development after the creation of a new tax office in the Treasury (which was to work closely with the proposed new Customs and Revenue Department). Some 150 staff worked in the new tax office, bringing the total number of Treasury staff to around 1,000 staff. While the Treasury remains a very small department, nonetheless, its control of expenditure provides it with a comprehensive overview of governmental activity. If 'knowledge is power', then the Treasury, uniquely, has 'a window into every ministry and departmental activity across Whitehall' (Hennessy 2001:394).

The ability of the Treasury to gain access through these knowledge 'windows' has increased in recent decades to the extent that the House of Commons' Treasury Select Committee expressed concern that 'the Treasury as an institution has recently begun to exert too much influence over policy areas which are properly the business of other departments' (HC 73

2001:para 21). In particular, the Treasury had assumed increased responsibility for the strategic direction of welfare reform (see Deakin and Parry
2000), and had substantially increased its influence over spending departments through Public Service Agreements (PSAs). PSAs are agreements
about the quality and level of service provision and delivery between the
Treasury and departments and other public bodies (or between departments and local authorities). They were introduced in 1998 as part of the
Comprehensive Spending Review (a biennial, medium-term expenditure
planning exercise) with the objective of linking the allocation of public expenditure to the targets and objectives specified by departments (see HC
378 1999; Thain 2000:228–30). The number of specific targets incorporated
in each Review declined from 250 in 1998 to 110 in 2004 as the government
sought to concentrate on its highest priorities. This still amounted to an average of six targets per department (Cm 6238 2004:7).

The government maintained that: 'The PSAs have contributed to a real
shift in culture in Whitehall away from inputs and processes towards
delivering outputs and results' (HC 62-x 2003:Memorandum by the Government). What worried some observers, however, was that PSAs simply
enhanced the capacity of the Treasury to 'delve inside departments to influence the management of resources' (HC 73 2001:para 38). What worried others was that the Treasury was now engaged in 'direct policy-making
and agenda control' (Thain 2000:232) in departments which extended far
beyond its traditional control and coordination roles. What is equally important to note, however, is that PSAs were not simply conceived as a mechanism for negotiating changes with individual departments, they were also
intended, as James (2004:400) points out, 'to improve the coordination
of priority setting where policy or delivery issues cut across departmental
boundaries'. As such PSAs were designed to institute a 'system-wide performance regime to reduce fragmentation' within the broader institutional
context of the core executive (James 2004:400).

Concerns remained, nonetheless, that the PSA system encouraged the
Treasury to micro-manage other department's business (HC 73 2001:para
31) and, in part, reflected the interventionist and innovative aspirations
of Gordon Brown as Chancellor of the 'New Treasury'. Indeed, the personal imprint of Brown upon major domestic policies, most particularly in
health and welfare was clearly visible (see Thain 2000; Deakin and Parry
2000; Richards and Smith 2002:224; Smith 2003:78). Certainly, the forceful

personality and strategic position of Brown within the Labour party has to be factored into any explanation of the changed role of the Treasury since 1997, but, as the Chancellor frequently stressed, his personality, his personal preferences, and even his personal relationship with Tony Blair, was not the fundamental issue:

> I think that the real story of decision-making in politics is about ideas and ideals, and is about the policies that reflect the concerns of people. The central question[s] ... cannot be reduced to personality issues without trivialising what are great and major questions about our future. (*The Times* 21 May 2003:8)

Conclusion

Gordon Brown's assessment of the importance of personality in UK executive politics is accurate: personality is not the fundamental issue. Certainly, matters of personal 'style', of individual 'agency', have some impact upon both the workings of the core executive and the outputs from Whitehall, but these actors operate within an institutional framework—a 'structure'—which mediates their actions. Moreover, in turn, these institutions reflect a fundamental set of ideas about the UK's political system itself. In essence, the norms, beliefs and political culture observable within the core executive in the 21st century are still informed by wider, systemic notions of accountability within a parliamentary state. As Marsh et al (2003:312–14) note, this view has shaped both the institutions and processes of the core executive and the way in which members of the core executive perform their various roles. This does not mean that these institutions are immutable and monolithic in form. In fact, as this chapter has revealed, the reverse is the case—the core executive has been subject to persistent and rapid change in recent decades and is characterized by a diversity of organizational structures. But these changes have been effected within the overall frame of notions of external accountability as specified in the Westminster model (see chapter 2). Indeed, the continued centrality of this model was acknowledged by Sir Andrew Turnbull, Cabinet Secretary and Head of the Home Civil Service in 2004:

This doctrine of indirect accountability, that Ministers are accountable to Parliament and the Civil Service are accountable to Ministers, has been there for 150 years at least. The question is: is that still an accepted keystone in the whole edifice? I think it is. (HC 423 2004:Q3)

Manifestly some institutional changes have chafed against the perimeters of this model, and some have been held to have transgressed the boundaries of traditional conventions altogether, but, ultimately, alternative conceptions of executive organization—managerialism, agencification, delayering, holistic governance—have to be legitimized by recourse to traditional conceptions of a 'public ethos' and of 'ministerial accountability'. In themselves, ideas about 'efficient service delivery' and 'joined-up' government, and the language of 'output legitimacy', are insufficient principles for institutional design they have to be located (often uneasily and paradoxically) within the wider frame of norms and values which condition 'appropriate behaviour' within a 'parliamentary state'.

KEY TERMS

- accountability culture
- bureaucracy
- cabinet
- cabinet system
- central government
- civil service
- civil service culture
- collective ministerial responsibility
- combined centre
- coordination
- core executive
- delayering
- executive agencies
- individual ministerial responsibility
- joined-up government

- managerialism
- ministerial code
- ministerial departments
- new public management
- non-departmental public bodies
- non-ministerial departments
- political accountability
- political executive
- prime ministerial government
- public sector ethos
- public service agreements
- special advisers
- Treasury
- Whitehall

GUIDE TO FURTHER READING

FOLEY, M. (2000) *The British Presidency: Tony Blair and the Politics of Public Leadership*, (Manchester, Manchester University Press).

A sustained argument in support of the idea that a *de facto* presidency has developed in the UK.

HENNESSY, P. (2001) *Whitehall*, (London, Pimlico).

A big book, both in terms of its dimensions and of its magisterial overview of the historic and contemporary roles of the civil service.

MARSH, D., RICHARDS, D. and SMITH, M. (2001) *Changing Patterns of Governance in the United Kingdom: Reinventing Whitehall?* (London, Palgrave Macmillan).

One of the few empirically grounded studies of Whitehall.

SMITH, M. (1999) *The Core Executive in Britain*, (London, Macmillan).

Remains the best introduction to the debates surrounding the concept of the 'core executive'.

WOODHOUSE, D. (1994) *Ministers and Parliament: Accountability in Theory and Practice*, (Oxford, Clarendon Press).

An extensive examination of the specifics of ministerial accountability.

5

Territorial Institutions

Overview

The UK's 'territorial' institutional structure both before 1999, and post-devolution, is examined in this chapter. The extent to which the 'new' territorial institutions post-1999 represent institutional continuity rather than fundamental change is considered. While the institutional structure of territorial management in the UK before 1999 was relatively simple, the position post-1999 is remarkably complex. This complexity stems not only from a quantitative increase in the number of new institutions but also from a qualitative change in interinstitutional interactions. To understand territorial institutions in the 21st century requires some historical understanding, and an appreciation that 'territorial' differences have had explicit institutional recognition in the UK.

Introduction

Before 1999, the UK state was commonly characterized as essentially 'centralized' and 'unitary'. It was centralized in the sense that there was no elected institution with primary legislative powers in the UK other than the Westminster parliament. It was unitary in the sense that although four different nations existed within the boundaries of the UK state, and that the UK had long been acknowledged as a multi-national state, these nations were governed primarily through unitary political institutions focused upon Westminster and Whitehall. Indeed, Vernon Bogdanor (1999a:1) noted, immediately pre-devolution, that the UK:

remained a highly centralized country, more so even than France, traditionally the paradigm of centralized government ... Britain has been, amongst
stable democracies, the largest of unitary states, apart from Japan; no other
democracy seeks to manage the affairs of so large a population through a
single parliament.

Bogdanor then proceeded to identify the concept of parliamentary sovereignty as a major impediment to an accommodation in the UK with
'structures of government ... whose raison d'etre is that of power sharing'
(Bogdanor 1999a:1). If the utility of the concept as a 'powerful ideology
of centralisation' was long acknowledged in the UK (see Judge 1993:193);
equally, in reverse, the potential of the concept to restrict the practice of
decentralization was of major concern to the proponents of devolution. In
either direction, the notion of parliamentary sovereignty has been at the
centre of the development of 'territorial' institutions in the UK both pre-
and post-devolution.

In this chapter the concept of parliamentary sovereignty will form
the analytical spine of the discussion. It will be used to explain the
'territorial' institutional structure pre-1999, and to understand the
variegated/asymmetrical nature of devolution in the UK post-1999. If
the 'territorial' institutional structure before 1999 was relatively simple;
what strikes many observers after 1999 is the 'complexity, indeed intricacy,
of the arrangements of devolution' (HL 28 2002:para 6). If the concept
of parliamentary sovereignty links both the pre- and post-devolutionary
institutional configuration, then the extent to which the 'new' territorial institutions post-1999 represent institutional continuity rather than
fundamental change also needs to be considered. Any discussion of the
institutions of territorial management in the contemporary UK has to
consider both the genesis and the conscious design of those institutions,
and to understand the norms and values incorporated into that design. This
will circle back to the issues raised in chapter 1, but, before then, we need
to know a little about the historical development of the UK's territorial
institutions.

Pre-1999: Simple but not undifferentiated institutions

While it is accurate to describe the pre-1999 institutional structure in the UK as essentially centralized and unitary, the very existence of ministerial departments for Scotland, Wales and Northern Ireland pointed to the fact that 'territorial' differences had explicit institutional recognition. Indeed, the continuance of these territorial institutions post-devolution points to an underlying continuity of territorial institutional relationships which underpins the devolution settlement, for, in part, the logic of devolution was simply to 'democratize' an already existing system of 'administrative devolution' (see Judge 1993:204). The fact that there was no 'grand design', no 'standardized options' (Urwin 1982:68) for the formation of 'territorial' institutions in the UK before devolution, also provides a clue as to why the post-1999 devolution settlement itself did not reveal a clear, symmetrical blueprint or comprehensive institutional design throughout the UK.

The United Kingdom came into existence through 'a series of historical contingencies' (Bogdanor 1999a:4; see also Judge 1993:160–80), and although the details of the UK's historical development need not detain us here, four broad themes are worthy of note. First, is the fact that the political institutions of England came to dominate the later creations of the British and United Kingdom states. Second, the UK parliament was 'the linchpin of the whole structure' (Bulpitt 1983:83). The various nations were incorporated into the UK through simple Acts of Parliament, not through any special constitutional contracts, and with the concept of parliamentary sovereignty providing a powerful ideology of centralization. The UK parliament served both as a means of integration and as a symbol of unity (see Judge 1993:164). Third, if the UK state was unitary it was not uniform. Indeed, a more accurate descriptive term was a 'union state' rather than a unitary state. The distinction was stated most clearly by Rokkan and Urwin (1982:11):

The unitary state [is] built up around one unambiguous political centre which ... pursues a more or less undeviating policy of administrative standardisation. All areas of the state are treated alike, and all institutions are directly under the control of the centre. . . . [In] the union state integration is less than perfect. While administrative standardisation prevails over most of the territory, [there is] survival of pre-union rights and institutional infrastructures which preserve some degree of regional autonomy and serve as agencies of indigenous elite recruitment.

A fourth theme is that, at any particular time, the differentials in the institutional balance between unity and diversity reflected the calculations of metropolitan, English-dominated executives in their relationships with the 'outer peripheries' of Scotland and Northern Ireland, as well as with the 'inner peripheries' of Wales and the regions of England.

Central departments

On entering office in 1997 the Labour government inherited three central departments with specifically 'territorial' concerns: the Scottish Office, the Northern Ireland Office and the Welsh Office. All three were a direct institutional recognition of the multi-national nature of the UK state, and each reflected, in turn, a different institutional relationship between the peripheries and the core administration in London. In parallel, 20 per cent of MPs returned to Westminster at the 1997 election represented constituencies in Scotland (72), Wales (40) and Northern Ireland (18), again as a direct acknowledgement of the territorial differences within the UK.

Scottish Office

In 1997 the Scottish Office had a core staff of just under 5,000 civil servants, with most based in Edinburgh but with a small contingent working out of Dover House, the Whitehall base of the Secretary of State and the other four Scottish Ministers. Within the Scottish Office five functional departments administered the responsibilities of the Secretary of State: Agriculture and Fisheries; Education; Environment, Home and Health; and Industry. In addition a number of executive agencies were accountable directly to Scottish Office Ministers: the Scottish Agricultural Science Agency; Registers of Scotland; Historic Scotland; Scottish Fisheries Protection Agency; Scottish Pensions Agency; Scottish Prison Service; and the Scottish Record Office. Other government departments included the Scottish Courts Administration which dealt with the organization and

administration of the Scottish courts. The existence of such distinct administrative institutions was a manifestation of the continued survival and importance of a separate Scottish legal system and legal institutions, as well as
other distinct institutions of 'civil society'—the Presbyterian church (as the
established church in Scotland), the education system; and the 'regional' institutions required to implement national welfare policies in the territorial
context of Scotland (for example Health Boards, and Scottish Homes).

Indeed, the history of 'territorial' institutions in Scotland is of some importance in understanding devolution post-1999 (see below). In a prescient
sentence, the White Paper *Scotland in the Union*, produced by the then Conservative government to defend the union, started with the words: 'in considering the future we must understand the past' (Cmnd 2225 1993). What
the past revealed for Scotland was that the Act of Union of 1707 created, in
Tom Nairn's (1993) vivid phrase, 'a decapitated nation state'. In essence the
Act of Union abolished the separate parliaments of Scotland and England
and replaced them with a single parliament of the United Kingdom of Great
Britain. In the event, the Scottish parliament, which had largely atrophied in
the century before union, was the only major institution to be 'lopped off'
in 1707. Other distinctly Scottish institutions—the legal system, the established church, and the system of local administration operating through the
royal burghs—remained intact and served both to represent and to sustain
a distinct social and, ultimately, political culture (see Nairn 1993; Kellas 1989;
Brown et al 1998).

From the outset in 1707 the administrative distinctiveness of Scotland was
recognized in the posts of the Secretary for Scotland and the Lord Advocate.
After the Jacobite rebellion of 1745 the post of Secretary was abolished,
leaving formal responsibility for administration in Scotland in the hands
of the Home Secretary advised by the Lord Advocate. If the existence of
a distinct legal system and the corresponding post of Lord Advocate continued to underline the distinctiveness of Scotland within the UK state, so
too did the continuance of a separate system of Scottish local government.
As the importance of the local provision of services and the regulation of
social relations in a rapidly industrializing and urbanizing society grew in
the early 19th century, the need for greater supervision and coordination of
these activities grew correspondingly. A series of 'intermediate' authorities
developed—of distinctively Scottish Boards and Departments interposed
between Scottish localities and central government in London. In sum,

by the early 19th century, the actual business of Scottish administration was conducted by burgh, and, later, county councils, in conjunction with a series of ad hoc boards. Eventually, the inefficiencies of this ad hocery, along with the growing gap between expanding functions and diminishing central supervision, and an attendant belief that London was benignly neglectful of Scottish affairs, generated demands within Scotland for administrative reform. The culmination of these and other demands came in 1885 with the establishment of the Scottish Office headed by a Secretary for Scotland.

Once established, the Scottish Office incrementally accrued to itself significant administrative responsibilities. Even so it took a long time before the old board system was rationalized into a coherent system of Scottish Office control (see Midwinter et al 1991:51–4; Mitchell 2003b:92–148). Only with the Reorganisation of Offices (Scotland) Act of 1939 were the remaining boards eventually absorbed into the Scottish Office, and the modern Scottish Office established with a Secretary of State serving formally as a member of the UK cabinet and exercising full ministerial responsibility for his department (Midwinter et al 1991:53–61; Mitchell 2003b:117–142). Thereafter, the Scottish Office remained a powerful institutional symbol of Scotland's incorporation, but not its assimilation, into the UK.

Northern Ireland Office

The Northern Ireland Office (NIO) was established in 1972 after direct rule was imposed from London, initially as a temporary measure in response to continued civil disorder, yet it was still in existence in 1997. The NIO was headed by a Secretary of State who was a member of the UK cabinet and who was supported by a team of three ministers. The Northern Ireland Secretary was responsible for 1,200 staff, organized in two Sections in Belfast and in London, who oversaw the administration of political, judicial and security matters in the province (see Carmichael and Osborne 2003:207–12). NIO staff remained distinct, however, from the 30,000 Northern Ireland civil servants who worked in the six functional departments (Finance and Personnel, Agriculture, Economic Development, Education, Environment, and Health and Social Services) and associated agencies (for example the NI Prison Service, NI Social Security Agency (for details see Tonge 1998:67–9; Greer 1999:143–5)).

While 'superficially' the existence of the NIO made 'the government of the province analogous to Scotland and Wales' (Rose 1982:59) the grafting of the

NIO onto pre-existing Northern Ireland ministries, the existence of a separate civil service, and the attendant need for careful administrative coordination through a Policy Coordination Committee distanced the NIO from its other sub-national counterparts.

What also distanced the government of Northern Ireland from its counterparts in Scotland and Wales was the removal of many of the powers associated with local government when direct rule was imposed in 1972. Under direct rule health, social services and education were managed by joint boards, while public housing was administered by a regional agency, the Northern Ireland Housing Executive (see Tonge 1998:69; Knox 1999: 317–21).

As with the other peripheries in the UK, history is of importance in understanding the institutional structure of government in Northern Ireland immediately before devolution in 1999. Given the complexity of the history of Northern Ireland, and given the significant parliamentary dimensions of that history, the necessary historical background will be provided below.

Welsh Office

After the two Acts of Parliament in 1536 and 1543 which extended the authority of the English monarch over the whole of Wales, Wales was gradually assimilated legally and politically into England, to the extent that, ultimately, it 'was governed as if it were England' (Rose 1982:57). Unlike Scotland, where distinct administrative institutions were established out of recognition of the distinctiveness of Scottish civil society, in Wales distinctiveness came to be defined, paradoxically, by the central government in London. Admittedly, recognition of the importance of the Welsh language in the school system led, in part, to a separate Welsh Department of the Board of Education in 1907. Thereafter, the requirements of central government itself, as well as the institutional 'fall-out' from developments in Scotland and Northern Ireland (for example the creation of sub-national Pension Commissions and Boards of Agriculture (for details see Bogdanor 1999a:156–9)), incrementally ratcheted-up the degree of the administrative distinctiveness of Wales from England.

What characterized the growth of Welsh administrative institutional distinctiveness was that there was no overall plan or deep-rooted political nationalist demand for such 'administrative devolution'. When the Welsh Office was created in 1964, with its own Secretary of State in the UK cabinet, it was as a much a reflection of heightened inner Labour party sensitivities in Wales as a coherent institutional response to administrative needs. At its creation the Welsh Office employed some 200 civil servants with an annual expenditure of just under £250 million. By 1999 it employed over 2,000 civil servants and spent some £7 billion, accounting for 70 per cent of all public expenditure in Wales. The expansion of the Welsh Office was largely as a result of it taking responsibility for policies formerly administered by other central departments in Wales (Rose 1982:58; Bogdanor 1999a:160).

If the Welsh Office, immediately before devolution, was acknowledged as 'the expression and means of government in Wales' (Jones 2000:19) the expression was largely of English legislation in a Welsh voice. (In fact, after the creation of the Welsh Language Board in 1988 all public bodies were required to adopt bilingual policies). Unlike Scotland with its separate legal system and often distinctly different legislation, the Welsh Office remained primarily responsible for implementing policies and legislation formulated in London-based central departments.

Territorial representation in the UK parliament

> Union was achieved by placing England, Wales, Scotland and Ireland under a common and supreme parliament, and by abolishing the parliaments of England, Scotland, Wales and Ireland. It is representation in a common and supreme parliament that has been the crucial feature, the very essence of the process of union. (Bogdanor 1999a:4)

While this statement captures the essence of the process, it also misses the asymmetries of that process.

England and Wales

As was noted in chapter 2, territorial representation was a characteristic feature of the English parliament from early medieval times. From 1215, and the signing of Magna Carta, the English monarch conceded both that the 'community of the realm' had the right to be consulted upon vital matters of policy and that extraordinary taxation should not be levied without consent. What the periodic meetings of parliament achieved subsequently was the representation of local communities, initially from the south-east of England, and policy accommodations between territorial magnates and the monarch. Legislation and taxation were formulated at a parliamentary level, while administration and the maintenance of order remained at the local level.

Beyond the 'core' of south-east England was an 'inner periphery' of northern English shires, Cornwall, and Wales. Wales had, since 1277, been controlled in roughly equal portions directly by the monarch, who assumed ownership of half of the land of the principality, and by quasi-autonomous magnates who, like their counterparts in the northern shires of England, ruled in the monarch's name but exercised considerable local autonomy. These separate jurisdictions were abolished in 1536. In the same year the Act of Union incorporated Wales into the English parliamentary system and a further Act of 1542 incorporated Welsh representation at Westminster. The institutional manifestation of this unity was the subsuming of Welsh representation in a single parliament of England.

Similarly, the incorporation of the 'outer peripheries' of Scotland and Ireland into a union state was also effected through parliamentary means. There was, however, nothing predetermined in this incorporation. Indeed, the different time-frames, the differing modes of integration and the divergent institutional forms of 'union' all point to the absence of some grand strategy. Whereas Anglo-Scottish union was implemented peacefully by treaty between independent states in the period 1689 to 1707, in contrast, the crucial period in the Anglo-Irish union, was characterized by intermittent violence and the suppression of the Irish parliament effectively by a colonial power (see Keating 1988:30–2). In both cases, however, what provided the unitary credentials of the subsequent states of Great Britain and of the United Kingdom was the Westminster parliament. It served both as the means of integration and as the symbol of unity. Moreover, what underpinned these credentials was the fact that the Westminster parliament, after 1689, acted as a sovereign parliament (see chapter 2). Hence, even though the parliament established after the Act of Union in 1707 was a new British institution, nonetheless, it had embodied within its foundations the preexisting English notion of parliamentary sovereignty.

Scotland

Originally, in 1707, 45 Scottish MPs and 16 peers were returned to Westminster. At the time this was an under-representation in terms of population but an over-representation (by a factor of three) in terms of taxation (see Birch 1977:25; Urwin 1982:55). Scottish representation was increased by the 1832 and 1867 Reform Acts respectively to 53 and 60, and it was deemed prudent thereafter to maintain relative over-representation of Scotland in the House of Commons. Indeed, this discrepancy was institutionalized in the 1944 Redistribution Act which set the minimum number of Scottish MPs at 71. (72 were returned at the general elections between 1992 and 2001. In December 2003 the final report of the fifth periodical review conducted by Boundary Commission for Scotland recommended that the number of Scottish constituencies should be reduced to 59). The very presence of Scottish MPs, irrespective of their number or, indeed, of whether or not they displayed distinctive patterns of legislative behaviour, was of significance in itself for the operation of territorial politics in the UK. The simple fact was that the UK parliament symbolized union.

Yet the paradox remained that, if the very presence of Scottish MPs at Westminster was a symbol of integration, they were also a constant reminder of the lack of uniformity within the UK. This found institutional reflection in the distinctive parliamentary arrangements for dealing with Scottish issues at Westminster that had to be devised. Procedurally, this distinctiveness found reflection in the various Grand and Standing Committees of the House which were exclusively focused upon Scottish legislation and policy; the separate opportunities afforded for questioning Scottish Office ministers; and for scrutiny through the Select Committee on Scottish Affairs (see Kellas 1989:85–95; Midwinter et al 1991:64–70). What emerged, therefore, was a 'Scottish parliamentary sub-system within the House of Commons' (Bogdanor 1999a:116); a sub-system that highlighted the essential 'duality' of Scottish 'peripheral' representation in a unitary parliament.

Northern Ireland

From the 13th century the English parliament claimed a right to legislate for Ireland: a right which was asserted in 1494 under Poyning's Law and its subjugation of the Irish parliament to that of England. Although periodic attempts were made to secure greater legislative autonomy it was not until 1782 that the Irish parliament regained its legislative independence, and not until 1793 that Catholics were enfranchised. Even so, Catholics still could not sit in the Irish parliament. Throughout, Irish parliamentary politics continued to be overshadowed by the British connection, with English politicians continuing to see Ireland primarily in security and imperial trading terms; and, in reverse, significant protectionist pressures building up in Ireland

and culminating in a series of recurring crises over commercial relations in the late 18th century. In 1798 resentment spilled onto the streets precipitating 'the most concentrated episode of violence in Irish history' (Foster 1989:280). The response from London was suppression and an enforced Act of Union in 1800.

The union abolished the Irish parliament and transferred Irish representation to the 'sovereign' parliament of Westminster, while restricting the number of representatives to 100. Constitutional union was clearly identified at the time, in London at least, as an integrative force—both economically and politically. From the outset in Ireland, however, powerful voices argued otherwise.

The details of the struggle for Home Rule between 1850 and 1922, though innately intriguing, lie beyond the scope of the present discussion; rather, what is of concern here is the importance of the UK parliament as an arena and a symbol of struggle, and as part of the 'problem' itself. The 'Irish problem' was imported into Westminster after 1880 by Parnell as leader of the Irish party. Parnell harnessed the Home Rule movement to militancy over the land issue. Moreover, Irish MPs consciously exploited parliamentary procedures to obstruct proceedings in Westminster. The clear message was that Britain would not be allowed to govern itself until greater self-government was conceded to Ireland. This message was heeded in 1886, 1893 and 1912 in successive Home Rule Bills—none of which were ultimately successful.

It was not until 1920, however, that legislation was introduced which, for the first time, entailed the creation of two legislatures in Ireland—one for the south and one for the six counties in the north. The intention of the Government of Ireland Act was to retain the whole of Ireland within the United Kingdom. Whilst formalising partition, through the proposal for two parliaments, the Act envisaged a temporary partition. In the event the 'all-Ireland' aspirations of the 1920 Act were rapidly dashed by the continuing 'troubles' in the south and the intensified military campaign of the Irish Republican Army (IRA). In December 1921 an agreement, officially entitled Articles of Agreement for a Treaty, was worked out between the British government and Sinn Féin; the essence of which was the creation of an Irish Free State of 26 counties in the south with dominion status.

The provisions of the 1920 Act, suitably amended, subsequently came into effect for the six counties of the north alone. A bicameral Northern Ireland parliament was established at Stormont; yet the UK parliament retained its sovereignty. For over half a century the Government of Ireland Act 1920 remained the basic statute underpinning the constitution of Northern Ireland. Until its suspension in 1972, the Act had established and maintained legislative devolution in a constitutionally unitary state. When suspension came, however, it provided 'an exemplary lesson in the sovereignty of parliament at Westminster'; for 'in just thirty-three hours of debate, the powers vested in Stormont were stripped away' (O'Leary et al 1988:58).

Nonetheless, while it existed, devolution in Northern Ireland demonstrated the compatibility of 'having a devolved parliament and affirming Unionism' (Rose 1982:176). Equally, it demonstrated that devolution in Northern Ireland reflected a desire in London for non-involvement in Northern Ireland's domestic affairs. As Wilford and Wilson (2003:79) note, 'virtually the whole British political class has been united for decades on the desirability of offloading responsibility for that "troubled" region [Northern Ireland] to its inhabitants'. This was reflected in the general 'hands-off' approach, except in the field of finance, of the UK government and the specific prohibition of MPs at Westminster from asking questions about devolved matters (see Connolly 1990:35–6).

Ultimately, what the experience of Northern Ireland served to underscore was that, behind the 'immutability' of parliamentary sovereignty and the centralization of authority within the UK state, there was an essential 'malleability' which allowed for, variously, institutional innovation, administrative devolution and a practical decentralization of authority to the peripheries.

Local government pre-1999

> To summarize: the United Kingdom has a constitutionally subordinate system of local government, without historically the wide-ranging competence of many European continental systems, yet which is far more than a network of field agencies of central government. It could be described as semi-autonomous. (Wilson and Game 2002:28–9)

In the UK, local government has historically been subordinate to central government. This status was succinctly stated in the Widdicombe Report on the *Conduct of Local Authority Business*: 'All current local authorities are the statutory creations of Parliament and have no independent status or right to exist' (Cmnd 9797–I 1986:45). One manifestation of this subordination has been the capacity of UK governments to reorganize local authorities almost at whim. In the four years before devolution in 1999, for example, reorganization of the structure of local authorities in the constituent parts of the United Kingdom reduced the number of local councils from 540 to 463. In England between 1995 and 1998 46 unitary councils replaced 63 existing authorities. In Wales 22 new single-tier councils replaced the existing 45 units in 1996, and in the same year in Scotland 32 new councils replaced 63 former regions and districts. This resulted in the largest local authorities and the highest ratio of citizens to elected councillors of any Western European country (Wilson and Game 2002:70). (There was no restructuring of local government in Northern Ireland in the 1990s. 26 District Councils remained in existence but, as noted above, they were responsible for far fewer services than local authorities in the rest of the UK).

The legal position of local government is subject to the *ultra vires* rule which holds that local authorities 'may properly incur expenditure only for purposes authorised by statute' (Bradley and Ewing 2003:646). In effect this has meant that there has been no general competences exercised by local authorities only specific actions sanctioned by UK legislation. If a local council acted outside these specific powers then it was deemed to have acted *ultra vires*—beyond its powers—and hence to have acted illegally. The extent to which central government controlled the activities of local government was illustrated vividly in the period 1979 to 1997 when the Conservative government introduced over 210 Acts of Parliament which affected local authorities, in addition to a deluge of secondary legislation and 'circulars' from central government departments 'advising' them how to exercise their responsibilities. Moreover, much of this legislation and 'advice' was regulatory in nature and designed to rework local government into 'an instrument of central policy' (Loughlin 2001:163). As part of the new institutional design for local government the provision of services—which had long been the preserve of, and a significant rationale for, local government—was radically restructured.

Despite the streamlining of local service provision in the decades before 1999 local government still accounted for more than a quarter of all public expenditure at the end of the 20th century. It was, in Wilson and Game's (2002:115) view, 'extremely big business'. Local authorities remained large and diverse organizations, employing a significant section of the workforce, and retaining responsibility for hundreds of different services (the main ones included the administration of school education, the provision of personal social services, strategic planning and development control, and environmental health and consumer protection). By the late 1990s many of these services were carried out in partnership with private sector and voluntary organizations or other public bodies. Indeed, the notion of 'local governance' became rooted in academic analyses and the practical discourse of local authority officials in the 1990s (see Stoker 1998; 2000). Wilson and Game (2002:138) provide a succinct definition:

> Local governance brings together governmental and non-governmental agencies in flexible partnerships ... Local governance is not based on a single authority, the provision of a specialised service, or a new set of structures, but on a fusion of different styles and different working relationships.

Elected local authorities were thus entwined by 1999 in a complex web of organizations providing local service delivery. Locked into a series of formal and informal partnerships and networks the institutional boundaries of local government proved to be permeable and often indistinct. But what continued to mark out the institutions of local government from the wider interinstitutional networks of local governance was the legitimacy derived from the electoral process.

In essence, 'local councils, being ... subject to direct periodic election ... are accorded a degree of political legitimacy which other agencies of government do not possess' (Loughlin 1996:39). This legitimacy, derived from the local representative process, allows for the articulation of local policy priorities, for policy variation (within nationally prescribed frameworks), and for locally elected politicians to 'govern'. As noted above, however, the 'degree of legitimacy' of local authorities, and the extent of policy discretion, is contingent upon a grant of authorization from Westminster and the national representative process. Nonetheless, the fact of 'local democratic approval' provides local councillors with a 'uniquely potent bargaining counter' (Wilson and Game 2002:30) both in negotiations with UK government and with 'local governance partners'. The extent to which this uniqueness continued post-1999 after devolution will be considered below.

The institutions of devolution post-1999

On 1 July 1999 two new representative institutions—a parliament in Edinburgh and a National Assembly in Cardiff—met for the first time. An Assembly for Northern Ireland came into existence later in the same year in December 1999. The creation of these new institutions marked a significant departure from 'territorial' management in the past, yet equally reflected continuities with the past, and held the potential to precipitate further discontinuities in the future. The primary concerns here, however, are the manner in which these institutions were designed and the way in which they have operated since 1999.

Institutional change and design

As noted in chapter 1, historical institutionalism normally assumes that institutions are 'change resistant' and are locked into established internal organizational patterns and external interactions with other institutions. Explaining institutional change has thus been both a challenge and a problem for theories rooted in notions of 'path dependency'. Variously, change has been explained by notions of 'critical junctures', which suggest that institutional development may be characterized by periods of continuity punctuated by 'branching points' where the institution moves onto a new path; or 'rapid bursts of institutional change'; or 'disruptions' which precipitate a sharp break with the past and stem from external change in the environment of an institution.

Various explanations of change in the UK have been advanced, and although a full listing of explanatory variables is not required here, what is worth noting, however, is that common to most explanations is a recognition of various asymmetries in the demands for change, and in the degree of change; as well as the contingency of change in different parts of the UK.

One, overly deterministic, institutional explanation is that the pre-existence of distinctive parliamentary institutions in Scotland and Ireland served, post-union, as powerful national symbols in the consciousness of political nationalists. Certainly, the experience of a devolved parliament in Northern Ireland for half of the 20th century provided some institutional pointers towards parliamentary reincarnation in the province in the future. In other words, from the outset, 'territorial' institutional ghosts haunted the corridors of the new Westminster parliament of Great Britain and ultimately of the United Kingdom.

A second explanation is that change resulted from the paradoxes of territorial representation within the UK parliament itself. As noted above, just as Westminster served as a symbol of the unity of the UK, representation of the peripheries also served to underline the distinctiveness, and asymmetries, of territorial representation. Thus, for example, the over-representation of MPs from Scotland contrasted with the under-representation of Northern Ireland MPs. Equally, the differing capacity of Westminster MPs to raise issues on matters covered by their respective decentralized administrations, and the different parliamentary procedures for dealing with legislation and the scrutiny of policy in the three peripheries, all pointed to distinctive patterns of territorial management in the UK.

A third, and related, explanation is that, as the significance of 'administrative devolution' became more pronounced both in terms of political contestation and executive competences, so the paradoxes of the nature and purpose of territorial representation at Westminster were spotlighted. In Wales the gradual accretion of administrative responsibilities to the Welsh Office after 1964, and the rapid doubling of the number of quangos under successive Conservative governments after 1979, led to a recognition of both the extent of administrative decentralization and of the weakness of executive accountability in the principality (see Jones 2000:20–1; Mitchell 2003c:36). In fact, the speed of 'administrative creep' (Jones 2000:16) in Wales increased as the pace of the implementation of neo-liberal policy programmes by the Thatcher and Major governments quickened. If the enhancement of 'the semi-secret world' of the executive institutions in Wales after 1979 gave constitutional observers cause for concern, the fact that this world was controlled primarily by a political party with only minority (and diminishing) electoral support provided political activists with the motivation and rationale for institutional change.

Certainly, in parallel with developments in Wales, the Thatcher years contributed to a major redirection of politics in Scotland and managed to turn 'the sense of grievance in Scotland [that] had been persistent and inchoate ... [into something] more coherent, with a left-progressive agenda forming around the case for a parliament or assembly' (Mitchell 2003d:247).

The sense of grievance stemmed from a belief in the 'relative deprivation' in Scotland—that the Scottish economy and social provision had fared adversely in comparison to England, and, in particular, that its collective welfare had been undermined by an English-dominated and, hence, 'unrepresentative' party. In fact, so unpopular did the Conservative party become in the 1990s that, after the 1992 election with only 11 Conservative MPs returned for Scottish constituencies, the Scottish Office depended upon 'parachutists' from English constituencies to fill the junior ministerial posts of Parliamentary Private Secretary.

Institutional design

Most institutional theories have a common concern with identifying the defining characteristics of institutions and with conceptualising, or at a minimum describing, institutional development and change. The question of institutional design, however, tends to separate, on the one hand, those theories which start from idealized prescriptions or assumptions (such as rational choice/game theories), or from the premise that designers have virtually a free choice (empirical institutionalism); from those, on the other, which stress historical legacies and constraints rather than rational design principles (historical institutionalism).

The creation of two new sub-national legislatures and the resurrection of another in 1999 certainly provided the opportunities both for theoretical reflection and practical consideration of issues of institutional design. At one level, as will be seen below, 'designers' consciously sought to inculcate novel values and norms in the new institutions, and to work from an institutional blueprint that explicitly did *not* replicate the 'Westminster model'. Yet, at another level, despite the good intentions of the 'designers', they were constrained by the existing configuration of political institutions in the wider UK. Their designs had to take into account that:

> prospective constitutional sites [were] more 'brownfield' than 'greenfield', containing the ruins of older buildings and potentially serious but hidden problems of subsidence. Meanwhile, the designers [had] to accommodate their plans to the awkwardly shaped sites created by much larger already constructed neighbouring buildings. This metaphor graphically illustrates how past events constrain individual actions in the present. (Laffin 2000:535)

Before examining the institutional designs that guided the construction of the new devolved institutions after 1999, it is worth stating briefly who the 'designers' were in the first place. Not surprisingly, different designers produced different designs in each of the three peripheries. Some common blueprints already existed from the 'Home Rule All Round' days of Gladstone in the 19th century (see Bogdanor 1999a:44–50) and from various Commissions, such as the Kilbrandon Commission in the 1970s (with its recognition that it was not necessary to have a uniform system in all parts of Great Britain (Cmnd 5460 1973:para 1217)). But each set of designers in the 1990s sought to construct institutions suited to the specific political contours of their own respective periphery.

In Scotland the very process of design engendered new institutional forms. A Scottish Constitutional Convention was formed in March 1989 to devise a 'final scheme' for the future government of Scotland (Scottish Constitutional Convention 1990:3). The Convention's membership was drawn from a 'wide spectrum of Scottish civil society' (Brown 2000:547) with representatives from political parties (with the notable exceptions of the Conservatives and SNP), trade unions, churches, local authorities and other organizations. The Convention's genealogy, in turn, could be traced back to the Campaign for a Scottish Assembly (latter renamed Campaign for a Scottish Parliament) which had been formed in the wake of the 1979 devolution referendum defeat. The Campaign was 'an all party, non-party organization, independent of all political parties' (Mitchell 1996:102) which produced *A Claim of Right for Scotland* in 1988. This *Claim* was signed by all members of the Constitutional Convention at its inaugural meeting, and in so doing they accepted the assertion of 'the sovereign right of the Scottish people to determine the form of Government best suited to their needs'. Apologists for the Convention emphasized the radical challenge posed by the *Claim*, both in its rejection of the notion of the sovereignty of the UK parliament and in its emphasis upon the superior rights (participatory and civil) of Scottish civil society (see Wright 1997:30–8). Yet, even its supporters had to acknowledge that the Convention produced 'a curious combination of rhetoric about a renewal of democracy with a continuation of the semi-secret world of the committees and boards that had run the Scottish welfare state' (Brown et al 1998:66). In essence the 'rhetoric was radical but the proposals were reformist' (Mitchell 2002:249).

In Wales the design process was less inclusive and was centred primarily within the Labour party. In 1992 the party in Wales appointed a Constitutional Policy Commission on devolution. In part this was to head-off support for the creation of a cross-party Welsh Constitutional Convention to parallel that in Scotland (see Morgan and Mungham 2000:35). However, sensitive to the accusations that any recommendations would simply constitute a Labour 'stitch-up', the Commission—guided by Ron Davies as Shadow Secretary for State—emphasized the values of participation, openness, inclusiveness and cooperation in framing its proposals. In so doing, the designers made clear their aspiration for a 'new model' to structure the government of Wales. In particular, a new Welsh assembly was to mark a 'sharp break with the traditions of a hidebound, anachronistic Westminster Parliament' (Laffin and Thomas 2000:559).

While the design processes for Scottish and Welsh devolution in the 1990s proceeded without the direct involvement of the Conservatives, the Conservative government, nonetheless, pursued pro-active policies for the reinstatement of devolution in Northern Ireland throughout this period. Indeed, the process of negotiation that was to culminate in the Belfast Agreement of 1998 started in 1996 under the government of John Major (see Wilford 2000:577). Without examining the details of this process, what is notable is that the designers included (intermittently) both nationalist and major unionist parties, along with the UK government and, significantly, the Irish government. The design process was a classic example of the UK government's belief in 'variable geometry' and of its desire to effect devolution in one part of the UK; Northern Ireland, but not in others, Scotland and Wales. Moreover, it represented a practical demonstration of the malleability of the concept of 'parliamentary sovereignty' where institutional design was concerned (see below).

Interior designers

Of necessity, consensus and consociationalism (power sharing) were integral to the design of the Northern Ireland Assembly. The exceptionalism of Northern Ireland had long been accommodated within the Westminster system. Yet in trying to import the values of participation, inclusion, openness and cooperation into the new representative institutions in Scotland and Wales, the designers both misread the Westminster system and underestimated the complexities of any subsequent interinstitutional inter-actions in an asymmetrically devolved UK. As noted above, the Convention in Scotland and the Commission in Wales worked on the basis of aspiration rather than detailed understanding of institutional design. In Scotland the vision was of a new Scottish parliament with substantial legislative powers but it was a vision expressed in the 'language of hope' (Scottish Constitutional Convention 1990:13). What was required was the translation of this language into detailed plans for the organization and operating procedures of the new parliament.

Once the referendum results were recorded in favour of the new representative bodies in September 1997 the task of translation fell primarily to the Consultative Steering Group in Scotland and the Devolution Implementation Group and the Assembly Advisory Group in Wales (for details see Brown 2000:548–50; and Laffin and Thomas 2000:560–6). Whereas the process of 'interior design' might have generated expectations of detailed deliberation upon the technicalities and intricacies of organizational structures and parliamentary procedures, the process itself was characterized as much by 'consensus-working and alliance-building' (Brown 2000:550; see also Laffin and Thomas 2000:562). The result was the enunciation both in Scotland and Wales of general guiding principles. In Scotland the new parliament was to work in accordance with the principles of power sharing, accountability, access and participation, and equal opportunities (Consultative Steering Group 1999:3). In Wales the remit of the Assembly Advisory Group was to develop an Assembly that was 'democratic, effective, efficient and inclusive' (Jones 2000:191).

The membership of both advisory groups included representatives from the major parties, local authorities, business, and civic groups and organizations. Both were advised by civil servants in the respective territorial department and both engaged in public consultation exercises. In Scotland the CSG also commissioned research on devolved governance in other countries. The emphasis upon inclusiveness and consultation in the design processes did embed certain general values into the institutional architecture of the new representative bodies, but arguably at the expense of detailed consideration of other key considerations about interinstitutional relations in the wider UK and about the specifics of internal organizational design. Indeed, members of both advisory groups are open to the charge of institutional naïveté, of aspiring to new political relationships and of asserting new forms of institutional interactions, but without fully appreciating the extent to which the 'old politics' and the old interinstitutional connections would intrude into the post-devolution structures (see Mitchell 2000:610; McAllister 2000:603; Mitchell 2004:34–7; see below). What is also apparent is that the institutional design of both representative bodies 'embrace[d] as many old practices as new' (McAllister 2000:603).

New institutions

The Scottish parliament

Section 1(1) of the Scotland Act 1998 states simply 'there will be a Scottish Parliament'. The first meeting of the 129 members of the Scottish parliament (MSPs) was convened in temporary accommodation in Edinburgh in September 1999. Indeed, the issue of the new parliament building was to plague the new parliament throughout its first four year term, as the costs spiralled from an initial estimate of £40 million to over £430 million by the time the building was officially opened in October 2004. For many in the Scottish media the intracacies of the architectural design and subsequent problems with construction on the Holyrood site served as a metaphor of the inherent deficiencies of institutional design.

One novel institutional design-feature of the Holyrood parliament was the introduction of an additional member electoral system, where 73 MSPs were elected from single member constituencies by simple majority vote and the remaining 56 'additional members' were elected from party lists from eight regions under a proportional system. The electoral arrangements mirrored the proposals contained within the Constitutional Convention's 1995 document *Scotland's Parliament, Scotland's Right*, and were an explicit recognition that the Labour party's electoral hegemony in Scotland would be curbed in the new parliament (as well as an astute calculation that the possibility of any future nationalist electoral dominance would also simultaneously be defused). Equally, the electoral system was designed to impact upon the internal workings of the parliament and upon executive-legislative relations by reducing the adversarial nature of party competition.

The outcomes of the two elections of 1999 and 2003 can be seen in Table 5.1

TABLE 5.1 Scottish Parliament Election Results 1999 and 2003

	Constituency MSPs				Regional list MSPs				Total MSPs			
	1999		2003		1999		2003		1999		2003	
	seats	% vote	seats	% vote	seats	% vote	seats	% vote	seats	% seats	seats	% seats
Labour	53	38.8	46	34.6	3	33.6	4	29.3	56	43.4	50	38.8
SNP	7	28.7	9	23.8	28	27.3	18	20.9	35	27.1	27	20.9
Lib Dem	12	14.2	13	15.4	5	12.4	4	11.8	17	13.2	17	13.2
Conservative	0	15.6	3	16.6	18	15.4	15	15.5	18	13.9	18	14.0
Green	0	0.0	0	0.0	1	3.6	7	6.9	1	0.8	7	5.4
Scot Soc Party	0	1.0	0	6.2	1	2.0	6	6.7	1	0.8	16	4.7
Other	1	2.6	2	3.4	0	5.7	2	8.9	1	0.8	4	3.0
Total	73	100.0	73	100.0	56	100.0	56	100.0	129	100.0	129	100.0

Under section 28(1) of the 1998 Act the Scottish parliament is granted the broad power to make laws for Scotland. Essentially the parliament legislates in the policy areas covered by the former Scottish Office, these are known as 'devolved matters' and include: health services; local government; education; housing; transport; the police, courts and judiciary; agriculture; the arts; and social work. However, copious exceptions to the legislative competences of the Scottish parliament were listed in Schedule 5 of the 1998 Act. These are known as 'reserved matters' and include: financial and economic matters; home affairs, including immigration and nationality issues; trade and industry; energy; social security; regulation of the professions; employment; health and medicines; the constitution; foreign affairs; defence; and the 'regulation of activities in outer space'. Any incursion by the Scottish parliament into these reserved areas would not be deemed to be law under section 29(1) of the Scotland Act.

The 'residual competence' of the Scottish parliament followed the model adopted for the Stormont parliament in Northern Ireland between 1922 to 1972. Equally, as with Stormont, the sovereignty of the UK parliament was asserted under section 28(7) of the 1998 Act which recognized the unfettered 'power of the Parliament of the United Kingdom to make laws for Scotland'. Moreover, a series of procedural and judicial restraints were designed to prevent the Scottish parliament from acting *ultra vires* (see Bogdanor 1999a:205–9; Forman 2002:90). Formally the sovereignty of Westminster was asserted from the outset; yet there was also an immediate recognition that 'politically, [the Scottish parliament] will be anything but subordinate. For the Scotland Act creates a new locus of political power' (Bogdanor 1999b:185). The expectation, both in London and in Edinburgh, was that conventions or standard operating procedures would evolve that would limit the capacity of Westminster to legislate with regard to devolved matters (see Page and Batey 2002:501). If the 'usual rule' (Donald Dewar, Scottish Parliament Official Record June 23 1999:col 69) was that Westminster would not legislate in devolved areas, the practice turned out to be significantly different. In the first parliament between 1999 and 2003 nearly as many bills (39) in Scotland originated in Westminster 'for devolved purposes' as originated in the Scottish parliament (50 Executive Bills). The purpose of such Westminster legislation was primarily to include Scotland in reform schemes which applied to the rest of the UK, or implemented provisions in accordance with the UK's international and European Union obligations, or enabled the Scottish Executive to subscribe to UK administrative arrangements (see Page and Batey 2002:508–13). With hindsight, as Page and Batey (2002:518) observe, 'it is clear that claims about Westminster legislation being a rare occurrence underestimated the strength of the pull towards uniformity in the devolution settlement'. What the Lords' Constitutional Committee found 'strange' was that 'an issue which is fundamentally about co-operation between legislatures has turned in practice into co-operation between executives' (HL 28 2002:para 130). This dimension of interinstitutional relations will be examined below, but, for the moment, our attention remains focused upon intra-institutional arrangements within the Scottish parliament.

In terms of the internal procedures of the Scottish parliament it was clear from the CSG's report that a 'different kind of Parliament' was envisaged with 'procedures that would be quite different from those used at Westminster' (Oliver 2003:261). This difference was made manifest in the creation of a Parliamentary Bureau, composed of the Presiding Officer and representatives of the main political parties, to arrange the work programme of the parliament and the composition and remit of committees. The intention was to initiate 'an inclusive and transparent' process for organising parliamentary business (Consultative Steering Group 1999:4), in contrast to the secretive and executive dominated process in Westminster. Similarly, the Westminster characteristics—of executive control of the legislative process and the government's ability to avoid detailed scrutiny—were to be minimized by the introduction of all-purpose committees which would combine the roles of standing and select committees at Westminster. The explicit purpose of having a strong committee system was to facilitate the 'sharing of power' between the Scottish Parliament and the Scottish Executive (Consultative Steering Group 1999:5–6). Committees were also identified as an integral part of the new procedures which were 'designed to ensure that the Executive is fully accountable to the Scottish Parliament for its actions' (Consultative Steering Group 1999:8). More generally the culture of openness and accessibility was to infuse the workings of the parliament at Holyrood and its relations with the Executive and the Scottish people. The procedures were also designed to maximize participation and consultation.

The distance between design aspiration and procedural practice, however, has been marked. An initial assessment of the operation of the

Bureau concluded that it had been 'more a formalization of Westminster-style "usual channels"' than had been intended by the CSG' (Winetrobe 2001:2). The fact that the Executive had a majority on the parliamentary Bureau allowed it to dominate the legislative programme and ensured predictability in securing the successful passage of its legislation. Indeed, a detailed study of legislative amendments in the first Scottish parliament (1999–2003) revealed that the extent of Executive dominance was such that: 'the degree of success of ministers is remarkably similar to the ministerial success . . . found in . . . the House of Commons' (Shephard and Cairney 2005). Similarly, the Procedures Committee of the Scottish Parliament, in reviewing the extent to which the CSG's principles guided the work of the parliament, concluded that: 'The evidence we received conveyed a powerful picture of the unequal strengths of the Scottish governance partners [Parliament and Executive]' (SP Paper 818 2003:para 45). While the committees had tempered 'to an extent' the dominance of the Executive, there was 'clear evidence that the committee system in the Scottish Parliament is under severe pressure of work and that the quality of output is threatened' (SP Paper 818 2003:para 1016). Indeed, there was a danger that: 'If Parliament [and its committees] becomes a conveyer belt for passing legislation, it will not serve as a vehicle for sharing power' (SP Paper 818 2003: para 1016).

Scottish Executive

Under the provisions of the Scotland Act 1998 ministers of the Scottish Executive have to be MSPs, and along with the law officers—the Lord Advocate and the Solicitor General—are accountable to parliament and must resign if parliament resolves that the Executive no longer retains its confidence. In this sense executive-legislative relations closely resemble those at UK level. The powers of the Executive are transferred from the UK government. Included within the powers of the Scottish Executive (derived from the Scottish Parliament) was the capacity to alter the standard rate of income tax levied in Scotland within a range of plus or minus three per cent of the UK level.

A First Minister is nominated by parliament and appointed by the Queen. In turn, the First Minister then chooses a ministerial team (in 2004 of 18 members) including a Deputy First Minister, who, since 1999, has been the leader of Labour's coalition partner, the Liberal Democrats. One of the consequences of the more proportional composition of the Scottish parliament has thus been the impact on the structure and operation of the Executive itself. Equally, the interactions between the coalition parties have been reoriented by experience of joint working in the Executive.

Officials of the Executive are members of the UK civil service, and the Permanent Secretary is appointed by the UK's Civil Service Commission (a fact that generated some political controversy upon the appointment of John Elvidge in July 2003). Nonetheless, Executive civil servants are accountable to Scottish ministers, and are organized primarily in eight functional departments: Development; Education; Enterprise; Transport and Lifelong Learning, Finance, and Central Services Department (FCSD); Health; Justice; Environment; and Rural Affairs. Fifteen executive agencies were also responsible to Scottish Executive ministers in late 2004.

In tandem with the creation of the Scottish Executive in 1999 the Scottish Office was reconstituted as the Scotland Office. However, considerable scepticism was expressed over the continuing significance of the role of the Secretary of State and of the Scotland Office, most volubly by the Lords' Constitution Committee (HL 28 2002:paras 54–68). Such criticism contributed in part, in June 2003, to the decision to merge the Scotland Office (and the Wales and Northern Ireland Offices) into a new Constitutional Affairs Department. In this merger the role of Secretary of State for Scotland (and those for Wales and Northern Ireland) was effectively downgraded. (After initial considerable confusion, the Scottish post was given to Alistair Darling—who happened to be Scottish and to represent a Scottish constituency—but whose primary responsibility remained as Secretary of State for Transport (for the complexities of this arrangement see HC 815 2003)). In 2004, the Scotland Office had a staff of 80, and its stated roles were 'to represent Scottish interests at Westminster' and to 'act as guardian of the devolution settlement' (www.scotlandoffice.gov.uk).

To ease the relations between the Scottish Executive (and the other devolved administrations) a Memorandum of Understanding and four Overarching Concordats (on International Relations, the EU, Financial Assistance to Industry, and Statistics) were agreed with the UK Government. More detailed bilateral Concordats were also signed between the

Scottish Executive and individual UK Government Departments. The Concordats are non-legally binding agreements and they are underpinned by Devolution Guidance Notes issued by the Office of the Deputy Prime Minister after consultation with the devolved administrations (for details see HL 28 2002:paras 18–48). In addition to these informal agreements, a Joint Ministerial Committee (JMC) formally brings together in plenary the UK Prime Minister and Deputy Prime Minister, the Chancellor of the Exchequer, and the Secretaries of State and the First and Deputy First Ministers from each devolved administration. But plenary JMC meetings are only the 'tip of the iceberg of intergovernmental contact' (HL 28 2002:para 30) as the JMC also meets in functional format, and there are occasional informal working meetings of ministers outside of the JMC framework. What worried many commentators, however, was that the consensual interinstitutional interactions had been dependent upon a party political consensus among likeminded ministers in London, Edinburgh and Cardiff, and that, almost inevitably, 'the present levels of goodwill will diminish over time' (HL 28 2002:para 26). This fear was invoked by Ian McCartney, the Labour party chairman, in his statement that a Conservative victory at the 2005 general election posed 'a threat to devolution because it would undermine the positive partnership that exists between both parliaments. Only Labour can be trusted to ensure a strong and stable UK' (*Sunday Herald* 19 December 2004).

Scottish local government

Most areas of devolved responsibility have major implications for local government in Scotland. Not surprisingly, therefore, the Scottish Executive has become the 'key focus' of local authorities' attention. A survey of local authority councillors and officials discovered a widespread perception that the 'Executive, while better than the Scottish Office before it, was still a centralising political force and as such attempted to dominate relations with local government' (Bennett et al 2002:19). In this survey, 78 per cent of councillors believed that the creation of the Executive had increased interference in local government affairs. Yet, paralleling this belief, was a recognition that devolution had provided a new capacity—a 'legislative space'—in which the Scottish parliament could enact provisions that would not have found a place before 1999 in Westminster's timetable.

Indeed, it is perhaps of significance that the first debate of the new Scottish parliament was on the relations between local government and the new devolved institutions (SP OR 2 July 1999 vol 1, no 13). The focus of the debate was upon the Report of the McIntosh Commission, which had been established by the Scottish Office prior to devolution to examine post-devolution interinstitutional relations. In turn, a range of new organizations were established to advance the Report's recommendations; the most important of these dealt with the renewal of local democracy (and resulted in the Kerley report of 2000), the Leadership Advisory Panel (which reported in 2001 on political management structures), and a Community Leadership Forum (for details see McGarvey 2002). In February 2003 *The Local Government in Scotland Bill* received Royal Assent, and placed a duty on local authorities to secure 'Best Value' 'having regard to efficiency, effectiveness, economy and the need to meet equal opportunities requirements'. Additionally, the Bill gave local authorities the power to advance the 'well being of their area' and placed a duty on local authorities to engage with other public sector partners in community planning. In November 2003 the Executive published its *Local Governance (Scotland) Bill*, which proposed the introduction of the single transferable vote system for local elections, and which was eventually passed in June 2004.

What was apparent from the first four years of devolution was that interinstitutional relations between local authorities and 'the centre' of the Scottish Executive had attained a distinctiveness from those pertaining elsewhere in the UK. Regulatory oversight, via Best Value, was less intrusive; and a more integrated approach to local government was apparent (see McGarvey 2002:43–4). Ultimately, however, as McGarvey (2002:45) concludes: just as a 'strong streak of centralism' remains in Whitehall in its relations with English local authorities, so the Scottish Executive's 'streak may not be as strong but it is still evident'. Thus, even after the *Local Government in Scotland Act 2003*, the policy discretion of local authorities remained closely circumscribed by the Executive. As McConnell (2004:213) noted: '[u]nless forced to do so, the Scottish Executive had no desire to see its political priorities undermined by giving "excessive" political freedoms to councils'. Moreover, what struck McConnell (2004:236) forcibly was 'that enormous similarities remain' with key policies for local government continuing to 'be virtually identical north and south of the border'.

The National Assembly for Wales

Unlike the Scottish parliament the Welsh National Assembly does not have primary legislative powers, its competences extend only to delegated or secondary legislation. In this sense it is at best a form of 'quasi-legislative devolution' (Oliver 2003:274) or more accurately 'executive devolution'. The UK parliament is still the legislature for Wales.

Equally, unlike the Scottish parliament, the National Assembly does not have the capacity to vary the basic rate of income tax. Like the Scottish parliament, however, the Assembly is funded essentially from a block grant from Westminster calculated under the Barnett Formula (for details see HL 28 2002:paras 82–109). Once in receipt of the block grant the devolved administration is free to spend the money in accordance with its own priorities.

Schedule 2 of the 1998 Government of Wales Act listed 18 areas in which responsibility was to be transferred to the National Assembly. These included: agriculture, education, economic development, health and health services, industry, local government, social services and transport. This supplemented Section 22 of the Act which allowed for the 'transfer to the Assembly of any function so far as exercisable by a Minister of the Crown in relation to Wales'. In essence these were powers that had formerly been exercised by the Secretary of State for Wales. Yet, the transfer of responsibilities within the designated areas was often piecemeal, and reflected the fact that the functions of the Welsh Office had accumulated incrementally and through specification in over 300 separate statutes or statutory instruments (see Osmond 2003:37). Thus, for example, not all areas of agriculture were devolved to the Assembly, as Welsh ministers found to their political cost during the Foot and Mouth epidemic of 2001. The 'patchwork pattern' of the National Assembly's powers, and the difficulties encountered in identifying what the Assembly could do, has been likened to a 'jigsaw of constantly changing pieces, none of which has straight edges' (Patchett in HL 28 2002:para 121). Concern over the flawed delineation of powers of the Assembly led to the appointment of the Richard Commission in July 2002 to examine the Assembly's 'powers and electoral arrangements' (www.richardcommission.gov.uk/content/termsref/index.htm). During its enquiries the Commission received compelling evidence of the failures of the initial institutional design of the Assembly (see for example Lord

Dafydd Elis Thomas, www.richardcommission.gov.uk/content/evidence/oral/podpo/index.htm; and Vernon Bogdanor, www.richardcommission.gov.uk/content/evidence/oral/bogdanorv/index-e.htm; see below).

From Executive Committee to Welsh Assembly Government

If the powers of the Assembly were occasionally indeterminate, the actual status of the institution was equally fuzzy. Patchett characterized the National Assembly as 'an institution without constitutional precedent' (2000: 229). The 1998 Government of Wales Act under section 1(2) created 'a body corporate'. Under section 53 the Assembly was required to elect a First Secretary, who, in turn, would then choose other Assembly Secretaries to serve on an Executive Committee. The 1998 Act also created subject committees to parallel the allocation of functions of the Assembly Secretaries. Each Secretary was to be a member of the appropriate subject committee, though not its chair, and it was envisaged that each committee would exercise collective scrutiny and make 'informed contribution to the development by its Secretary of policy in its field' (Patchett 2000:238). Clearly this design reflected the desire of the NAAG to develop a more inclusive, collective and consensual approach to policy formulation (see above), but, equally clearly and from the outset, the Assembly effected a differentiation of executive and 'parliamentary' roles and privileged the former over the latter.

This distinction was increasingly formalized after the report of the Assembly's Review of Procedure was published in February 2002. The review was commissioned in the light of concern over how the Assembly had operated in its first year (www.wales.gov.uk/subiassemblybusiness/procedures/assemblyreview.htm). The starting point was an acknowledgement that: 'While the Assembly is, in law, a corporate body, the political reality is that a separation has emerged between Assembly Ministers and the officials supporting them on the one hand, and Assembly Members supported by the staff of the Presiding Office on the other' (Para 2.2). In recognition of this fact the Report proposed that the term 'Minister' should be used instead of Secretary. Beyond this the review was unable to reach a consensus on the nomenclature to be used to describe the Executive, though effectively this issue had been decided during the course of the review by the decision of the First Minister, announced in November 2001, to call it the 'Welsh Assembly Government' and by the adoption of the term 'cabinet' for the Executive Committee. The Review also sought a clarification of the respective roles of ministers and other Assembly members on committees as well as of the interconnected issue of the policy and scrutiny roles of the committees.

What emerged during the lifetime of the first Assembly was a clearer separation of legislative and executive roles, to the extent that Osmond (2003: 13) concluded that the Assembly had taken on the appearance of a 'virtual parliament'. Within this 'virtual' institution there was a strong executive authority and the importation of several key elements of the pre-existing Westminster system; the most fundamental of which was that the 'executive has governed and the backbenchers have been left to exert influence as and when they can' (Osmond 2000:45).

Assembly composition

The fact that Assembly members were elected under an additional member system similar to that used in Scotland was supposed to encourage a 'new style' of collegial, if not actually consensual, politics and to undermine the possibility of the monolithic control of a majority party in the Assembly. Despite the seeming altruism of the institutional designers, the proportion of 'constituency' to 'additional' members in Wales (at 60 to 40, in contrast to the 57 to 43 in Scotland), revealed a pragmatic calculation of the relative advantage to be gained by the Labour party in securing support, in the first instance of its own members for the devolution scheme, and, in the second instance of the voters at elections for the Assembly.

At the first Assembly elections in May 1999 Labour was returned as the largest party (see Table 5.2), which was no surprise, but did not obtain a majority in the National Assembly, which did come as a surprise to some commentators (see Balsom 2000:218). The first 18 months witnessed a minority Labour administration that was eventually terminated by a vote of no confidence in Alun Michael as First Secretary. An interim informal 'cohabitation' agreement then followed between Labour and Plaid Cymru; before a formal Partnership Agreement was signed between Labour and Liberal Democrats in October 2000. As part of this Agreement two cabinet posts were allocated to the Liberal Democrats as members of a coalition government. After the 2003 election, Labour, with just 30 of the 60 seats, resolved to govern alone rather than enter into another coalition with the Liberal Democrats. In these circumstances party unity among the Government party, and hence support for executive measures, was almost guaranteed, yet, in practice, this marked little change from the pre-2003

TABLE 5.2 **Welsh National Assembly Election Results 1999 and 2003**

	Constituency MSPs				Regional list MSPs				Total MSPs			
	1999		2003		1999		2003		1999		2003	
	seats	% vote	seats	% vote	seats	% vote	seats	% vote	seats	% seats	seats	% seats
Labour	27	37.6	30	40.0	1	35.5	0	36.6	28	46.7	30	50.0
Plaid Cymru	9	28.4	5	21.2	8	30.6	7	19.7	17	28.3	12	20.0
Conservative	1	13.5	1	19.9	8	16.5	10	19.2	9	15.0	11	18.3
Lib Dem	3	14.2	3	14.1	3	12.5	3	12.7	6	10.0	6	10.0
Other	0	6.3	1	4.8	0	4.9	0	11.8	0	0.8	1	1.7
Total	40	100.0	40	100.0	20	100.0	20	100.0	60	100.0	60	100.0

position. Indeed, loyal support by coalition backbenchers for ministers was a characteristic feature of the first Assembly. As Bradbury and McGarvey (2003:224) noted, coalition Assembly Members (AMs) 'remained broadly loyal, voting as a block'.

National Assembly 'executive'

As in Scotland, civil servants working for the National Assembly and the Assembly Government (4,290 in 2004) remain members of the UK civil service subject to the Civil Service code (see chapter 4). Civil servants working for the Assembly Government have developed, however, a 'new administrative culture' following the creation of a stronger executive machine. One manifestation of the strengthened executive within the Assembly is the increased supervision of executive agencies in the principality. Pre-devolution, agencies led 'relatively autonomous lives' (Osmond 2003:19). Post-devolution, agencies responsible to the Assembly were redesignated 'assembly sponsored public bodies' (ASPBs) and became more 'corralled and disciplined, becoming more like state departments along Whitehall lines than free-standing, arm's length organisations' (Osmond 2003:19).

At the start of 2004 there were 15 executive and 18 advisory ASPBs and five tribunals (Richard Commission 2004:125). In July 2004, First Minister Rhodri Morgan announced that the Welsh Development Agency, the Wales Tourist Board, and the National Council for Education and Training for Wales would cease to be quangos by April 2006, and would be merged with their sponsor departments to become part of the Assembly administration. In November 2004, the First Minister announced further changes to be implemented by 2007. These included the merging of 12 advisory agricultural ASPBs into a single body, the transfer of the Welsh Language Board to the Welsh Assembly Government, the redesignation of the Ancient Monuments Board for Wales and the Historic Buildings Council for Wales as advisory panels within the Welsh Assembly Government, the merging of the strategy, policy and planning capabilities of several other quangos with those of the Welsh Assembly Government, and the abolition of Health Professions Wales.

The Richard Commission

The Richard Commission, as noted above, had been appointed in July 2002 to examine the adequacy of the National Assembly's powers and its electoral arrangements. When it reported in March 2004 it started from the premise that the status quo was not 'a sustainable basis for future development' (Richard Commission 2004:255). What was required, instead, was a new and distinctive model for a legislative assembly; but, in the interim, there should be a progressive transfer of delegated powers from Westminster to the Assembly in relation to devolved services. A corollary of the increase in legislative competencies would be the need for a formal distinction between the executive and the legislature in Cardiff and the replacement of the corporate body with two separate institutions (2004:258). A further consequence of increased legislative powers, in the Commission's opinion, would be the need to increase the Assembly's membership to 80, and the preferred option of the Commission was for the enlarged Assembly to be elected under the single transferable vote system. The hope of was that the new Assembly would be in place by 2011 (2004:261)

This hope looked a little forlorn, however, within a few months of the publication of the Commission's report. The initial response of the Secretary of State for Wales, Peter Hain, was that there was much 'food for thought' in the Commission's report, and that a formal response would be made after hearing from representations from the Welsh Assembly Government and after consultations with Welsh MPs and within Whitehall. But the Wales Secretary sought to make it 'crystal clear' that a referendum would be required on a Scottish model, and that any reform to the electoral system would have to be based upon maintaining the existing number of Welsh parliamentary constituencies (www.walesoffice.gov.uk/pn_20040331a.html). More worryingly for the Commission, the First Minister, Rhodri Morgan, began to question some of its fundamental proposals—the need for full legislative powers (*Western Mail* 26 June 2004:1), and the need for an enlarged Assembly (WNA Official Record 28 April 2004:30)—and so lengthened the odds against the implementation of the Commission's recommendations by 2011.

Local government in Wales

The creation of the National Assembly left existing local government structures and responsibilities in Wales untouched. Such was the importance of local government in Welsh politics generally, and in internal Labour party politics specifically (see Morgan and Mungham 2000:46), that the Government of Wales Act 1998 expressly required the Assembly 'to sustain and promote local government' (section 113(1)), and to establish a Partnership Council of representatives of the Assembly and local authorities to advise on local government matters (section 113(2)). This combination—of a National Assembly and a fully fledged system of local authorities—was very unusual in comparison with other devolved or federal systems. As Laffin et al (2002:4) point out: 'Federal countries like America, Canada and Australia combine strong state governments and weak local governments with few powers and functions. Such international comparisons underline the potential for ambiguity and dispute in post-devolution Wales'.

One possible dispute was over the extent to which the Assembly might encroach upon the functions of local authorities. Yet, the findings of research into relations between the National Assembly and local government in the first two years of devolution did not find that the former had 'crowded' Welsh policy space or reduced local discretion. If anything, 'post-devolution local discretion and autonomy had increased' (Laffin et al 2002:35). This view found further substantiation in the evidence of the Welsh Local Government Association to the Richard Commission: 'Since 1999 Assembly and local government relations have developed and prospered' (www.richard-commission.gov.uk/content/evidence/written/wlga/changes-e.htm). Yet, the room for policy discretion was ultimately limited by the fact that 'the Assembly has to work within the constraints of an England-and-Wales policy system' (Laffin et al 2002:35). New Labour's commitments—to modernize local government and to influence its internal structures and management, to impose externally audited regimes through 'Best Value', to enter into Local Public Service Agreements—had all been 'imported' into Wales through Westminster initiated legislation. In fact, Edwina Hart, the National Assembly Government's Minister for Finance, Local Government and Communities, acknowledged that in some areas of common England and Wales legislation, such as the Local Government Act 2000, there were 'deficiencies where the Assembly was only given partial powers or powers that did not reflect its wishes' (www.richardcommission.gov.uk/content/evidence/oral/ehart/index.htm).

Northern Ireland

Two basic points need to be made in preface to an examination of political institutions in Northern Ireland post-1999. The first is that the institutional arrangements specified in the Belfast Agreement of 1998 were far more detailed and 'jurified' (see Oliver 2003:265) than in other parts of the UK. This is a direct reflection of the need for precision in specifying procedures and powers to achieve power sharing—consociationalism—in a divided community. Second, Northern Ireland remains part of the UK and is subject to the parliamentary sovereignty of the UK parliament. History in the province since 1972 has revealed that just as devolution could be given it could also be taken away. Although not presaged in the Belfast Agreement, 'an alternative system of government under the Secretary of State for Northern Ireland [was] on stand-by in the Province' (Oliver 2003:265). This default option was triggered four times in the first two years of the Northern Ireland Assembly's existence (see below).

The Belfast Agreement

The Belfast Agreement (Cm 3883 1998) was signed by eight of the province's major nationalist and unionist parties on Good Friday, 10 April 1998. The Agreement's model of devolution was consociationalist in essence (a term popularized by Arend Lijphart (1977)). A consociation is an association of communities and is achieved on the basis of bargains reached by political leaders of ethnic or religious groups. The bargains are guided by the principles of cross-community executive power-sharing, proportionality rules throughout public sector organizations, community self-government, equality in cultural life, and veto rights for minorities (see O'Leary 2001:49). However, the Agreement also included a confederal element of cross-border agreements and institutions which linked Northern Ireland not only to the UK but also to the Republic of Ireland. This combination of consociationalist and confederal principles led some commentators to identify the Belfast Agreement as an example of 'consociationalism plus' (Wilford 2000:578). What is of importance for the present discussion is how these principles and values were translated into the design of the devolved institutions after 1999.

The Belfast Agreement was endorsed by referendums in both Northern Ireland and in the Republic of Ireland on 22 May 1998. The Northern

Ireland Act 1998 then translated the Agreement's major provisions into UK legislation. The institutions envisaged in the Agreement and incorporated in the Act reflected three interrelated strands that had formed the basis of UK governments' strategy since the early 1990s. The first was concerned with institutional arrangements within Northern Ireland; the second with 'north-south' cross-border institutional relations between Belfast and Dublin; and the third with 'east-west' relations between both parts of Ireland and the rest of the UK. The very interconnectedness of the three strands provided each party to the negotiations with the opportunity to accommodate concessions in one strand with gains in the others (see Wilford 1999:286).

Strand One: Northern Ireland Assembly

The impact of consociational theory was apparent in the design of the 108 Member Assembly. Members of the Legislative Assembly (MLAs) were elected under the highly proportional single transferable vote (STV) system. STV had been used in the Province in all elections, other than those for Westminster, since 1972. The principle of proportionality was carried through into the Assembly itself as the composition of the Executive Committee (cabinet), Assembly committees, and the allocation of committee chairs were determined in accordance with party strengths. The 'safeguards to ensure that all sections of the community [could] participate and work together' (Cm 3883 1998:section 5) also required qualified majority voting on 'key decisions'. These decisions included the election of the First Minister and Deputy First Minster, and, within the Assembly, its standing orders, budget and election of the Chair of the Assembly were to be determined on a 'cross-community basis' (Cm 3883 1998:section 5). Cross-community support was to be demonstrated and measured on the basis of each MLA having registered his or her party identity as a 'nationalist', 'unionist' or 'other'.

The Assembly was given the authority to pass primary legislation for devolved matters in devolved areas. As with the Scottish parliament, residual legislative competence was transferred to the Assembly with certain matters reserved to the UK parliament (NI Act 1998:Schedule 3). There was the possibility that at some future date any reserved matter could, with cross-community support, be transferred to the Assembly (NI Act 1998:section 4(2)). Unlike the Scotland Act, however, certain matters were deemed to be 'excepted' (Schedule 2). These included subjects that were 'reserved' in Scotland—such as the Crown, UK elections, international obligations, defence, nationality and immigration, and national security. There was no provision for excepted matters to be transferred to the Northern Ireland Assembly. A further distinctive feature of the NI Act was section 6(2e) which stated that a provision was outside the competence of the Assembly if 'it discriminates against any person or class of person on the ground of religious belief or political opinion'. The Assembly's competence did not extend either to matters that formed part of the law of a country other than Northern Ireland, or were incompatible with the Human Rights Act 1998, or with European Union legislation. Neither did the Assembly have the power to vary the rate of UK income tax.

In terms of the internal operation of the Assembly, standing orders were not to be made, amended, or repealed without cross-community support (section 41(2)). Under its standing orders, a Business Committee was established, which was chaired by the Presiding Officer and included members of all parties prepared to participate in committee work (the Northern Ireland Unionist party and the UK Unionist Party refused membership of the committees). Ten statutory/departmental committees were established to advise on the formulation of policy and to scrutinize legislation. They were also given the power to initiate legislation, though this power remained unused before the Assembly was suspended in October 2002. In practice, the Assembly's legislative procedures largely reflected those at Westminster with the notable addition of a 'consideration' stage in committee, and a 'further consideration' stage to allow for additional amendments to be proposed and examined after committee scrutiny. The average time to complete the legislative process was 16 weeks, and 21 bills were considered by the Assembly between December 1999 and the end of the session of 2001.

Six other 'standing' committees' were created under Standing Order 48 (Procedures, Business, Public Accounts, Standards and Privileges, Audit and 'the Centre'—the latter to monitor 13 specified areas covered by the Office of the First Minster and Deputy First Minister). The limited experience of the operation of the committee system tended to echo experience at Westminster, with the committees dominated by executive parties, with the agendas of departmental/statutory committees firmly structured by executive priorities (Wilford and Wilson 2003:106), and with ministers ignoring or rejecting committee recommendations 'with impunity' (Oliver 2003:270; see also Tonge 2005:140–1).

Northern Ireland executive

Section 16 of the Northern Ireland Act 1998 incorporated the principle of power sharing into the heart of the Executive. At the centre of the Executive, was what O'Leary (2001:52) called 'a novel dyarchy' of 'two quasi presidential figures'—the First Minister and the Deputy First Minister, who were elected and held office in tandem. Both had to stand for election together and to secure the support of a majority of the MLAs voting in the election, including a majority of the designated nationalists and a majority of the designated unionists. Both had identical powers. In effect this institutional design ensured that the top Executive posts were shared by a unionist and a nationalist (respectively David Trimble of the UUP and Seamus Mallon of the SDLP).

The posts were *quasi* presidential because neither the First nor the Deputy First Minister were empowered to choose the other ten ministers in the Executive Committee. The principle of proportionality was reflected in the choice of the other ministers on the basis of the d'Hondt rule (supplemented after July 1999 by the requirement that the Executive had at least three designated nationalists and three designated unionists). Ministers in accepting office were expected under their Pledge of Office to serve all the people equally, to promote equality and to prevent discrimination (Cm 3883 1998:Strand One Annex A). Significantly, the appointment of ministers did not require the endorsement of the Assembly. If they lost the confidence of the Assembly, however, the 1998 Act allowed for ministers to be removed if sufficient cross-community support was secured. Yet, the loss of confidence did not constitute ministerial responsibility in the sense conventionally accepted in Westminster or Holyrood or Cardiff. Confidence was lost if a minister was 'not committed to nonviolence and exclusively peaceful and democratic means'; or because of any failure to observe any other terms of the pledge of office (NI Act 1998 section 30(1)).

In terms of performance the Executive rarely appeared to act as a cohesive institution. In its early years its ministers were embroiled in a number of sectarian controversies over health and education provision and Tonge (2005:153) characterized the Executive as a 'non-congenial collective, neither cabinet nor coalition'. Indeed, Tonge (2005:150) summarizes the deficiencies of this institutional arrangement thus:

the lack of a formal system of government and opposition meant that scrutiny of executive action was confined largely to committees: it was difficult to remove incompetent ministers; ministers would play to the gallery of their party's MLAs; ministers in the executive did not support the interlinked institutions established under the Good Friday agreement (the DUP) or some institutions of the state (Sinn Féin, on policing); there was little sense of collective responsibility; and key financial decisions rested with Whitehall and Westminster.

Civic Forum

Paragraph 34 of the Belfast Agreement provided for a Civic Forum to be established. In turn, section 56 of the Northern Ireland Act required the First Minister and Deputy First Minister 'to make arrangements for obtaining from the Forum its views on social, economic and cultural matters'. When it was established, with the consent of the Assembly, it comprised 60 representatives from non-government organizations, business, agriculture, arts, churches and trade unions. According to Oliver (2003:271), 'it can be seen as an example of an institutionalized extra-parliamentary, and therefore non-party, deliberative democracy mechanism, which was regarded as necessary by those in favour because of expected shortcomings and exclusiveness of the Assembly and the executive'. Oliver then proceeds to note that the Forum 'experienced problems'. Some of these derived from the nature of sectarian politics in the Province, with members of the Orange Lodge complaining that the Lodge did not have formal representation; others were rooted more fundamentally in the very concept of 'consultative bodies' operating in conjunction with parliamentary assemblies (see Judge 1999:122–8). In the event, the Forum was short-lived, meeting for the first time in October 2000 and being suspended upon the resumption of direct rule two years later.

Strand Two: North-South institutions

If the Belfast Agreement was internally consociational, with its cross community executive power sharing, proportionality norms, recognition of community autonomy and equality and mutual veto rights, it was also externally confederal. O'Leary (2001:62) provides the stipulative definition that a confederation exists when 'political units voluntarily delegate powers and functions to bodies that exercise power across their jurisdictions'. The North-South Ministerial Council (NSMC), established under section 52 of the 1998 Act, constituted an explicit confederal institution. Modelled in part upon the European Union's Council of Ministers (see O'Leary 2001:63), the intention was to enable Ministers from both parts of Ireland to exercise considerable policy discretion in reaching cross-border decisions, while they still remained accountable to their respective domestic legislatures. Indeed, the EU impinged more directly on the work of the NSMC as one of the Council's responsibilities was to 'consider the European Union dimension of relevant matters, including the implementation of EU policies and programmes' and to ensure the appropriate representation of the Council's views at relevant EU meetings (Cm 3883 1998:Strand Two:para 17).

To enable the NSMC to operate, the Irish government had to amend the Irish constitution to allow the Council and its implementation bodies to exercise island-wide jurisdiction. Correspondingly, the UK government had to stretch the 'malleability' of parliamentary sovereignty to allow for the outputs of cross-border cooperation by two separate executives in Ireland to have effect within a part of the UK.

The fate of the NSMC was linked directly to that of the Assembly. The Belfast Agreement (Cm 3883 1998: Article 2(13)) stated that the Assembly and the Council were 'mutually interdependent, and that one cannot successfully function without the other'. What happened after the suspension of the Assembly in 2002 will be examined below, but, for now, the operation of the NSMC between December 1999 and October 2002 needs to be outlined.

Article 2(1) of the Belfast Agreement stipulates that the North/South Ministerial Council 'will bring together those with executive responsibilities in Northern Ireland and the Irish Government to develop consultation, co-operation and action within the island of Ireland—including through implementation on an all-island and cross-border basis—on matters of mutual interest and within the competence of each Administration, North and South'. The first meeting of the Council was held in December 1999 and was attended by the full Irish cabinet and by ten Ministers from Northern Ireland. Agreement was reached on the creation of six cross-border implementation bodies, and where they were to be located, as well as on an outline programme of work for discussion in sectoral meetings. The Council met four times in plenary format, while 60 sectoral meetings were held in the period up to October 2002. Twelve sectors were identified in the

Belfast Agreement for cooperation. In six sectors implementation bodies were established: Waterways Ireland; Food Safety Promotion Board; Trade and Business Development Body (InterTradeIreland); Special European Union Programmes Body; the Language Body; and the Foyle, Carlingford and Irish Lights Commission. These bodies employed some 600 directly recruited staff. The other six sectors—Agriculture, Education, Environment, Health, Tourism, and Transport—were designated 'Areas of Co-operation' in which common policies and approaches were agreed in the North-South Ministerial Council but implemented separately in each jurisdiction.

Although conceived in 'functional' terms the NSMC could not escape the intrusion of Northern Ireland's sectarian politics. From its inaugural meeting onwards ministers from the Democratic Unionist Party boycotted the Council's meetings, and, from late 2000 to October 2001, the First Minister refused to nominate Sinn Féin Ministers to attend its meetings (this was in protest at the slow progress made by the IRA towards arms decommissioning). Nonetheless, the Council in reviewing progress in June 2002 maintained that 'valuable work' was being performed by the sectoral bodies and looked forward to 'the delivery of further tangible benefits' (www.northsouthministerialcouncil.org/plenary/pm020628.htm). However, such benefits looked increasingly in doubt upon the suspension of the Northern Ireland Assembly a few months later. Given that the NSMC and the Assembly were supposedly 'mutually interdependent', Unionists were incensed when the UK and Irish governments agreed a new treaty in November 2002 to sustain the NSMC on a 'care and maintenance' basis and to allow its sectoral work to continue, for the jobs of its staff to be secured and for reappointments to the sectoral bodies to be made. What suspension of the Assembly did stall, however, was further consideration of a North-South Consultative Forum (an outline structure for which had been agreed in June 2002) and the development of a Joint Parliamentary Forum (as envisaged in Article 2(18) of the Belfast Agreement).

Strand Three: East-West institutions

A second confederal institution, the British-Irish Council (BIC) was established under section 52 of the Northern Ireland Act 1998. Membership of the BIC was to be drawn from representatives of the British and Irish Governments, devolved institutions in Northern Ireland, Scotland and Wales, and the Isle of Man and the Channel Islands (and eventually, if established, from devolved institutions in England). The stated purpose of the BIC was 'to promote the harmonious and mutually beneficial development of the totality of relationships among the peoples of these islands'. The inclusion of the BIC in the Agreement was to offer reassurance to the Ulster unionists and was designed to provide an institutional expression of East-West relations as a balance to the North-South arrangements of Strand Two (Walker 2001:130).

The BIC was conceived primarily as a mechanism to exchange information, discuss, consult and 'use best endeavours' to reach agreement on cooperation on matters of mutual interest. Suitable issues for early discussion in the BIC were identified as transport links, agricultural, environment, culture, health, education and the EU. The Council itself stressed its institutional uniqueness in that it is the only international forum in which the constituent subnational units of the British Isles participate.

The BIC meets in different formats, including at summit level and in specific sectoral format. By the end of 2004 the Council had convened six times at summit level. Specific sectoral meetings also focused on particular areas of policy. Ministerial meetings were held on Transport in December 2000 in Belfast, and on Environment in October 2000 in London, February 2002 in Edinburgh, and London in January 2003. Sectoral meetings were held on the misuse of drugs in Dublin in March 2002 and February 2003, and in Edinburgh in November 2004. What is apparent is that the BIC, which was created in large part to allay Ulster unionist sensitivities, has continued to operate without the direct representation of members from Northern Ireland after the suspension of the Northern Ireland Assembly.

England

It is no coincidence that Vernon Bogdanor's book *Devolution in the United Kingdom* has individual chapters on Scotland, Wales and Northern Ireland but England is dealt with in a few pages under the chapter subheading of 'The English Dimension' (1999a:264–76). This was despite Bogdanor's acknowledgement that: 'England is, in many respects, the key to the success of devolution' (Bogdanor 1999a:264). While this verdict might be true in the long-term, in the short-term, as already noted earlier in this chapter, the key to the successful implementation of devolution legislation immediately after 1997 was the avoidance of the 'English question' by focusing upon those nations and sub-nations that actively sought, and had historical claims to, devolution. Under Labour, devolution was for the 'converted' and not for the politically agnostic or the plain disinterested. While the Labour government subsequently sustained criticisms that: '[c]hanges to the territorial management of the United Kingdom were thus made as much in terms of pragmatic political adjustment as of a logical constitutional settlement' (Peele 2003:204; see also Johnson 2001:339–40; Forman 2002:366–7), nonetheless, the very expediency of its proposals allowed it to initiate its devolution programme *precisely* because it avoided detailed discussion of an overarching scheme for the UK as a whole.

Unlike Scotland, Wales and Northern Ireland, England and its regions have not had a Secretary of State or a designated English Office in Whitehall to represent its territorial interests. Nor have there been distinct English committees at Westminster to parallel the territorial parliamentary committees for Scotland, Wales and Northern Ireland. Nor for that matter did Westminster enact specific English legislation pertaining only to England and its regions. In part this reflected an unconscious blurring of the identities 'Englishness' and 'Britishness', and an unthinking acceptance that the ties that bound the UK state together were functional issues and common economic and social concerns (see Bogdanor 2003:232). Certainly issues of service provision structured discourse about locality and regionalism in England far more than notions of regional identity. Key state services—health, employment, social security, environment, law and protective services, and tax collection—traditionally have been organized and administered on a regional basis while still being accountable to central departments and ministers located in Whitehall. The key to understanding English regional structures according to Hogwood (1996a:1) is that:

> they are primarily concerned not with the management of *territory* but with the delivery of *functions*. . . . The use of regional or other territorial administrative units at one or more levels is . . . an administrative convenience to enable certain tasks to be carried out rather than being primarily concerned about the distinctive features of each or some general view about having a 'regional tier'.

Before 1997 much debate about English regions had been devoted to identifying the most logical boundaries within which to provide services. That such boundaries were essentially artificial constructs resulted in a plethora of cross-cutting and overlapping boundaries which made the identification of unambiguous regions difficult to discern. While there were a number of regionally based institutions—outposts of central departments or executive agencies or NDPBs—there were no common boundaries and no regional government institutions in their own right in England until the creation of ten Government Offices for the Regions (GOs) in 1994.

The Government Offices were designed to integrate the regional activities of four major central departments—then entitled, Environment, Trade and Industry, Transport, and Employment. The new integrated offices administered a single budget for urban regeneration and development and assumed responsibility for programmes formerly operated by the individual departments. They were designed as a single point of contact for local councils and economic and social interests to access central government departments. As such they did not provide services directly, but were concerned primarily with nationally determined distributive policies and their implementation. 'Crucially', as Hogwood (1996b:31 original emphasis) noted at the time, GOs would 'continue to be regarded as offices of *central* government'. Even then, many major aspects of the regional activities of central government remained beyond the coordination of the GOs. Indeed, even within the four constituent departments their respective Next Steps agencies did not come under the auspices of the GOs, with each agency retaining the right to determine its own regional organization (Hogwood 1996a: 22–3). Similarly the regional offices of major NDPBs were not included. Moreover, at the same time as regional Government Offices were being established the abolition of distinct Regional Health Authorities was under way. The culmination of successive restructuring exercises within the NHS immediately before 1997 was an increase in central control and direction as Regional Health Authorities were replaced by regional offices of the Department of Health (see Greenwood et al 2002:206–7).

English regions post-1997

Under the Conservative government before 1997 the emphasis of the Government Offices of the Regions was clearly upon effecting central control through regional coordination rather than enabling regional control or accountability. As the Performance and Innovation Unit's report *Reaching*

Out: The Role of Central Government at Regional and Local Level (PIU 2000b:AB3) noted: 'The degree of policy control by parent Departments over GOs is generally tight with GOs regarded as the delivery arm'. Formal accountability of the Government Offices and their regional directors remained unambiguously in Whitehall. While the creation of GOs did strengthen interdepartmental coordination at the centre (Hogwood 1996a:28), there was no inherent logic leading either in the direction of the creation of an English Department of the Regions, or for that matter in the direction of regionally elected assemblies to oversee the activities of GOs.

The simple, but crucial, point made repeatedly by Hogwood (1996a;1–2; 1996b:30) was that the regional administrative structures in place before 1997 were not concerned in essence with the management of territory but with the delivery of functions. Moreover, there was no single 'regional tier' as such upon which democratic accountability could be focused, but, rather, a diversity of structures, roles and boundaries (some 100 were identified by Hogwood (1996b:30)).

In the absence of a strong tradition of regional government in England, and for that matter the historic absence of elected regional representative institutions, the Labour party in opposition after 1979 scoured relatively virgin territory to construct a case for English democratic regional government. Although 'instinctively sympathetic to regional devolution in England' (Bogdanor 1999a:272), New Labour in its election pledges and in its first term of office promoted two distinct visions of what English regionalism entailed. The first was what Oliver (2003:282–3) terms a 'bottom up process' of establishing regional chambers or assemblies (see below). The second envisaged 'top-down decentralising arrangements' and was driven by the substantive policy objective of promoting economic development and regeneration in the English regions. In this view what was required was nationally determined regional policy (Tomaney and Hetherington 2003:53) or, in the Government's own words, was to provide regions with the capacity to make judgements on their 'needs and priorities within a national framework' (Cm 5511 2003:para 1.24). The institutional manifestation of this view came with the creation of eight Regional Development Agencies (RDAs) under the Regional Development Agencies Act 1998 (a London Development Agency was subsequently established in 2000 (see below)).

Regional Development Agencies

Regional Development Agencies are NDPBs that work within the bound-aries of the Government Offices of the Regions. Their Boards are appoin-ted and are directly accountable to ministers in Whitehall. Each RDA has a chair and between eight and 15 members, who are collectively charged with furthering the economic development and the regeneration of the re-gion; as well as promoting business efficiency, investment and competit-iveness; and employment. RDAs also have a statutory duty to formulate a regional strategy. Significantly the government emphasized its pleasure that 50 per cent of board members, appointed for the second three-year term between 2001 and 2004, had 'current or recent business experience' (House of Commons Research Paper 2002:14). The government underlined its sup-port for these business-led partnership bodies by increasing their funding in the 2000, 2002 and 2004 spending reviews (to a projected collective an-nual budget of £2.3 billion in 2007–08). Moreover, from April 2002, RDAs were allowed to allocate these extra resources flexibly to promote the prior-ities identified in their regional strategies. Monitoring of RDA performance is undertaken by the Government Offices. In turn, in spring 2000, the activ-ities of the GOs were themselves brought under the management of the Re-gional Coordination Unit (RCU). The RCU describes itself as the 'corporate centre' of the GOs and regional policy networks (www.rcu.gov.uk)).

Regional Assemblies

Included in the Regional Development Agencies Act 1998 was provision for the creation of Regional Chambers. Section 18 of the Act conceived of a scrutiny role whereby RDAs would provide information to, and answer questions from, representatives of regional interests. These were conceived as 'voluntary, multi-party, regional chambers' with their members drawn from local authorities, and representatives from 'the social, economic, and environmental sectors in the region' (Cm 5511 2002:para 2.14). Although 'voluntary', Chambers were established rapidly in all eight RDA regions, and soon styled themselves 'Assemblies'. They were not directly elected, though over two thirds of their members indirectly represented local au-thorities (Tomaney 2001a:117). Their core funding was provided by local au-thorities, though from March 2001 central government provided £15 million to promote their activities over a three-year period.

From the outset Regional Assemblies were open to the accusation that they were a 'wishy-washy attempt to provide English RDAs with a modicum of democratic oversight and accountability inside the territorial boundaries within which they operate' (Forman 2002:126). Their 'insipidness' was not helped by the fact that these were largely artificial boundaries that attracted little, and varying, sense of regional identity. Indeed, Hogwood (1996b:33) had noted earlier the irony of attempting to represent 'regional' opinion in Chambers based on boundaries 'devised by central government for its own purposes'.

More positively, Oliver (2003:283) credited the Labour government with a desire to encourage the articulation of regional interests through a 'bottom-up' process of democratization (see above). While the extent to which centrally designated Chambers initially constituted a bottom-up process is open to debate, nonetheless, once established, the 'Chambers have proved the adage that a tier of government with no function will go out and find one' (Sandford 2002:792). The function they found was to develop regional networks where none existed before. In which case the 'small-scale policy shifts' made by RDAs in response to concerns articulated in the Chambers were not the best measure of their accomplishments, for, as the government argued: 'the chambers have a meaningful role beyond scrutinising the work of their regional Development Agencies' (Cm 5511 2002:para 2.16).

This role—of 'joining up' a large number of 'partnerships', 'stakeholders', 'social and environmental partners', 'agencies', 'government offices', and of identifying an 'overarching regional strategy' (Cm 5511 2002:para 4.12) and securing its implementation—was to be developed formally in the government's proposals for the transformation of the voluntary Chambers into elected Regional Assemblies.

Elected regional assemblies

In May 2003 The Regional Assemblies (Preparation) Act received Royal Assent. The Act fulfilled the commitment in the regional governance White Paper (Cm 5511 2002) to allow each of the English regions to establish an elected assembly, if approved in a referendum. Once at least one region had voted for an elected assembly, the government intended to introduce a further Bill to enable assemblies to be set up. The first referendum was expected to be held in Autumn 2004 at the earliest. Section 13(2) of the 2003 Act required the government to ascertain the level of interest in a region in holding a referendum. To help the Deputy Prime Minister (who was deemed responsible for determining the level of interest) a 'soundings exercise' was conducted and the results were published in June 2003 in the report *Your Regions, Your Say* (ODPM 2003). What became apparent was what was already known: support for regional devolution was patchy. Only three regions—the North East, North West, and Yorkshire and the Humber—recorded more than a 50 per cent response in favour of a referendum. On this basis, the Deputy Prime Minister announced that before referendums were held in these three regions a review of local government would be conducted. This reflected the conclusion of the White Paper *Your Region, Your Choice* that elected regional assemblies should be established in tandem with the introduction of a 'wholly unitary local government structure' in that area (Cm 5511 2002:para 9.6). Thus, although regional assemblies were to derive most of their functions from those currently exercised by central departments, a single tier of local government would help both to clarify which elected body was responsible for which functions, and to simplify relations between elected councils and elected assemblies.

The proposed assemblies were to be based on the existing administrative boundaries used by the Government Offices and Regional Development Agencies. There would be between 25 and 35 members, depending upon the population of a region. Assembly members would be elected under the Additional Member System (AMS). A leader and cabinet of up to six members would constitute an executive and would be chosen by, and be fully accountable to, the full assembly. Scrutiny committees should be established to probe specific policy areas and to hold the assembly executive to account. In addition, the government was 'very keen' that key regional stakeholders (from business, trade unions, voluntary organizations and environmental groups) should be involved directly in the work of the assemblies (Cm 5511 2002:paras 7.8–7.9). Equally, indirect modes of participation, through 'some form of consultative/partnership forum' (Cm 5511 2002:para 7.9), were also to be contemplated. The assemblies would be funded primarily through a single government grant, though they would also be able to raise additional funds through the council tax.

Despite the continuing commitment of the Labour government, or more particularly the Deputy Prime Minister, to the cause of regional devolution, only one referendum was ultimately held in November 2004. In an all-postal ballot on 4 November in the North East the vote was overwhelmingly against the creation of a regional assembly (78 per cent against in a 49 per cent turnout). The other two referendums, in the North West, and Yorkshire and Humberside, had been postponed in July 2004. These postponements had been confirmed in September by the Minister for Local and Regional Government, Nick Raynsford (HC Debates 13 September 2004: vol 424, col 988).

London

In making proposals for elected regional assemblies the Labour government drew directly upon experience in London where, in May 2000, elections had been held for the Greater London Authority (GLA) consisting of a Mayor and Assembly (Cm 5511 2002:para 3.11). Indeed, the extent to which the experience of the GLA was invoked (along with experience in Scotland and Wales) in making the case for elected regional assemblies can be gauged from Box 5.1.

BOX 5.1   *Your Region, Your Choice* **(Cm 5511 2002)**

4.22   The Regional Development Agencies will become directly accountable to the relevant elected assembly. . . . as in London.

4.46   The role of elected regional assemblies on public health will reflect that of the GLA in London.

5.7   The simplest means for an elected assembly to raise money from people within its region is a precept on the council tax. This is the means by which the Greater London Authority can raise additional funds.

6.11   The Government proposes to adopt the Additional Member System (AMS) for regional assembly elections. This system is already used for elections to . . . the Greater London Assembly.

7.3   The Government believes that there should be a split between the executive and scrutiny functions within an elected assembly [as characterised by] . . . the Greater London Authority.

7.7   The Government proposes that assemblies should have between 25 and 35 members. . . . this size would be consistent with the Greater London Authority, which has 25 elected members in its assembly.

7.9   . . . stakeholders might be involved directly in the work of regional assemblies . . . in some form of consultative/partnership forum or sounding board [such as] the London Civic Forum [whose] aim is to engage the capital's civic society in the new governance of London through democratic

continues

Box 5.1 continued

> debate and effective consultation with the Mayor and the Greater London Assembly.
>
> 9.1 The Government's Manifesto said that provision should be made for directly elected regional government to go ahead in regions where people decided in a referendum to support it. That is how we determined whether there was popular support for ... a Greater London Authority.
>
> 9.6 ... We have therefore concluded that in any region where an elected assembly is established, there should be an associated move to a wholly unitary local government structure. There are clear precedents for such a structure ... London [has a] wholly unitary structure of local government.

While the GLA provided a partial template for elected regional government in the rest of the England, there were also several unique provisions of the GLA Act 1999 that limited potential 'policy learning' from its experience. The first was the unique institutional position of a directly elected Mayor—for a single constituency of 'Greater London' with its population of 7.3 million and over 5 million electors. When the 1999 Act was passed the London Mayor became the first directly elected local executive in the UK. (After the Local Government Act 2000 a further eleven mayors were elected in English local authorities). The London Mayor was empowered to set and control the £4.7 billion budget (in 2002 prices) for the GLA. The Mayor was also charged with the formal determination of policies in four key functional areas. Four boards—the London Development Agency, Transport for London, the London Fire and Emergency Planning Authority, and the London Metropolitan Police Authority—administer these functions. Most board members are appointed by the Mayor. In addition, the Mayor has responsibilities for environment, culture, public health, media and sport, and inward investment, as well as a legal requirement to produce a number of strategies.

The position of the London Mayor is also unique in that, although in possession of executive powers, the staff responsible for the delivery of mayoral policies and budget decisions—the Chief Executive and Authority officials—are appointed by the Assembly. In no other elected governmental institution in the UK does the legislative/scrutiny institution make key executive/administrative appointments (Travers 2002:784). In these circumstances, therefore, it was of little surprise that the GLA in its first 18 months was preoccupied with making appointments and establishing new officer structures. Unlike the new administrations in Scotland and Wales which inherited the accumulated experience of pre-existing departments, there were no direct, continuous institutional structures upon which the GLA could draw. Moreover, the system of governance that immediately pre-dated the GLA was renowned for being 'highly complex; [and] characterized by a proliferation of institutions and partnerships operating in the absence of any strategic coordination and with limited democratic accountability' (Syrett and Baldock 2003:73). While the founding logic of the GLA was rooted in 'joined-up' strategic vision and action, the sheer complexity and crowdedness of the institutional landscape (with some 500 organizations involved in the funding, management and delivery of economic development and regeneration alone in 2000) impeded the production of coherent London-wide policy programmes.

Institutional complexity has thus been the hallmark of London government post-1997. Travers (2002:787) points out that there are in effect four different kinds of governmental institutions: central government departments, government appointed boards, local authorities, and the GLA itself (see also Sweeting 2002:13–15). Indeed, an inbuilt dynamic in the design process has been discerned whereby central departments and local authorities simultaneously resisted conceding significant powers or service delivery to the GLA (see Tomaney 2001b:228–30; Travers 2002:781,787; Syrett and Baldock 2003:81). The resultant institutional configuration in London can thus be explained, in historical institutionalist terminology, in the following manner:

> The evolution of London's current system of network governance out of past practice illustrates the interrelationship between the formal and informal institutional environment and how particular institutional arrangements arise at particular historical and geographical junctures. The evolutionary and path-dependent nature of change is evident in a number of respects, not least the long-standing local-central opposition between a highly centralized state and powerful world city. (Syrett and Baldock 2003:81)

England at Westminster

Although charged by its nationalist detractors as being the 'English parliament' Westminster still remains the parliament of the UK as a whole.

Ironically, while its procedures have been altered to accommodate devolution in Scotland, Wales and, intermittently, in Northern Ireland, the procedures of the House of Commons remain basically unaltered as far as England is concerned. At the inception of devolution much was made of the 'English dimension' and the potential problems that asymmetrical devolution would import into Westminster (see HC 460 1998:para 47–53). The danger was that England would be treated as an unequal partner in a union parliament of equal parts. As the then leader of the Conservative party, William Hague, argued in July 1999:

> the real loser from Labour's chaotic approach to the constitution is England. The people of England now find themselves governed by political institutions that are manifestly unfair to them. First, the English are under-represented in parliament; . . . second the English do not have an exclusive say over English laws. (Hague 1999)

The second unfairness related directly to the 'West Lothian Question'. This question had been posed by Scottish Labour MP Tam Dalyell, who represented the then constituency of West Lothian, and who remorselessly pointed to the fact that after devolution Scottish MPs at Westminster would no longer be able to vote on Scottish domestic policies but would still be able to vote on English domestic policies. In addition, it would be possible for a future Labour government to legislate successfully on English domestic matters on the strength of support from MPs from Scotland (see Judge 1999:187–90). The immediate response of the Labour government after 1999 was that the best answer was to stop asking the question. Indeed, for the most part, the question receded in the minds of most MPs until May 2003 when a vote to introduce foundation hospitals in England was decisively influenced by Scottish Labour MPs who off-set the effect of a rebellion by 65 other Labour Members. The question reverberated more loudly in January 2004 when the Higher Education Bill was approved at its second reading with only a majority of five. 72 Labour MPs voted against the government making it the largest revolt on domestic legislation since 1997. Significantly, 46, of 55, Scottish Labour MPs voted in favour. On such occasions, the Opposition was quick to point out that: 'The Government were effectively bailed out . . . by Scottish Labour Members voting on an English matter' (HC Debates 8 May 2003:col 838). Equally, on these occasions, the government maintained that the West Lothian Question remained a 'non-issue' (*The Times* 27 February 2004:2), and that it intended to do nothing about this anomaly: 'The last thing that we want is the creation of three or four categories of Members with different rights according to the level of devolution that has been given to their areas' (HC Debates 8 May 2003:col 838).

If the West Lothian Question remained unanswered (and some argued that it was unanswerable anyway (see Bogdanor 1999a:232)), so too was the issue of introducing distinct procedures for processing 'English' legislation. The government was generally dismissive of proposals to allow English MPs to deal with 'English' bills, in large part on the grounds that there was no such thing as exclusively English legislation (see HC 814 1999:para 8; Hazell 2001:275). Recognition of an 'English dimension' came, however, in May 2001 with the reincarnation of a Regional Affairs Committee. A standing Committee on Regional Affairs had been in existence since 1975, but had met on only 13 occasions before 2001. In its initial guise, all English MPs were entitled to attend meetings of the standing committee, but after changes to its standing orders in 2000 a core membership of 13 English MPs was stipulated. The Committee met on seven occasions between May 2001 and June 2004; but such a parliamentary device hardly constituted 'the use of Westminster as a proxy for an English parliament' (Sandford 2002:790).

Generally, as Lodge et al (2004:193) note, 'the impact of devolution on Westminster remains minimal' and that Westminster continued to look 'much the same as it did before devolution' (see also Gay 2003:173). In essence this means that exclusively 'English' procedures and processes remain undeveloped, while Scotland, Wales and Northern Ireland retain their distinct Select Committees and Grand Committees and each still has a designated question time in the Commons. If the expectation was that procedures in Westminster for Scotland, Wales and Northern Ireland would be labelled 'devolution minus'—'minus' territorial committees, swathes of specific legislation, and many parliamentary questions—the practice is 'devolution plus'. Only with regard to England does a position of 'devolution minus' pertain in Westminster—'minus' exclusive English committees, legislative procedures, and deliberative forums.

While proposals to create 'devolution plus' in England, through the creation of a parliament for England, have been proposed they have tended also to be just as rapidly dismissed (for details see Forman 2002:123–5). In essence, such proposals seek to resolve the 'problem of England' by redressing the asymmetry of the post-1999 devolution settlement with an institutional symmetry in the form of four devolved parliaments for each of the constituent territories of the UK. If the logic is simple it is also warped. Asymmetry would continue to underpin such schemes for parliamentary symmetry. One parliament would continue to represent some 83 per cent of the total UK population, and this English parliament 'would inevitably compete with Westminster itself' (Sandford 2002:791). In which case, it would 'not resolve the problem to which devolution is the answer' (Bogdanor 1999a:268). The answer, according to the Labour government at least, has been more devolution—but to English regions (see above).

Conclusion

If the institutional structure of territorial management in the UK before 1999 was relatively simple, the position post-1999 is remarkably complex. This complexity stems not simply from a quantitative increase in the number of new institutions but also from a qualitative change in interinstitutional interaction.

The new institutions include sub-national parliaments and assemblies; sub-national executives, regional development agencies, regional assemblies, elected local mayors, a Greater London Authority, as well the new central departments in Whitehall—the Office of the Deputy Prime Minister and the Department of Constitutional Affairs both with major 'territorial' roles. The sheer scale of institutional innovation is impressive in its own right, but equally noteworthy is an inherent dynamic for further, and seemingly perpetual, institutional change.

While some analysts wish to argue that this dynamic is a conscious strategy built into the design of the new territorial institutions (see Stoker 2002), others are concerned that 'little or no effort has been made to think in a consistent and connected way about the case for decentralizing powers' (Johnson 2001:341). This debate will be revisited in chapter 7 but, here, all that is required to note is the specificity and contingency of institutional design on the one hand, and the uncertain and almost random institutional consequences stemming from the initial design process on the other.

The designs were specific insofar as there were three discrete devolution settlements, one each for Scotland, Wales and Northern Ireland, and an, as of yet, unspecified number of regional settlements in England. Similarly, the creation of the GLA with its elected Mayor was a 'one-off' design, but with explicit capacity for spill-over into elected city mayors and into regional assemblies elsewhere in the UK. Each design was contingent upon the historical institutional legacies and political imperatives pertaining in each periphery. In this sense there was no overarching or all encompassing blueprint covering the whole of the UK. While accepting that there was no UK-wide institutional plan (and without making a judgement at this stage as to whether this constituted a 'failing' on the part of the Labour government), nonetheless, there are manifest deficiencies with the designs of the territorial institutions and these 'problems' have been acknowledged by the institutions themselves. Thus, for example, the National Assembly of Wales had occasion to review its procedures after the first year of operation and made 45 recommendations in order to rectify the anomalies of a 'body corporate'. Rectification came in the form of a divorce of the executive from the legislature and the importation of Westminster-type relations. As the Presiding Officer of the Assembly noted:

> The National Assembly was not designed to replicate the conventional West-minster model of a relatively clear divide between legislature and executive. . . . [Yet] to all intents and purposes . . . we have transformed ourselves into as much of a simulacrum of the conventional Westminster model as the constraints of the Government of Wales Act allow us. (HL 147 2002, Memorandum, Lord Elis-Thomas)

Moreover, concern at the 'fundamental flaws' of the Wales Act 1998 contributed directly to the creation of the Richard Commission to examine the powers and electoral arrangements of the Assembly. When asked about the confusion of powers under the 1998 Act the Presiding Officer remarked that: 'My short answer to that is anything is better than what we have got' (HL 147 2002:Q 919).

Similarly the Scottish parliament felt the need to review its procedures in light of the experience of its first term. The Procedures Committee's report (SP 818 2003) produced 135 recommendations aimed at aligning the practice of the parliament to the principles outlined in the CSG's institutional design. Even then the Committee maintained that a further 'roots and branch' review was necessary to address 'a number of fundamental points . . . about pressures in our legislative procedures' (Recommendation 37). Moreover, former Presiding Officer Sir David Steel, when reflecting upon the experience of the first parliament, was moved to recommend fundamental reforms to the system of legislative scrutiny, financial powers, and the electoral system which he argued had been an 'expensive mistake' (quoted in *The Times* 19 August 2003). In turn these observations echoed some of the 'flaws' and 'problems' identified by the Scottish Affairs Select Committee (HC 460 1998) even before the inception of the Scottish parliament.

If deficiencies were apparent within the devolved parliaments in Scotland and Wales then parallel doubts were expressed about the reformed institutional structure of London government. After only a year in operation, Assembly members announced their intention to review the GLA model in light of their dissatisfaction with the new institutional structure (Tomaney 2001b:246). Certainly, imposing new institutions onto a 'preexisting complex and fragmented institutional landscape' (Syrett and Baldock 2003:77) simply contributed to the complexity of interinstitutional relations in the capital.

More generally, interinstitutional relations have become a major feature of territorial management in the UK. As the Lords' Committee on the Constitution (HL 28 2002:11) pointed out, devolution 'makes intergovernmental relations inevitable, and integral to the UK's system of government'. New institutions such as the Joint Ministerial Committee, the British-Irish Council, the North-South Ministerial Council in Ireland, and, within Whitehall, the creation of a Department of Constitutional Affairs and the Office of the Deputy Prime Minister, all indicate the importance of coordinating the activities of territorial institutions. Equally importantly, a number of informal mechanisms and procedures—concordats, agreements in specific policy areas, bilateral meetings, and informal contacts—have had to be devised to provide a framework for interinstitutional cooperation. Overall, what struck the Lords' Committee (HL 28 2002:para 6) when reviewing post-1999 developments in the UK was the complexity and intricacy of interinstitutional relations in a system of asymmetric devolution.

KEY TERMS

- additional member electoral system
- administrative devolution
- asymmetric devolution
- Belfast Agreement
- confederal
- consociationalism
- corporate body
- English dimension
- local government
- multi-national state
- new politics

- quasi-legislative devolution
- regional assemblies
- regional government
- reserved matters
- Scottish civil society
- sub-national legislatures
- territorial representation
- union state
- unitary state
- *ultra vires*
- West Lothian Question

GUIDE TO FURTHER READING

BOGDANOR, V. (1999) *Devolution in the UK*, (Oxford, Oxford University Press).

An accessible introduction to the history of devolution and its contemporary importance in the UK.

TRENCH, A. (ed) (2004) *Has Devolution Made a Difference? The State of the Nations 2004* (Exeter) (Imprint Academic).

A collection of essays reflecting upon the experience of the first four years of devolution throughout the UK.

MITCHELL, J. (2003) *Governing Scotland*, (London, Palgrave).

A detailed exploration of the origins and development of the Scottish Office which

engages with wider debates about Scotland's position within the UK's union state.

TONGE, J. (2005) *The New Northern Irish Politics* (London, Palgrave Macmillan).

A sanguine analysis of institutional change since the Good Friday Agreement rooted firmly within a wider critical debate about a 'new politics' in Northern Ireland.

WILSON, D. and GAME, C. (2002) *Local Government in the United Kingdom* (3rd edn.), (London, Palgrave).

An accessible textbook which provides a comprehensive overview of the major institutional and political dimensions of local government.

6

Judicial and Regulatory Institutions

Overview

Within any political system there exist a series of public institutions with responsibilities for the oversight and regulation of 'political' institutions. In most political systems the judiciary has served as a key regulator of the activities of political institutions. Indeed, from the 1990s onwards, interinstitutional interactions in the UK became more judicialized. Moreover, in addition to the increase in 'hard law' regulation and judicial review of the activities of political institutions, other forms of regulation have developed in recent decades. The extent of this development is such that some commentators now believe that the UK can be characterized as a new 'regulatory state'. At the same time, traditional notions of public accountability through parliament have come under challenge from a seemingly exponential growth of demands for 'inquiries' into the activities of government in the 21st century.

This chapter starts with an examination of the related concepts of a 'separation of powers' and 'judicial independence' and notes that in the UK, as in all liberal democracies, complete separation across three main dimensions—functions, institutions and personnel—has never been achieved in practice. The interconnectedness of the three branches of government in the UK—the legislative, executive and judicial—is illustrated in relation to the Human Rights Act, devolution, the growth of judicial review, regulation, inquiries, and other institutional processes of citizen redress and accountability.

Introduction

The preceding chapters have had as their focus institutions that are explicitly 'political'—insofar as they are directly concerned with the formulation, implementation and delivery of public policies and programmes. Yet, within any political system there exist a series of other public institutions with responsibilities for the oversight, regulation, and resolution of disputes concerning aspects of the working procedures and outputs of 'political' institutions. Clearly, a rigid demarcation does not exist between policy making, implementation, oversight and adjudication. Thus, for example, one of the classic functions of legislatures has been 'oversight'—through the control and scrutiny of executive institutions and the redress of misdemeanours and maladministration. Similarly, executives have their own internal mechanisms of control, coordination and oversight to regulate the activities of state officials and to cultivate 'appropriate behaviour' in accordance with both internal norms and the values of the broader political culture. Yet, it is the third so-called 'branch of government'—the judiciary—that has historically fulfilled the role of the interpretation and adjudication of the policies and actions of the legislative and executive branches of government. The judiciary has served in most political systems as a key regulator of the activities of political institutions. Undoubtedly, the law has provided the fundamental framework for the conduct of much political activity in the United Kingdom. In the words of Harlow and Rawlings (1997:67) the law has acted both as a 'green light' to empower governments and as a 'red light' to control executive actions.

From the outset of this chapter, therefore, it has to be acknowledged that there is no rigid and unambiguous distinction between the roles performed by 'political' and 'judicial' institutions. Traditionally the institutional norms associated with the 'Westminster model'—particularly those derived from the notion of parliamentary sovereignty—served to delimit the relationships between the legislature, executive and judiciary in the UK. Interinstitutional interactions between the courts and political institutions have been guided by, what Oliver (2003:19) terms as, 'comity' and the recognition of reciprocal conventions, understandings and sensitivities. While 'comity' emphasized the independence and partisan neutrality of the judiciary, it also reflected the subordinate institutional status of the courts.

What became increasingly apparent from the 1990s onwards, however, was that interinstitutional interactions were becoming more judicialized—as political processes and decisions became increasingly subject to regulation by 'hard law' enforceable in the courts. In fact, two decades earlier, accession to the European Community had changed fundamentally the relationship between the courts, executive and parliament by enabling UK courts to review the compatibility of UK legislation with 'superior' EU law. The challenge posed to the concept of parliamentary sovereignty was both profound and contested (see Loveland 2003:358–423). Similarly, the Scotland, Wales, and Northern Ireland Acts, and the Human Rights Act passed in 1998 all posed further challenges to the notion of parliamentary sovereignty and impacted upon the relations between the courts and political institutions. These Acts gave the courts jurisdication to enforce the provisions in statutes, and so to subject political decisions and some aspects of interinstitutional interactions to court-enforced legal regulation.

In addition to the increase in 'hard law' regulation and judicial review of the activities of political institutions, other forms of regulation have developed in recent decades. The extent of this development is such that some commentators now believe that the UK can be characterized as a new 'regulatory state' (see Moran 2003:4–5). Importantly, for present purposes, the growth in regulatory institutions has been identified as a further challenge to the institutional prescriptions of the Westminster model. Equally, however, as will be seen later in this chapter, the form and working of regulatory institutions has also been influenced by those very prescriptions.

Judicial and political institutions

Most discussions of the relationship between judicial and political institutions start from an examination of the related concepts of a 'separation of powers' and 'judicial independence' (for comparative examples see Elgie 2003:178; Schmidt 2003:107). In the UK a contrast is often drawn with the separation of powers incorporated in the written constitutions of the United States and France, and, in turn, a recognition is then made of the different meanings ascribed to the concept of 'separation' in both countries (see Bradley and Ewing 2003:82–4).

Three different dimensions of 'separation' are normally identified: a separation of functions, institutions, and personnel (see Le Sueur and Sunkin 1997:41; Bradley and Ewing 2003:84). Taking each of these dimensions in turn: first, three basic functions—of legislation, execution and adjudication—can be discerned in any political system, irrespective of whether they are performed by separate institutions or institutional actors. Second, institutions can be categorized as legislative, executive or judicial in accordance with the roles performed, but a normative prescription is usually made that there *should* be a diffusion of state power amongst these three institutional categories. Third, in terms of personnel, 'separation' means that each institution has a distinct membership, and, normally, a prescription—that there should not be overlapping membership—accompanies this notion of separation.

While conceptions of a separation of powers have proved influential in the institutional designs, or eventual institutional configurations, of all liberal democracies, complete separation across all three dimensions—functions, institutions and personnel—has never been achieved in practice. Certainly in the case of the UK, and as noted in preceding chapters, there is at best an asymmetrical separation of institutions and personnel. In practice, there is an extensive overlap of functions and personnel between the legislature and the political executive. There is also an overlap of personnel between the judiciary, executive and legislature, with the head of the judiciary, the Lord Chancellor, serving as a member of the cabinet as well as a member of the upper chamber (along with thirty or so leading members of the judiciary who sit as Lords of Appeal). Equally, although the concept of parliamentary sovereignty prescribes that parliament (and the executive therein) has exclusive legislative power, judicial decisions have proved 'important as a source of law on matters where the government is unwilling to ask Parliament to legislate' (Bradley and Ewing 2003:88). As Johnson (1999: 59) observes, 'for the tidy-minded' this asymmetrical differentiation 'might appear to be a strange mix-up', but there is in fact a sharper separation between the judiciary and executive and legislative branches than a too narrow focus 'on the points at which they intersect' would suggest.

Indeed, judicial independence has been a fundamental constitutional precept since 1688. In its modern formulation it means 'independence from any direct or indirect interference or influence by the Executive' (Hobhouse 2003:D.1). However, the very appointment procedures for judicial posts would seem to infringe the notion of independence. The most senior posts have traditionally been appointed under Royal prerogative after consultation with the prime minister and, in turn, the Lord Chancellor appointed or made recommendations for the appointment of a wide range of judicial appointments (for example, in 2001–02 the Lord Chancellor made over 900 judicial and tribunal appointments (CP 10/03 2003:para 31)). While an Independent Commission for Judicial Appointments had, since March 2001, scrutinized the appointments process and considered complaints in individual cases about appointment procedures, nonetheless, as the government's consultation paper of 2003 on the appointment of judges acknowledged, the entire appointment process was still effectively in the hands of the Lord Chancellor (CP 10/03 2003:para 22). The potential for patronage inherent within the power of appointment was one that had not been exercised in recent times but, nonetheless, it had 'no place in a modern democratic society' (CP 10/03 2003:para 22). In proposing a 'truly independent' Judicial Appointments Commission the Labour government proposed to 'end this breach of the separation of powers, and . . . bolster judicial independence' (CP 10/03 2003:para 23). Yet, its initial preference was for a 'recommending commission' which would still leave the final decision on appointment with the minister. The preferred organizational model was for the Commission to be a non-departmental public body with its own staff. Ultimately, 'overall policy in relation to judicial appointments should remain a Government responsibility' (CP 10/03 2003:para 92). If executive involvement was still to feature in the judicial appointment process there remained, nonetheless, a traditional and over-riding concern to preserve judicial independence. In fact, given the constitutional significance of protecting judicial independence, the government considered enshrining this responsibility in statute.

Once appointed, permanent judges hold office 'during good behaviour' and so can only be removed from office in exceptional circumstances. Moreover, judges of the High Court and superior courts can only be removed by the Crown after a resolution from both Houses of Parliament. This has served, historically, to protect the judiciary from undue executive interference. The independence of the judiciary has also been buttressed through institutional norms and a professional ethos which have emphasised insulation from participation in political controversies and from partisan identification in public. More fundamentally, the judiciary in the UK, since the late 17th century, has subscribed to the doctrine of parliamentary sovereignty and an attendant subordinate role to that of the legislature. This finds reflection in the interpretation of statutes which has primarily entailed the judiciary giving effect to the latest expression of the will of parliament (Barnett 2002:124). This does not mean that judges merely discover the 'true meaning of legislation' without in some way contributing to the 'making or creating of law' through their interpretation. Instead, it simply means that the judiciary has devised institutional rules which limit judicial creativity and dampen 'dynamic law making tendencies' (Barnett 2002:124). It is this restrictive approach of the judiciary to the interpretation of statutes that has 'worked in favour of judicial independence' (Johnson 1999:60). This does not mean, of course, that governments have not at various times expressed anxiety about the infringement of these rules—famously and vehemently articulated by Home Secretaries Michael Howard (Conservative, in 1995–6) and David Blunkett, (Labour, serially throughout his period in office 2001–04). Blunkett's concern was most pithly expressed in the statement: 'Frankly, I'm fed up with having to deal with a situation where parliament debates issues and judges then overturn them' (quoted in HL Debates 21 May 2003, col 894).

Judicial review

The courts, since the 17th century, have had an important role in ensuring that executive bodies operated within the powers conferred by parliament. In the application of the rule of law in Britain judicial review has been a vital element. Judicial review is, in essence, the procedure 'by which action (or inaction) of public bodies may be challenged in the courts on the grounds that such bodies have exceeded or abused their legal powers' (Sunkin 2001:9). In short, it is the nearest that the law gets to having 'a specialised and exclusive process for handling litigation against the executive and public bodies on the grounds that they have exceeded or abused their legal powers—or propose to' (Weir and Beetham 1999:441). Increasingly, in recent years, this 'political' role of the courts has developed, to the extent that the number of applications for judicial review nearly quadrupled within the space of two decades to a total of over 3,400 in 2000 (the year that the Human Rights Act 1998 came into effect in England and Wales (see below)). In 2003 it was estimated that some 5,000 applications had been made. But the aggregate figures reveal little about whether there was a change in the proportion of applications for review in relation to the number of decisions taken by public bodies. Moreover, even with such an increase, the total number of applications remains 'tiny when compared with the millions of decisions taken by public bodies that are potentially subject to challenge' (Sunkin 2001: 10). In addition, 60 per cent of the applications made for judicial review in 2000 related to immigration issues (with asylum decisions alone constituting 45 per cent of all applications). If the number of applications is 'tiny', and their spread across policy areas is remarkably limited, it should also be noted that central government was not the major target of such applications. As Sunkin (2001:11) discovered, only four per cent of cases concerned central government, whereas local government attracted 20 per cent of all applications.

Nonetheless, despite the limited number and the restricted focus of judicial review applications, their expansion did increase concern about the potential for creating a highly visible, pro-active and 'politicized' judiciary. These concerns merely heightened when the quantitative increase was matched by a qualitative change in the rationale for judicial review. As a process designed to ensure that public bodies act within the powers conferred upon them by parliament, the initial primary focus of judicial review was upon establishing the limits of executive action. In particular it was concerned with the extent to which bodies had acted within their statutory powers (*intra vires*). Any action outside of the limits of parliament's grant of authority could be deemed *ultra vires*. Traditionally three *ultra vires* grounds have been stipulated: illegality, procedural impropriety, and irrationality (see Madgwick and Woodhouse 1995:108–113; Weir and Beetham 1999:453–6; Loveland 2003:426–51). Other grounds have developed alongside the traditional ones—most notably disproportionality (which is a ground for review in European Community law and under the Human Rights Act (see below)). Whereas the interpretation of 'legality' and 'procedural impropriety' may be complex they are at least relatively formalistic and may be justified by reference to the rule of law. Notions of irrationality and disproportionality, however, are far more contestable and controversial. The danger is that these grounds may prompt a judge to reach an independent view on the merits or wisdom of an executive decision and so challenge the role of the decision maker. This may prove to be a particularly 'provocative' course of action if the decision maker is a minister (Oliver 2003:91). In these circumstances the wider institutional norms of the judiciary have been invoked to self-limit the scope for the questioning of ministerial decisions.

The most pressing constraint is the judiciary's 'own acceptance of the sovereignty of Parliament' (Oliver 2003:95) and its 'deference to Parliament' (Weir and Beetham 1999:458). Judges have traditionally invoked parliamentary sovereignty as good grounds for exercising restraint in challenging executive decisions. This 'self-limitation' of the judiciary is itself based upon an idealized conception of parliamentary sovereignty rooted in an acceptance of the 'Westminster model'. Rarely does the reality of executive dominance and 'executive sovereignty' intrude into this view. Indeed, one powerful strand of the conceptualization of judicial review sees deference to the sovereignty of parliament as an acceptance by judges of a 'democratic doctrine' and of the legitimacy derived from the process of election. This view is encapsulated in Lord Lester's (2001:687) statement that: 'When the courts interpret legislation, develop the principles of the common law, and decide issues of legal public policy, they need a firm understanding of the concepts of democracy from which their judicial powers and duties derive, and of the way in which those concepts are put into practice'.

Another, more plausible strand, in the view of Oliver (2003:104), is rooted in 'good governance theory'. In essence Oliver (2003:19) takes this to mean the existence of comity between institutions. At the heart of interinstitutional relations among the courts, executive and parliament are a series of conventions and informal understandings which serve as self-denying ordinances and which limit infringements of discrete institutional boundaries. Should interinstitutional comity be fractured, based as it is upon mutual understandings and reciprocity, then the chances of juridicialization would increase. In these circumstances an 'appreciation of the risks to both sides if comity breaks down lies behind the deference of the courts to Acts of Parliament' (Oliver 2003:104).

> It is to preserve this comity that the courts defer to Parliament, rather than because they are committed to the idea that whatever a majority in Parliament enacts is democratic until it is repealed. If comity were to be overstretched, either Parliament would limit the powers of the Courts, or legislation would be introduced to limit the powers of the government. (Oliver 2003:104)

What remains of importance is that the foundations of comity between the courts, executive and parliament, date back to the 17th century and the Bill of Rights of 1689. The institutional prescriptions underpinning the Glorious Revolution (see chapter 2) have continued to delimit the interactions of the courts, executive and parliament ever since.

Human Rights Act 1998

The passage of the Human Rights Act 1998, which came into effect in England in October 2000 (and earlier in Scotland, Wales and Northern Ireland under devolution legislation), was deemed to be a defining 'critical moment' in the interinstitutional relationship between the courts, executive and parliament. Opponents of the Act maintained variously that it would 'politicize' the judiciary, have a 'defining influence on the balance of power between the legislature and the judiciary' (in Lord Kingsland, then shadow Lord Chancellor, HL Debates 3 November 1997: vol 582, col 1234), and provide 'an immense new impetus to the judge's law-making power' (Lord Waddington, HL Debates 3 November 1997: vol 582, col 1254). Proponents, most notably the then Lord Chancellor Lord Irvine, were convinced that incorporation of the European Convention into domestic law would 'deliver a modern reconciliation of the inevitable tension between the democratic right of the majority to exercise political power and the democratic need of individuals and minorities to have their human rights secured' (HL Debates 3 November 1997: vol 582, col 1234).

The Human Rights Act (HRA) enables the main articles of the European Convention on Human Rights (ECHR) to have effect in the UK's legal system. In essence, the HRA grafts a human rights layer onto existing UK law. The UK had ratified the Convention in 1951, and, indeed, had been the first state to do so. The Convention does not provide a comprehensive listing of human rights, with only limited coverage of economic and social rights for example, and with many of the rights that are included being subject to exceptions or qualifications. The Convention does include, however, such basic liberties as: the right to life; freedom from torture or inhuman or degrading treatment or punishment; freedom from slavery and forced labour; liberty and security of person; fair trial; respect for private and family life, home and correspondence; freedom of thought, conscience and religion;

freedom of expression; freedom of peaceful assembly and freedom of association.

Before the Human Rights Act came into effect any individual who felt aggrieved by an action of the executive or by the effect of the existing law, and who believed it to be contrary to the European Convention, could petition the European Court of Human Rights (ECtHR) at Strasbourg (via an indirect route before a new direct procedure was introduced in November 1998 (see Ewing 1999:83)). If the Court found a violation of a Convention right, the United Kingdom, like all other parties to the Convention, consented to abide by the decisions of the Court. In cases where violations were found, states were expected to ensure that deficiencies in domestic laws were rectified so as to bring them into line with the Convention. Importantly, however, a finding by the ECtHR of a violation of a Convention right did not have the effect of automatically changing domestic law and practice. It remained the responsibility of national legislatures and executives to effect such changes. Indeed, in at least two of the 35 cases (in the period 1975–1995) where the ECtHR found breaches of the Convention in the UK, the government was 'unwilling to give effect of decisions of the European Court and [took] steps to avoid doing so' (Bradley and Ewing 2003:415).

The HRA 1998 introduced a general requirement that all legislation— past, present and future—should be compatible with the Convention. It was made unlawful for public authorities to act in a way that was incompatible with Convention Rights. Under section 3 of the Act the courts are required to interpret primary and secondary legislation, wherever possible, in a manner consistent with the Convention. This does not allow UK courts to strike down, or 'disapply' legislation, or make new law. Instead, where legislation is deemed to be incompatible with Convention rights, superior courts may make a declaration of incompatibility (under section 4.2). Such a declaration does not 'affect the validity, continuing operation or enforcement' of legislation nor is it binding on the parties to the proceedings (section 4.6). If a declaration of incompatibility is made it is then up to the government and parliament to decide how to proceed. The government may decide to amend primary legislation, or not as the case may be. Equally the HRA (section 10) provides for 'fast-track' remedial orders whereby primary legislation can be amended through secondary/delegated legislation (see chapter 2).

In this manner, in limiting the primary role of the courts to interpretations of incompatibility, the legislative sovereignty of the UK parliament is preserved. Indeed, before introducing the 1998 Act the government considered the possibility of empowering the courts to set aside an Act of Parliament believed to be incompatible with the Convention rights (following the Canadian model). However, it decided against this option precisely because of 'the importance which the Government attaches to Parliamentary sovereignty' (Cm 3782 1997:para 2.11). In a classic statement of parliamentary sovereignty the government took the concept to mean:

> that Parliament is competent to make any law on any matter of its choosing and no court may question the validity of any Act that it passes. In enacting legislation, Parliament is making decisions about important matters of public policy. The authority to make those decisions derives from a democratic mandate. Members of Parliament in the House of Commons possess such a mandate because they are elected, accountable and representative. To make provision in the Bill for the courts to set aside Acts of Parliament would confer on the judiciary a general power over the decisions of Parliament which under our present constitutional arrangements they do not possess, and would be likely on occasions to draw the judiciary into serious conflict with Parliament. (Cm 3782 1997:para 2.13)

Despite this classic statement, early assessments of the impact of the HRA indicated that while 'as a matter of constitutional legality, parliament may well be sovereign, . . . as a matter of constitutional practice it has transferred significant power to the judiciary' (Ewing 1999:92). Flinders (2001:63) went even further and argued that: 'Although the Human Rights Act 1998 is purported to reconcile the protection of human rights with the sovereignty of parliament, it represents an unprecedented transfer of political power from the executive and legislature to the judiciary'. However, as the operation of the Act unfolded, more nuanced assessments of interinstitutional interactions emerged. One strand of analysis emphasized the notion of 'judicial deference' and the extent to which this idea had become 'a firmly established feature of judicial review in cases involving the British Human Rights Act' (Edwards 2002:860). There are principled reasons—primarily the absence of the democratic legitimacy of the courts—as to why the courts defer to the executive and legislature; but, equally, there is a belief that the judiciary is 'institutionally incompetent' to deal with complex issues of public policy (Edwards 2002:859). Whatever the specific reasons the courts appear to have tried to avoid political controversy. Certainly, the House of Lords has generally been cautious in its interpretation of the HRA (Woodhouse 2003b: 932). Indeed, only ten declarations of incompatibility were made in the first three years of the operation of the Act (Falconer 2004).

Whilst there is no disputing that the HRA 1998 blurred the interface between judicial and political institutions (Woodhouse 2003b:932), the self-limiting institutional norms of the judiciary ultimately minimized the extent of conflict between courts and legislature. That there was conflict is apparent from the periodic outbursts of the then Home Secretary, David Blunkett (see Stevens 2002:131; Woodhouse 2003b:924). That the scope of conflict was relatively restricted underlined, however, the continued significance of judicial deference and associated notions of parliamentary sovereignty. More particularly, the provisions of the 1998 Act pertaining to declarations of incompatibility and discretionary remedial action 'preserve comity between the courts and parliament by preventing the courts from challenging parliament' (Oliver 2003:115). While the ruling of the Law Lords in December 2004, that the detention of foreign nationals without trial under the provisions of the Anti-Terrorism, Crime and Security Act 2001 was incompatible with the ECHR, was seen by large sections of the media to breach such comity, both the Law Lords and ministers acknowledged that it was parliament alone that had the obligation to reconsider the provisions of the 2001 Act. As Charles Clarke, the new Home Secretary, made clear: 'Let me reaffirm that the case is about the compatibility of our domestic legislation with the European convention on human rights. As the Human Rights Act 1998 makes clear, Parliament remains sovereign and it is ultimately for Parliament to decide whether and what changes should be made to the law' (HC Debates 20 December 2004: vol 428 col 1913).

In maintaining the theoretical supremacy of parliament, the HRA underscored the distinctiveness of the normative systems, and integral notions of 'appropriate behaviour', operating within judicial and political institutions in the UK. Institutional norms and the 'logic of appropriateness' do change however. The scale of change, as calibrated in the enactment of the HRA, has been likened to a 'paradigm shift in the foundations of British constitutional law' (Edwards 2002:866). Yet, notable features of the new paradigm pre-date the HRA. Certainly under the provisions of the HRA the courts enter into a dialogue with the executive, acting through the legislature, by requiring justification for legislation which infringes convention rights. Before the HRA, however, the courts had already developed, in cases involving common law rights and freedoms, a capacity of alerting the executive and parliament to principles that might have been disregarded (Edwards 2002:867).

More profoundly, perhaps, the HRA has begun to affect the institutional norms of the executive (see Feldman 2004:93). As Lord Irvine (2002) concluded in his speech commemorating the first two years of the operation of the HRA: 'The Act represents one small manageable step for our Courts; but a major leap for our constitution and our culture'. Proponents of the incorporation of human rights had long argued that an important facet of the HRA would be its effect on the institutional culture and internal norms of Whitehall. Certainly, the 1997 White Paper *Rights Brought Home* emphasized that:

> The ... requirement to make a statement about the compliance of draft legislation with the Convention will have a significant and beneficial impact on the preparation of draft legislation within Government before its introduction into Parliament. It will ensure that all Ministers, their departments and officials are fully seized of the gravity of the Convention's obligations in respect of human rights. (Cm 3782 1997:para 3.4)

Part of the reason for the delayed introduction of the HRA, in England at least, was to enable government departments and their associated agencies and other public bodies to prepare for the 'mainsteaming' of Convention rights within the work of the executive. Management systems, training programmes, a Human Rights Taskforce, a Human Rights Unit (initially based in the Home Office but transferred later to the Department of Constitutional Affairs), were established to inculcate a 'human rights culture' in Whitehall and beyond. The initial impact of these initiatives was highly variable both within and between public bodies (see Feldman 2001:21); and the effort expended on them, in comparison with the parallel training programme for the judiciary, was limited (see HL 67–I/HC 489–I 2003:para 34, paras 61–2). If a change in 'culture', to be internalized within formal institutions and externalized to civil society, was one of the primary objectives of the HRA it was also recognized that this would be a long-term process (see HL 66–i/HC 332–i 2001:para 6).

At the time of the passage of the 1998 Act the government had considered the case for a Human Rights Commission to act as a champion for the promotion of a new rights culture, but had deferred a decision until the HRA had 'bedded in' and its impact upon other 'rights' bodies—such as the Commission for Racial Equality and the Equal Opportunities Commission—could be determined (see Cm 3782 1997:paras 3.8–3.12).

In March 2003 the Joint Committee on Human Rights—which is a parliamentary body created to consider human rights matters, proposals for remedial orders and whether the attention of parliament should be drawn to such remedial orders—considered the case for establishing a Commission and found it 'compelling' (HL 67–I/HC 489–I 2003:1). The Joint Committee reached this conclusion after observing that: 'The culture of human rights has yet to be internalized within public authorities or their inspectorates. More worryingly perhaps, the momentum to develop this culture appears to us to be slowing—in some areas to a standstill' (HL 67–I/HC 489–I 2003:para 95). This institutional inertia, along with the finding that public knowledge of human rights' issues was at best 'partial or ill-informed', convinced the Joint Committee of the need for the creation of a Commission on Human Rights.

Following the Joint Committee's recommendations, the government announced in November 2003, its intention to create a Commission for Equality and Human Rights. The prime purpose of this Non-Departmental Public Body would be to build 'a new, inclusive sense of British citizenship and identity . . . [and] promote a culture of respect for human rights, especially in the delivery of public services' (www.dca.gov.uk/hract/sosannouc. htm). The Commission would not be established, however, until late 2006 'at the earliest'. In the meantime consideration was to be given as to how the new Commission would operate in relation to Scotland and Wales.

Asymmetry and judicial institutions

As the Joint Committee on Human Rights observed, 'Asymmetry is one of the inevitable consequences of devolution' (HL 67–I/HC 489–I 2003:para 215). Two separate Commissions had been in existence in Northern Ireland as a result of the Northern Ireland Act 1998—the Human Rights Commission, and the Equality Commission for Northern Ireland. Even with the creation of a UK-wide body, these Commissions would continue to operate as independent bodies accountable to the Secretary of State for Northern Ireland.

Similarly in Scotland, the Scottish Executive had already confirmed, in December 2001, that an independent and statutory Human Rights Commission for Scotland was to be created. In February 2003 a consultation document was published (Scottish Executive 2003a) which proposed the creation of a 'devolved body' dealing with matters raised in relation to the Scottish Executive and Parliament. Responses to the consultation were largely supportive (Scottish Executive 2004) though it was recognized that the creation of a single UK Equality and Human Rights Commission alongside a Scottish Human Rights Commission would generate problems of overlapping competences and the need for coordinated activities (Scottish Executive 2004: 43–5; HL 67–I/HC 489–I 2003:paras 215–218). In Wales there was little debate about, and few calls for, the creation of a Human Rights Commission.

The asymmetrical arrangements with regard to the promotion of human rights reflect broader institutional differences between the various legal systems within the UK. As noted in chapter 5, for example, the Act of Union 1707 maintained the separate identity of the Scottish legal and judicial systems. The organization of the judicial system in 21st century Scotland remains largely devolved. There are distinct criminal and civil courts north of the border. In criminal matters the High Court of Justiciary, the Sheriff Courts and the District Courts adjudicate. Alongside their criminal jurisdiction the Sheriff Courts also deal with most civil law cases. Appeals can be made to the Sheriff Principal and then to the Court of Session. The House of Lords may hear appeals in civil matters from Scotland, though these have been relatively infrequent occurrences. Since the creation of the Scottish parliament the Judicial Committee of the Privy Council has had jurisdiction to consider disputes over devolved powers (see below). Also since devolution the Scottish Executive Justice Department, under the Minister for Justice, has been responsible for aspects of criminal and civil justice and civil law, for courts administration, for legal aid, and liaison with the legal profession. The Lord Advocate and Solicitor General for Scotland, are law officers of the Scottish Executive and provide the Executive with advice on legal matters. After devolution a new post of Advocate General was created to provide advice on Scots law to the UK government.

In Northern Ireland jurisdiction is exercised by the Supreme Court of Judicature which comprises the Court of Appeal, the High Court and the Crown Court. The Crown Court deals with all serious criminal cases; the High Court deals with civil cases; and the Court of Appeal has the power to review both civil and criminal law decisions. The inferior courts in Northern Ireland are the county courts and magistrates courts. Overall, the UK Lord Chancellor is responsible for court administration through the Northern Ireland Court Service. Policy and legislation concerning criminal law, the police and the penal system are the responsibility of the Northern Ireland Office, under the Secretary of State.

Supreme Court

In November 2003 the UK government included in the Queen's Speech a commitment to establish a Supreme Court (HL Debates 26 November 2003 vol 655, col 1). Three factors converged to prompt the government's proposal. All three arose in some form from the wider constitutional reforms effected by the Labour government; and all, jointly, contributed to the logic for the creation of a new court as 'a single apex' for the UK's judicial system (CP 11/03 2003:para 20). The first factor arose from the fact that after devolution the Judicial Committee of the Privy Council determined cases relating to the legal competence of the devolved administrations, assemblies and parliament. Its judgments were binding on all parties. (The Judicial Committee also acted as the final court of appeal for some Commonwealth jurisdictions and for the Crown Dependencies of Jersey, Guernsey and the Isle of Man; as well having other technical jurisdictions (see Bradley and Ewing 2003:366–7)). In proposing that the jurisdiction of the Judicial Committee should be transferred to a Supreme Court, the government acknowledged that this would remove the possibility of a conflict of interest arising from the fact that judgments are made by a party to the dispute—the UK parliament—with an interest in the outcome of the case. The separation of the new court from the UK parliament would remove doubts as to judicial independence from the legislature and the UK executive. This proposal was welcomed by the Scottish Executive with the proviso that appropriate arrangements were made to ensure that Scottish judges sat in cases raising devolution issues (Scottish Executive 2003b).

The second factor arose from the reform of the House of Lords, and the spotlight that had been focused during the reform process upon the conduct of judicial business in the Lords (see chapter 2; HC 494 2002:paras 150–3; HL 17/HC 171 2002:para 25). The government was persuaded of the need for the separation of the highest level of the judicial system from the executive and legislative systems. This view extended beyond the specific proposal for a Supreme Court and was explicitly linked to the separation of the judicial, executive and legislative roles traditionally performed by the Lord Chancellor (see Department of Constitutional Affairs 2003), as well as to the procedures for appointing judges (CP 10/03 2003). A persistent theme was to 'put the relationship between the executive, the judiciary and the legislature on a modern footing' (www.lcd.gov.uk/consult/lcoffice/index.htm: para 6; CP 11/03 2003:para 1). Part of the 'modern' context to which the three institutions had to react was the unfolding impact of the HRA. This constituted the third factor prompting change. Article 6 of the ECHR, and its incorporation in the HRA 1998, required a stricter view to be taken on the independence and impartiality of the judiciary. Thus, as the government's consultation paper acknowledged, 'The Human Rights Act 1998, itself the product of a changing climate of opinion, has made people more sensitive to the issues and more aware of the anomaly of the position whereby the highest court of appeal is situated within one of the chambers of Parliament' (CP 11/03 2003:para 11).

In their combination, the HRA, devolution, and the growth in judicial review had increased the visibility of the highest courts. The potential for conflicting judgments issued by the Law Lords (acting in the Appellate Committee) and by the Judicial Committee over human rights issues was noted both by the UK government (CP 11/03 2003:para 19) and by the Scottish Executive (Scottish Executive 2003b:para 1). To remove this potential for conflict the case was made that: 'it is essential that there is a single UK-wide court at which all matters of a constitutional nature, such as devolution issues . . . [or] involving breaches of ECHR, whether arising under the Human Rights Act or by operation of section 57(2) of the Scotland Act, should be considered by the same court' (Scottish Executive 2003b:para 1).

The proposed new body was thus to be a new court with a UK-wide jurisdiction. The Supreme Court would be separate from the courts in England and Wales, Scotland, and Northern Ireland. It would combine the roles of the Appellate Committee of the House of Lords with those of the Judicial Committee of the Privy Council. Correspondingly, its members would be separated from the executive and the legislature. While the initial members of the new Court would be the 12 full-time Law Lords, they would not sit or vote in the House of Lords while acting as members of the Court (CP 11/03

2003:para 36). The Law Lords themselves were split on this issue, with eight voicing the opinion that the President of the Supreme Court (along with the most senior judges in England and Wales, Scotland and Northern Ireland) should be appointed members of the Lords (CP 11/03 2003: para 21).

Significantly, the government rejected the model of the Supreme Court of the United States or of the German Federal Constitutional Court. There was no intention to create a specific constitutional court, and there was no perceived need to extend the jurisdiction of the Court into areas not already covered by the Appellate Committee and the Judicial Committee. The reason stated was simple: 'In our democracy, Parliament is Supreme. There is no separate body of constitutional law which takes precedence over all other law' (CP 11/03 2003:para 23).

Certainly, the manner in which the radical proposal for the creation of a supreme court was announced in June 2003 did little to secure support. On the one side, the government was accused of not appreciating the constitutional significance of its initial announcement (see Lord Woolf *The Times* 3 March 2004), and, on the other, some observers were 'mystified as to the driving force behind the proposal' (Carnwath 2004:251–2). Nonetheless, the Constitutional Reform Bill, with its provisions for establishing a supreme court, abolishing the office of Lord Chancellor and creating a Judicial Appointments Commission was introduced in February 2004. Perhaps not surprisingly, given its genesis and constitutional sensitivity, the Bill encountered deep resistance within the House of Lords. In March 2004 it was referred, unusually, to a Select Committee (this procedure had been little used since the early 20th century). In turn, when the Select Committee reported in June 2004, it was so evenly divided in its opinion over the creation of a supreme court that it made no recommendation on the issue (HL 125 2004:para 132). In July the government suffered a defeat at Committee Stage, of 240 votes to 208, on abolition of Lord Chancellor. The bill continued to be examined in the Lords through October 2004 and a decision was taken to carry the bill over into session 2004–2005 to allow the government the opportunity to reverse in the House of Commons some of the Lords' defeats. The bill received Royal Assent in March 2005.

Regulation

Beyond the courts and the legislature there has developed a diverse set of institutions concerned with 'secondary regulation'. 'Secondary regulation' applies both to government regulation of the private sector and to regulation inside government and public sector organizations.

Regulation of the private sector

A discussion of the regulation of private sector institutions might appear to be somewhat tangential to the concerns of a book on 'political institutions'. Certainly, such a discussion is a relatively recent innovation in the consideration of political institutions. Indeed, 'until the 1980s regulation was little discussed, and in particular hardly any concern existed with designing institutions to undertake this task' (Prosser 1997:1). What contributed to this change in the 1980s was the movement towards the wholesale privatization of public, 'nationalized' industries (alongside fears about the adverse effects of structural changes in the financial sector (see below)). Yet, regulation was not a new phenomenon. If anything, the management of nationalized industries through public corporations in the post-war period up to 1984 was the exception to a longer historical pattern of state regulation of private and quasi-public industries (see Prosser 1997:33–45). Thus, for example, by the beginning of the 20th century a series of regulatory institutions already existed for a range of privately owned utilities, such as the Railway and Canal Commission and the Electricity Commission. These were supplemented later with regulatory institutions for newly emerging sectors such as the Air Transport Licensing Authority (created in 1938) and the Independent Broadcasting Authority (established in 1954).

However, such was the change in the scale and scope of regulation accompanying the programme of privatization after 1984 that it became commonplace to talk of the 'rise of the regulatory state' (see Loughlin and Scott 1997: 205; Moran 2001:20; HL 68–I 2004:para 17). The 'regulatory state' is commonly identified as 'a style of governance' in which there has been a move 'away from the direct provision of public services ... towards oversight of provision of public services by others' (Scott 2000:44). With each privatization a parallel regulatory institution was created: telecommunications

(Oftel in 1984); gas supply (OfGas, 1986); water services (Ofwat, 1989); electricity supply (Offer, 1989); railways (ORR in 1993); and the creation of a single energy regulator in the Office of Gas and Electricity Markets (Ofgem in 1999). Without going into the details of the rationales underpinning regulation—which basically distil into 'economic' reasons (with regulation acting as a surrogate for market forces), or 'public interest' arguments (with regulation serving to secure consideration of broader social and environmental concerns)—the issue of greater concern for present purposes is how the regulatory institutions interacted with existing state institutions. The first point to note is that the new regulatory bodies 'reflected the tradition of strong executive power' (Loughlin and Scott 1997:209) in the UK. They were created as non-ministerial government departments (see chapter 4; see Prosser 1997:47). Thus, while individual regulators were vested with specific personal powers, they shared joint statutory responsibilities with ministers (see Bradley and Ewing 2003:298–300). (The creation of the Gas and Electricity Markets Authority to head Ofgem, rather than a single Director General, marked a move away from 'personalized' regulation. Similarly the Railways and Transport Act of 2003 replaced the single statutory office of the Rail Regulator with a new board structure in the Office of Rail Regulation). Certainly ministers are expected to exercise their routine responsibilities at arm's length, but regulators are required to have regard to any general guidance issued by an appropriate minister. As one regulator noted, however, '"Have regard" is not the same as "do as you are told"' (Memorandum by Rail Regulator, HL 68–II 2004: para39). More importantly perhaps, the initial design of regulatory institutions was 'path dependent' in the sense that ministers had pre-determined the structure of privatized industries and the competitive environment in which they were to operate.

While the rise of the 'regulatory state' has been identified as a fundamental challenge to existing notions of public accountability through ministers (see Prosser 1997:52; Moran 2001:31), it can just as easily be maintained that a 'regulatory state can never be fully achieved' in the UK precisely because of the continued impact of the 'tradition of ministerial responsibility' (Loughlin and Scott 1997:218). Regulators recognize the need both to establish and maintain effective working relationships with government departments (Memorandum by Ofgem, HL 68–II 2004:para 52). They are required to make an annual report to the relevant Secretary of State, and to provide 'information, advice and assistance' to ministers. This may take the form of providing answers to written parliamentary questions, or of pursuing 'a policy of "no surprise" so that Ministers are aware in advance of any significant ... decisions' (Memorandum from Ofgem HL 68–II 2004:para 52). Regulators also have a formal, and extensive, accountability to parliament for the exercise of their powers (see for example HL 68–II 2004:Q597; HL 68–II 2004: Memorandum from Tony Prosser). As the House of Lords' Select Committee on the Constitution noted:

> Parliament is crucial to ensuring accountability. It not only creates the regulators by statute, it also calls ministers to account for the policy that is implemented by the regulators and acts on behalf of citizens in ensuring that ministers and regulators are acting in the public interest. (HL 68–I 2004: para 174)

Moreover, during the course of its inquiry into the 'Regulatory State', the Lords' Committee received evidence of the effectiveness of the system for holding regulators to account, particularly through parliamentary select committees. Perhaps not surprisingly, therefore, in responding to concerns about the depth of accountability, the Committee recommended the creation of a dedicated committee, preferably a joint committee of both Houses, to improve scrutiny of the 'regulatory state' (HL 68–I 2004:paras 199–200). Significantly, regulators themselves believed that 'strong accountability is not inconsistent with independence' and, if anything, there is a new 'matrix of accountability which is probably more specific and more intense than ever applied to a minister' (Tom Winsor, former Rail Regulator, HL 68–II 2004:Q 597).

The move away from self-regulation

Historically the financial sector in the UK, primarily the City of London, was the most important example of 'self-regulation'. Self-regulation in the UK was distinctive in comparative terms because of its informality, both in the absence of specialized regulators and codified rules, and in the fact that private associations (rather than public institutions) have been central to self-regulation. As Moran (2003:68) observes, 'low levels of institutionalization, codification, and juridification have marked the system [of self-regulation]'. Yet, in the last two decades of the 20th century the state, and hence public institutions, became increasingly involved in what remained nominally 'self-regulatory systems'. In this process, the institutional structure of financial regulation 'has been transformed into a 'more centralized, more state controlled hierarchy' (Moran 2003:77). In this respect the creation of the Financial Services Authority typifies the degree to which the 'institutional innovation' of the specialized regulatory agency empowered by law straddles the private sphere of 'markets' and the public sphere of state institutions.

Financial Services Authority

The Financial Services Authority (FSA) is an independent non-governmental body, given statutory powers by the Financial Services and Markets Act 2000. It is a limited company financed by the financial services industry. Over 9,250 financial firms operate under FSA regulation. The FSA's Board is appointed by the Treasury and is responsible for overall policy. It is accountable to Treasury Ministers and, through them, to parliament. It has a statutory duty to produce an annual report for presentation to Treasury ministers and to parliament. It also regularly provides evidence to the House of Commons' Treasury Select Committee (see www.fsa.gov.uk/accountability).

Food standards agency

One other example of the transformation of regulatory regimes in the UK in the late-1990s also highlights the move away from self-regulation. Although the food industry had been regulated with regard to adulteration and dangerous products by statute since 1875, the producers had dominated the enforcement process to the extent that it approximated something close to self-regulation (Moran 2003:62). The BSE crisis, and the announcement in 1996 that BSE was likely to have been transmitted to humans, led to reform of the regulation of the food industry and the creation of a new Food Standards Agency that would not be 'tied to any vested interests' (Cm 3830 1998:Foreword). The Food Standards Agency was established in 2000, under the provisions of the Food Standards Act of 1999, as a non-ministerial department operating at arm's length from ministers. The Agency was headed by a Board appointed to act in the public interest and not to represent particular sectors, and is accountable to parliament through Health ministers, and to the devolved administrations in Scotland, Wales and Northern Ireland for its activities within their areas. In turn, the Meat Hygiene Service became an executive agency of the Food Standards Agency. For Moran (2003:150) the Food Standards Agency is of importance as a 'manifestation of the regulatory state' and as a project involving 'modernization, standard-ization, surveillance, and control'.

The committee on standards in public life

The 1990s witnessed increased questioning of the extent to which the major political institutions—parliament, executive, parties—should remain self-regulating. A series of widely publicized misdemeanours and indiscretions by MPs, ministers, and civil servants; accusations of partisan influence in the appointment and workings of quangos; and the opaqueness of the finan-cing of political parties gave rise to perceptions of 'sleaze' and of a malaise in ethical standards at the heart of the political system. In response to increased concern, the Committee on Standards in Public life was established under the chairmanship of Lord Nolan in October 1994. The Committee is an ad-visory Non-Departmental Public Body of the Cabinet Office charged with examining 'current concerns about standards of conduct of all holders of public office' and making recommendations 'to ensure the highest stand-ards of propriety in public life'. The initial scope of the Committee included: Members of Parliament; Members of the European Parliament; members and senior officers of all NDPBs and NHS bodies; non-ministerial office holders; and elected members and senior officials of local authorities. In November 1997 the terms of reference of the Committee were extended to include 'issues in relation to the funding of political parties'.

In less than a decade from its inception the Committee issued nine reports and made 342 recommendations (some 80 per cent of which were accepted in one form or another). One major impact of the Committee has been the propagation of Codes of Conduct throughout state institutions. Codes of conduct now guide the activities of members of both Houses of the UK parliament, ministers, civil servants, special advisers, NDPBs, local authorities, the Scottish Parliament, Welsh Assembly, Northern Ireland Assembly, and even the Committee of Standards in Public Life itself. Such codes make explicit reference to the seven principles of public life—selflessness, integrity, objectivity, accountability, openness, hon-esty and leadership—which were enunciated in the Committee's first report (Cm 2850–I 1995:14). Equally the Committee has overseen the introduction of a series of 'Standards' Commissioners in the various in-stitutional forms of: the Parliamentary Commissioner for Standards; the

Commissioner for Public Appointments; the Standards Commission for Scotland; the Northern Ireland Assembly's Commissioner for Standards; the Standards Board for England (to examine conduct in local authorities); and the Electoral Commission.

The Electoral Commission was established by the Political Parties, Elections and Referendum Act 2000. Before this Act political parties in the UK had remained largely unregulated by law, in comparison with most other western democracies. The Electoral Commission is an independent statutory authority which reports directly to parliament through a committee chaired by the Speaker of the House of Commons. It is responsible, among other duties (see chapter 2) for the registration of political parties, monitoring significant donations to registered parties and regulating national party spending on elections campaigns. The 2001 general election witnessed the first imposition of limits on national campaign expenditure. After the Political Parties, Elections and Referendum Act parties were incorporated into 'their own special regulated domain' and displayed the characteristic features of the 'regulatory state' namely 'the use of a specialized agency to control newly colonized domains' (Moran 2003:151).

The office of the Parliamentary Commissioner for Standards is of particular interest, as the office demonstrates the continued significance of the concept of parliamentary sovereignty even within a perceived transition to a 'regulatory state'. As the then Leader of the House informed the Committee on Standards in Public Life: 'self-regulation in the House of Commons has a constitutional importance because the House is sovereign. In order to fulfil its responsibilities as a sovereign institution, Parliament must have the freedom of privilege so that it is protected from outside interference' (Cm 5663 2002:para 2.15). In this sense, the model of regulation within the Commons remains one of self-regulation, and, importantly, one that precludes judicial review (see Cm 5663 2002:para 2.19). From the outset the Commons resisted appointing the Commissioner under statute—in part out of fear of exposing the office to judicial review. The Commissioner is, therefore, an Officer of the House whose role and powers are specified in standing orders rather than statute. While the office of Commissioner constitutes a 'significant independent element with a system which remains essentially self-regulating' (Cm 2850–I 1995:para 99) critics maintain that what is required is an 'external element' of regulation (see Cm 5663 2002:para 9.8). Just such a view was expressed by the Committee on Standards in Public life

when it reviewed, in 2002, the implementation of its earlier recommendations on standards of conduct in the Commons. It recommended that an
'external element' should be introduced at every stage of the process of regulation—development of standards of conduct, investigation and adjudication of complaints (Cm 5663 2002:para 9.9). Perhaps not surprisingly, the
House's Committee on Standards and Privileges was concerned at the degree of 'externalization' proposed by the Standards Committee (see HC 403
2003:paras 23–47).

Regulation inside government

The secondary regulation of government is characterized by Hood et al
(2000:284) as entailing 'oversight of bureaucracies by other public agencies
operating at arm's length from the direct line of command, the overseers being endowed with some sort of official authority over their charges'. In the
following discussion the term 'regulation' will be used broadly to encompass institutions of audit, inspection and regulation. (Though some maintain that audit, inspection and regulation are distinct but complimentary
activities and what distinguishes regulator institutions is the possession of
executive powers to secure compliance (see Public Audit Forum 2002a:2)).

The 'particular institutional manifestation' of secondary regulation is
characterized by: 'i) one public bureaucracy in the role of an overseer aiming
to shape the activities of another; ii) an organizational separation between
the "regulating" bureaucracy and the "regulatee" . . . ; iii) some official
"mandate" for the regulator organization to scrutinize the behaviour of the
"regulatee" and seek to change it' (Hood et al 2000:284). In combination,
these three institutional features serve to distinguish 'secondary' from
'primary' regulation, while also providing the defining, common characteristics of a diverse range of 'regulator' organizations.

In the two decades before 1997 there was a marked increase in secondary
regulation of government. Yet, throughout this period, there was no clearly
articulated policy of government regulation, it simply grew in an ad hoc and
unplanned manner. The scale of increase is quantified by Hood et al (1999:
28–33; 2000:286) who estimated that, between 1976 and 1995, the number of
regulator organizations increased by 20 per cent to over 200, their total staff
grew by around 90 per cent to nearly 20,000, and expenditure on regulation
of government more than doubled to nearly £1bn. Under Labour the

increase continued and included 'inertia growth'—of bodies established after 1997 but initiated by preceding Conservative governments (for example the Benefit Fraud Inspectorate and the Trading Standards Council)—as well as new regulator bodies initiated by Labour, such as the Best Value Inspectorate for England and Wales, created in 1999 within the Audit Commission, and the Standards Board for England, established in 2001 to promote high standards of ethical behaviour in local authorities. While there was continuity in quantitative terms there was, however, a qualitative change in the 'institutional design ideas' underpinning public sector regulation after 1997 (Hood et al 2000:291).

One reason for this change was the increased emphasis placed upon the capacity of regulator institutions to assist the government in fulfilling its manifesto pledges of securing more effective and efficient delivery of public services. In recent decades, as noted in chapters 3 and 4, the core executive has been confronted by the organizational dilemmas associated with 'governance' and a 'differentiated polity'. One such dilemma stemmed from the distinction drawn between 'steering' and 'rowing'. While governments sought to control the policy agenda (to 'steer') they found it more difficult to do so given their increased dependence upon an expanded range of delivery ('rowing') bodies—executive agencies, quangos, local authorities, and private sector organizations. In these circumstances, regulatory bodies could be conceived as 'control mechanisms' of value to central government. Indeed, Cope and Goodship (2002:34) argued that regulatory bodies have been used by the core executive 'as its "eyes and ears" in steering an increasingly fragmented governance'. In this sense, regulation is associated with control and accountability. Both regulation and accountability involve the exercise of authority, 'but regulation focuses on authority relationships where an organization controls another at "arm's length" ... and places particular emphasis on the role of standards or "rule-like" structures in mediating those relationships' (James 2000:328).

However, the proliferation of regulatory bodies and regulatory regimes inside government also led to other dilemmas, not the least of which were the potential for 'accountability overload' (Hogwood et al 2000:222), excessive 'regulatory compliance costs' (Hood et al 2000:291), and the 'frustration of joined-up service delivery' (Cope and Goodship 2002:36). Explicit acknowledgement of some of the potential pathologies of regulation was found in the White Paper *Modernising Government* (Cm 4310 1999: 16;23;37) and in the Report *Wiring it Up* (PIU 2000:52–3). The solutions proposed by the Labour government included more cooperation and coordination among regulators (Cm 4310 1999:43; PIU 2000:55), encouraging regulators to look across organizational boundaries (PIU 2000:54), and allaying departmental suspicions that auditors would punish sensible risk-taking (PIU 2000:56).

The institutional effects of the qualitative change in the 'institutional design ideas' can be seen in the activities of the major audit institutions.

The National Audit Office

The National Audit Act of 1983 created the National Audit Office (NAO) in its present form. Before then the Exchequer and Audit Department had assisted the Comptroller and Auditor General (C&AG) in auditing the accounts of all government departments and of reporting to parliament accordingly. The Comptroller and Auditor General was also empowered under the Exchequer and Audit Departments Act of 1866 to authorize the issue of public money to government from the Bank of England. Yet it was not until the 1983 Act that the C&AG formally became an Officer of the House of Commons with the independent discretion to report on the manner in which government bodies had used public funds. Since the Government Resources and Accounts Act of 2000 the C&AG has been required to examine a department's use of 'resources' as well as finances. The NAO is responsible for auditing the accounts of all government departments, agencies, and Non-Departmental Public Bodies (see chapter 4).

The cycle of NAO audit and accountability culminates in the consideration of C&AG reports by the House of Commons' Select Committee of Public Accounts (PAC). A number of NAO Reports (49 in session 2002–03 and 50 in session 2003–04) are then investigated further and reported upon by the PAC. By convention, government responds to any recommendations made by the PAC within two months. Other select committees have been encouraged to make greater use of the NAO's services, and session 2001–02 witnessed the innovation of the then Transport, Local Government and Regions Committee taking evidence from the National Audit Office following an NAO report on the London Underground Public Private Partnership.

Under the 1983 Act the NAO is empowered to examine and report on the 'economy, efficiency and effectiveness of public spending'. On this basis the NAO presents around 50 'value-for-money' audits each year. Value-for-money audits are essentially performance audits which examine aspects of corporate governance, the systems and processes of internal management, and the use of resources in delivering services, or implementing programmes or specific projects. In addition, given the emphasis placed upon Public Service Agreements (see chapter 4), the NAO has developed a programme of work in response to the growing importance of performance measurement in government, and many recent value-for-money reports have examined departments' performance measurement systems or validated performance data (HC 62 2003:para 61).

Auditors general: Scotland, Wales and Northern Ireland

Since devolution, and the creation of the Scottish Parliament and the Welsh National Assembly, separate Auditor Generals have been appointed in Scotland and Wales. The UK C&AG remains responsible for audits in all matters reserved to the UK government (see chapter 5), and is also charged with auditing the payment of the block grants made to the devolved executives as well as the direct expenditure of the Scotland Office, Wales Office, and Northern Ireland Office.

The Scotland Act 1998 established the post of Auditor General for Scotland. The Auditor General is responsible for auditing a total of 19 departments of the Scottish Executive and associated government agencies, 23 NDPBs, 52 NHS trusts and health boards, 42 further education colleges, and Scottish Water. The Auditor General does not scrutinize local councils, or police or fire boards. Audit Scotland is the body charged under the Public Finance and Accountability (Scotland) Act 2000 with conducting audits and of preparing reports on behalf of the Auditor General to the Scottish Parliament. In Parliament, the Audit Committee takes the lead role in considering and reporting on the Auditor General's reports.

An Auditor General for Wales (AGW) was also created under the Government of Wales Act 1998. Sir John Bourn, the Comptroller and Auditor General for the UK was appointed as the first AGW and was supported by staff in the Cardiff Office of the National Audit Office. Certainly Bourn's dual position 'considerably assisted the transition to devolution and the development of new audit arrangements for Wales' (Public Audit Forum 2002b:25). The Welsh Assembly is required by the 1998 Act to publish all financial and value-for-money reports produced for it by the AGW and for the Assembly's Audit Committee to take evidence and produce its own reports. The National Assembly government is required by the Assembly's standing orders to respond formally and promptly to each Audit Committee Report. In April 2003 a draft Public Audit (Wales) Bill proposed the creation of a single Wales Audit Office, headed by the AGW, to provide a unified audit regime of Welsh public bodies. This was to be achieved through combining the existing functions of the AWG with most of those exercised by the Audit Commission in Wales (see below). The Wales Audit Office would be responsible for the financial audit and value for money audit of the National Assembly for Wales and its sponsored bodies as well as health and local government bodies in Wales. In November 2003 the Public Audit (Wales) Bill was published (as the third Wales-only bill since devolution), and received its Royal Assent in September 2004.

The Comptroller and Auditor General for Northern Ireland heads the Northern Ireland Audit Office (NIAO), and undertakes financial audit and value for money audits. The NIAO is responsible for the external audit of central government bodies in Northern Ireland, including Northern Ireland Departments and their Executive Agencies; Executive Non-Departmental Public Bodies and health and personal social service bodies. (Some NIAO staff are also designated by the Department of the Environment as local government auditors). The Comptroller and Audit General for Northern Ireland reports to the Northern Ireland Assembly, or to the UK Parliament during the suspension of devolution.

Audit Commission

The Audit Commission is a Non-Departmental Public Body established in 1983 to regulate the external auditors of local authorities in England and Wales. Its role was extended in 1990 to include the NHS (Strategic Health Authorities, Local Health Boards, NHS trusts and Primary Care Trusts in England and Wales), and, by the late 1990s, it had been empowered to conduct joint reviews with the relevant inspectorates of social service provision and local education authorities. In 2000 its role was expanded again to enable it to carry out 'Best Value' inspections of local government services, and in 2003 it attained responsibility for inspecting housing associations through a new and extended Housing Inspectorate. Since its inception, therefore, the Audit Commission has been in almost perpetual institutional evolution as it responded to the changing 'institutional design ideas' of successive governments.

The stated aim of the Audit Commission is to 'promote the best use of public money by ensuring the proper stewardship of public finances and by helping those responsible for public services to achieve economy, efficiency and effectiveness' (www.auditcommission.gov.uk/aboutus/downloads/ StrategicRegBurdenWEB.pdf). In this regard its 'priorities ... dovetail with those of the government in office' (Humphrey 2001:37) and so serve to enhance the 'steering capacity' of government (Cope and Goodship 2002:35–6; Wilson and Game 2002:158). This does not mean, however, that the Commission is subservient to central government. It has been willing to criticise central government policies and to support individual council's spending priorities where it has deemed appropriate (Wilson and Game 2002:159; Kelly 2003:467). Certainly the relationship between the UK government, the Audit Commission, and regulated bodies and the public has been far from top-down and uni-directional as the discourse of 'control' seems to suggest. Indeed, Clive Grace (2003:73–5), as newly appointed director of the Audit Commission, identified a 'new paradigm' of regulation in the 21st century in which there were multi-directional interactions between government, regulators, regulatees and the public as 'consumers' and 'users'. Increasingly the relationship between regulators and delivery agents has become more interactive and far more complex than traditional notions of 'central control' would allow.

This new complexity was evident in the Audit Commission's 2003 document *Strategic Regulation*. While recognising that 'regulation is an absolutely vital part of the public sector', the Commission acknowledged that regulation was 'fragmented' and that there were 'legitimate concerns about the cost, value and accountability of regulation' (Audit Commission 2003:2). To address these concerns the Audit Commission proposed the adoption of 'strategic regulation' which was designed to 'minimise the burden of regulation on audited and inspected bodies, while maximising the impact of regulation on improvement in services for users' (2003:4). The former objective was to be achieved through 'managed audits', a 'lighter-touch approach' to the audit of the very smallest councils (parish, town and community councils), and the adoption of a single performance management framework. In 2002, the introduction of Comprehensive Performance

Assessments (CPA) allowed the Commission to produce 'score cards' of council performance derived from information held by councils, government departments, auditors and inspectors; as well as a 'corporate assessment' of councils' ability to improve. The perceived value of the CPA regime was that it would reduce the level of audit and inspection required for better performing councils (Audit Commission 2003:6). In addition, the Commission sought to reduce the auditing burden still further by requesting the government to remove the statutory requirement of the Local Government 1999 Act for Best Value performance plans to be audited.

The Audit Commission in Wales

This body conducts local audit and inspection of Welsh public services. With a staff of 180 it works closely with the Audit Commission in England, but has developed distinct modes of operation to reflect the differences in organization and policy priorities amongst Welsh public bodies that have emerged since 1999. (The Audit Commission in England may still be called upon to give evidence to the National Assembly on the findings of its work.)

The Accounts Commission in Scotland

The Commission examines how Scotland's 32 local authorities and 34 joint boards manage their finances. Its 12 members are appointed by Scottish Executive ministers. It is assisted by specialist staff from Audit Scotland. Under the Local Government Scotland Act 2003 local authorities were given the power to promote or improve the 'well-being' of the people living in their area as well as to improve their performance in the delivery of services through 'Best Value'. The Accounts Commission was given audit responsibilities in relation to the provision of the 2003 Act and developed new arrangements (based largely on experience since 1997) to conduct Best Value audit.

Public Audit Forum

In October 1998 a consultative and advisory Public Audit Forum was established following a government recommendation in 1997. In essence, the Forum's remit was concerned with the development of 'joined-up' thinking through: the promotion of cooperation among national audit agencies; advice on the application of standards and practices of public auditors; advice on resolving common technical problems; provision of a 'strategic focus on issues cutting across the work of national audit agencies'; as well as the dissemination of good practice (www.public-audit-forum.gov.uk/about.htm). After reconstitution in November 2002 as an 'Audit Group', the Forum's membership included the National Audit Office, the Northern Ireland Audit Office, the Audit Commission for Local Authorities and the National Health Service in England and Wales, Audit Scotland; and Accounts Commission for Scotland; representatives from private sector accountancy firms and an observer from the Treasury.

Ombudsmen

The ombudsman model in the UK was initially derived from the Ombudsman in Scandanavian countries and New Zealand (see Gregory and Giddings 2002:5–6). However, what is of particular significance about the creation of the first ombudsman, for the purposes of this book at least, was that 'the British model was designed to fit within existing institutions' (Bradley and Ewing 2003:685). Indeed, the official title of the first ombudsman created in 1967—the 'Parliamentary Commissioner for Administration' (PCA)—gave a very clear indication as to which institution the new post had to be accommodated. From the outset it was made clear that the intention in creating a Parliamentary Commissioner was 'not to create any new institution which would erode the functions of MPs' (Gregory and Giddings 2002:28). Instead the purpose was to 'develop and reinforce' the existing institutional arrangements for protection of the individual against state maladministration.

The concern of institutional designers to locate the new ombudsman within the institutional contours of the UK's parliamentary state is revealed in several distinctive features of the UK model (see Gregory and Giddings 2002:24–9). First, the Ombudsman is, in essence, an Officer of the House of Commons appointed by the Crown and reports to parliament. Second, unlike all other countries, with the exception of France, the PCA in the UK is not authorized to act upon complaints received directly from members of the public. Instead, the PCA can only investigate complaints referred to her from Members of the House of Commons. Third, the PCA is also unique in the method of reporting the results of her investigations, as the report is made to the referring MP rather than to the initial complainant.

Fourth, whereas most other ombudsman have wide jurisdictional remits, the UK PAC is empowered only to investigate complaints made against central government departments and associated bodies for which ministers are deemed responsible (though some 228 public bodies are included on an indicative list of the bodies the PCA is able to investigate (see www.ombudsman.org.uk/pca/investigate.html)). Fifth, the PCA in the UK is distinctive in not having the authorization to initiate investigations in her own right, nor to adjudicate or resolve complaints. As Gregory and Giddings conclude: 'Much that is distinctive about the United Kingdom variant of the Ombudsman institution is to be found in its origins and in the efforts its architects felt constrained to make in order to accommodate the Ombudsman idea within the existing institutional framework of British government'.

From this initial design, the office of the PCA has developed incrementally and has been supplemented by a variety of 'speciality ombudsmen'. In 1994 the jurisdiction of the PCA was extended to include complaints about problems in obtaining access to official information under the Code of Practice on Access to Government Information.

The Health Service Ombudsman (HSO) investigates complaints about the National Health Service (NHS). Since its inception in 1973 the PCA has held coterminously the post of Health Service Commissioner (or more accurately 'posts', as, until 2002, there were nominally three Commissioners for England, Wales and Scotland). One major difference between the PCA and the HSO is that the latter may receive complaints directly from individuals. In other words, there is no MP filter. In part, the absence of the requirement for an MP filter can be accounted for in the perception of MPs that NHS matters were of a 'local character', given the sub-national organization of the service; and, in part also, by the institutional status of the NHS—with mediated arm's length responsibility of ministers. A second major difference is that the HSO can consider complaints beyond 'maladminstration' and so investigate 'poor service delivery' and complaints about 'care and treatment' (www.ombudsman.org.uk/hse/england/what_can. html).

Sub-national Ombudsmen

There are three Local Government Ombudsmen in England who investigate, for three different parts of the country, complaints of injustice arising from maladministration by local authorities and certain other bodies. A Local Government Ombudsman for Wales has also been in existence since 1974.

Devolution brought in its wake a restructuring of the ombudsmen systems in the UK. Both the Scotland Act and the Wales Act of 1998 made provision for the creation of respective Parliamentary Commissioners for Administration to investigate maladministration arising from the actions of the devolved executives. In October 2002 a single office of the Scottish Public Services Ombudsman replaced the existing Scottish Parliamentary, Health Service, Local Government and Housing Association Ombudsmen.

In March 2003 the Welsh Assembly Government announced its intention to create an integrated office of the Public Services Ombudsman for Wales by bringing together the separate offices of the Welsh Administration Ombudsman, the Health Service Ombudsman for Wales and the Commissioner for Local Administration in Wales. As an interim measure, while primary legislation was produced, it was agreed that the incumbent Commissioner for Local Administration in Wales was to succeed to the office of Health Service Commissioner for Wales in November 2003 and to the Welsh Administration Ombudsman in the autumn of 2004.

The Office of the Northern Ireland Ombudsman had been established in 1969 and since 1996 has included the two offices of the Assembly Ombudsman for Northern Ireland and the Northern Ireland Commissioner for Complaints. The combined Ombudsman's jurisdictions cover maladministration by government departments and public bodies, and complaints relating to local councils, education boards, health and social services boards, and housing in Northern Ireland.

Review of the public sector Ombudsmen

The proliferation of 'complaints-handling systems' since the introduction of the PCA in 1967, and the fact that they had been 'introduced with little thought that they should fit any systemic model or to whether the multiplicity or variety of arrangements would confuse the public' (Cabinet Office 2000a:para 2.18), was highlighted in a *Review of the Public Sector Ombudsmen in England* published in April 2000 (Cabinet Office 2000a). The Review was proposed in the *Modernising Government* White Paper and was seen as part of the overarching programme to encourage 'more joined-up and responsive services' (Cm 4310 1999:32). Given the developments outlined above, the Review concluded that the existing system was, indeed, confusing to the public and militated against the effective consideration of 'cross-boundary' complaints. Moreover the Review acknowledged that the organization of the public sector ombudsmen in England could not be considered in isolation from the arrangements in other parts of the UK (Cabinet Office 2000a:para 7.7). The general conclusion was reached that the pace and scope of change in the modernisation of government was 'leaving behind the public sector ombudsman' (2000a:para 8.1).

Flowing from this general conclusion came 51 specific recommendations. The most important for the present discussion were: the creation of a new College/Commission of ombudsmen which would combine the PCA, HSO and CLA, and which would provide a 'single gateway' for complaints; the collective 'direct answerability' of the Commission to the UK parliament; the removal of the MP filter; for public sector ombudsmen in Scotland, Wales and Northern Ireland to a have 'associate' status with the new Commission; and for the Commission to be able to report to parliament on a UK basis. However, after acceptance of the major recommendations of the Review in July 2001, the government hesitated in introducing the primary legislation required to bring a new Commission into effect (much to the concern of the House of Commons Public Administration Select Committee (see HC 448 2003:paras8−11)).

Indeed, the Public Administration Select Committee identified several 'worrying trends' which made the necessity of reform of the Ombudsmen system even more pressing. The first was the increase in the number of complaints received by the Parliamentary Ombudsman (1,973 in 2002−03; 1,981 in 2003−04). The Committee believed that the increased workload of the Ombudsman revealed 'disturbing evidence about routine administrative failure, departmental indifference and political intrusion into administrative matters . . . [which went] to the heart . . . of the issue of the quality of the public service that citizens should expect' (HC 448 2003:para 14). Moreover, the Committee concluded that: 'If the Government wishes to make public services responsive to citizens, as it claims, it must ensure that public service agencies take their obligations to the Ombudsman more seriously' (HC 448 2003:para 33).

If the Review, and the Public Administration Committee's response, provides some indication of how the Labour government's reformist conception of public service delivery impacted upon the institutional form of the ombudsmen, then, equally, the Review also provided an insight into the changing interinstitutional relationships among 'accountability' institutions in the UK. Of particular resonance for the 'Westminster model' was the recommendation to remove the MP filter; for, as the Cabinet Office's consultation paper on the Review noted, 'the original reasons for introducing the filter no longer apply. Modernisation of government and constitutional change have brought about many means by which the citizen can seek redress. .... The role of the MP as champion of the citizen is no longer exclusive' (Cabinet Office 2000b:para 2.14). More particularly, the Review voiced the opinion that the extensive development of partnerships (especially those between central and local government) meant that 'the MP filter can no longer be sustained in an era of joined up government' (Cabinet Office 2000a:para 3.52).

Yet the creation of a single integrated ombudsmen office in England would still leave unresolved the problem of coordinating the activities of Ombudsmen across the UK. As Ann Abraham, Parliamentary Commissioner, pointed out, she still had a role in considering complaints from Scotland, Wales and Northern Ireland about matters reserved at Westminster. Indeed, she believed that a more seamless service for citizens in England 'would complicate the handling of complaints from those not living in England about matters not devolved to Cardiff, Belfast or Edinburgh' (Memorandum HC 506–I 2003:para 8). What she believed was required was joint working amongst all public sector ombudsmen in the UK.

Inspection

The official definition of inspection is 'the process of periodic, targeted scrutiny to provide an independent check, and to report, on whether services are meeting national and local performance standards, legislative and professional requirements and the needs of Service users' (Public Audit Forum 2002a:5). The intention is to promote accountability and to contribute to the development of public policy through the provision of information to government and the public about the quality of service delivery. A series of national agencies carry out inspection of the major public services in the four sub-nations in the UK. The Office for Standards in Education

(Ofsted) is a non-ministerial government department (see chapter 4), is highly visible, and conducts inspections in England, along with its sister inspectorates in Scotland, Wales and Northern Ireland. In England, since 2002, social service and health care provision has been inspected by two agencies—the Commission for Healthcare Audit and Inspection and the Commission for Social Care Inspection. The police services are inspected by Her Majesty's Inspectorates for England and Wales, for Scotland, and for Northern Ireland. Since 2003, a single Housing Inspectorate, located in the Audit Commission (see above), has inspected both local authorities and re-gistered social landlords.

Inquiries

One manifestation of public disquiet about existing mechanisms of re-dress of grievances or general oversight of government is the seemingly exponential growth of demands for 'inquiries' into the activities of gov-ernment in the 21st century. Indeed, one Labour minister expressed his concern at the incessant demands for inquiries in his statement that: 'We cannot run the government on the basis of public inquiries. They may be good for lawyers but they are not good for the governance of this country' (Adam Ingram quoted in HC 606 2004:Q249). Yet, inquir-ies are an accepted part of the structure of administrative justice in the UK, and take several different institutional forms. *Public Inquiries* are stat-utory inquiries mostly concerned with planning issues or land develop-ment, as well as being used to examine electoral boundaries, or to in-vestigate major public disasters. *Tribunals of Inquiry* are appointed in ac-cordance with the provisions of the 1921 Tribunals of Inquiry (Evidence) Act. Such tribunals investigate 'matters of concern which requires thor-ough and impartial investigation to allay public anxiety' (Bradley and Ewing 2003:683). Recent examples of inquiries conducted on a statutory basis include the investigation of the Dunblane Primary School shootings in 1996, the 'Bloody Sunday' Inquiries—instigated respectively in 1972 and 1998—into events surrounding the shootings in Londonderry, Northern Ireland in 1972; and into the Shipman case in 2000, in which a doctor was found guilty of murdering scores of his patients. In addition, *ad-hoc non-statutory inquiries* have been used increasingly to investigate such disparate matters as standards in public life (the Nolan Inquiry, 1995), the sale of arms-making equipment to Iraq (the Scott Inquiry, 1996), the foot and mouth crisis (Anderson Inquiry, 2001), the circumstances surrounding the death of civil servant Dr David Kelly (Hutton Inquiry, 2004), and the review of intelligence on weapons of mass destruction (Butler Inquiry, 2004).

What is notable about the last mentioned group of inquiries is that they addressed perceived failures of the political system and processes of government. As such they were highly contentious, and although established to conduct independent investigations, and often headed by senior judges (as in the case of Nolan, Scott, and Hutton, and with nearly 60 per cent of major inquiries since 1990 chaired by serving judges (CP 12/04 2004: Annex B)) their manner of appointment (by ministers) and the specification of their terms of reference (again by ministers) served to politicize the very process of inquiry. As Beatson (2004:24) noted: 'Where a topic is politically controversial and the report is neither a binding enforceable decision nor correctable by an appeal, those disagreeing with it may be unable to resist the temptation of seeking to discredit its findings by fierce criticism of the judge [or, in the case of Lord Butler, an ex-permanent secretary]'. The temptation to dismiss the findings of the Hutton and Butler inquiries as 'establishment whitewashes' proved too great for opposition parties, and most UK newspapers and news media in 2004. If the purpose of the inquiries was to 'provide a dispassionate account of what happened' (Lord Falconer HC 606 2004: Q197), or, in a more idealized view, to 'restore order and legitimacy to institutions and to serve as an extra-parliamentary means of ensuring public accountability' (Beatson 2004:2) the questioning of the very inquiry processes, let alone the respective conclusions, did little to depoliticize the narrative of events or to 're-legitimize' the political process.

Conclusion

Inquiries provide a clear example of the intermingling of judicial and political institutional roles. As Beatson (2004:6) observes: 'At a point of crisis in Britain, almost no one except some academics, questions the appropriateness of turning to a judge'. Frequently, inquiries blur notions of the separation of powers and the distinction between political and judicial roles. Even a government that seeks to reinforce the separation elsewhere—in its proposals for a supreme court and the abolition of the office of the Lord

Chancellor—willingly concedes that 'it can be appropriate for judges to chair inquiries, because their experience and position make them particularly well-suited to the role' (CP 12/04 2004:para 46). In part, it is the 'long tradition of independence from politics' and the broad acceptance that judges are 'free from any party political bias' (CP 12/04 2004:para 46) that enhances the qualifications of the judiciary to chair inquiries. But equally the very virtues of independence and partisan neutrality—the very foundations of the legitimacy of the institutions of inquiry—are the first to be questioned by dissenters from the conclusions of inquiries into politically sensitive issues. Lord Hutton's inquiry into the events surrounding the death of Dr David Kelly, and the opprobrium heaped upon him and his findings, provided a vivid illustration of the intertwining of political and judicial institutional roles and how partisan political norms came into direct conflict with, and were used to challenge, the 'institutionally apolitical' norms of independence of the inquiry process and outcomes (see Beatson 2004).

The potential for politicization of the judiciary has also been highlighted in the growth of judicial review. Concerns about 'judicial activism'—with the courts scrutinising executive actions—led to claims that 'judges had moved over the line from the judicial to the political' (Stevens 2002:68). Similar claims were voiced in relation to the discretion exercised by the judiciary in relation to EU legislation and in response to the Human Rights Act of 1998. Cumulatively, these changes led to the conclusion that the judiciary had benefited from an unprecedented transfer of political power away from the legislature and the executive. In parallel, the growth of the 'regulatory state' raised questions about traditional institutional patterns of accountability within the parliamentary state. Proponents of the concept of the 'regulatory state' believed that the historic interinstitutional interactions between executive and legislature had been re-pivoted with the growth of regulatory institutions.

The changing interinstitutional relationships noted in this chapter have both empirical and normative dimensions. The extent to which the roles of judicial, executive and legislative institutions have become intertwined and overlap has been monitored in the preceding pages. Underpinning these empirical developments has been a normative proposition that the judiciary has become more proactive, the regulatory state more extensive, and the inquiry system more expansive because the historic institutional modes of redress—through parliament—have been undermined. Hence, judicial review 'may be vital to ensure fairness in society now that Parliament is increasingly ineffective in controlling executive decisions' (Stevens 2002:68); the 'regulatory state' may be a response to the deficiencies of ensuring accountability in the 'parliamentary state'; and inquiries may reflect doubts 'whether Parliament has the will to exercise an appropriate level of regulation over government in politically controversial matters' (Beatson 2004:22).

But, as this chapter has made clear, the extent and direction of interinstitutional change are not only prompted by fundamental questioning of parliament's historic institutional roles, but are also framed within a set of constitutional answers provided by parliament's institutional position itself. At it starkest, institutional development in the UK in the 21st century is constrained by a path determined by the pre-existing configuration of the 'parliamentary state'. This is apparent in the comity and self-limitation observable on the part of the judiciary, and the attendant deference to the democratic legitimacy of the legislature and the political executive. Similarly, there is recognition that 'regulation starts with Parliament' and that 'the ultimate responsibility for regulation rests with Parliament' (HL 68–I 2004:para 29), and that there is a basic institutional interconnectedness within the regulatory framework (HL 68–I 2004:para 40). Equally, although major inquiries are conducted independently of the parliamentary process, their findings ultimately prompt a ministerial statement to parliament and so reignite the political controversies they were designed, in part, to smother (see for example on the Butler Inquiry, HC Debates 14 July 2004:cols 1431–1451). The simple point is that although judicial review, regulation and inquiries, each in their own way, are institutional responses to perceived failings of the traditional institutional processes of accountability associated with the 'parliamentary state'; ultimately—in the 'last instance'—these institutional responses have to accommodate themselves to the pre-existing political institutional framework.

KEY TERMS

- accountability
- asymmetry
- audit
- comity

- declaration of incompatibility
- Human Rights Act 1998
- inquiries
- inspection
- judicial deference
- judicial independence
- judicial review
- ombudsman

- oversight
- politicized judiciary
- regulation
- regulatory state
- self-regulation
- separation of powers
- supreme court

....

GUIDE TO FURTHER READING

GREGORY, R. and GIDDINGS, P. (2002) *The Ombudsman, the Citizen and Parliament*, (London, Politicos).

An exhaustive and definitive account of the origins and development of the Ombudsman system.

LOVELAND, I. (2003) *Constitutional Law, Administrative Law and Human Rights: A Critical Introduction*, 3rd edn. (London, LexisNexis Butterworths).

A readable constitutional law textbook. Its readability stems in part from its willingness to locate the study of law within broader political and historical contexts.

MORAN, M. (2003) *The British Regulatory State: High Modernism and Hyper-Innovation*, (Oxford, Oxford University Press).

An incisive and challenging examination of new regulatory institutions and the debates concerning the 'regulatory state'.

OLIVER, D. (2003) *Constitutional Reform in the UK*, (Oxford, Oxford University Press).

A broad ranging text but specifically of value for its examination of the interconnections of judicial, regulatory and political institutions.

STEVENS, R. (2002) *The English Judges: Their Role in the Changing Constitution*, (Oxford, Hart Publishing).

A short and enlightening examination of the two-way flow of influence between political and judicial institutions.

7

···

Conclusion

Overview

The extent of institutional change since 1997, and the extent to which the UK continues to be characterized as much by institutional continuity as by institutional revolution, are assessed in this chapter. The main explanations of institutional change are examined and the paradoxes stemming from the formulation of institutional change within the parameters of the Westminster model are analysed. Despite the speed and scope of institutional change, the institutional prescriptions of the Westminster model still dominate the discourse of UK politicians in the 21st century.

Introduction

Institutional continuity was taken both as a 'given' and as a 'concern' in the UK in the latter part of the 20th century. In fact, a basic conservatism towards traditional political institutions had pervaded both major political parties for much of that century and had ensured the continuance of institutions whose political DNA could be dated back to the 17th century and beyond. In particular, the UK post-war state was characterized by institutional continuity rather than institutional change. Without doubt there had been discontinuities and change, but these tended to be specific, pragmatic and, in essence, piecemeal. In these circumstances, notions of path dependency—with political institutions displaying 'change resistance' and a 'self reinforcing dynamic' (see chapter 1)—appeared to have particular resonance in explaining the relative institutional inertia in the UK. Yet, since 1997, the scale and scope of institutional change has been such that it has been identified as a 'constitutional revolution', with change being greater than 'during any comparable period since at least the middle of the 18th century' (King 2001:53). If this has been the case, then what needs to be explained is institutional change—and the extent to which 'critical junctures', 'branching points', and 'punctuated equilibria' have characterized political institutional development in recent years.

This final chapter is thus structured around four main themes: first, the extent of institutional change; second, the precipitants of institutional change, third, the coherence of institutional change; and finally the paradoxical nature of institutional change.

Extent of institutional change

The scale of institutional change is indicated in Table 7.1. This table simply lists the major 'new' political institutions created between 1997 and 2004. 'New' is defined here as those institutions which were newly created, or whose role and functions had been sufficiently restructured to warrant a new title. Excluded from this list are many institutions which were reconstituted or reformulated, such as many executive agencies and NDPBs, or which were internally 'modernized' such as the House of Commons, House of Lords, the civil service, the Cabinet Office, and local authorities. In other words, the true extent of institutional change was far more extensive than captured in Table 7.1.

The sheer scale, rapidity and incessantness of institutional change in these years gave rise to academic concerns about the pathological consequences of such change. In particular, anxieties over the 'unintended consequences' of institutional change continued to mount (see below). Certainly, if political institutions have to be understood in terms of their interactions and interdependencies (as argued in chapter 1), then the task of comprehending political institutions in the UK in the mid-2000s was far more complicated than it had been a decade earlier.

Equally, concern about the financial costs of new representative institutions began to mount and to be deployed in the party conflict preceding the 2005 general election. Thus, for example, in the autumn of 2004 the Shadow Financial Secretary to the Treasury, Andrew Tyrie, published a paper which estimated the costs of the new representative institutions in Scotland, Wales,

TABLE 7.1	**Institutional Change Post-1997***

Sub-national/regional/local

England
 Elected Mayors (11)
 English Regional Chambers/Assemblies
 Greater London Authority
  Elected Mayor and Assembly,
  London Development Agency,
  Transport for London,
  London Fire and Emergency Planning Authority,
  London Metropolitan Police Authority
 Central-Local Partnership
 Regional Coordination Unit
 Regional Development Agencies
 Standards Board for England
 Sub-national partnerships (60 different types)

Northern Ireland
 Civic Forum NI
 Equality Commission for Northern Ireland
 Human Rights Commission (NI)
 NI Assembly's Commissioner for Standards
 Northern Ireland Assembly
 Northern Ireland Executive

Scotland
 Audit Scotland
 Auditor General for Scotland
 Civic Forum Scotland
 Scottish Executive
 Scottish Human Rights Commission
 Scottish Information Commissioner
 Scottish Parliament
 Scottish Public Services Ombudsman
 Standards Commission for Scotland

continues

Table 7.2 continued

Wales

  Auditor General for Wales

  Public Services Ombudsman for Wales

  Wales Audit Office

  Welsh National Assembly

  Welsh National Assembly Government

Devolution Related

  British-Irish Council

  Joint Ministerial Committee

  North-South Ministerial Council

Executive Institutions

  Departments

    Constitutional Affairs

    Culture, Media and Sport

    Education and Skills

    Environment, Food and Rural Affairs

    Office of Deputy Prime Minister

    Office of Leader of the House of Commons

    Scotland Office

    Wales Office

    Work and Pensions

    HM Revenue and Customs

  Task Forces

Judicial, Regulatory, Redress Institutions

  Commission for Equality and Human Rights

  Electoral Commission

  House of Lords Appointments Commission

  Information Commissioner (FoI)

  Judicial Appointments Commission

  Public Audit Forum/Audit Group

  Supreme Court

*Changes implemented or to be implemented by 2006

Northern Ireland, and London (reported in *The Times* 10 November 2004). Excluding the capital costs of some £560 million, the annual running costs for these devolved institutions were recorded as £188 million. In total, Tyrie estimated that the 'cost of democracy' (including, for example, MPs' salaries and allowances and local government management costs), was 80 per cent higher in 2004 than it had been in 1997 and stood at £1.3 billion. Even discounting for partisan inflation of the actual figures, nonetheless, the scale of institutional change brought not only perceived benefits but also manifest financial costs.

Precipitants of institutional change

As noted in chapter 1 several explanations of institutional change can be found in new institutional theories. One common explanation revolves around the idea that rapid change is associated with the punctuation of existing institutional equilibria, when 'branching points' are reached that move the trajectory of institutional development onto a new path. While new institutional theories, particularly historical institutionalism, have been capable of identifying such branching points after the event, they have been less successful in predicting such changes. Even when change has been identified, explanations of why 'branching points' or 'critical moments' occur at particular times have tended to stress exogenous rather than endogenous factors. External change in the environment of an institution (whether empirical or ideational) becomes a major explanatory variable of institutional change.

A globalising economy

Mark Evans (2003:42) argues that the late 1980s and 1990s represented a 'critical moment' for democratic institutions in the UK in the face of 'relative economic decline, the unresolved Irish and Scottish questions, mounting pressures of European integration and public dissatisfaction with the way the UK was governed'. Evans identifies the 'global economic structure' as a major precipitant of institutional change. On the one side, national governments were constrained by politico-economic events elsewhere in the world (though the exact strength of these constraints distinguishes theorists of, respectively, 'globalization', 'europeaniza-tion', and 'national governance' (see Gamble 2000:290–2; Hay 2002:5–7; Richards and Smith 2002:122–45)). On the other, the UK's economy had performed relatively poorly within the globalising economy. Moreover, although the 'state of the British economy has preoccupied and constrained the British political class with a consistency and potency unmatched by any other' (Coates 2002:155) these preoccupations and constraints had been more pronounced in some periods than in others. Historically, a pattern had emerged whereby heightened concern over the performance of the economy tended to be accompanied by increased critical scrutiny of the performance of political institutions. This was the case in the periods 1919–22, 1930–33, and from the late 1970s through to the 1980s (see Judge 1990b:39–50). Indeed, in this latter period, 'the economic failures and social tensions of the 1970s reinforced the impression of institutional failure' (Johnson 2004:3). Certainly, by the 1990s, the connection between a failing economy and failing political institutions became something of an orthodoxy amongst the chattering classes. Best selling books, by for example Will Hutton, propounded the view that economic and social malaise in the UK could be redressed by 'nothing less than root and branch overhaul of the Westminster version of democracy' (Hutton 1996:25). These popular diagnoses were confirmed in more academic treatises, with, for example, Marquand (1988:246) identifying 'the conception of power and authority which has underpinned Britain's political order since the 18th century' as 'an obstacle to successful [economic and social] adjustment'.

Europeanization

If the concerns about a globalising economy were general (and arguably 'generalized' in the sense of not drawing direct and detailed connections between global economic constraints and specific institutional failings), more precise institutional concerns were apparent in the debate over con-tinuing membership of the European Union and the process of 'european-ization'. The most acute of these concerns pivoted around the impact of membership upon the institutional values associated with 'parliamentary sovereignty'. There was little dissent from the view that 'membership of the European Community, with its doctrines of primacy and direct effect, has undermined the doctrine of the legal sovereignty of Parliament' (Oliver

2003:84). Moreover, there was little doubt that 'in any normal interpretation of the matter Parliament has surrendered both legal and political sovereignty to a substantial degree' (Johnson 2004:265). Such 'surrender' exercised the thoughts not only of 'eurosceptics' in both major parties (and beyond in the UK Independence Party) but also concerned those who identified a paradox—that the policy independence of the executive within the UK had increased as its policy dependence upon other member states had also increased during a deepening process of 'europeanization' (see Judge 1993:210–11; Page 2004:48).

Predictably perhaps, contention amongst and between party politicians (with the EU revealing significant fractures within both major parties since accession in 1973) focused upon challenges posed to the constitutional precept of parliamentary sovereignty. Yet, the irony was that a more sustained challenge to the very model itself came in the institutional reconfiguration of 'national government' into 'multi-level governance'. Indeed, as Geddes (2004:161) notes, the 'trend towards new patterns of governance is one to which Eurosceptic rhetoric has been slow to adapt because of its strong focus on the classic locations of power, authority and accountability: namely parliament and the notion of parliamentary sovereignty'.

Yet the trend towards 'new patterns of governance' provided a far more profound challenge to the Westminster model than the debate about parliamentary sovereignty could encapsulate. As noted in chapter 3, proponents of 'governance' and associated models of 'networks', 'differentiated polity', and the 'hollowed-out state' maintained that the Westminster model was 'limited and misleading' (Pierre and Stoker 2000:31) and failed to capture the institutional diversity and complexity of the modern UK state. This complexity was a characteristic of new institutional interconnections, where traditional state political institutions were interlocked with non-governmental institutions in a web of networks. The importance of membership of the EU was that these networks extended beyond state borders to incorporate 'europeanized' interactions and interdependencies centred upon 'Brussels'. Membership of the EU (and other international organizations) was identified as an external hollowing-out of the UK state as UK governments became intermeshed in convoluted power-dependency relations beyond the level of the nation state. In this sense, the process of 'europeanization' and the practice of multi-level governance highlighted 'important empirical gaps in the Westminster model' (Bevir and Rhodes 2003:198).

Multi-level UK

The UK's membership of the EU not only spotlighted the issue of the devolution of power *upwards* to EU institutions but also illuminated devolution *downwards* to regions and local authorities within the UK itself. Admittedly, for most of the period between 1979 and 1997 the issue of internal devolution was framed and developed in the half-light of the national peripheries and regions, and away from the glare of London-based institutions. While, for much of this period, the flames of Thatcherite neo-liberal social and economic policies shone brightly in central state institutions they cast scorching and destructive shadows over traditional political institutions associated with the peripheries. Indeed, the centralising dynamic of Mrs Thatcher's statecraft (see below) contributed to a 'perception in Scotland and Wales that the old territorial consensus and all that accompanied it was being undermined by the Conservatives' (Mitchell 2002:247). Support for devolution after 1979 was thus largely negative in intent—to prevent future English dominated governments in London acting regressively in the peripheries. In part, however, support reflected a positive desire to match the political institutional structure in Scotland and Wales to existing (and threatened) national social and civic institutions in those countries.

Moreover, the very concept of internal devolution within the UK gathered 'external' legitimation through the broader processes of 'europeanization' noted above. Indeed, powerful constitutional substantiation of sub-national political institutions found formal acknowledgement in the doctrine of subsidiarity in the Maastricht Treaty of 1992. For most member states such sub-national institutions were already in existence and, hence, the Maastricht Treaty simply confirmed the legitimate role of regions within the overarching frame of the EU. For many in Scotland, Wales and Northern Ireland, however, subsidiarity provided a goal to be attained. Yet this goal was contested in the UK, and revealed starkly the divergence between the peripheries and a centralist Conservative government in London. On the one side, the UK government sought to define subsidiarity in terms of a dispersion of powers between two levels—nation states and the EU. On the other, supporters of devolution argued that subsidiarity conceived of delegation amongst at least three levels—sub-nations, nation states and the EU.

Centralization: Westminster model rampant

Despite the 'empirical gaps' revealed in the development of multi-level governance and the challenges posed to the Westminster model through 'europeanization', the model was deployed by successive Conservative governments after 1979 to moderate the tendencies towards governance (see Judge 1993:195–7). Yet this was itself paradoxical. On the one side, 'far from decentralising the state, the policies of successive Thatcher administrations are widely regarded as having actually increased the degree of centralization in British government and society' (Foley 1999:54). Of particular relevance to the argument of this book: 'Margaret Thatcher's governments earned a thoroughly deserved reputation for arrogance and authoritarianism, but they did so by using the large powers conferred on central government by the Westminster system ... The Thatcher programme ... exploited to the hilt the quite traditional structures of the UK state to legitimate and realize the government's objectives' (Blackburn 1992:6). Certainly, Mrs Thatcher invoked the Westminster model and the legitimatory capacity of the notion of parliamentary sovereignty to defuse the perceived threats to the neo-liberal project posed by trade unions (see Judge 1993:120); institutions of collective provision (education, National Health Service (see Bogdanor 1989:137)); the professions; and, especially, local government (see Kavanagh 1990:286–8).

Existing state institutions, configured in the Westminster model, were further deployed simultaneously to enhance collective state power and to reduce the scope of individual civil liberties under successive Conservative governments (for details see Ewing and Gearty 1990). These sustained challenges to civil liberties not only galvanized opposition to the authoritarian tendencies of the Thatcherite neo-liberal project, but also underscored the simple fact that they had been effected through existing institutions. In using the established institutional structures of the Westminster model Mrs Thatcher managed both to reaffirm the potency of an executive-centric institutional configuration and to generate demands for new institutional forms and structures to address the pathologies of an over-centralized state. Indeed, Ewing and Gearty (1990:7) prophesized that 'Mrs Thatcher's greatest service to the nation may yet be the institutional reforms that take place on her departure'.

The Third Way

Undoubtedly, the Thatcherite project radicalized politics in the UK and stretched further the conventional and consensual nature of institutional interactions into the mutated form of the Westminster model characterized as 'elective dictatorship'. (The term 'elective dictatorship' had originally been coined by the Conservative politician Lord Hailsham to criticize the governing style of Labour governments in the 1970s (Hailsham 1978)). So great were the effects of 'over-government' and the transformation of economic and social relations after 1979, however, that the cumulative effects have been likened to 'regime change'. Certainly, the rapidity and scope of socio-political transformation was sufficient to fuel demands for radical constitutional change (Bogdanor 1989:141–2; Brazier 1998:8–12; Gamble 1996:22–3; Foley 1999:49–53; Johnson 2004:163).

What is significant about the Labour party's response (and ultimately that of successive Labour governments) to the Thatcherite period is that it was comprehensive. In accepting the need for 'modernisation', such renewal was to be wide-ranging and was to encompass Labour's own internal organization and philosophy, as well as attempting to reconceptualize political, social and economic relationships in a rapidly changing and globalising world. Moreover, although 'New Labour' and its underpinning 'Third Way' project have been dismissed as vacuous (Fielding 2003:81), the party's leadership should be credited with seeking to identify the ideological parameters which defined the Labour party as it headed into a new century. A searching inventory and assessment of the ideological baggage inherited from the preceding century was a necessary part of this reorientation. Equally, recognition of the changed ideological and policy terrains upon which the Labour party had to compete, as a result of Conservative electoral and governmental dominance after 1979, had to be factored into the party's reconstitution as an electoral and ideological force. Indeed, as Andrew Gamble (1996:34) observed, 'the transformation of the Labour party is sometimes regarded as Thatcherism's greatest achievement'.

Here is not the place, and this is not the book, to provide a detailed discussion of the 'Third Way' (see Giddens 1998; 2000). What is of importance for present purposes is that the Third Way 'starts off from what it is not. A third or middle way must necessarily stand in relation to two others'

(Driver and Martell 2002:69). The 'two others' in Labour's case were the 'old left'—the social democratic politics of the post-war period characterized as statist, keynesian and welfare oriented; and the 'new right'—the neo-liberal social and economic individualism of Thatcherite Conservatism. The Third Way was designed:

> to promote wealth creation and social justice, the market and the community; that will embrace private enterprise but not automatically favour market solutions; that can endorse a positive role for the state ... while not assuming that governments provide public services directly; and that can provide a communitarian rather than an individualist view of society in which individuals are embedded in social relations which give structure and meaning to people's lives; and that it is the role of governments to promote 'the community' as a way of enriching individual lives. (Driver and Martell 2002:70).

Whether these general principles amount to a coherent ideology or translate into specific policy prescriptions is beyond the immediate focus of this chapter. What is of concern, however, is to note that the Third Way sought to identify new forms of public intervention in society and the economy and to countenance the reform or 'reinventing' of government and public administration (Driver and Martell 2002:79). In this sense democratic renewal was a core, if somewhat nebulous, element of the Third Way. Thus the 'reconstruction of government' can be seen clearly in the conceptions of key Third Way propagandists (see, for example Mandelson and Liddle 1996; Giddens 1998). If 'New Labour [was] a new type of politics' (Mandelson and Liddle 1996:17) then a 'new party', a 'new government', and a 'new enthusiasm for constitutional change' were essential elements of the new polity. Institutional change, therefore, was at the heart of the new project and included the following specific ingredients: a new relationship between citizen and subject (through the incorporation of the ECHR into UK law), the revival of local government; regional and subnational devolution; parliamentary reform; electoral reform; and open government (Mandelson and Liddle 1996:189–210). These ingredients eventually found reflection in the Labour party's manifestos of 1997 and 2001. In this manner, Third Way ideas were transmuted into specific elements of New Labour's programmes for government.

Party pragmatism

Before entering government, leading strategists in the Labour party recognized that a 'big bang' approach to institutional reform would be inappropriate, and that instead 'steady, piecemeal reform' was the way forward (Mandelson and Liddle 1996:210). More cynical observers maintained, however, that piecemeal institutional change would be as much a reflection of political and partisan expediency as of principled strategy. The devolution settlements in Scotland and Wales exemplified such thinking: 'Each devolution scheme appears to have been tailored to deal with what were perceived as problems and attitudes specific to that part of the United Kingdom where it was to be applied' (Johnson 2001:335). Not the least of these problems were partisan calculations about the powers to be devolved, the electoral systems to be adopted (including the relative weighting of constituency and additional members), the structures of legislative and executive relations, and the very size of the respective representative bodies (see chapter 5). Arguably, therefore, commitment to the principles of devolution was mediated through an equally powerful commitment to maximize partisan advantage in any devolution settlement. Similarly, the failure to introduce electoral reform for Westminster elections; the anaemic nature, and delayed implementation, of freedom of information legislation; the severe qualification of the commitment to revive democratically elected local government (manifested in the preference for managed local service delivery effected through targets and regulation); and the residual, undemocratic composition of the 'interim' House of Lords, have all variously been caricatured as the partisan calculations of the Labour leadership in government.

Coherence: Where's the blueprint?

Even when New Labour governments escaped accusations of partisan expediency or ideological zealotry, they were subjected to the charges that their institutional reforms were ill-conceived, uninformed, haphazard and under-researched. There were two dimensions to such charges. One identified 'ignorance of, and apparent indifference to, the nation's constitutional arrangements' (Norton 2003:554) on the part of Tony Blair and his ministers. The absence of 'rigorous intellectual underpinning' and 'the obsessive desire for quick results' was claimed to have resulted in a 'huge muddle' (Smith 2003:593). Thus, for all that Labour governments were obsessed with notions of 'joined-up' government, critics lamented the absence of joined-up thinking about institutional reform (see Johnson 2001:343). In this view, reforms were seen as ad hoc, stand-alone initiatives, lacking a 'coherently devised overall plan' (Smith 2003:591) and 'were not the fruits of a grand design' (Lester 2001:693). New Labour stood accused of 'a blank refusal to examine constitutional matters in the round' (Smith 2003:592).

Many analyses of specific institutional reforms noted the absence of an overarching blueprint. For example, even before the Scottish Parliament was established, the Scottish Affairs Select Committee had expressed concern that: 'As far as we can see, this reform is being conceived piecemeal; if there is an overall blue-print showing how all the pieces will fit together, none of our witnesses were aware of it' (HC 460 1998:para 31). Similarly, Lord Woolf, in commenting upon the proposals for the creation of a Supreme Court (see chapter 6) expressed concern about the 'torrent of constitutional changes' and that 'there is hardly an institution performing functions of a public nature which has not been the subject of change. The changes have ... been introduced in separate legislation, but little attention has been paid to their cumulative effect' (*The Times* 3 March 2003).

While there was widespread consensus that there was no grand design, the reasons why this was the case varied. First, there was the view that there was a tradition in the UK of 'pragmatic ad-hoc adaptation' (Johnson 2004:284); in which case, New Labour governments simply conformed to tradition. Second, and more radically, the absence of an overarching blueprint was explained in terms of New Labour's adoption of a strategy of change which was 'deliberately designed to be a muddle in order to both search for the right reform formula and create a dynamic for change by creating instability but also space for innovation' (Stoker 2002:418). By this argument, New Labour's approach to institutional reform was premised on the principle of a lottery. Stoker propounded the view that Labour's strategy with regards to English regional government (see chapter 5) was not the result of confusion, but represented a conscious strategy. This strategy had been designed, in part, to disorientate existing local/regional institutions; in part, because of a lack of trust between New Labour and the institutions of devolved governance (2002:426), in part, to build winning coalitions and provide 'prizes for all' (2002:428), and, in part, as a means of reconciling the tensions between New Labour's reputation for 'control freakery' and its Third Way vision of creating a decentralized, empowering and enabling state (2002:431). Stoker clearly identified this as a winning strategy, insofar as it 'has allowed a plethora of decentralized units and reform initiatives to find favour' (2002:417). Yet, the other dimensions of a lottery—that there are losers as well as winners, and risks as well as opportunities—is not examined. The negative result of the referendum on an elected regional assembly in the North East of England in November 2004 (see chapter 5), and the earlier rejections of elected mayors in 19 cities, provided empirical challenges to Stoker's logic: 'my point is not that the programme is incoherent but that it is incoherent with reason and for a purpose' (Stoker 2002:418). The voters in these regions and cities appeared to share an alternative and broader conception that: 'Extensive though the reforms introduced by Labour have been, it is difficult to see in them a new constitutional settlement in the sense of a coherent set of ideas that can be expected to take root' (Peele 2000:116).

Change and continuity

> [V]iewed in retrospect, the second half of the 20th century was a period of unusual constitutional quiescence ... the extended period of inertia ended with the election of the Labour government on 1 May 1997. (Flinders 2004:127)

Whilst Flinders' statement identifies the step-change in the UK's institutional development after 1997, it understates the significance of some of the changes that had occurred during the preceding 18 years of Conservative government. In fact 'Mrs Thatcher made many institutional changes' (Rhodes 1997:95). Indeed, institutional change after 1997 can be seen as both an incremental advancement of changes implemented between 1979 and 1997 and as a reaction to some of those changes. The 'reaction' has been noted already in the pages of this chapter. The 'advancement' has been noted in earlier chapters, but it is worth recapping here some of the strands of development.

Significantly for the present discussion, the institutional hall-marks of the Thatcherite 'revolution' came to be burnished in the Blairite 'revolution' after 1997: agencification, new public management, marketization, regulation and audit, the propagation of an efficiency ethos, enhanced central control of local authorities, the pursuit of a consociational strategy in Northern Ireland, and the embedding (albeit reluctantly) of 'europeanization'. Hence, not only did institutional innovation pre-date 1997, but the changes effected by the Blair governments also incorporated several vital elements of earlier Thatcherite reforms.

Underpinning such continuity was a further, more fundamental continuity. This was a pervasive, and often uncritical, deployment by successive governments of the norms and values of the Westminster model. Despite espousing the 'reconstruction of government'—variously through the importation of alternative norms and values associated with private sector institutions (managerialism, marketization, performance measurement, regulation and service delivery); or with Third Way 'modernisation' (partnerships, social inclusion, holistic government)—both Conservative and Labour governments simply layered these ideas on top of existing norms associated with the Westminster model. When questions were raised about the compatibility of these new institutional norms with the traditional institutional norms of representative and accountable government, successive administrations, by default or design, sought answers in an idealized version of the Westminster model (see particularly chapters 4 and 6).

Testimony to the hold of the traditional Westminster model over a 'modernising' Labour government came from a diverse range of analytical perspectives (a few examples will suffice here):

'Labour, like its predecessors, remains a party of traditional loyalty to the Westminster model of government'. (Driver and Martell 2002:56–7)

'Labour politicians have been conditioned, as much as Conservatives, by the Westminster model'. (Richards and Smith 2002:232)

'New Labour has taken great care to implement its constitutional reforms, however precariously, within the traditional Westminster model of British government. Crucially, the conventional arrangements have not been replaced with any discernible conception of an alternative constitution'. (Flinders 2004:143)

'Labour has introduced significant innovations ... within the context ... of an acceptance of the precepts of the Westminster model'. (Richards and Smith 2004:124)

'The constitution has not been reshaped or recast in a new form ... the Blair government undertook reform in what was in reality a more or less traditional way: it sought pragmatically to make changes where it could by adapting, changing and adding to the familiar institutional landscape'. (Johnson 2004:308–9)

After 1997 the familiar institutional landscape continued to follow the contours of the Westminster model. Why exactly, still requires some explanation.

The most persuasive explanation derived from the analysis threaded through the preceding chapters is that the Westminster model still symbolizes the elemental values of representation and accountability that serve as the prescriptions of legitimate government in the UK. As argued in chapter 2 the Westminster model retains its significance as an organizing perspective in the sense of identifying a set of norms, values and meanings that legitimate the actions and interactions of state institutions. These might very well be idealized—in their specification of a serial flow of legitimacy from the people through their elected representatives to an accountable and responsive executive. Nonetheless, in this process, government has been conceived as 'limited', with its outputs controlled and authorized by representatives of the 'political nation' (treated synonymously with 'the people' since the mass franchise) and so legitimized. These values and their institutional embodiment in an elected parliament have been at the 'core of the theory and practice of British government for [over] three hundred years, (Miliband 1982:20). Given both the longevity and the centrality of these prescriptions there are grounds 'for believing that the ideals of parliamentary government ... still command widespread, though diffused and diluted loyalty in society at large. There is after all no evidence of substantial and committed support for plausible alternatives to parliamentary government fashioned in the image of the Westminster tradition' (Johnson 2004:135).

If the Westminster model is still the one to which the electorate subscribes, or at least acquiesces, it is also the model that informs how the major political actors—politicians, civil servants and judges—operate and relate to each other, and how institutional norms—of the executive, legislative and judicial branches—are defined in the UK (Judge 2004:696). In declaring repeatedly that 'there is no intention to begin from first principles' (HL Debates 21 June 2001:vol 626, col 52) New Labour governments have confirmed their continuing attachment to the 'appropriate behaviour' encompassed within the 'old principles'. Thus, Labour governments since 1997 have persistently defended their actions, and formulated institutional change, within the parameters of the Westminster model. Each institutional and constitutional reform—whether of the House of Lords, devolved parliaments and assemblies, incorporation of the ECHR, or the creation of a supreme court—has been accompanied by a ritual reaffirmation of the continuing centrality of the model, and especially parliamentary sovereignty, to the legitimation of the state and government. Labour governments have not sought to challenge the 'critical constitutional morality' prescribed in this model. Far from it, the key notions of consent, representation and accountability still provide the normative foundations of the UK's political institutional structure.

New Labour has been accused of being 'short-sighted', 'suffering from a paucity of imagination' and failing to provide 'any discernible conception of an alternative constitution' (Flinders 2004:143). Certainly, there are alternative conceptions of representation other than those provided in a majoritarian, parliamentary model. Equally, there are other notions of consent and legitimation, and other forms of accountability. Manifestly, some of these alternative principles have found reflection in Labour's institutional innovations, for example in: the consociational nature of the Good Friday agreement in Northern Ireland; citizens' juries; the increased use of referendums; the expanded scope of regulation; the advancement of an accountability culture through ombudsmen, inquiries, and judicialization; and a growing emphasis upon the rights of the 'consumers' of public services and the propagation of a culture of 'service delivery'. Beyond conscious institutional innovation, other forms of participation—massive demonstrations in opposition to government policies on Iraq; or civil disobedience by the Countryside Alliance, or by fuel protesters; and other forms of accountability—especially through the voracious and incessant questioning of government activities by the media—have chaffed against the principles of the Westminster model.

Nonetheless, despite these alternative institutional forms and normative propositions, which, undoubtedly, pose both conscious as well as unthinking challenges to the Westminster model, the institutional prescriptions of that model still dominate the discourse of UK politicians. As seen throughout this book, the norms, values and meanings of the Westminster model still inform the institutional interactions of state institutions—the legislature, executive and judiciary—and still prescribe the relationship between formal political institutions and citizens. That these principles—which stipulate accountability, openness and responsiveness—have been inverted in the routine interactions of political institutions has posed an elemental paradox at the heart of the modern UK state (see Judge 1993).

This is a paradox that remains unresolved. While UK governments have displayed a profound understanding of the advantages to be gained from an executive-centric system legitimated through a parliamentary-centric theory, they have shown less understanding of the corrosive effects that the very practice of government has upon the legitimating theory. The challenge for 21st century governments, therefore, is to reconnect the daily interactions of political institutions to the 'appropriate behaviour' prescribed in the 'Westminster model'. What is required is both an understanding of why this reconnection is necessary and why failure to 'reconnect' will exacerbate the 'disconnect' between citizens and political institutions. Without sustained understanding of the context, contingency and interconnectedness of institutions (of the 'path' of institutional development), and of the norms, values and meanings prescribing 'appropriate behaviour', the paradox at the heart of UK government will remain unresolvable.

....

KEY TERMS

- constitutional blueprint
- elective dictatorship
- europeanization
- globalization
- institutional continuity
- precipitants of institutional change
- subsidiarity
- Third Way
- unintended consequences

....

GUIDE TO FURTHER READING

EVANS, M. (2003) *Constitution-Making and the Labour Party*, (London, Palgrave Macmillan).

A broad-ranging, if uneven, account of the dynamics behind New Labour's constitutional reform 'project', and assessment of

reform from the perspectives provided by policy analysis.

FOLEY, M. (1999) *The Politics of the British Constitution*, (Manchester, Manchester University Press).

An early attempt to understand the constitutional fuels driving New Labour's institutional revolution.

JOHNSON, N. (2004) *Reshaping the British Constitution: Essays in Political Interpretation*, (London, Palgrave Macmillan).

A sceptical assessment of constitutional change from an 'old school' institutionalist perspective.

LUDLAM, S. and SMITH, M. J. (eds.) (2004) *Governing as New Labour: Politics and Policy Under Blair*, (London, Palgrave Macmillan).

A broad examination of New Labour's second term in office with chapters on governance, the constitution, and public services illuminating many of the issues associated with institutional change.

REFERENCES

ASPINWALL, M. D. and SCHNEIDER, G. (2000) 'Same Menu, Separate Tables: The Institutional Turn in Political Science and the Study of European Integration', *European Journal of Political Research*, 38, 1:1–36.

Audit Commission (2003) *Strategic Regulation: Minimising the Burden, Maximising the Impact*, London, Audit Commission, (available at www.audit-commission.gov.uk/Products/ NATIONAL–REPORT/C6A0FAB4– 4B68–4A92–9F4B–B35E8FC281B6/ StrategicRegBurdenWEB.pdf).

BAGGOT, R. (1995) *Pressure Groups Today*, (Manchester, Manchester University Press).

BARA, J. and BUDGE, I. (2001) 'Party Policy and Ideology: Still New Labour?', *Parliamentary Affairs*, 54, 4:590–606.

BARBERIS, P. (1998) 'The New Public Management and a New Accountability', *Public Administration*, 76, 3:451–70.

BARNETT, H. (2002) *Constitutional and Administrative Law*, 4th edn., (London, Cavendish Publishing).

BATES, R. H. (1991) 'The Economics of Transitions to Democracy', *PS: Political Science and Politics*, 24, 1:24–7.

BEATSON, J. (2004) 'Should Judges Conduct Public Inquiries', Paper based on 51st Liolen Cohen Lecture, Jerusalem, June 2004, (available at www.dca.gov.uk/judicial/speeches/ jb070704.pdf).

BEETHAM, D., BYRNE, I., NGAN, P. and WEIR, S. (2002) *Democracy Under Blair: A Democratic Audit of the United Kingdom*, (London, Politicos).

BENN, T. (2003) *Free Radical: New Century Essays*, (London, Continuum).

BENNETT, M., FAIRLEY, J. and McATEER, M. (2002) *Devolution in Scotland: The Impact on Local Government*, (London, Joseph Rowntree Foundation).

BERGMAN, T. MÜLLER W. C., STRØM K. and BLOMGREN, M. (2004) 'Democratic Delegation and Accountability: Cross-national Patterns', in K. STRØM, W. C. MÜLLER and T. Bergman (eds.), *Delegation and Accountability in Parliamentary Democracies*, (Oxford, Oxford University Press).

BEVIR, M. and RHODES, R. A. W. (2003) *Interpreting British Governance*, (London, Routledge).

BICHARD, M. (2000) 'Creativity, Leadership and Change', *Public Money and Management*, April-June, 41–6.

BIRCH, A. H. (1964) *Representative and Responsible Government*, (London, Allen & Unwin).

BIRCH, A. H. (1971) *Representation*, (London, Macmillan).

BIRCH, A. H. (1977) *Political Integration and Disintegration in the British Isles*, (London, Allen & Unwin).

BLACKBURN, R. (1992) 'The Ruins of Westminster', *New Left Review*, 191:5–35.

BLACKBURN, R. and KENNON, A. (2003) *Parliament:Functions, Practice and Procedures* (London, Sweet and Maxwell).

BLACKBURN, R. and PLANT, R. (1999) 'Monarchy and the Royal Prerogative', in R. BLACKBURN and R. PLANT (eds.), *Constitutional Reform. The Labour Government's Constitutional Reform Agenda*, (London, Longman).

BOGDANOR, V. (1989) 'The Constitution', in D. KAVANAGH and A. SELDON (eds.), *The Thatcher Effect*, (Oxford, Clarendon Press).

BOGDANOR, V. (1999a) *Devolution in the UK*, (Oxford, Oxford University Press).

BOGDANOR, V. (1999b) 'Devolution: Decentralisation or Disintegration?' *Political Quarterly*, 70, 2:185–94.

BOGDANOR, V. (2001) 'Civil Service Reform: A Critique', *Political Quarterly*, 72, 3:291–9.

BOGDANOR, V. (2003) 'Asymmetric Devolution: Toward a Quasi-Federal Constitution', in P. DUNLEAVY, A. GAMBLE, R. HEFFERMAN, and G. PEELE (eds.), *Developments in British Politics 7*, (London, Palgrave).

BONNEY, N. (2003) 'The Scottish Parliament and Participatory Democracy: Vision and Reality', *Political Quarterly*, 74, 4:459–67.

Boundary Commission for England (2000) *The Review of Parliamentary Constituencies in England*, London, Boundary Commission for England

BRADBURY, J. and MCGARVEY, N. (2003) 'Devolution: Problems, Politics and Prospects', *Parliamentary Affairs*, 56, 2:219–36.

BRADLEY, A. W. and EWING, K. D. (2003) *Constitutional and Administrative Law* 13th edn., (London, Longman).

BRAZIER, R. (1998) *Constitutional Reform: Reshaping the British Political System*, (Oxford, Oxford University Press).

BROWN, A. (2000) 'Designing the Scottish Parliament', *Parliamentary Affairs*, 53, 3:542–56.

BROWN, A., MCCRONE, D. and PATERSON, L. (1998) *Politics and Society in Scotland* 2nd edn., (London, Macmillan).

BUDGE, I., CREWE, I., MCKAY D., and NEWTON, K. (2004) *The New British Politics*, 3rd edn., (London, Pearson Longman).

BULPITT, J. (1983) *Territory and Power in the United Kingdom*, (Manchester, Manchester University Press).

BURCH, M. and HOLLIDAY, I. (1996) *The British Cabinet System*, (London, Prentice Hall/Harvester Wheatsheaf).

BURCH, M. and HOLLIDAY, I. (2004) 'The Blair Government and the Core Executive', *Government and Opposition*, 39, 1:2–21.

BURKE, E. [1774] (1801), Speech to the Electors of Bristol, in *Works*, vol 3, (Rivington, London).

BUTT, R. (1969) *The Power of Parliament*, (London, Constable).

Cabinet Office (1997) *Opening Up Quangos: A Consultation Paper*, London, Cabinet Office.

Cabinet Office (1998) *Quangos: Opening the Doors*, London, Cabinet Office, (available at www.cabinet-office.gov. uk/central/1998/pb/open/index. htm).

Cabinet Office (1999) *Report to the Prime Minister from Sir Richard Wilson, Head of the Home Civil Service*, London, Cabinet Office.

Cabinet Office (2000a) *Review of the Public Sector Ombudsmen in England*, Report by the Cabinet Office, London, Cabinet Office, (available at www. cabinet-office.gov.uk/central/2000/ ombudsmenreview.pdf).

Cabinet Office (2000b) *Review of the Public Sector Ombudsmen in England*, Consultation Paper, June, London, Cabinet Office.

Cabinet Office (2001) *Ministerial Code: A Code of Conduct and Guidance on Procedures for Ministers*, Machinery of Government Secretariat, London, Cabinet Office, (available at www.cabinet-office.gov.uk/central/2001/mcode/p01.htm).

Cabinet Office (2003a) *List of Ministerial Responsibilities*, November, London, Cabinet Office, (available at www.knowledgenetwork.gov.uk/eLMR/Minister.nsf/).

Cabinet Office (2003b) *Public Bodies 2003*, London, The Stationery Office.

Cabinet Office (2003c) *How to Review Agencies and NDPBs*, London, Cabinet Office, (available at www.cabinet-office.gov.uk/agencies-publicbodies/agencies/exec_sum. shtm).

Cabinet Office (2003d) *Delivery and Reform: Progress and Plans for the Future*, London, Cabinet Office.

Cabinet Office (2004) *Civil Service Reform: Delivery and Values*, London, Cabinet Office.

CAMPBELL, C. and WILSON, G. K. (1995) *The End of Whitehall: Death of a Paradigm*, (London, Blackwell).

CARMICHAEL, P and OSBORNE, R. (2003) 'The Northern Ireland Civil Service Under Direct Rule and Devolution', *International Review of Administrative Sciences*, 69, 2:205–17.

CARNWORTH, R. (2004) 'Do We Need a Supreme Court?', *Political Quarterly*, 75, 3:249–56.

CHESTER, N. (1981) *The English Administrative System*, (Oxford, Clarendon Press).

Cm 2850–I (1995) *Standards in Public Life*, First Report of the Committee on Standards in Public Life, Chairman Lord Nolan, London, HMSO.

Cm 3782 (1997) *Rights Brought Home: The Human Right Bill*, London, The Stationery Office.

Cm 3830 (1998) *The Food Standards Agency: A Force for Change*, London, The Stationery Office.

Cm 3883 (1998) *The Belfast Agreement: An Agreement Reached in Multi-Party Negotiations*, London, The Stationery Office.

Cm 4183 (1999) *Modernising Parliament: Reforming the House of Lords*, London, The Stationery Office.

Cm 4310 (1999) *Modernising Government*, London, The Stationery Office.

Cm 4534 (2000) *A House for the Future*, Royal Commission on the Reform of the House of Lords (Chairman: The Rt Hon Lord Wakeham), London, The Stationery Office.

Cm 4997 (2001) *Review of Parliamentary Pay and Allowances*, Review Body on Senior Salaries, London, The Stationery Office.

Cm 5291 (2001) *The House of Lords: Completing the Reform*, London, The Stationery Office.

Cm 5429 (2002) *Departmental Report 2002: Cabinet Office*, London, The Stationery Office, (available at www.cabinet-office.gov.uk/2002/co_report).

Cm 5456 (2002) *Audit and Accountability for Central Government: The Government's Response to Lord Sharman's Report 'Holding to Account'*, London, The Stationery Office.

Cm 5511 (2002) *Your Region, Your Choice*, London, The Stationery Office, (available at www.odpm.gov.uk/stellent/groups/odpm_regions/documents/page/odpm_regions_607900.hcsp).

Cm 5628 (2002) *Government Response to the Procedure Committee Report on*

Parliamentary Questions (HC 622), London, The Stationery Office.

Cm 5663 (2002) *Standards of Conduct in the House of Commons*, Eighth Report, Committee on Standards in Public Life, London, The Stationery Office.

Cm 5775 (2003) *Defining the Boundaries within the Executive: Ministers, Special Advisers and the Permanent Civil Service*, Ninth Report from the Committee on Standards in Public Life, London, The Stationery Office.

Cm 5926 (2003) *Departmental Report 2003: Cabinet Office*, London, The Stationery Office.

Cm 6163 (2004) *Financing Britain's Future: Review of the Revenue Departments*, (chairman Gus O'Donnell), London, HM Treasury.

Cm 6226 (2004) *Departmental Report 2004: Cabinet Office*, London, The Stationery Office.

Cm 6238 (2004) *2004 Spending Review: Public Service Agreements 2005–2008.*, London, The Stationery Office.

Cm 6373 (2004) *A Draft Civil Service Bill: A Consultation Document*, London, The Stationery Office.

Cmnd 2225 (1993) *Scotland in the Union: A Partnership for Good*, Edinburgh, HMSO.

Cmnd 4506 (1970) *The Reorganisation of Central Government*, London, HMSO.

Cmnd 5460 (1973) *Royal Commission on the Constitution 1969–1973*, Report, London, HMSO.

Cmnd 9230 (1918) *Report of the Machinery of Government Committee of the Ministry of Reconstruction*, (Haldane Report), London, HMSO.

Cmnd 9797–I (1986) *The Conduct of Local Authority Business*, Report of the Committee of Inquiry into the Conduct of Local Authority Business, London, HMSO.

COATES, D. (1975) *The Labour Party and the Struggle for Socialism*, (Cambridge, Cambridge University Press).

COATES, D. (2002) 'The New Political Economy of Postwar Britain', in C. HAY (ed.), *British Politics Today*, (Cambridge, Polity).

CONNOLLY, M. (1990) *Politics and Policy Making in Northern Ireland*, (London, Philip Allan).

Conservative Party (1997) *The 114th Conservative Party Conference, Speeches*, London, Conservative Party.

Conservative Party (1998) *The Fresh Future*, London, Conservative Party.

Conservative Party (2001) *An Introduction to the Conservative Party*, London, Conservative Party, (available at www.conservatives.com).

Consultative Steering Group (1999) *Shaping Scotland's Parliament*, The Consultative Steering Group on the Scottish Parliament, Edinburgh, HMSO.

COOK, R. (2003) *The Point of Departure*, (London, Simon & Schuster).

COPE, S. and GOODSHIP, J. (2002) 'The Audit Commission and Public Services: Delivering for Whom?', *Public Money and Management*, 22, 4:33–40.

COWLEY, P. (2002) *Revolts and Rebellions: Parliamentary Voting Under Blair*, (London, Politicos).

COWLEY, P. and STUART, M. (2003) 'Parliament, More Revolts, More Reform', *Parliamentary Affairs*, 56, 2:188–204.

COWLEY, P. and STUART, M. (2004) 'More of the Same? Backbench Behaviour at the Beginning of the Fourth Session', (available at www.revolts.co.uk).

COXALL, B. ROBINS, L. and LEACH, R. (2003) *Contemporary British Politics*, 4th edn., (London, Palgrave Macmillan).

CP 10/03 (2003) *Constitutional Reform: A New Way of Appointing Judges*, Consultation Paper, London, Department of Constitutional Affairs, (available at www.dca.gov.uk/consult/jacommission/index.htm).

CP 11/03 (2003) *Constitutional Reform: A Supreme Court for the United Kingdom*, Consultation Paper, London, Department for Constitutional Affairs. (available at www.dca.gov.uk/consult/supremecourt).

CP 12/04 (2004) *Effective Inquiries*, Consultation Paper, London, Department of Constitutional Affairs, (available at www.dca.gov.uk/consult/inquiries/inquiries.pdf).

CP 14/03 (2003) *Constitutional Reform: Next Steps for the House of Lords*, Consultation Paper, London, Department of Constitutional Affairs, (available at www.dca.gov.uk/consult/holref/index.htm).

DAINTITH, T. and PAGE, A (1999) *The Executive in the Constitution: Structure, Autonomy and Internal Control*, (Oxford, Oxford University Press).

DAUGBJERG, C. and MARSH, D. (1998) 'Explaining Policy Outcomes: Integrating the Policy Network Approach with Macro-level and Micro-Level Analysis', in D. MARSH (ed.), *Comparing Policy Networks*, (Buckingham, Open University Press).

DEAKIN, N. and PARRY, R. (2000) *The Treasury and Social Policy*, (London, Macmillan).

DEARLOVE, J. and SAUNDERS, P. (2000) *Introduction to British Politics* 3rd edn., (Cambridge, Polity).

DENVER, D., HANDS, G., FISHER, J. and McALLISTER, I. (2003) 'Constituency Campaigning in Britain 1992–2001', *Party Politics*, 9, 5:541–59.

Department of Constitutional Affairs (2003) *Constitutional Reform: Reforming the Office of the Lord Chancellor*, Consultation Paper, London, Department of Constitutional Affairs, available at www.lcd.gov.uk/consult/lcoffice/index.htm.

Department for Constitutional Affairs (2004) *The House of Lords: Frequently Asked Question*, April, (available at www.dca.gov.uk/constitution/holref/lordsfaq2004.htm).

DICEY, A. V. [1885] (1959) *An Introduction to the Study of the Law of the Constitution*, 10th edn., (London, Macmillan).

DOHERTY, B., PATERSON, M., PLOWS, A. and WALL, D. (2002) 'The Fuel Protests of 2000: Implications for the Environmental Movement in Britain', *Environmental Politics*, 11, 2:165–73.

DOHERTY, B., PATERSON, M., PLOWS, A. and WALL, D. (2003) 'Explaining the Fuel Protests', *British Journal of Politics and International Relations*, 5, 1:1–23.

DOWDING, K. (1995) 'Model or Metaphor? A Critical Review of the Policy Network Approach', *Political Studies*, 43, 1:136–58.

DOWDING, K. (2001) 'There Must be an End to Confusion: Policy Networks, Intellectual Fatigue, and the Need for Political Science Methods Courses in British Universities', *Political Studies*, 49, 1:89–105.

DRIVER, S. and MARTELL, L. (2002) *Blair's Britain*, (Cambridge, Polity).

DUNLEAVY, P. (1989) 'The Architecture of the British Central State: Part 1: Framework for Analysis', *Public Administration*, 67, 3:249–75.

DUVERGER, M. (1959) *Political Parties* 2nd edn., (London, Methuen).

EDWARDS, R. A. (2002) 'Judicial Deference under the Human Rights Act', *Modern Law Review*, 65, 6:859–82.

Efficiency Unit (1998) *Improving Management in Government; The Next Steps*, London, HMSO.

ELGIE, R. (2003) *Political Institutions in Contemporary France*, (Oxford, Oxford University Press).

EVANS, M. (2003) *Constitution-Making and the Labour Party*, (London, Palgrave Macmillan).

EWING, K. D and GEARTY, C. A. (1990) *Freedom Under Thatcher: Civil Liberties in Modern Britain*, (Oxford, Clarendon Press).

EWING, K. D. (1999) 'The Human Rights Act and Parliamentary Democracy', *Modern Law Review*, 62, 1:79–99.

FALCONER, C. (2004) 'Human Rights and Constitutional Reform', Speech to the Law Society and Human Rights Lawyers Association, 17 February, London, (available at www.dca.gov.uk/speeches/2004/lc170204.htm).

FELDMAN, D. (2001) 'Whitehall, Westminster and Human Rights', *Public Money and Management*, 21, 3:19–24.

FELDMAN, D. (2004) 'The Impact of Human Rights on the UK Legislative Process', *Statute Law Review*, 25, 2:91–115.

FIELDING, S. (2003) *The Labour Party: Continuity and Change in the Making of 'New' Labour*, (London, Palgrave Macmillan).

FLINDERS, M. (2001) 'Mechanisms of Judicial Accountability in British Central Government', *Parliamentary Affairs*, 54, 1:54–71.

FLINDERS, M. (2001) *The Politics of Accountability in the Modern State*, (Aldershot, Ashgate).

FLINDERS, M. (2002) 'Shifting the Balance? Parliament, the Executive and the British Constitution', *Political Studies*, 50, 1:23–42.

FLINDERS, M. (2004) 'New Labour and the Constitution', in S. LUDLAM and M. J. SMITH (eds.), *Governing as New Labour: Politics and Policy Under Blair*, (London, Palgrave Macmillan).

FOLEY, M. (1999) *The Politics of the British Constitution*, (Manchester, Manchester University Press).

FOLEY, M. (2000) *The British Presidency: Tony Blair and the Politics of Public Leadership*, (Manchester, Manchester University Press).

FOLEY, M. (2004) 'Presidential Attribution as an Agency of Prime Ministerial Critique in a Parliamentary Democracy: The Case of Tony Blair', *British Journal of Politics and International Relations*, 6, 3:292–311.

FORMAN, F. N. (2002) *Constitutional Change in the United Kingdom*, (London, Routledge).

FOSTER, C. D. (2001) 'The Civil Service Under Stress: The Fall in Civil Service Power and Authority', *Public Administration*, 79, 3:725–49.

FOSTER, R. F. (1989) *Modern Ireland 1600–1972*, (London, Penguin Books).

FOX, C. J. and MILLER, T. (1995) *Postmodern Public Administration: Toward Discourse*, (Thousand Oaks, CA, Sage).

FRY, G. (1979) *The Growth of Government*, (London, Frank Cass).

GAINS, F. (1999) *Understanding Department-Next Steps Relationships*, Unpublished PhD, Sheffield, University of Sheffield.

GAINS, F. (2004a) 'Adapting the Agency Concept: Variations within "Next Steps"', in C. POLLITT and C. TALBOT (eds.), *Unbundled Government: A*

Critical Analysis of the Global Trend to Agencies, Quangos and Contractualisation (London, Routledge).

GAINS, F. (2004b) ' "Hardware, Software or Network Connection?" Theorizing Crisis in the UK Next Steps Agencies', *Public Administration*, 82, 3:547–66.

GAMBLE, A. (1990) 'Theories of British Politics, *Political Studies*, 37, 3:404–20.

GAMBLE, A. (1996) 'The Legacy of Thatcherism', in M. PERRYMAN (ed.), *The Blair Agenda*, (London, Lawrence & Wishart).

GAMBLE, A. (2000) 'Policy Agendas in a Multi-Level Polity', in P. DUNLEAVY, A. GAMBLE, I. HOLLIDAY and G. PEELE (eds.), *Developments in British Politics 6*, (London, Palgrave Macmillan).

GARNER, R. and KELLY, R. (1998) *British Political Parties Today*, 2nd edn., (Manchester, Manchester University Press).

GAY, O. (2003) 'Evolution from Devolution: The Experience at Westminster', in R. HAZELL (ed.), *The State and the Nations 2003*, (Exeter, Imprint Academic).

GEDDES, A. (2004) *The European Union and British Politics*, (London, Palgrave Macmillan).

GIDDENS, A. (1998) *The Third Way: The Renewal of Social Democracy*, (Cambridge, Polity).

GIDDENS, A. (2000) *The Third Way and its Critics*, (Cambridge, Polity).

GRACE, C. (2003) 'Regulation: The Modern Idiom', *Public Money and Management*, 23, 2:73–5.

GRANT, W. (1978) 'Insider Groups, Outsider Groups and Interest Group Strategies in Britain', *Department of Politics Working Paper No 19*, Warwick, University of Warwick.

GRANT, W. (2000) *Pressure Groups and British Politics*, (London, Macmillan).

GRANT, W. (2001) 'Pressure Politics: From "Insider" Politics to Direct Action?', *Parliamentary Affairs*, 54, 2:337–48.

GREENLEAF, W. H. (1987) *The British Political Tradition, Volume Three: A Much Governed Nation Part I*, (London, Methuen).

GREENWOOD, J., PYPER, R. and WILSON, D. (2002) *New Public Administration in Britain*, 3rd edn., (London, Routledge).

GREER, A. (1999) 'Policymaking', in P. MITCHELL and R. WILFORD (eds.), *Politics in Northern Ireland*, (Boulder, Westview Press).

GREER, A. (2002) 'Policy Networks and Policy Change in Organic Agriculture: A Comparative Analysis of the UK and Ireland', *Public Administration*, 80, 3:453–73.

GREGORY, R. and GIDDINGS, P. (2002) *The Ombudsman, the Citizen and Parliament*, (London, Politicos).

GRIFFITH, J. A. G. (1974) *Parliamentary Scrutiny of Government Bills*, (London, George Allen & Unwin).

GRIFFITH, J. A. G. (1982) 'The Constitution and the Commons', in RIPA, *Parliament and the Executive*, RIPA, London.

GUNTHER, R. and DIAMOND, L. (2003) 'Species of Political Parties: A New Typology, *Party Politics*, 9, 2:167–99.

HAGUE, W. (1999) *Strengthening the Union After Devolution*, Speech to the Centre for Policy Studies, 15 July, London, Centre for Policy Studies.

HAILSHAM, Lord (1978) *The Dilemma of Democracy*, (Glasgow, Collins).

HALL, P. A. (1986) *Governing the Economy: The Politics of State*

Intervention in Britain and France, (Oxford, Oxford University Press).

HALL, P. A. and TAYLOR, R. C. R (1996) 'Political Science and the Three New Institutionalisms', *Political Studies*, 44, 5:936–57.

HALL, P. A. and TAYLOR, R. C. R (1998) 'The Potential of Historical Institutionalism: A Response to Hay and Wincott', *Political Studies*, 46, 5:958–62.

HANHAM, H. J. (1969) *The Nineteenth Century Constitution*, (London, Cambridge University Press).

Hansard Society (2001) *The Challenge for Parliament: Making Government Accountable*, Report of the Hansard Society Commission on Parliamentary Scrutiny, (London, Vacher Dod Publishing).

HARLOW, C. (1999) 'Accountability, New Public Management, and the Problems of the Child Support Agency', *Journal of Law and Society*, 26, 2:150–74.

HARLOW, C. and RAWLINGS, R. (1997) *Law and Administration*, 2nd edn., (London, Butterworths).

HASSAN, G. (2002) 'The Paradoxes of Scottish Labour: Devolution, Change and Conservatism', in G. HASSAN and C. WARHURST (eds.), *Tomorrow's Scotland*, (London, Lawrence & Wishart).

HAY, C. (2002) 'British Politics Today: Towards a New Political Science of British Politics', in C. HAY (ed.), *British Politics Today*, (Cambridge, Polity).

HAY, C. and WINCOTT, D. (1998) 'Structure, Agency and Historical Institutionalism, *Political Studies*, 46, 5:951–7.

HAZELL, R. (2001) 'The English Question: Can Westminster be a Proxy for an English Parliament?', *Public Law*, Summer: 268–80.

HC 19 (1990) *The Working of the Select Committee System*, Second Report, Select Committee on Procedure, Session 1989–90, House of Commons, London, HMSO.

HC 48 (2000) *Delegated Legislation*, First Report, Procedure Committee, Session 1999–2000, House of Commons, London, The Stationery Office.

HC 62 (2003) *On Target? Government By Measurement*, Fifth Report, Public Administration Committee, Session 2002–03, London, The Stationery Office.

HC 62-x (2003) *Memorandum by the Government (PST 60): Minutes of Evidence for Thursday 24 March 2003*, Public Administration Committee, Session 2002–03, London, The Stationery Office.

HC 73 (2001) *HM Treasury*, Treasury Select Committee, Third Report, Session 2000–01, London, The Stationery Office.

HC 94 (2001) *Making Government Work: The Emerging Issues*, Seventh Report of the Public Administration Committee, Session 2000–01, House of Commons, London, The Stationery Office.

HC 115 (1996) *Report of the Inquiry into the Export of Defence Equipment and Dual-Use Goods to Iraq and Related Prosecution*, Chairman Sir Richard Scott, London, HMSO.

HC 128 (2003) *A Draft Civil Service Bill: Completing the Reform*, Public Administration Committee, Session 2003–4, London, The Stationery Office.

HC 136 (2002) *Ministerial Accountability and Parliamentary Questions: The Government Response to the Committee's Ninth Report of Session 2001–02*, First Report, Public Administration Committee, Session 2002–03, House of

Commons, London, The Stationery Office.

HC 152 (1996) *Delegated Legislation*, Fourth Report, Procedure Committee, Session 1995–96, House of Commons, London, The Stationery Office.

HC 165 (2003) *Government by Appointment: Opening Up the Patronage State*, Public Administration Select Committee, Fourth Report, Session 2002–03, London, The Stationery Office.

HC 190 (1997) *The Legislative Process*, First Report, Modernisation of the House of Commons Committee, Session 1997–98, House of Commons, London, The Stationery Office.

HC 209 (1999) *Quangos*, Public Administration Select Committee, Sixth Report, Session 1998–99, London, The Stationery Office.

HC 224 (2002) *Select Committees*, First Report, Modernisation of the House of Commons Committee, Session 2001–02, House of Commons, London, The Stationery Office.

HC 238 (2000) *Making Government Work*, Minutes of Evidence Taken Before the Public Administration Committee, Session 1999–2000 House of Commons, London, The Stationery Office.

HC 293 (2001) *Special Advisers: Boon or Bane?*, Fourth Report, Public Administration Committee, Session 2000–01, House of Commons, London, The Stationery Office.

HC 300 (2000) *Shifting the Balance: Select Committees and the Executive*, First Report, Liaison Committee, Session 1999–2000, House of Commons, London, The Stationery Office.

HC 310-i (2004) *The Prime Minister: Oral Evidence Given by the Rt Hon Tony Blair MP*, Liaison Select Committee, Session

2003–04, House of Commons, London, The Stationery Office.

HC 325 (2004) *Programming of Legislation*, Fourth Report, Procedure Committee, Session 2003–04, House of Commons, London, The Stationery Office.

HC 333 (2003) *Procedures for Debates, Private Members' Bills and the Powers of the Speaker*, Fourth Report, Procedure Committee, Session 2002–03, House of Commons, London, The Stationery Office.

HC 367 (2001) *Mapping the Quango State*, Fifth Report, Public Administration Select Committee, Session 2000–01, London, The Stationery Office.

HC 378 (1999) *Public Service Agreements*, Seventh Report, Treasury Select Committee, Session 1998–99, London, The Stationery Office.

HC 403 (2003) *Standards of Conduct in the House of Commons*, Eighth Report, Committee on Standards in Public Life, Session 2002–03, London, The Stationery Office.

HC 422 (2004) *Taming the Prerogative: Strengthening Ministerial Accountability to Parliament*, Fourth Report, Public Administration Committee, Session 2003–04, House of Commons, London, The Stationery Office.

HC 423 (2004) *Oral Evidence given by Sir Andrew Turnbull KCB CVO, Secretary of the Cabinet and Head of the Home Civil Service*, Public Administration Committee, Session 2003–4, London, The Stationery Office.

HC 440 (2001) *Memorandum Submitted by the Leader of the House of Commons. Modernisation of the House of Commons: A Reform Programme for Consultation*, Modernisation of the House of Commons Committee,

Session 2001–02, House of Commons, London, The Stationery Office.

HC 446 (2004) *Annual Report for 2003*, Liaison Committee, Session 2003–04, House of Commons, London, The Stationery Office.

HC 448 (2003) *Ombudsman Issues*, Third Report, Public Administration Committee, Session 2002–03, London, The Stationery Office.

HC 460 (1998) *The Operation of Multi-layer Democracy*, Second Report from the Select Committee on Scottish Affairs, House of Commons, Session 1997–98, London, The Stationery Office.

HC 494 (2002) *The Second Chamber: Continuing the Reform*, Fifth Report, Public Administration Committee, Session 2001–02, House of Commons, London, The Stationery Office.

HC 501 (2003) *Delegated Legislation: Proposals for a Sifting Committee*, First Report, Procedure Committee, Session 2002–03, House of Commons, London, The Stationery Office.

HC 506-i (2003) *The Work of the Ombudsmen*, Minutes of Evidence 6 March, Ann Abraham, Parliamentary Commissioner for Administration and Health Service Commissioner for England, Public Administration Committee, Session 2002–03, London, The Stationery Office.

HC 556 (2004) *The Merger of Customs and Excise and the Inland Revenue*, Ninth Report, Treasury Committee, Session 2003–04, London, The Stationery Office.

HC 558 (2003) *Annual Report for 2002*, First Report, Liaison Committee, Session 2002–03, House of Commons, London, The Stationery Office.

HC 588 (1978) *First Report from the Select Committee on Procedure*, Session 1977–78, London, HMSO.

HC 588 (2003) *Annual Report for 2002*, First Report, Liaison Committee, Session 2002–03, House of Commons, London, The Stationery Office.

HC 589 (2000) *Programming of Legislation and Timing of Votes*, Second Report, Modernisation of the House of Commons Committee, Session 1999–2000, House of Commons, London, The Stationery Office.

HC 590 (2002) *The Work of Select Committees 2001*, First Report, Session 2001–02, House of Commons, London, The Stationery Office.

HC 600 (1998) *Modernisation of the House of Commons*, Fourth Report, Select Committee on Modernisation of the House of Commons, Session 1997–98, London, HMSO.

HC 606–ii (2004) *Government by Inquiry*, Oral Evidence given by Rt Hon Lord Falconer of Thoroton, QC, Public Administration Committee, Session 2003–04, London, The Stationery Office.

HC 622 (2002) *Parliamentary Questions*, Third Report, Procedure Committee, Session 2001–02, House of Commons, London, The Stationery Office.

HC 684 (2003) *Delegated Legislation: Proposals for a Sifting Committee: The Government's Response to the Committee's First Report*, Second Report, Procedure Committee, Session 2002–03, House of Commons, London, The Stationery Office.

HC 748 (2000) *Independence or Control? The Government's Reply to the Committee's First Report of Session 1999–2000 — Shifting the Balance: Select Committees and the Executive*, Second Report, Liaison Committee, Session

1999–2000, House of Commons, London, The Stationery Office.

HC 814 (1999) *Procedural Consequences of Devolution: Government Response to the Fourth Report from the Committee*, First Special Report of the Procedure Committee, House of Commons, Session 1998–99, London, The Stationery Office.

HC 815 (2003) *Scotland Office Departmental Report 2003*, Uncorrected Evidence presented by Rt Hon Alistair Darling MP, Mrs Anne McQuire MP and Mr David Crawley, on 17th June 2003, Scottish Affairs Committee, House of Commons, Session 2002–03, London, The Stationery Office.

HC 906 (2000) *Sittings in Westminster Hall*, Fourth Report, Modernisation of the House of Commons Committee, Session 1999–2000, House of Commons, London, The Stationery Office.

HC 1095 (2002) *Evidence Presented by the Right Hon Tony Blair MP, Prime Minister on 16th July 2002*, Liaison Select Committee, House of Commons, London, The Stationery Office.

HC 1168 (2002) *Modernisation of the House of Commons: A Reform Programme*, Second Report, Modernisation of the House of Commons Committee, Session 2001–2, House of Commons, London, The Stationery Office.

HC 1169 (2004) *Programming of Legislation: The Government's Response to the Committee's Fourth Report*, Fifth Special Report, Procedure Committee, House of Commons, London, The Stationery Office.

HC 1180 (2004) *Evidence To Committees*, Oral Evidence Given by Peter Hain MP, Liaison Committee, Session 2003–04,

House of Commons, London, The Stationery Office.

HC 1222 (2003) *Programming of Bills*, First Report, Modernisation Committee, Session 2002–03, House of Commons, London, The Stationery Office.

HC Research Paper (2002) *House of Lords Reform—The 2001 White Paper*, 02/2002, Parliament and Constitution Centre, House of Commons Library, London, House of Commons.

HEFFERNAN, R. (2003) 'Political Parties and Political Systems' in P. DUNLEAVY, A. GAMBLE, R. HEFFERNAN and G. PEELE (eds.), *Developments in British Politics 7*, (London, Palgrave Macmillan).

HENNESSY, P. (2000) *The Prime Minister: The Office and its Holders Since 1945*, (London, Penguin Books).

HENNESSY, P. (2001) *Whitehall*, (London, Pimlico).

HERB, M. (1999) 'Taxation, Collective Action, and the Origins of Representative Institutions', paper delivered at Annual Meeting of the American Political Science Association, Atlanta, September 2–5.

HILL, B. W. (1976) *The Growth of Political Parties, 1689–1742*, (London, Allen & Unwin).

HL 9 (2003) *The Work of the Committee*, Special Report, Delegated Powers and Regulatory Reform Committee, Session 2003–04, House of Lords, London, The Stationery Office.

HL 17/HC 171 (2002) *House of Lords Reform*, First Report, Joint Committee on House of Lords Reform, Session 2002–03, House of Lords and House of Commons, London, The Stationery Office.

HL 28 (2002) *Devolution: Inter-Institutional Relations in the United Kingdom*, Second Report, House of

Lords Select Committee on the Constitution, Session 2002–03, London, The Stationery Office.

HL 58/HC 473 (2001) *Making Remedial Orders*, Seventh Report of the Joint Committee on Human Rights, Session 2001–02, House of Lords and House of Commons, London, The Stationery Office.

HL 66–i/HC 332–i (2001) *Memorandum by the Home Office*, Minutes of Evidence taken on Wednesday 14th March 2001, Joint Committee on Human Rights, Sixth Report, House of Lords and House of Commons, Session 2001–02, London, The Stationery Office.

HL 67–I/HC 489–I (2003) *The Case for a Human Rights Commission*, House of Lords, House of Commons Joint Committee on Human Rights, Sixth Report, Session 2002–03, London, The Stationery Office.

HL 68–I/II (2004) *The Regulatory State: Ensuring its Accountability*, House of Lords Select Committee on the Constitution, Sixth Report, Session 2003–04, London, The Stationery Office.

HL 97/HC 668 (2003) *House of Lords Reform*, Second Report, Joint Committee on House of Lords Reform, Sessions 2002–03, House of Lords and House of Commons, London, The Stationery Office.

HL 125 (2004) *Constitutional Reform Bill [HL]*, First Report, Select Committee on the Constitutional Reform Bill [HL], Session 2003–04, London, The Stationery Office.

HL 147 (2002) *Devolution: Inter-Institutional Relations in the United Kingdom, Minutes of Evidence*, House of Lords Select Committee on the Constitution, Session 2001–02, London, The Stationery Office.

HL 151/HC 1109 (2002) *House of Lords Reform*, Special Report, Joint Committee on House of Lords Reform, Session 2001–02, House of Lords and House of Commons, London, The Stationery Office.

HL 155/HC 1027 (2003) *House of Lords Reform, Government Reply to the Committee's Second Report*, Special Report, Joint Committee on House of Lords Reform, Session 2002–03, House of Lords and House of Commons, London, The Stationery Office.

HL 173 (2004) *Parliament and the Legislative Process*, Select Committee on the Constitution, Fourteenth Report, Session 2003–04, London, The Stationery Office.

HOBHOUSE, J. (2003) *The Law Lords' Response to the Government's Consultation Paper on Constitutional Reform: A Supreme Court for the United Kingdom: Supplementary Response of Lord Hobhouse of Woodborough*, (available at www.parliament.uk/documents/upload/JudicialSCR071103.pdf).

HODGSON, G. (1981) *Labour at the Crossroads*, (Oxford, Martin Robertson).

HOGWOOD, B. W. (1995) 'Whitehall Families: Core Departments and Agency Forms in Britain', *International Review of Administrative Sciences*, 61, 4:511–30.

HOGWOOD, B. W. (1996a) *Mapping the Regions: Boundaries, Coordination and Government*, (London, Joseph Rowntree Foundation).

HOGWOOD, B. W. (1996b) 'Devolution: the English Dimension', *Public Money and Management*, 16, 4:29–34.

HOGWOOD, B. W., JUDGE, D. and McVICAR, M. (2000) 'Agencies and

Accountability', in R. A. W. Rhodes (ed.), *Transforming British Government. Volume 1 Changing Institutions*, (London, Macmillan).

Hood, C, and James, O. (1997) ' The Central Executive' in P. Dunleavy, A. Gamble, I. Holliday and G. Peele (eds.), *Developments in British Politics 5*, (London, Macmillan).

Hood, C., James, O. and Scott, C. (2000) 'Regulation of Government: Has it Increased, Is it Increasing, Should it be Diminished', *Public Administration*, 78, 2:283–304.

Hood, C., James, O. Jones, G. W. and Travers, A. (1999) *Regulation Inside Government*, (Oxford, Oxford University Press).

House of Commons (2004) *Session Information Digest 2002–3*, (available at www.publications. parliament.uk/ pa/cm200304/cmsid/contents.htm).

House of Commons Department of Finance and Administration (2004) *The Quick Guide: Salaries, Allowances etc. for Members of Parliament*, London, House of Commons, (available at www. Parliament.uk/documents/upload/ HofCpsapQG.pdf).

House of Commons Information Office (2003a) *Members' Pay, Pension and Allowances*, Factsheet M5, London, House of Commons.

House of Commons Information Office (2004) *Parliamentary Questions*, Factsheet P1, London, House of Commons.

House of Commons Research Paper (2002) *Regional Development Agencies*, House of Commons Library, Research Paper 02/50, London, House of Commons, (available at www. parliament.uk/commons/lib/research/ rp2002/rp02-050.pdf).

House of Lords (2003) *Annual Report 2002–03*, London, House of Lords, (available at www.publications. parliament.uk/pa/ld200203/ldbrief/ 14602.htm).

House of Lords (2004) *The Work of the House of Lords*, House of Lords, Information Office, London, House of Lords.

Humphrey, J. C. (2001) 'Bewitched or Bewildered? "Facts" and "Values" in Audit Commission Texts', *Local Government Studies*, 27, 2, 19–43.

Hutchinson, I. G. C. (2001) *Scottish Politics in the Twentieth Century*, (London, Palgrave Macmillan).

Hutton, W. (1996) *The State We're In*, (revised edn.) (London, Vintage).

Ingle, S. (2000) *The British Party System* 3rd edn., (London, Pinter).

Irvine, Lord (2002) 'The Human Rights Act Two Years On:An Analysis', The Inaugural Irvine Human Rights Lecture, Durham University, 1 November, (available at www.dca. gov.uk/speeches/2002/lc011102.htm).

James, O. (2000) 'Regulation Inside Government: Public Interest Justifications and Regulatory Failures', *Public Administration*, 78, 2:327–43.

James, O. (2004) 'The UK's Core Executive's Use of Public Service Agreements as a Tool of Governance', *Public Administration*, 82, 2:397–419.

James, S. (1999) *British Cabinet Government*, 2nd edn., (London, Routledge).

Johnson, N. (1999) 'The Constitution', in I. Holliday, A. Gamble and G. Parry (eds.), *Fundamentals in British Politics*, (London, Macmillan).

Johnson, N. (2001) 'Taking Stock of Constitutional Change', *Government and Opposition*, 36, 3:331–54.

JOHNSON, N. (2004) *Reshaping the British Constitution: Essays in Political Interpretation*, (London, Palgrave Macmillan).

JONES, B., KAVANAGH, D., MORAN, M. and NORTON, P. (2004) *Politics UK*, 5th edn., (London, Longman).

JONES, J. B. (2000) 'Changes to the Government of Wales 1979–1997', in J. B. JONES and D. BALSOM (eds.), *The Road to the National Assembly for Wales*, (Cardiff, University of Wales Press).

JORDAN, A. G. (1990a) 'Sub-Governments, Policy Communities and Networks: Refilling the Old Bottles?', *Journal of Theoretical Politics* 2, 3:319–38.

JORDAN, A. G. (1990b) 'Policy Community Realism versus "New" Institutionalist Ambiguity', *Political Studies*, 38, 3:470–85.

JORDAN, A. G. and RICHARDSON, J. J. (1987) *Government and Pressure Groups in Britain*, (Oxford, Clarendon Press).

JORDAN, G. (1994) *The British Administrative System: Principles versus Practice*, (London, Routledge).

JUDGE, D. (1981) *Backbench Specialisation in the House of Commons*, (London, Heinemann Educational Books).

JUDGE, D. (1983) 'Considerations on Reform', in D. JUDGE (ed.), *The Politics of Parliamentary Reform*, (London, Heinemann Educational Books).

JUDGE, D. (1990a) 'Parliament and Interest Representation', in M. RUSH (ed.), *Parliament and Pressure Politics*, (Oxford, Clarendon Press).

JUDGE, D. (1990b) *Parliament and Industry*, (Aldershot, Dartmouth).

JUDGE, D. (1993) *The Parliamentary State*, (London, Sage).

JUDGE, D. (1999) *Representation: Theory and Practice in Britain*, (London, Routledge).

JUDGE, D. (2004) 'Whatever Happened to Parliamentary Democracy in the UK?', *Parliamentary Affairs*, 57, 3:682–701.

KATZ, R. and MAIR, P. (2002) 'The Ascendancy of the Party in Public Office: Party Organizational Change in Twentieth-Century Democracies', in R. GUNTHER, J. R. MONTERO and J. J. LINZ (eds.), *Political Parties: Old Concepts and New Challenges*, (Oxford, Oxford University Press).

KAVANAGH, D. (1990) *Thatcherism and British Politics: The End of Consensus?*, (Oxford, Oxford University Press).

KAVANAGH, D. (2004) 'The Cabinet and Prime Minister' in B. JONES, D. KAVANAGH, M. MORAN and P. NORTON (eds.), *Politics UK*, 5th edn., (London, Longman).

KEATING, M. (1988) *State and Regional Nationalism: Territorial Politics and the European State*, (London, Harvester Wheatsheaf).

KELLAS, J. G. (1989) *The Scottish Political System*, 4th edn., (Cambridge, Cambridge University Press).

KELLY, J. (2003) 'The Audit Commission: Guiding, Steering and Regulating Local Government', *Public Administration*, 81, 2:459–76.

KELLY, R. (2002) 'The Party Didn't Work: Conservative Reorganisation and Electoral Failure', *Political Quarterly*, 73, 1:38–43.

KELLY, R. N. (1989) *Conservative Party Conferences*, (Manchester, Manchester University Press).

KELSO, A. (2003) 'Where Were the Massed Ranks of the Parliamentary Reformers? "Attitudinal" and "Contextual" Approaches to Parliamentary Reform', *Journal of Legislative Studies*, 9, 1:57–76.

KING, A. (2001) *Does the United Kingdom Still Have a Constitution?*, The Hamlyn

Lectures 52nd Series, (London, Sweet & Maxwell).

KINGDOM, J. (2003) *Government and Politics in Britain: An Introduction*, 3rd edn. (Cambridge, Polity).

KLINGEMANN, H. D., HOFFERBERT, R. I. and BUDGE, I. (1994) *Parties, Policies and Democracy*, (Boulder, Westview Press).

KNOX, C. (1999) 'Northern Ireland: At the Crossroads of Political and Administrative Reform', *Governance*, 12, 3:311–28.

KRAUSNER, S. (1984) 'Approaches to the State: Alternative Conceptions and Historical Dynamics', *Comparative Politics*, 16, 2:223–46.

Labour Party (1935) *Annual Conference Report*, London, Labour Party.

Labour Party (1997a) *New Labour: Because Britain Deserves Better*, London, Labour Party.

Labour Party (1997b) *Partnership in Power*, London, Labour Party.

Labour Party (2001) *Ambitions for Britain*, London, Labour Party.

LAFFIN, M. (2000) 'Constitutional Design: A Framework for Analysis', *Parliamentary Affairs*, 53, 3:532–41.

LAFFIN, M. and THOMAS, A. (2000) 'Designing the National Assembly for Wales', *Parliamentary Affairs*, 53, 3:557–76.

LAFFIN, M., TAYLOR, G. and THOMAS, A. (2002) *A New Partnership? The National Assembly for Wales and Local Government*, (London, Joseph Rowntree Foundation).

LAFFIN, M., TAYLOR, G. and THOMAS, A. (2003) 'Devolution and Party Organisation: The Case of the Wales Labour Party', Paper presented to the Annual Conference of the Political Studies Association, April 2003, University of Leicester, (available at www.psa.ac.uk/cps/2003/Martin%20 Laffin.pdf).

LANE, J-E and ERSSON, S. (2000) *The New Institutional Politics: Performance and Outcomes*, (London, Sage).

LaPALOMBARA, J. and WEINER, M. (1966) 'The Origin and Development of Political Parties', in J. LaPALOMBARA and M. WEINER (eds.), *Political Parties and Political Development*, (Princeton, N.J., Princeton University Press).

LE SUER, A. and SUNKIN, M. (1997) *Public Law*, (London, Longman).

LESTER, A. (2001) 'Developing Principles of Public Law', *Public Law*, Winter: 684–94.

Liberal Democrats (2001) *A Real Chance for Real Change: General Election Manifesto 2001*, London, Liberal Democrats; (summary at www. libdems.org.uk/documentspolicies/ Manifestos/fed-mini.pdf).

Liberal Democrats (2003) *The Constitutions of the Liberal Democrats*, London, Liberal Democrats, (available at www.libdems.org.uk).

LIEBERMAN, E. S. (2001) 'Causal Inference in Historical Institutional Analysis', *Comparative Political Studies*, 34, 9:1011–35.

LIJPHART, A. (1977) *Democracy in Plural Societies: A Comparative Exploration*, (New Haven, Yale University Press).

LIJPHART, A. (1984) *Democracies: Patterns of Majoritarian and Consensus Governments in Twenty-One Countries*, (New Haven, Yale University Press).

LIJPHART, A. (1992) 'Introduction', in A. LIJPHART (ed.), *Parliamentary Versus Presidential Government*, (Oxford, Oxford University Press).

LIJPHART, A. (1999) *Patterns of Democracy: Government Forms and Performance in Thirty-Six Countries*, (New Haven, Yale University Press).

LING, T. (2002) 'Delivering Joined-Up Government in the UK, Dimensions, Issues and Problems', *Public Administration*, 80, 4:615–42.

LODGE, G., RUSSELL, M. and GAY, O. (2004) 'The Impact of Devolution on Westminster: If Not Now, When?', in A. TRENCH (ed.), *Has Devolution Made a Difference? The State of the Nations 2004*, (Exeter, Imprint Academic.)

LOUGHLIN, M. (1996) 'The Constitutional Status of Local Government', in L. PRATCHETT and D. WILSON (eds.), *Local Democracy and Local Government*, (London, Macmillan).

LOUGHLIN, M. (2001) 'The Restructuring of Central-Local Government Relations', in J. JOWELL and D. OLIVER (eds.), *The Changing Constitution* 4th edn., (Oxford, Oxford University Press).

LOUGHLIN, M. and SCOTT, C. (1997) 'The Regulatory State', in P. DUNLEAVY, A. GAMBLE, I. HOLLIDAY and G. PEELE (eds.), *Developments in British Politics 5*, (London, Macmillan).

LOVELAND, I. (2003) *Constitutional Law, Administrative Law and Human Rights: A Critical Introduction*, 3rd edn., (London, LexisNexis Butterworths).

LOW, S. (1904) *The Governance of England*, (London, Fischer Unwin).

LOWELL, A. L. (1920) *Government of England*, (London, Macmillan).

LOWNDES, V. (2002) 'Institutionalism', in D. MARSH and G. STOKER (eds.), *Theory and Methods in Political Science*, 2nd edn., (London, Palgrave).

LYNCH, P. (2002) 'Partnership, Pluralism and Party Identity: the Liberal Democcarts after Devolution', in G. HASSAN and C. WARHURST (eds.), *Tomorrow's Scotland*, (London, Lawrence & Wishart).

MADGWICK, P. and WOODHOUSE, D. (1995) *The Law and Politics of the Constitution*, (London, Harvester Wheatsheaf).

MAIR, P. (1994) 'Party Organizations: From Civil Society to the State', in R. S. KATZ and P. MAIR(eds.), *How Parties Organize*, (London Sage).

MAITLAND, F. W. (1908) *The Constitutional History of England*, (Cambridge, Cambridge University Press).

MANDELSON, P. and LIDDLE, R. (1996) *The Blair Revolution: Can New Labour Deliver?* (London, Faber and Faber).

MANIN, B. (1997), *The Principles of Representative Government*, (Cambridge, Cambridge University Press).

MARCH, J. G. and OLSEN, J. P. (1989) *Rediscovering Institutions: The Organizational Basis of Politics*, (New York, Free Press).

MARQUAND, D. (1988) *The Unprincipled Society*, (London, Fontana).

MARSH, D. (1998) 'The Development of the Policy Network Approach', in D. MARSH (ed.), *Comparing Policy Networks*, (Buckingham, Open University Press).

MARSH, D. and SMITH, M. (2000) 'Understanding Policy Networks: Towards a Dialectical Approach', *Political Studies*, 48, 1:4–21.

MARSH, D., RICHARDS, D, and SMITH, M. (2001) *Changing Patterns of Governance in the United Kingdom: Reinventing Whitehall?* (London, Palgrave Macmillan).

MARSH, D., RICHARDS, D, and SMITH, M. (2003) 'Unequal Plurality: Towards an Asymmetric Power Model of British Politics' *Government and Opposition*, 38, 3, 306–32.

MARSHALL, G. (1984) *Constitutional Conventions*, (London, Clarendon Press).

McALLISTER, L. (2000) 'The New Politics in Wales:Rhetoric or Reality?', *Parliamentary Affairs*, 53, 3:591–604.

McGARVEY, N. (2002) 'Intergovernmental Relations in Scotland Post-Devolution', *Local Government Studies*, 28, 3:29–47.

McKENZIE, R. T. (1963) *British Political Parties*, 2nd edn., (London, Mercury Books).

McLEAN, I., CLIFFORD, C. and McMILLAN A. (2000) 'The Organisation of Central Government Departments: A History 1964–92', in R. A. W. RHODES (ed.), *Transforming British Government*. Volume 1 Changing Institutions, (London, Macmillan).

McLEAN, I., SPIRLING, A. and RUSSELL, M. (2003) 'None of the Above: The UK House of Commons Votes on Reforming the House of Lords, February 2003', *Political Quarterly*, 74, 3:298–310.

MEZEY, M. (1979) *Comparative Legislatures*, (Durham, N.C., Duke University Press).

MIDWINTER, A., KEATING, M. and MITCHELL, J, (1991) *Politics and Public Policy in Scotland*, (London, Macmillan).

MILIBAND, R. (1982) *Capitalist Democracy in Britain*, (Oxford, Oxford University Press).

MILL, J. S. [1861] (1910) *Considerations on Representative Government*, (London, Dent)

MINKIN, L. (1980) *The Labour Party Conference*, (Manchester, Manchester University Press).

MINKIN, L. (1992) *The Contentious Alliance*, (Edinburgh, Edinburgh University Press).

MITCHELL, J. (1990) *Conservatives and the Union*, (Edinburgh, Edinburgh University Press).

MITCHELL, J (1996) *Strategies for Self-Government: The Campaigns for A Scottish Parliament*, (Edinburgh, Polygon).

MITCHELL, J. (2000) 'New Parliament, New Politics in Scotland', *Parliamentary Affairs*, 53, 3:605–21.

MITCHELL, J. (2002) 'Towards a New Constitutional Settlement', in C. HAY (ed.), *British Politics Today* (Cambridge, Polity).

MITCHELL, J. (2003a) 'Political Parties', in *Nations and Regions: Quarterly Report August 2003*, London, Constitution Unit, (available at www.ucl.ac.uk/constitution-unit/monrep/scotland/scotland_august_2003.pdf).

MITCHELL, J. (2003b) *Governing Scotland*, (London, Palgrave Macmillan).

MITCHELL, J. (2003c) *Devolution and the Future of the Union*', in J. FISHER, D. DENVER and J. BENYON (eds.), *Central Debates in British Politics*, (London, Longman).

MITCHELL, J. (2003d) 'Towards a New Constitutional Settlement', in C. HAY (ed.), *British Politics Today*, (Cambridge, Polity).

MITCHELL, J. (2004) 'Scotland: Expectations, Policy Types and Devolution', in A. TRENCH (ed.), *Has Devolution Made a Difference? The State of the Nations 2004*, (Exeter, Imprint Academic).

MORAN, M. (2001) 'The Rise of the Regulatory State in Britain', *Parliamentary Affairs*, 54, 1:19–34.

MORAN, M. (2003) *The British Regulatory State: High Modernism and Hyper-Innovation*, (Oxford, Oxford University Press).

MORGAN, K. and MUNGHAM, G. (2000) 'Unfinished Business: Labour's Devolution Policy', in J. B. JONES and D. BALSOM (eds.), *The Road to the National Assembly for Wales*, (Cardiff, University of Wales Press).

NAIRN, T. (1988) *The Enchanted Glass: Britain and Its Monarchy*, (London, Radius).

NAIRN, T. (1993) *The Break-up of Britain*, 2nd edn., (London, New Left Books).

NORRIS, P. (2001a) 'The Twilight of Westminster? Electoral Reform and its Consequences', *Political Studies*, 49, 5:877–900.

NORRIS, P. (2001b) 'Apathetic Landslide: The 2001 British General Election', *Parliamentary Affairs*, 54, 4:565–89.

Norton Commission (2000) *Strengthening Parliament*, The Report of the Commission to Strengthen Parliament, London, Conservative Party.

NORTON, P (1981) *The Commons in Perspective*, (Oxford, Martin Robertson).

NORTON, P. (1990) 'Parliament and Policy In Britain: the House of Commons as a Policy Influencer', in P. NORTON (ed.), *Legislatures*, (Oxford, Oxford University Press).

NORTON, P. (1993a) *Does Parliament Matter?* (London, Harvester Wheatsheaf).

NORTON, P. (1993b) 'Questions and the Role of Parliament', in M. FRANKLIN and P. NORTON (eds.), *Parliamentary Questions*, (Oxford, Clarendon Press).

NORTON, P. (1994) 'Factions and Tendencies within the Conservative Party', in H. MARGETTS and G. SMITH (eds.), *Turning Japanese?*, (London, Lawrence & Wishart).

NORTON, P. (1997) 'The Case for First-Past-The-Post', *Representation*, 34, 2:84–8.

NORTON, P. (1998) 'Nascent Institutionalisation: Committees in the British Parliament', *Journal of Legislative Studies*, 4, 1:143–62.

NORTON, P. (2001) 'Playing By the Rules: the Constraining Hand of Parliamentary Procedure', *Journal of Legislative Studies*, 7, 3:13–33.

NORTON, P. (2003) 'Governing Alone', *Parliamentary Affairs*, 56, 4:543–59.

NORTON, P. (2004) 'The House of Commons', in B. JONES, D. KAVANAGH, M. MORAN, and P. NORTON (eds.), *Politics UK*, 5th edn., (London, Longman).

O'GORMAN, F. (1975) *The Rise of Party in England 1760–82*, (London, Allen & Unwin).

O'LEARY, B. (2001) 'The Character of the 1998 Agreement: Results and Prospects', in R. WILFORD (ed.), *Aspects of the Belfast Agreement*, (Oxford, Oxford University Press).

O'LEARY, B., ELLIOTT, S. and WILFORD R. A. (1988) *The Northern Ireland Assembly*, (London, Hurst and Co).

ODPM (2003) *Your Regions, Your Say*, London, Office of the Deputy Prime Minister, (available at www.odpm. gov.uk/stellent/groups/ odpm_regions/documents/page/ odpm_regions_023485.hcsp).

Office of the Civil Service Commissioners (2003) *Report of the Civil Service Commissioners to Her Majesty the Queen for the Period 1 April 2002 to 31 March 2003*, London, Office of the Civil Service Commissioners, (available at www.civilservicecommissioners.gov.uk/ documents/annual/cscrep02.pdf).

OLIVER, D. (2003) *Constitutional Reform in the UK*, (Oxford, Oxford University Press).

OSMOND, J. (2000) 'A Constitutional Convention by Other Means: The First Year of the National Assembly for Wales', in R. HAZELL (ed.), *The State and the Nations: The First Year of Devolution in the United Kingdom*, (Exeter, Imprint Academic).

OSMOND, J. (2003) 'From Corporate Body to Virtual Parliament: The Metamorphosis of the National Assembly for Wales', in R. HAZELL (ed.), *The State of the Nations 2003*, (Exeter, Imprint Academic).

OSMOND, J. (2004) 'Nation Building and the Assembly: The Emergence of a Welsh Civic Consciousness', in A. TRENCH (ed.), *Has Devolution Made a Difference? The State of the Nations 2004*, (Exeter, Imprint Academic).

PACKENHAM, R. A. (1970) 'Legislatures and Political Development', in A. KORNBERG and L. MUSLOFF (eds.), *Legislatures in Developmental Perspective*, (Durham, N.C., Duke University Press).

PAGE, A. (2004) 'Balancing Supremacy: EU Membership and the Constitution', in P. GIDDINGS and G. DREWRY (eds.), *Britain and the European Community: Law, Policy and Parliament*, (London, Palgrave Macmillan).

PAGE, A. and BATEY, A. (2002) 'Scotland's Other Parliament: Westminster Legislation about Devolved Matters in Scotland since Devolution', *Public Law*, Autumn: 501–23.

PAGE, A. and DAINTITH (2000) 'Internal Control in the Executive and its Constitutional Significance, in R. A. W. RHODES (ed.), *Transforming British Government*. Volume 1 Changing Institutions, (London, Macmillan).

PANEBIANCO, A. (1988) *Political Parties: Organization and Power*, (Cambridge, Cambridge University Press).

PANITCH, L. and LEYS, C. (1997) *The End of Parliamentary Socialism*, (London, Verso).

PARRIS, H. (1969) *Constitutional Bureaucracy*, (London, Allen & Unwin).

PASQUINO, G. (1997) 'Nomination: Semi-Presidentialism: A Political Model at Work', *European Journal of Political Research*, 31, 1:128–37.

PATCHETT, K. (2000) 'The New Welsh Constitution: The Government of Wales Act 1998', in J. B. JONES and D. BALSOM (eds.), *The Road to the National Assembly for Wales*, (Cardiff,University of Wales Press).

PATTERSON, S. C. and MUGHAN, A. (2001) 'Fundamentals of Institutional Design: The Functions and Powers of Parliamentary Second Chambers', *Journal of Legislative Studies*, 7, 1:39–60.

PEELE, G. (2000) 'The Law and the Constitution', in P. DUNLEAVY, A. GAMBLE, I. HOLLIDAY and G. PEELE (eds.), *Developments in British Politics 6*, (London, Palgrave Macmillan).

PEELE, G. (2003) 'Politics in England and Wales', in P. DUNLEAVY, A. GAMBLE, R. HEFFERMAN, and G. PEELE (eds.), *Developments in British Politics 7*, (London, Palgrave Macmillan).

Perri 6, LEAT, D., SELTZER, K. and STOKER, G. (2002) *Towards Holistic Governance: The New Reform Agenda*, (London, Palgrave Macmillan).

PETERS, B. G. (1996) 'Political Institutions, Old and New', in R. E. GOODIN and H. KLINGEMANN (eds.), *A New Handbook of Political Science*, (Oxford, Oxford University Press).

PETERS, B. G. (1999) *Institutional Theory in Political Science: the 'New Institutionalism'*, (London, Pinter).

PETERS, B. G. and PIERRE, J. (1998) 'Institutions and Time: Problems of Conceptualization and Explanation', *Journal of Public Administration Research and Theory*, 8, 4:565–74.

PIERRE, J. and PETERS, B. G. (2001) *Governance, Politics and the State*, (London, Macmillan).

PIERRE, J. and STOKER, G. (2000) 'Towards Multi-Level Governance', in P. DUNLEAVY, A. GAMBLE, I. HOLLIDAY and G. PEELE (eds.), *Developments in British Politics 6*, (London, Palgrave Macmillan).

PIERSON, P. (1996) 'The Path to European Integration: A Historical Institutionalist Perspective', *Comparative Political Studies*, 29, 2:123–63.

PIERSON, P. (2000) 'The Limits of Design: Explaining Institutional Origins and Change', *Governance*, 13, 4:475–99.

PIERSON, P. and SKOCPOL, T. (2002) 'Historical Institutionalism in Contemporary Political Science', in I. KATZNELSON and H. V. MILLER (eds.), *Political Science: The State of the Discipline*, (New York, W. W. Norton & Company).

PIU (2000a) *Reaching Out: The Role of Central Government at Regional and Local Level*, Performance and Innovation Unit.

PIU (2000b) *Wiring it Up: Whitehall's Management of Cross-Cutting Policies and Services*, Performance and Innovation Unit, London, The Stationery Office.

POLSBY, N. W. (1968) 'The Institutionalization of the US House of Representatives', *American Political Science Review*, 62, 144–67.

POLSBY, N. W. (1975) 'Legislatures', in F. I. GREENSTEIN and N. W. POLSBY, *Handbook of Political Science, Governmental Institutions and Processes*, Volume 5, (MA, Addison Wesley).

PRESSMAN, J. L. and WILDAVSKY, A. (1974) *Implementation*, (Berkeley, University of California Press).

Prime Minister's Office of Public Services Reform (2002) *Better Government Services: Executive Agencies in the 21st Century*, London, Cabinet Office.

PROSSER, T. (1997) *Law and the Regulators*, (Oxford, Clarendon Press).

Public Audit Forum (2002a) *The Different Roles of External Audit, Inspection and Regulation: A Guide for Public Service Managers*, Consultation Paper, London, Public Audit Forum, (available at www.public-audit-forum.gov.uk/PAF.pdf).

Public Audit Forum (2002b) *Central Government Audit in the UK After Devolution*, London, Public Audit Forum, (available at www.public-audit-forum.gov.uk/devolution.pdf).

RADCLIFFE, J. (1991) *The Reorganisation of British Central Government*, (Aldershot, Dartmouth).

REDLICH, J. (1908) *The Procedure of the House of Commons: A Study of its History and Present Form*, (London, Constable).

REEVE, A. and WARE, A. (1992) *Electoral Systems: A Comparative and Theoretical Introduction*, (London, Routledge).

REICH, S. (2000) 'The Four Faces of Institutionalism: Pubic Policy and a Pluralistic Perspective' *Governance*, 13, 4:501–22.

RHODES, R. A. W. (1988) *Beyond Westminster and Whitehall*, (London, Unwin Hyman).

RHODES, R. A. W. (1990) 'Policy Networks: A British Perspective',

Journal of Theoretical Politics, 2, 3:292–316.

RHODES, R. A. W. (1995a) 'The Study of Political Institutions', in D. MARSH and G. STOKER (eds.), *Theory and Methods in Political Science*, (London, Macmillan).

RHODES, R. A. W. (1995b) 'Introducing the Core Executive', in R. A. W. RHODES and P. DUNLEAVY (eds.), *Prime Minister, Cabinet and Core Executive*, (London, Macmillan).

RHODES, R. A. W. (1996) 'The New Governance: Governing without Government', *Political Studies*, 44, 4:652–67.

RHODES, R. A. W. (1997) *Understanding Governance: Policy Networks, Governance, Reflexivity and Accountability*, (Buckingham, Open University Press).

RHODES, R. A. W. and MARSH, D. (1992) 'Policy Networks in British Politics', In D. MARSH and R. A. W. RHODES (eds.), *Policy Networks in British Government*, (Oxford, Oxford University Press).

Richard Commission (2004) *Report of the Richard Commission*, Commission on the Power and Electoral Arrangements of the National Assembly for Wales, Cardiff, The Stationery Office.

RICHARDS, D. (1997) *The Civil Service Under the Conservatives 1979–1997*, (Brighton, Sussex Academic Press).

RICHARDS, D. and SMITH, M. J. (2002) *Governance and Public Policy in the UK.* (Oxford, Oxford University Press).

RICHARDS, D. and SMITH, M. (2004) 'The "Hybrid State": Labour's Response to the Challenge of Governance', in S. LUDLAM and M. J. SMITH (eds.), *Governing as New Labour: Policy and Politics under Blair*, (London, Palgrave Macmillan).

RICHARDSON, J. (2000) 'Government, Interest Groups and Policy Change', *Political Studies*, 48, 5:1006–25.

RICHARDSON, J. J. (1993) 'Introduction: Pressure Groups and Government', in J. J. RICHARDSON (ed.), *Pressure Groups*, (Oxford, Oxford University Press).

RICHARDSON, J. J. and JORDAN, A. G. (1979) *Governing Under Pressure*, (Oxford, Martin Robertson).

RIDDELL, P. (2000) *Parliament Under Blair*, (London, Politicos).

ROBINSON, N. (2002) 'The Politics of the Fuel Protests: Towards a Multi-Dimensional Explanation', *Political Quarterly*, 73, 1:58–66.

ROGERS, R. and WALTERS, R. (2004) *How Parliament Works*, 5th edn., (London, Pearson, Longman).

ROKKAN, S. and URWIN, D. W. (1982) 'Introduction: Centres and Peripheries in Western Europe', in S. ROKKAN and D. W. URWIN (eds.), *The Politics of Territorial Identity: Studies in European Regionalism*, (London, Sage).

ROSE, R. (1982) *Understanding the United Kingdom: The Territorial Dimension in Government*, (London, Longman).

ROSE, R. (2001) *The Prime Minister in a Shrinking World*, (Cambridge, Polity).

ROTHSTEIN, B. (1996) 'Political Institutions: An Overview', in R. E. GOODIN and H. KLINGEMANN (eds.), *A New Handbook of Political Science*, (Oxford, Oxford University Press).

RUSH, M. (2001) *The Role of the Member of Parliament Since 1868: From Gentleman to Players*, (Oxford, Oxford University Press).

RUSH, M. (2005) *Parliament Today*, (Manchester, Manchester University Press).

RUSH, M. and ETTINGHAUSEN, C. (2002) *Opening Up: The Usual Channels*, (London, Hansard Society).

RUSSELL, M. (2003) 'Is the House of Lords Already Reformed?', *Political Quarterly*, 74, 3:311–18.

SANDFORD, M. (2002) 'What Place for England in an Asymmetric Devolved UK?', *Regional Studies*, 36, 7:789–96.

SCHMIDT, M. G. (2003) *Political Institutions in the Federal Republic of Germany*, (Oxford, Oxford University Press).

Scotland Office (2003) *Departmental Report 2003*, London, The Stationery Office, (available at www.scottish secretary.gov.uk/Publications/ Scotland%20Office%20-%20Contents. htm).

SCOTT, C. (2000) 'Accountability in the Regulatory State', *Journal of Law and Society*, 27, 1:38–60.

Scottish Constitutional Convention (1990) *Towards Scotland's Parliament*, Edinburgh, Scottish Constitutional Convention.

Scottish Constitutional Convention (1995) *Scotland's Parliament, Scotland's Right*, Edinburgh, Scottish Constitutional Convention.

Scottish Executive (2003a) *Scottish Human Rights Commission: Consultation Paper*, Edinburgh, Scottish Executive, (available at www.scotland. gov.uk/consultations/justice/shrs-00.asp).

Scottish Executive (2003b) *Constitutional Reform, Scottish Executive Response: Supreme Court for the United Kingdom*, Edinburgh, Scottish Executive, (available at www.scotland.gov.uk/about/JD/JD-BSU/00018515/SEresponse.pdf).

Scottish Executive (2004) *The Scottish Human Rights Commission: Analysis of Consultation Responses*, Legal Studies, Social Research, Scottish Executive, Edinburgh, The Stationery Office.

Scottish Socialist Party (2003) *Scottish Socialist Party Constitution as Amended at Annual Conference, February 2003*, (available at www.scottishsocialist party.org/pages/constitution.html).

SEARING, D. D. (1994) *Westminster's World*, (Cambridge, MA, Harvard University Press).

SEAWRIGHT, D. (2002) 'The Scottish Conservative and Unionist Party: "The Lesser Spotted Tory"?', in G. HASSAN and C. WARHURST (eds.), *Tomorrow's Scotland*, (London, Lawrence & Wishart).

SHAW, E. (2002) 'New Labour in Britain: New Democratic Centralism', *West European Politics*, 25, 3:147–70.

SHELL, D. (1992) *The House of Lords*, 2nd edn., (London, Harvester Wheatsheaf).

SHELL, D. (2001) 'The History of Bicameralism', *Journal of Legislative Studies*, 7, 1:5–18.

SHEPHARD, M. and CAIRNEY, P. (2005) 'The Impact of the Scottish Parliament in Amending Executive Legislation' *Political Studies*, 53, 2:303–19.

SIMEON, R. (2002) 'Free Personal Care: Policy Divergence and Social Citizenship', in R. HAZELL (ed.), *The State of the Nations 2003*, (Exeter, Imprint Academic).

SMITH, M. J. (1999a) *The Core Executive in Britain*, (London, Macmillan).

SMITH, M. J. (1999b) 'The Institutions of Central Government', in I. HOLLIDAY, A. GAMBLE and G. PARRY (eds.), *Fundamentals in British Politics*, (London, Macmillan).

SMITH, M. J. (2003) 'The Core Executive and the Modernization of Central Government' in P. DUNLEAVY,

A. Gamble, R. Heffernan and G. Peele (eds.), *Developments in British Politics 7*, (London, Palgrave).

Smith M. J., Marsh, D. and Richards, D. (1995) 'Central Government Departments and the Policy Process', in R. A. W Rhodes and P. Dunleavy, *Prime Minister, Cabinet and Core Executive*, (London, Macmillan).

Smith, T. (2003) ' "Something Old, Something New, Something Borrowed, Something Blue": Themes of Tony Blair and His Government', *Parliamentary Affairs*, 56, 4:560–79.

SP Paper 818 (2003) *The Founding Principles of the Scottish Parliament: the Application of Access and Participation, Equal Opportunities, Accountability and Power Sharing in the Work of the Parliament*, Third Report of the Procedures Committee, Edinburgh, Scottish Parliament (available at www.scottish.parliament.uk/S1/official_report/cttee/proced–03/prr03–03–01.htm).

Stevens, R. (2002) *The English Judges: Their Role in the Changing Constitution*, (Oxford, Hart Publishing).

Stewart, J. D. (1958) *British Pressure Groups*, (Oxford, Clarendon Press).

Stoker, G. (1998) 'Governance as Theory: Five Propositions', *International Social Science Journal*, 155:17–28.

Stoker, G. (2000) *The New Politics of British Local Governance*, (London, Macmillan).

Stoker, G. (2002) 'Life is a Lottery: New Labour's Strategy for the Reform of Devolved Governance', *Public Administration*, 80, 3:417–34.

Strategy Unit (2004) *Briefing May 2004*, The Prime Minister's Strategy Unit, (available at www.strategy.gov.uk).

Strøm, K. (1998) 'Parliamentary Committees in European Democracies', *Journal of Legislative Studies*, 4, 1:21–59.

Study of Parliament Group (1976) *Specialist Committees in the British Parliament: The Experience of a Decade*, PEP, 42, no 564.

Sunkin, M. (2001) 'Trends in Judicial Review and the Human Rights Act', *Public Money and Management*, 21, 3:9–12.

Sweeting, D. (2002) 'Leadership in Urban Governance: The Mayor of London', *Local Government Studies*, 28, 1:3–20.

Syrrett, S. and Baldock, R. (2003) 'Reshaping London's Economic Governance: The Role of the London Development Agency', *European Urban and Regional Studies*, 10, 1:69–86.

Talbot, C. (1995) 'The Prison Service: A Framework of Irresponsibility?', *Public Finance Review*, 8:16–19.

Tether, P. (1996) 'The Party in the Country II', in P. Norton (ed.), *The Conservative Party*, (London, Prentice Hall).

Thain, C. (2000) 'Economic Policy', in P. Dunleavy, A. Gamble, I. Holliday and G. Peele (eds.), *Developments in British Politics 6*, (London, Macmillan).

Thelen, K. and Steinmo, S. (1992) 'Historical Institutionalism in Comparative Politics', in S. Steinmo, K. Thelen, and F. Longstreth (eds.), *Structuring Politics: Historical Institutionalism in Comparative Analysis*, (Cambridge, Cambridge University Press).

Tilly, C. (1992) *Coercion, Capital, and European States* (rev. edn.), (Oxford Blackwell).

Toke, D. and Marsh, D. (2003) 'Policy Networks and the GM Crops Issue: Assessing the Utility of a Dialetical

Model of Policy Networks', *Public Administration*, 81, 2:229–51.

TOMANEY, J. (2001a) 'Reshaping the English Regions', in A. TRENCH (ed.), *The State of the Nations 2001*, (Exeter, Imprint Academic).

TOMANEY, J. (2001b) 'The New Governance of London: A Case of Post-democracy?', *City*, 5, 2:225–48.

TOMANEY, J. and HETHERINGTON, P. (2003) 'England Arisen?', in R. HAZELL (ed.), *The State of the Nations 2003*, (Exeter, Imprint Academic).

TONGE, J. (1998) *Northern Ireland: Conflict and Change*, (London, Prentice Hall).

TONGE, J. (2005) *The New Northern Irish Politics?*, (London, Palgrave Macmillan).

TOPF, R. (1994) 'Party Manifestos', in A. HEATH, R. JOWELL and J. CURTICE (eds.), *Labour's Last Chance*, (Aldershot, Dartmouth).

TRAVERS, T, (2002) 'Decentralization London–style: The GLA and London Governance', *Regional Studies*, 36, 7:779–88.

Treasury (2001) *Holding to Account: The Review of Audit and Accountability for Central Government*, Review by Lord Sharman, London, The Treasury (available at www.hm-treasury.gov.uk/media//928E1/Holding%20to%20Account.pdf).

TURPIN, C. (1989) 'Ministerial Responsibility: Myth or Reality?', in J. JOWELL and D. OLIVER (eds.), *The Changing Constitution* 2nd edn., (Oxford, Clarendon Press).

URWIN, D. W. (1982) 'Territorial Structures and Political Developments in the United Kingdom', in S. ROKKAN and D. W. URWIN (eds.), *The Politics of Territorial Identity: Studies in European Regionalism*, (London, Sage).

WALKER, G. (2001) 'The British-Irish Council', in R. WILFORD (ed.), *Aspects of the Belfast Agreement*, (Oxford, Oxford University Press).

WALKLAND, S. A. W. (1979) 'Introduction', in S. A. W. WALKLAND (ed.). *The House of Commons in the Twentieth Century*, (Oxford, Clarendon Press).

WEAVER, R. K. and ROCKMAN, B. A (1993) *Do Institutions Matter?*, (Washington, D. C., Brookings Institution).

WEBB, P. (2000) *The Modern British Party System*, (London, Sage).

WEBB, P. (2003) 'Parties and Party System: Prospects for Realignment', *Parliamentary Affairs*, 56, 2:283–96.

WEBB, P. D. (1994) 'Party Organizational Change in Britain: The Iron Law of Centralization', in R. S. KATZ and P. MAIR (eds.), *How Parties Organize*, (London Sage).

WEIR, S. and BEETHAM, D. (1999) *Political Power and Democratic Control in Britain*, (London, Routledge).

WHEELER-BOOTH, M. (2001) 'Procedure: A Case Study of the House of Lords', *Journal of Legislative Studies*, 7, 1: 77–92.

WHITELEY, P, SEYD, P. and RICHARDSON, J. J. (1994) *True Blues: The Politics of Conservative Party Membership*, (Oxford, Oxford University Press).

WILFORD, R, and WILSON, R. (2003) 'Northern Ireland: Valedictory?', in R. HAZELL (ed.), *The State of the Nations 2003*, (Exeter, Imprint Academic).

WILFORD, R. (1999) 'Epilogue', in P. MITCHELL and R. WILFORD (eds.), *Politics in Northern Ireland*, (Boulder, Westview Press).

WILFORD, R. (2000) 'Designing the Northern Ireland Assembly', *Parliamentary Affairs*, 53, 3:577–90.

WILSON, D. and GAME, C. (2002) *Local Government in the United Kingdom*, 3rd edn., (London, Palgrave).

WINETROBE, B. (2001) *Realising the Vision: A Parliament with a Purpose*, (London, Constitution Unit).

WOODHOUSE, D. (1994) *Ministers and Parliament: Accountability in Theory and Practice* (Oxford, Clarendon Press).

WOODHOUSE, D. (2003a) 'Ministerial Responsibility', in V. BOGDANOR (ed.), *The British Constitution in the Twentieth Century*, (Oxford, Oxford University Press).

WOODHOUSE, D. (2003b) 'The English Judges, Politics and the Balance of Power', *The Modern Law Review*, 66, 6:920–35.

WRIGHT, K. (1997) *The People Say Yes: The Making of Scotland's Parliament*, (Argyll, Argyll Publishing).

WRIGHT, T. (2000) *The British Political Process: An Introduction*, (London, Routledge).

INDEX

A

Accountability
    Audit Commission, 249–51
    Auditors General, 248–9
    Executive Agencies, 137
    ministerial accountability
        centrality of departments, 120–3
        civil service culture, 127–8
        collective responsibility, 117, 148–51
        delayering, 133
        individual responsibility, 117, 120–3, 127
    Scottish Executive, 187
    National Audit Office, 247–8
    non-departmental public bodies, 139–42
    ombudsmen, 256
    overload from secondary regulation, 246
    parliamentary questions, 53–4
    paradoxical nature of change, 279
    policy communities, 109–11
    Public Audit Forum, 251–2
    rise of regulatory state, 240
Additional member electoral system, 193–5
Administrative devolution, 178
Annual conferences
    Conservative Party, 86, 88
    Labour, 92
    Labour Party, 91–2
    Plaid Cymru, 102–3
    Scottish National Party, 99–100
    Scottish Socialist Party, 101
    Welsh Liberal Democrats, 103
Appropriate behaviour see Rules of the game
Aspinwall, M.D., 8
Asymmetry
    bicameralism, 64
    devolution, 177
    judicial institutions, 234–6
Audit Commission, 249–51
Auditors General, 248–9

B

Baggot, R., 104–5
Baldock, R., 214, 219

Balsom, 193
Bara, J., 114
Barberis, P., 138
Barnett, H., 226
Bates, R.H., 28
Batey, A., 185–6
Beatson, J.
    inquiries, 258–9
    judiciary, 259–60
Beetham, D.
    House of Commons, 45
    judicial review, 226–8
    non-departmental public bodies, 140, 142
Belfast Agreement
    Civic Forum, 202
    confederalism, 203
    power sharing, 198–9
Benn, T., 78
Bennett, M., 189
Bergman, T., 56
Bevir, M.
    Europeanization, 268
    networks, 106–15
Bichard, M., 129
Birch, A.H.
    House of Commons, 38
    ministerial departments, 120
    Scottish representation, 171
    Westminster model, 27
Blackburn, R.
    centralized government, 270
    House of Commons, 49–51
    monarchy, 77
    Westminster model, 80
Block vote, 90
Bogdanor, V.
    centralized government, 270
    devolution, 180
    devolution in England, 205
    English Dimension, 216–17
    English regions, 208
    managerialism, 130
    ministerial departments, 122, 129
    Scottish Parliament, 185

Bogdanor, V. (*Continued*)
  Scottish representation, 172
  territorial institutions, 163–5
  territorial representation, 170
  Third Way, 271
  Welsh Assembly, 192
  Welsh Office, 169–70
Bradbury, J., 193
Bradley, A.W.
  human rights, 230
  judicial independence, 223–4
  local government, 175
  ministerial departments, 126
  Ombudsmen, 252
  regulation, 240
  Supreme Court, 236
Brazier, D., 271
British-Irish Council, 204–5
Brown, A.
  devolution, 180
  Scottish Office, 167
Budge, I.
  House of Commons, 37
  House of Lords, 66
  party system, 114
  Westminster model, 24
Bulpitt, J., 165
Burch, M., 118, 144
Bureaucracy
  civil service culture, 127–9
Burke, E., 41–2
Butt, R., 28
Byrne, I., 142

C

Cabinet system
  combined centre, 151–60
  coordination, 148–51
  individual ministerial responsibility,
    120–3
  joined-up government, 144–5
  move towards, 149
  prime ministerial government,
    145–8
Cadre parties, 84, 85
Campbell, C., 128
Carmichael, P., 168
Cause groups, 104–5
Central Criminal Court, 3

Central government
  combined centre, 151–60
  conclusions, 160–1
  Executive Agencies, 135–8
  joined-up government
    coordinating old and new, 143–51
    need for reform, 142–3
  ministerial accountability, 120–3
  ministerial departments
    civil service culture, 127–9
    definitions and organization, 124–7,
    managerialism, 129–32
  non-departmental public bodies,
    138–42
  non-ministerial departments, 133–5
  Northern Ireland, 174
  pre-devolution, 163–4
  precipitant of institutional change,
    270
Chester, N., 122
Civic Forum, 202
Civil service
  Committee on Standards in Public Life,
    243–5
  culture, 127–9
  delayering, 132–3
  managerialism, 129–32
  non-ministerial departments, 133–5
  Whitehall
    joined-up government, 142–51
    ministerial departments, 124–32
    Treasury, 158–60
Clifford, C., 71
Coates, D.
  globalization, 267
  Labour Party, 91
Coaxall, B., 105
Collective ministerial responsibility
  coordination, 148–51
  overview, 117
Combined centre
  Cabinet Office, 152–3
  Delivery and Reform Team, 154–6
  Deputy Prime Minister's Office, 154
  Prime Minister's Delivery Unit, 157
  Prime Minister's Office, 153–4
  Reform Strategy Group, 157
  Strategy Unit, 156–7
  Treasury, 158–60

Committee on Standards in Public Life,
243–5
Confederalism
Belfast Agreement, 198–9
British-Irish Council, 204–5
North-South Ministerial Council,
202–4
Connolly, M., 174
Consensus model, 20
Conservative Party
centralized government, 270
historical institutionalism, 30
House of Lords, 66–7
issue networks, 112
origins, 85–6
paradoxical nature of change,
276
party representation, 38
reorganization after 1997, 86–9
Scotland, 99
Thatcherite neo-liberalism, 269
Consociationalism
Belfast Agreement, 181, 198–9
Northern Ireland, 201–2
Scottish Parliament, 186–7
Conventions, 31–2
Cook, R., 59
Coordination
cabinet system, 148–51
joined-up government, 144–5
need for reform, 142–3
prime ministerial government,
145–8
Cope, S., 246, 250
Core executive
combined centre, 151–60
defining a government department,
124
joined-up government, 144–5
prime ministerial government,
145–8
secondary regulation of government,
246
Courts see also Judiciary
Supreme Court, 236–8
Cowley, P.
House of Commons, 40–1
House of Lords, 74
Westminster model, 79

Coxall, B., 105
Crewe, I., 37
Critical junctures, 14
Crown-in-parliament, 29–30, 32

D

Daintith, T., 122, 124, 126
Daugbjerg, C., 111
Deakin, M., 159
Dearlove, J., 24
Debates, 43–4
Declarations of incompatibility, 230–1
Delayering, 132–3
Delegated legislation, 50–2
Deliberative assemblies
importance, 41–3
types of debate, 43–4
Delivery and Reform Team, 154–6
Democratization as emasculation
Conservative Party, 89
Labour Party, 93
Denver, D.
Conservative Party, 88
Liberal Democrats, 97
Deputy Prime Minister's Office, 154
Development Agencies, 209
Devolution
administrative devolution, 178
alternatives to the Westminster model,
179–83
asymmetry of human rights, 234–6
conclusions, 217–19
English Dimension
avoidance of question, 205–7
London, 212–14
regions post-1997, 207–12
Westminster model, 214–17
establishment of Supreme Court,
237
Europeanization, 267–8
extent of institutional change, 265
institutional change, 177–9
Northern Ireland, 173–4
Belfast Agreement, 198–9
British-Irish Council, 204–5
North-South Ministerial Council,
202–4
Northern Ireland Assembly, 199–201
Northern Ireland Executive, 201–2

Devolution (*Continued*)
  precipitant of institutional change, 269
  Scotland
    alternatives to the Westminster model,
      179–83
    local government, 189–90
    Scottish Executive, 187–9
    Scottish Parliament, 183–7
  secondary regulation of government
    Auditors General, 248–9
    ombudsmen, 253–4
  Wales
    alternatives to the Westminster model,
      179–83
    local government, 196–7
    National Assembly for Wales, 191–6
Diamond, L., 83–4
Dicey, A.V., 5
Doherty, B., 113
Dowding, K., 106–14
Driver, S., 272, 276
Dunleavy, P., 123
Duverger, M., 83–4

E

Edwards, R.A., 231–3
Elections
  additional member electoral system,
    193–5
  Committee on Standards in Public Life,
    244
  elective dictatorship, 271
  electoralist parties, 84–5
  mandates
    London, 212–14
    party representation, 37
    pre-eminence of House of Commons,
      26
    Regional Assemblies, 210–12
    Scottish Parliament, 183–4
    West Lothian Question, 215–16
  professional parties, 84, 96
  volatility, 94–5
Elgie, R., 223
Elliott, S., 174
Empirical institutionalism, 1, 18–20
English Dimension
  avoidance of question, 205–7
  London, 212–14

  regions post-1997, 207–12
  Westminster model, 214–17
Ersson, S., 15
Ettinghausen, C., 39
Europeanization, 267–8
Evans, M., 266
Ewing, K.D.
  centralized government, 270
  human rights, 230–1
  judicial independence, 223–4
  local government, 175
  ministerial departments, 126
  Ombudsmen, 252
  regulation, 240
  Supreme Court, 236
Exchange relationships, 105
Executive
  combined centre, 151–60
  Committee on Standards in Public Life,
    243–5
  conclusions, 160–1
  core executive
    defining a government department,
      124
    joined-up government, 144–5
    prime ministerial government,
      145–8
    secondary regulation of government,
      246
  effect of human rights, 233
  Executive Agencies, 135–8
  extent of institutional change, 265
  individual ministerial responsibility,
    120–3
  introduction, 117–20
  joined-up government
    coordinating old and new, 143–51
    need for reform, 142–3
  judicial review, 226–9
  ministerial departments, 123–4
    civil service culture, 127–9
    definitions and organization, 124–7
    delayering, 132–3
    lead element, 123–4
    managerialism, 129–32
  National Assembly for Wales, 195
  non-departmental public bodies,
    138–42
  non-ministerial departments, 133–5

Northern Ireland, 201–2
overview, 117
Scottish Executive, 187–9
secondary regulation of government,
    244–7
Executive Agencies, 135–8

F

Fairley, J., 189
Falconer, Lord
  House of Lords, 72
  human rights, 232
  judiciary, 258
Feldman, D., 233
Fielding, S., 89, 271
Financial Services Authority, 242
Finer, H., 5
First-past-the-post system
  groups and parties distinguished, 104
  two-party system, 95
Fisher, J.
  Conservative Party, 88
  Liberal Democrats, 97
Flinders, M.
  executive agencies, 138
  House of Commons, 62
  human rights, 231
  institutional change, 275
  joined-up government, 143
  ministerial departments, 129
  New Labour, 278
Foley, M.
  centralized government, 270
  core executive, 145–6
  Third Way, 271
Food Standards Agency, 242–3
Forman, F.N.
  devolution in England, 206
  electoral systems, 95
  English Dimension, 216
  regional assemblies, 210
  Scottish Parliament, 185
Foster, C.D., 173
Foster, R.F.
  delayering, 132
  ministerial departments, 128, 129
Fox, C.J., 2
Freedom of information, 54
Fry, G., 123

G

Gains, F., 137–8
Gamble, A.
  coordination, 149
  globalization, 267
  old institutionalism, 5, 21
  Third Way, 271
  Westminster model, 24–5, 25
Game, C.
  Audit Commission, 250
  local government, 174–6
Garner, R.
  Conservative Party, 87
  Labour Party, 89
Gay, O., 216
Gearty, C.A., 270
Geddes, A., 268
Giddens, A., 271
Giddings, P., 252
Globalization, 266–7
Goodship, J., 246, 250
Governance
  combined centre, 151–60
  focus on networks, 106–7
  issue networks, 111–14
  joined-up government
    coordinating old and new, 143–51
    need for reform, 142–3
  judicial review, 228
  local government, 176
  policy communities, 107–11
  rise of regulatory state, 239
  Third Way, 272
Grace, C., 250
Grant, W.
  groups, 104–5
  issue networks, 113
  policy communities, 109
Greater London Authority, 3
Green Party, 101
Greenleaf, W.H., 158
Greenwood, J.
  coordination, 148–9
  devolution in England, 207
  executive, 118–19
  executive agencies, 138
  joined-up government, 143
  managerialism, 129

Greenwood, J. (*Continued*)
  ministerial departments, 123, 124
  non-departmental public bodies,
    139
Greer, A.
  issue networks, 112
  Northern Ireland Office, 168
Gregory, R., 252
Griffith, J.A.G., 31
Groups *see also* Party system
  conclusions, 114–15
  insider and outsider groups
    distinguished, 105
  networks
    focus of governance, 106–7
    issue networks, 111–14
    policy communities, 107–11
  parties distinguished, 104
  sectional and cause groups distinguished,
    104–5
Gunther, R., 83–4

H

Hague, W., 215
Hailsham, Lord, 271
Hall, P.A.
  historical institutionalism, 9–15
  new institutionalism, 6
  rational choice institutionalism, 8
  rules of the game, 7
Hands, G.
  Conservative Party, 88
  Liberal Democrats, 97
Hanham, H.J., 122
Harlow, C.
  executive agencies, 138
  judiciary, 222
Hassan, G., 98–9
Hay, C.
  globalization, 267
  historical institutionalism, 9
Heffernan, R.
  coordination, 149
  electoral systems, 94
  Liberal Democrats, 97
  party system, 84
Hennessy, P.
  cabinet office, 153
  core executive, 146

delivery and reform, 155
joined-up government, 143
ministerial departments, 129
non-ministerial departments, 135
Treasury, 158
Herb, M., 28
Hetherington, P., 208
Hill, B.W., 83
Historical institutionalism
  devolution, 177
  House of Lords, 64–6
  importance, 26–7
  London government, 214
  new institutionalism, 9–15
  parliamentary state, 27–31
  understandings and conventions, 31–2
Hobhouse, Lord, 224
Hodgson, G., 89
Hogwood, B.W.
  devolution in England, 206–7
  English regions, 208
  executive agencies, 138
  ministerial departments, 125
  non-departmental public bodies,
    140–1
  regulation inside government, 246
Holliday, I., 118, 144
Home Rule for Ireland, 173–4
Hood, C.
  executive, 118
  regulation inside government, 245–6
House of Commons
  pre-eminence, 26
  representation
    delegated legislation, 50–2
    deliberations, 41–4
    legislative process, 44–52
    linkage and territory, 32–4
    parties, 36–41
    principle of distinction, 34–6
    scrutiny and control, 52–64
House of Lords
  asymmetric bicameralism, 64
  composition, 66–8
  establishment of Supreme Court,
    236–7
  history, 64–6
  legislative process, 45
  role and functions, 73–6

Human rights
  asymmetry of devolution, 234–6
  establishment of Supreme Court, 237
  growth judicial review, 226–7
  remedial orders, 51
  scope and importance, 229–34
Humphrey, J.C., 250
Hutchison, I.J.C, 99
Hutton, W., 267

I

Identity politics, 83
Individual ministerial responsibility
  centrality of departments, 120–3
  Whitehall structures, 127
Ingle, S.
  Conservative Party, 86
  Scottish party system, 99
Inquiries, 257–8
Insider groups, 105, 107, 113
Inspection, 256–7
Institutional change
  combined centre
    Delivery and Reform Team, 154–6
    Reform Strategy Group, 157
  critical junctures, 14
  devolution, 177–9
  establishment of Supreme Court,
    236–8
  extent, 263–6
  historical institutionalism, 30
  House of Lords
    composition, 68–73
    removal of hereditary peers, 67–8
    role and functions, 73–6
  lack of cohesion, 273–5
  Liberal Democrats, 96
  National Assembly for Wales, 195–6
  normative institutionalism, 17
  ombudsmen, 254–6
  overview and introduction, 262–3
  paradoxical nature, 275–9
  party pragmatism, 273
  path dependency, 13–14
  precipitants
    central government, 270
    devolution, 269
    Europeanization, 267–8
    globalization, 266–7

    Third Way, 271–2
  select committees, 58–60
Institutionalism
  context, 19
  introduction, 2
  Westminster model, 24–5
Institutions
  definitions
    'brass plate' approach, 2–4
    new institutionalism, 5–21
    old institutionalism, 4–5
  formation, 13, 17
  territorial representation
    introduction, 163–4
    pre-1999, 165–76
Interim house, 67
Interinstitutional interactions
  cabinet system, 117
  devolution, 182
  empirical institutionalism, 19, 21
  House of Commons, 53
  House of Lords, 66
  issue networks, 112
  joined-up government, 144–5
  judicialization, 222–3, 259–60
  new patterns of governance, 268
  ombudsmen, 256
  Scotland, 190
  territorial representation, 219
Intra-party democratization, 91
Irvine, Lord, 229
Issue networks, 108, 111–14

J

James, O.
  coordination, 149
  regulation inside government, 245–6, 246
  Treasury, 159
James, S., 118
Johnson, N.
  coherence, 274
  devolution in England, 206
  Europeanization, 268
  globalization, 267
  judicial independence, 224, 226
  party pragmatism, 273
  territorial representation, 217
  Third Way, 271
  Westminster model, 277

Joined-up government
  absence of institutional reform, 274
  coordinating old and new, 143–51
  need for reform, 142–3
Jones, G.W., 24, 245
Jones, J.B., 169–70, 178, 182
Jordan, A.G.
  ministerial departments, 124
  policy communities, 106–14
Judge, D.
  accountability, 279
  centralized government, 270
  executive, 119
  executive agencies, 138
  globalization, 267
  House of Commons, 33, 36, 41–2, 52, 55–8, 62
  issue networks, 112–13
  ministerial departments, 121, 126, 128
  non-departmental public bodies, 140–1
  Northern Ireland, 202
  parliamentary state, 28
  party system, 83
  policy communities, 110
  regulation inside government, 246
  territorial institutions, 164–5
  West Lothian Question, 215
  Westminster model, 25, 79, 277
Judicial review, 226–9, 237
Judiciary
  asymmetry of devolution, 234–6
  establishment of Supreme Court, 236–8
  extent of institutional change, 265
  independence, 223–6
  introduction, 222–3
  overview, 221
  politicization
    human rights, 229
    judicial review, 227–9

K

Katz, R., 89
Kavanagh, D., 153, 270
Keating, M.
  Scottish Office, 168
  Scottish party system, 99
  Scottish representation, 172
  territorial representation, 171

Kellas, J.G.
  Scottish Office, 167
  Scottish party system, 98
  Scottish representation, 172
Kelly, J., 250
Kelly, R.
  Conservative Party, 86–7, 89
  Labour Party, 89
Kelso, A., 59–60
Kennon, A.
  House of Commons, 49–51
  Westminster model, 80
King, A., 263
Kingdom, J., 24
Knox, C., 169
Krausner, S., 14

L

Labour Party
  approval of first-past-the-post system, 95
  Blairite revolution, 275–7
  democratization after 1997, 92–3
  failure to embrace change, 278
  issue networks, 112
  joined-up government, 142–3
  origins, 89–92
  paradoxical nature of change, 276
  party representation, 38
  Scotland, 98–9
  Third Way, 96, 271–2
  Wales, 102
Laffin, M.
  devolution, 179, 181
  Welsh local government, 197
  Welsh party system, 102
Lane, J-E., 15
LaPolombara, J., 84
Law-making
  historical institutionalism, 31
  legislative process, 44–52
  pre-eminence of House of Commons, 26
Le Suer, A., 224
Leach, R., 105
Leat, D., 143
Legislative process
  English Dimension, 216
  House of Commons, 44–52
  House of Lords, 74–5
  National Assembly for Wales, 191

Northern Ireland Assembly, 199–201
    royal assent, 76–9
    Scottish Parliament, 185
Legitimation
    centralised government, 270
    House of Lords, 65
    human rights, 231
    legislative process, 52
    local government, 176
    policy communities, 110–11
    territorial representation, 32–4
    Westminster model, 24–6
Lester, Lord, 228, 274
Leys, C., 92
Liberal Democrats
    electoral professional model, 97
    historical institutionalism, 30
    origins, 95–6
    party representation, 38
    principles and constitution, 96
    Scotland, 100–1
    Wales, 103
Liddle, R., 272, 273
Lieberman, E.S., 11, 13, 14
Lijphart, A.
    empirical institutionalism, 18–20
    Northern Ireland, 198
Ling, T., 143
Linkage
    civil service culture, 127–8
    groups, 103–4
    House of Commons and territorial
        representation, 32–4
    overview, 82
Local government
    Audit Commission, 249–51
    Scotland, 189–90
    territorial representation, 174–6
    Wales, 196–7
Lodge, G., 216
Logic of appropriateness, 16
London government, 212–14, 264
Lord's reform
    composition, 68–73
    removal of hereditary peers, 67–8
    role and functions, 73–6
Loughlin, M.
    local government, 175–6
    regulation, 239–40

Loveland, I.
    House of Lords, 66
    judiciary, 223
Low, S., 147
Lowell, A.L., 4
Lowndes, V.
    new institutionalism, 6
    normative institutionalism, 15, 16
    old institutionalism, 4
    rules of the game, 7
Lynch, P., 100

M

Madgwick, P., 227
Mair, P., 89, 93
Majoritarian model, 19–20
Managerialism, 129–32
Mandelson, P., 272, 273
Manin, B., 33–6
March, J.G., 6, 15–17, 79
Marquand, D., 267
Marsh, D.
    coordination, 149
    core executive, 148
    executive politics, 160
    ministerial departments, 123–4,
        128
    networks, 106–15
Marshall, G., 121
Martell, L., 272, 276
Mass membership, 84, 85
Mass parties, 90
McAllister, L.
    Conservative Party, 88
    devolution, 183
    Liberal Democrats, 97
McAteer, M., 189
McCrone, D., 167, 180
McGarvey, N., 190
McKenzie, R.T., 85, 90
McLean, I., 71, 124
McMillan, A., 71
McVicar, M.
    executive agencies, 138
    non-departmental public bodies,
        140–1
    regulation inside government, 246
Members of Parliament, 35–6
Mezey, M., 18

Midwinter, A.
  Scottish Office, 168
  Scottish party system, 99
  Scottish representation, 172
Miliband, R., 25
  Westminster model, 277
Mill, J.S.
  House of Commons, 42
Miller, T., 2
Ministers
  accountability
    centrality of departments,
      120–3
    civil service culture, 127–8
    Scottish Executive, 187
  Code, 120
  departments
    civil service culture, 127–9
    delayering, 132–3
    lead element, 123–4
    managerialism, 129–32
    territorial representation
      pre-1999, 165–70
  Deputy Prime Minister's Office,
    154
  Prime Minister
    Delivery Unit, 157
    government system, 145–8
    Office, 153–4
  responsibility
    Executive Agencies, 136–8
    Northern Ireland Executive,
      201
Minkin, L., 90–1
Mitchell, J.
  devolution, 178, 180, 183
  Europeanization, 269
  Scottish Office, 168
  Scottish party system, 98–9, 99
  Scottish representation, 172
Monarchy, 76–9
Moran, M.
  judiciary, 223
  regulation, 239–42
  standards in public life, 244
Morgan, K., 197
Mughan, A., 64
Multi-party systems, 94
Mungham, G., 197

N

Nairn, T., 78, 167
National Assembly for Wales
  devolution, 191–6
  multi-party systems, 94
  non-departmental public bodies, 138
  subnational party systems, 102–3
National Audit Office, 247–8
Nationalist Parties, 99–100
Networks
  focus of governance, 106–7
  issue networks, 111–14
  policy communities, 107–11
New democratic centralism
  Conservative Party, 87–8
  Labour Party, 90–1, 93
New institutionalism
  conclusions, 21
  empirical institutionalism, 18–20
  exaggeration of previous neglect, 5–6
  historical institutionalism, 9–15
  normative institutionalism, 15–17
  overview, 1
  rational choice, 7–9
  rules of the game, 6–7
New Labour, 67–76
New public management, 136
Next Step Agencies, 125, 135–8
Ngan, P., 142
Non-departmental public bodies, 138–42,
  234, 249–51
Non-ministerial departments, 133–5, 256–7
Normative institutionalism, 1, 15–17
Norris, P.
  electoral systems, 95
  party system, 114
North-South Ministerial Council, 202–4
Northern Ireland
  asymmetry of human rights, 235–6
  Auditors General, 248–9
  devolution
    alternatives to the Westminster model,
      179–83
    Belfast Agreement, 198–9
    British-Irish Council, 204–5
    institutional change, 177–9
    North-South Ministerial Council,
      202–4

Northern Ireland Assembly, 199–201
Northern Ireland Executive, 201–2
multi-party systems, 94
territorial representation pre-1999, 168–9, 172–4
Norton, P.
coherence, 273
Conservative Party, 85
electoral systems, 95
empirical institutionalism, 18
House of Commons, 36, 39, 52–3, 56
House of Lords, 75
parliamentary state, 30
Westminster model, 80

O

O'Gorman, F., 85
O'Leary, B., 174, 198, 201, 202–3
Oliver, D.
English regions, 208
Europeanization, 267
human rights, 232
judicial review, 228
judiciary, 222
managerialism, 129
non-departmental public bodies, 139
Northern Ireland, 198, 200, 202
regional assemblies, 210
Scottish Parliament, 186
Welsh Assembly, 191
Olsen, J.P., 6, 15–17, 79
Ombudsmen
institutional design, 252–3
Parliamentary Commissioner, 244
recommendations for reform, 254–6
One Member One Vote
Conservative Party, 88
Labour Party, 91–2
Wales Labour Party, 102
Osborne, R., 168
Osmond, J.
Welsh Assembly, 191, 195
Welsh party system, 103
Outsider groups, 105, 107, 113

P

Packenham, R.A., 18
Page, A.

ministerial departments, 122, 124, 126
Scottish Parliament, 185–6
Panebianco, A., 83–4
Panitch, L., 92
Parliament see also Party system
Commissioner, 244
recommendations for reform, 254–6
role and powers, 252–3
House of Commons
pre-eminence, 26
representation, 32–64
House of Lords
asymmetric bicameralism, 64
composition, 66–8
establishment of Supreme Court, 236–7
history, 64–6
legislative process, 45
role and functions, 73–6
MPs, 35–6
state
Labour Party, 89
Westminster model, 27–31
systems
empirical institutionalism, 19
pre-eminence of House of Commons, 26
Parris, H., 122
Parry, R., 159
Partisan dealignment, 94
Party system see also Groups
conclusions, 114–15
Conservatives
centralized government, 270
historical institutionalism, 30
House of Lords, 66–7
issue networks, 112
origins, 85–6
paradoxical nature of change, 276
party representation, 38
reorganization after 1997, 86–9
Scotland, 99
Thatcherite neo-liberalism, 269
electoralism in 21st century, 84–5
introduction, 82–3
Labour
approval of first-past-the-post system, 95
Blairite revolution, 275–7

Party system (*Continued*)
democratization after 1997, 92–3
failure to embrace change, 278
issue networks, 112
joined-up government, 142–3
origins, 89–92
paradoxical nature of change, 276
party representation, 38
Scotland, 98–9
Third Way, 96, 271–2
Wales, 102
Liberal Democrats
electoral professional model, 97
historical institutionalism, 30
origins, 95–6
party representation, 38
principles and constitution, 96
Scotland, 100–1
Wales, 103
overview, 82
pre-eminence of House of Commons, 26
representation, 36–41
subnational parties
scope, 97
Scotland, 98–102
Wales, 102–3
two-party system, 94–5
typologies, 83–4
whips, 39–40
Pasquino, G., 18
Patchett, K., 192
Paterson, L., 37
Paterson, M.
devolution, 180
issue networks, 113
Scottish Office, 167
Path dependency, 13
Executive Agencies, 137
House of Lords, 64
judiciary, 260
parliamentary state, 27
Patterson, S.C., 64
Peele, G.
coherence, 275
Conservative Party, 89
coordination, 149
devolution in England, 206
Peers, 65, 67–8
Perri 6, 143

Peters, B.G.
empirical institutionalism, 18
historical institutionalism, 9–10, 11–15, 13, 14
institutional change, 14–15
networks, 106–15
normative institutionalism, 15, 17
old institutionalism, 4–5
rational choice institutionalism, 8
rules of the game, 7
Pierre, J.
Europeanization, 268
historical institutionalism, 14
networks, 106–15
Pierson, P., 9–15
Plaid Cymru, 102–3
Plant, R., 77
Plows, A., 113
Policy communities, 107–11, 113
Political accountability, 117, 139–42
Political executive, 144–5
Politicization of judiciary
conclusions, 259
effect of human rights, 229
judicial review, 227–9
Polsby, N.W., 35
Power sharing
Belfast Agreement, 181, 198–9
British-Irish Council, 202–4
North-South Ministerial Council, 202–4
Northern Ireland, 201–2
Scottish Parliament, 186–7
Precipitants of institutional change
centralised government, 270
devolution, 269
Europeanization, 267–8
globalization, 266–7
Third Way, 271–2
Prerogative powers
civil service culture, 128
Westminster model, 78–9
Presidential systems
electoral contests, 94
empirical institutionalism, 19
Northern Ireland Executive, 201
prime ministerial government, 145–8
Pressman, J.L., 18
Prime Minister
Delivery Unit, 157

Deputy Prime Minister's Office, 154
government system, 145–8
Office, 153–4
Principle of distinction, 34–6
Private sector regulation, 239–43
Prosser, T., 239–41
Public Audit Forum, 251–2
Public inquiries, 257–8
Public sector ethos, 132
Public service agreements, 159, 197
Punctuated equilibria, 14, 27
Pyper, R.
coordination, 148–9
devolution in England, 207
executive, 118–19
executive agencies, 138
joined-up government, 143
managerialism, 129
ministerial departments, 123, 124
non-departmental public bodies,
139

Q

Quangos *see* Non-departmental public
bodies

R

Radcliffe, J.
joined-up government, 143
ministerial departments, 123
Rational choice institutionalism
devolution, 179
new institutionalism, 7–9
overview, 1
Rawlings, R., 222
Redlich, J., 5
Reeve, A., 32
Reform *see also* Institutional change
Strategy Group, 157
Regional government
Assemblies, 209–12
Development Agencies, 209
pre-1997, 207–8
Regulation
Committee on Standards in Public Life,
243–5
conclusions, 258–60
extent of institutional change, 265
inquiries, 257–8

inspection, 256–7
move away from self-regulation, 241–3
ombudsmen
institutional design, 252–3
recommendations for reform, 254–6
sub-national institutions, 253–4
rise of regulatory state, 239–41
secondary regulation of government
Audit Commission, 249–51
Auditors General, 248–9
National Audit Office, 247–8
Public Audit Forum, 251–2
scope and importance, 244–7
Reich, S., 6
Remedial orders, 51–2
Representation
government, 37
historical institutionalism, 28–31
House of Commons
linkage and territory, 32–4
party representation, 36–41
principle of distinction, 34–6
House of Lords, 65
National Assembly for Wales, 193–5
policy communities, 110–11
Reserved matters
Northern Ireland Assembly, 199–201
Scottish Parliament, 185
Responsible government, 37, 42–3
Rhodes, R.A.W.
core executive, 144
Europeanization, 268
executive, 118
institutional change, 275
networks, 106–15
old institutionalism, 4–5
Westminster model, 24–5, 27
Richard Commission, 195–6
Richards, D.
coordination, 149
core executive, 148
delayering, 132
Deputy Prime Minister, 154
executive agencies, 135
executive politics, 160
globalization, 267
ministerial departments, 123–4, 128,
129
networks, 106–15

Richards, D. (*Continued*)
  Treasury, 159
  Westminster model, 24–5, 276
Richardson, J.J.
  Conservative Party, 86
  groups, 105
  policy communities, 106–14
Riddell, P., 24
Robins, L., 105
Robinson, N., 113
Rockman, B.A., 18–19
Rogers, R., 38, 43
Rokkan, S., 165–6
Rose, R.
  core executive, 146–8
  Northern Ireland Office, 168
  Welsh Office, 169–70
Rothstein, B., 6–7
Royal assent, 76–9
Royal Courts of Justice, 3
Rules of the game
  human rights, 232
  networks, 114
  new institutionalism, 6–7
  normative institutionalism,
    15–17
  paradoxical nature of change, 278
Rush, M., 36, 39, 79
Russell, M.
  English Dimension, 216
  House of Lords, 73

S

Sandford, M.
  English Dimension, 216–17
  regional assemblies, 210
Saunders, P., 24
Schmidt, M.G., 223
Schneider, G., 8
Scotland
  Audit Commission, 251
  Auditors General, 248–9
  devolution
    alternatives to the Westminster model,
      179–83
    institutional change, 177–9
    local government, 189–90
    Scottish Executive, 187–9
    Scottish Parliament, 183–7

  extent of institutional change, 264
  precipitants of institutional change, 269
  Scottish Parliament
    asymmetry of human rights, 234–5
    multi-party systems, 94
    non-departmental public bodies, 138
    subnational party system, 98–102
  territorial representation pre-1999
    parliamentary representation, 171–2
    Scottish Office, 166–8
Scott, C., 239–40, 245–6
Scottish civil society, 167
Scrutiny and control
  House of Commons
    parliamentary questions, 52–5
    select committees, 55–64
  House of Lords, 76
Searing, D.D., 79
Seawright, D., 99
Sectional groups, 104–5
Select committees, 55–64, 153
Self-regulation, 241–3
Seltzer, K., 143
Separation of powers, 223–6
Seyd, P., 86
Shaw, E., 92, 93
Shell, D., 65–6
Simeon, R., 100
Single-issue politics, 104
Skocpol, T., 9–15
Smith, M.
  coherence, 274
  coordination, 149
  core executive, 147, 148
  delayering, 132
  Deputy Prime Minister, 154
  executive, 118–19
  executive agencies, 135
  executive politics, 160
  globalization, 267
  joined-up government, 143
  ministerial departments, 123–4, 128, 129
  networks, 106–15
  Treasury, 159
  Westminster model, 24–5, 276
Socialist Party, 101–2
Sociological institutionalism, 7
Sovereignty
  centralised government, 270

effect of human rights, 231
historical institutionalism, 30–1
introduction, 24
judicial review, 228
National Assembly for Wales, 191
Northern Ireland, 173
pre-eminence of House of Commons, 26
Scottish Parliament, 185
separation of powers, 226
subsidiarity, 269
territorial representation, 164
understandings, 32
Westminster model, 25
Special advisers, 131
Standard operating procedures, 15
Standards in public life, 243–5
Standing committees, 46–7, 200
Statutory inquiries, 257–8
Statutory instruments, 50–2
Steinmo, S., 9–15
Stevens, R., 232, 259–60
Stewart, J.D., 104
Stoker, G.
   coherence, 274–5
   Europeanization, 268
   joined-up government, 143
   territorial representation, 217
Strategy Unit, 156–7
Strøm, K., 56
Stuart, M.
   House of Commons, 41
   House of Lords, 74
Sub-national legislatures
   institutional change, 177–9, 264
   institutional design, 179–83
Subnational party systems
   scope, 97
   Scotland, 98–102
   Wales, 102–3
Subsidiarity, 269
Sunkin, M., 224, 226–7
Supreme authority see Sovereignty
Supreme Court, 236–8
Sweeting, D., 214
Syrrett, S., 214, 219

T

Talbot, C., 138
Taxation
   historical institutionalism, 28
   National Assembly for Wales, 191
   Scotland, 171
   Treasury, 158–60
Taylor, G.
   historical institutionalism, 9–15
   new institutionalism, 6
   rational choice institutionalism, 8
   rules of the game, 7
   Welsh local government, 197
   Welsh party system, 102
Territorial representation see also
   Devolution
   conclusions, 217–19
   devolution post-1999
      institutional change, 177–9
   introduction, 163–4
   pre-1999
      local government, 174–6
      ministerial departments, 165–70
      parliamentary representation, 170–7
      Westminster model, 32–4
Tether, P., 86
Thain, C., 159
Thelen, K., 9–15
Third Way, 96, 271–2
Thomas, A.
   devolution, 181–2
   Welsh local government, 197
   Welsh party system, 102
Tilly, C., 28
Toke, D., 112
Tomaney, J.
   devolution, 219
   English regions, 208
   London government, 214
   regional assemblies, 209
Tonge, J., 168–9, 200–1
Topf, R., 37
Trade unions, 90
Travers. T., 213–14
Treasury, 158–60
Turpin, C., 121

U

Ultra vires
   judicial review, 227
   rule, 175
   Scottish Parliament, 185

Understandings, 31–2
Unintended consequences, 263
Union state, 171, 235
Unionist Party, 99
Unitary state, 163–4, 171, 178
Urwin, D.W.
  Scottish representation, 171
  territorial institutions, 165–6
Usual channels
  responsible government, 38–41
  Scottish Parliament, 187

W

Wales
  alternatives to the Westminster model,
    179–83
  Audit Commission, 251
  Auditors General, 248–9
  extent of institutional change, 265
  institutional change, 177–9
  local government, 196–7
  National Assembly for Wales
    devolution, 191–6
    multi-party systems, 94
    non-departmental public bodies, 138
    subnational party systems, 102–3
  precipitants of institutional change, 269
  territorial representation pre-1999
    parliamentary representation, 171
    Welsh Office, 169–70
Walker, G., 205
Walkland, S.A.W., 31
Wall, D., 113
Walters, R., 38
  House of Commons, 43
Ware, A., 32
Weaver, R.K., 18–19
Webb, P.D.
  Conservative Party, 85, 88–9
  electoral systems, 94
  Labour Party, 90–1
  Liberal Democrats, 96
  party organization, 92, 93
  party system, 83–4, 114
  subnational party systems, 97
Weiner, M., 84
Weir, S.
  House of Commons, 45
  judicial review, 226–8

non-departmental public bodies,
  140, 142
West Lothian Question, 215–16
Westminster Hall, 43–4
Westminster model
  centrality of institutional approach, 24–5
  devolution, 179–83
  English Dimension, 214–17
  historical institutionalism
    importance, 26–7
    parliamentary state, 27–31
    understandings and conventions, 31–2
  House of Commons
    delegated legislation, 50–2
    deliberations, 41–4
    legislative process, 44–52
    pre-eminence, 26
    representation, 32–41
    scrutiny and control, 52–64
  House of Lords
    asymmetric bicameralism, 64
    composition, 66–8
    history, 64–6
    role and functions, 73–6
  monarchy, 76–9
  networks as governance, 114–15
  paradoxical nature of change, 275–9
  pre-eminence of House of Commons, 26
Wheeler-Booth, M., 65–6
Whips, 39–40
Whitehall
  joined-up government
    coordinating old and new, 143–51
    need for reform, 142–3
  ministerial departments
    civil service culture, 127–9
    definitions and organization, 124–7
    delayering, 132–3
    managerialism, 129–32
    overview, 124
  non-ministerial departments,
    133–5
  overview, 117
  Treasury, 158–60
Whiteley, P., 86
Wildavsky, A., 18
Wilford, R.
  devolution, 181–2
  Northern Ireland, 174, 198–200

Wilson, D.
  Audit Commission, 250
  coordination, 148–9
  devolution in England, 207
  executive, 118–19
  executive agencies, 138
  joined-up government, 143
  local government, 174–6
  managerialism, 129
  ministerial departments, 123, 124, 128

non-departmental public bodies, 139
  Northern Ireland, 174
Wincott, D., 9
Winetrobe, B., 187
Woodhouse, D.
  human rights, 232
  judicial review, 227
  ministerial departments, 121
Wright, K.
  devolution, 180
  House of Commons, 39